SCIENCE FICTION: 101

ROBERT SILVERBERG'S WORLDS OF WONDER

Edited and with an Introduction by
ROBERT SILVERBERG

Introduction by
GREG BEAR

ibooks

new york

www.ibooksinc.com

DISTRIBUTED BY SIMON & SCHUSTER, INC

For Cliff Bennett and Jim Blish
and Damon Knight and Horace Gold
and Fred Pohl and Lester del Rey and Alfie Bester
and all the others who knew the secret
that I was trying so hard to learn.

SCIENCE FICTION: 101

ROBERT SILVERBERG's many novels include *The Alien Years*; the most recent volume in the Majipoor Cycle, *Lord Prestimion*; the bestselling Lord Valentine trilogy; and the classics *Dying Inside* and *A Time of Changes*. *Sailing to Byzantium*, a collection of some of his award-winning novellas, was published by ibooks in 2000. He has been nominated for the Nebula and Hugo awards more times than any other writer; he is a five-time winner of the Nebula and a four-time winner of the Hugo.

PRAISE FOR *SCIENCE FICTION: 101—ROBERT SILVERBERG'S WORLDS OF WONDER*

"The stories alone are worth the price of admission, examples of the best that science fiction can be. But the whipped cream on top is Silverberg's essay on the craft of each story."
—*Wilmington Morning News*

"I loved his writing insights and his personal understanding of the history of the field. The commentary . . . is exact and praiseworthy. Read it."
—*Ogre magazine*

"Scintillating stories, intriguing autobiography."
—*Kirkus Reviews*

"No science fiction fan can afford to miss this gem."
—*Marlboro Enterprise/Hudson Daily Sun*

"Inspiring, revealing and educational."
—*New Haven Register*

AVAILABLE NOW

COMING SOON

CONTENTS

CONTENTS

INTRODUCTION

by

GREG BEAR

Worlds of Wonder was a fresh breeze when it first appeared and is still bracing today. Literary criticism consists all too often of slipshod attempts to analyze one or two recent popular books and make broad, misleading, and sadly unfounded judgments. Robert Silverberg couldn't do that if he tried—he's read too much and knows too much. But what he knows has been filtered through his own experience—and honed by a razor-sharp sense of humor. Silverberg shines a light on pretension, and so spotted, dismisses it with the lift of an eyebrow and a weary smile.

Scary. But usually, dead on. You see, he's not only smart, he's good at what he does. No false sense of humility here. Instead, what we get is a personal (and often truly humble) appraisal of that literary playground he loves most dearly, that I love most dearly, and that all but the most jaundiced, deluded, and incompetent critics of our day regard as one of the premier branches of world literature: science fiction.

Worlds of Wonder functions in part as memoir, in part as a summing up, and in very large part as a guidebook for anyone who wants to write science fiction. Silverberg's appreciation and analysis of the included fine stories are exceptionally helpful to writers struggling to learn how to translate what they love into what readers will understand and embrace.

Along the way, you will meet Robert Silverberg himself, and learn what guided him, how his friends helped him, and what mistakes he made and later avoided.

It's an excellent place to begin. It's also a drink of pure spring water in the middle of a long career. In short, *Worlds of Wonder* is a classic that refreshes and serves us all.

FOREWORD

What you have here is actually three books in one. It's an anthology of some of the finest short stories in the history of science fiction; it's a series of essays intended to constitute a textbook of sorts on the art and craft of writing science fiction; and it's a collection of personal reminiscences by someone who has spent—or misspent, some might argue—more than forty years of his life reading the stuff and nearly as much time writing it. What it amounts to, then, is a three-level attempt to come to some understanding of what science fiction is and how one goes about creating it, and to convey some of that understanding to others.

The casual reader who has no interest in becoming a science-fiction writer or in knowing how science-fiction writers go about their tasks will nevertheless find much pleasure in the dozen or so stories I've gathered here. They are all marvelous tales, stories that lit up my mind with wonder when I first encountered them long ago. Not one, I think, shows its age in the slightest: they are still fresh, vivid, splendiferous works of the imagination that display marvelous pyrotechnics. And so I think this book is apt to have plenty to offer even the reader who chooses to skip all the commentary interspersed among the fiction.

There is a somewhat smaller but still significant group of readers—the class of people who want to be professional writers of science fiction—who will, I hope, find something of value in that commentary as well. I've assembled a collection of stories that, when they first were published, struck me as outstanding and, by their example, helped to guide me toward the formation of a set of criteria for writing science fiction. I think I *did* learn how to write science fiction and to do it pretty well, and I have an assortment of awards, fancy reviews, and affidavits from my mother and my former teachers to back me up. I realize that despite all those ostensible proofs of performance I may be deluded in my belief that I've done a good job over the years. But what is not a matter for debate is that I *have* been a professional science-fiction writer for an entire generation, supporting myself largely and most of the time since 1955 exclusively by making up stories and novels about times and places that don't exist. That makes me think I must have been doing something right. The essays here constitute, in their circuitous way, a statement of the principles on which I've based my approach to the writing of science fiction.

Finally, for an even smaller group of readers—those who have read my books or met me at some science-fiction convention and who have developed some curiosity about me as a result—there's a good bit of autobiographical material here. That probably won't interest the people who have bought this book purely for the stories, and it may not even interest the ones who hope to pick up some useful tips about how to write science fiction; but I think it will interest *someone*. At the very least it interests me.

I will not attempt to hide the self-indulgent nature of

this book. The whole thing is, in a real sense, an affectionate gift to that 12-year-old kid with my name who set out, in Brooklyn long ago, to be a science-fiction writer. Look, kid, I'm trying to say: here are all those stories you loved so much, the ones you wished you could have written. Here's what you think about them now, decades and decades later. And this is what happened to *you*. You grew up and wrote a bunch of books and got them published and everything worked out pretty well. So it wasn't a waste of time at all, the hours you spent reading *Amazing Stories* and *Startling Stories* and *Astounding Science Fiction.* You found your life's work that way. You would grow up to give pleasure to others and to find some satisfaction yourself in writing stories that you hoped were worthy companions to those that pleased you so much back then. So here's a book for you, kid—a birthday present from the future.

A self-indulgence, yes. But I think this book is going to be useful to others, or I would never have dared to propose it to my publisher. And I know it's been useful to me, both because it's given me the chance to reread some stories that I admire and because it's allowed me an opportunity to codify and clarify my own half-intuitive theories about science fiction and about fiction in general.

It's necessary, of course, for any writer to work out theories about what he thinks he's doing. Unless you have some idea of what a story ought to be, and what in particular a science-fiction story ought to be, I don't see how you can write one. But most of the time those theories remain subliminal, internalized, intuitive. A writer, a *professional* writer, goes about his work more or less as a juggler does, or a pianist, or a baseball player, by learning the technique of the job and turning it into automatic reflex. That's fine, as far as it goes. But from time to time I think it's important for a writer to ask himself, "What *is* a story? What *is* science fiction? What the hell *is* this whole business all about, anyway?"

I've been asking myself those questions for close to forty years. I ask them again in the pages ahead. And I try to provide some answers.

Not that I've come up with *absolute* answers. There aren't any. A story is many things, and the same story often is different things to different people. A story is a machine that enlightens: a little ticking contrivance that guides its reader to some bit of illumination. It is a pocket universe in which the reader can hide for a time from the pressure of the everyday world. It is an exercise in vicarious experience, a trip in someone else's mind, an essay in alternative realities. It is a verbal object, an incantation made up of rhythms and sounds.

A science-fiction story is all of those things at once, and something more. "Mainstream" fiction takes place in a world directly derived from our own—sometimes rather loosely modeled after our generally perceived reality, as in the fiction of Franz Kafka, and sometimes shaped with painstaking mimetic focus, as in that of John O'Hara or F. Scott Fitzgerald. Science fiction, though, is a branch of fantasy; it draws on the realities of our world at one remove, attempting to portray not what does exist but that which we know does not. At its purest extreme, fantasy portrays that which we know *cannot* exist, and tries to make the impossible plausible. The subset of fantasy that we call science fiction also aims for plausibility, but instead of dealing in impossiblities (werewolves, magic wands, nymphs turning into trees) it works with that which is or seems possible but not yet a reality (colonies on Mars, voyages to Alpha Centauri, androids that commit murder) and tries to give such unrealities the feel of reality, at least for the nonce, coaxing from the reader a "willing suspension of disbelief." That famous phrase of Coleridge beautifully describes what any writer, but most particularly the writer of fantasy or science fiction, must strive to achieve.

Evoking that suspension of disbelief is the basic trick of the trade. The fantasist—and I include in that class the science-fiction writer—does it by producing fiction that is realistic at its core, built about some set of rigorously held and internally consistent perceptions and assumptions. You will find such a set of perceptions and assumptions underlying the world created by Lewis Carroll, the one created by J.R.R. Tolkien, and those created by Robert A. Heinlein, Isaac Asimov, and Arthur C. Clarke. They may be wildly fantastic assumptions—should be, in fact. But they must have a strict inner reality of their own. Without it, fantasy becomes too easy, and thus incomprehensible, and thus boring.

This is about as close as I want to come to defining science fiction. I've been writing it for more than thiry-five years and still don't have a working definition for it that covers all cases, nor do I want one. (I came up with one once that, as someone else gently pointed out, excludes my own best s-f novel.) But these are some basic characteristics that I've isolated:

1. An underlying speculative concept, systematically developed in a way that amounts to an exploration of the consequences of allowing such a departure from known reality to impinge on the universe as we know it.

2. An awareness by the writer of the structural underpinnings (the "body of scientific knowledge") of our known reality, as it is currently understood, so that the speculative aspects of the story are founded on conscious and thoughtful departures from those underpinnings rather than on blithe ignorance.

3. Imposition by the writer of a sense of limitations somewhere within the assumptions of the story. The magical ability to turn anything into anything without effort all too easily vitiates the tensions necessary to good fiction of any sort. On the other hand, subjecting the powers of magic to the laws of thermodynamics turns a story from fantasy to

science fiction, though that story may be full of sorcerers in pointy hats.

4. A subliminal knowledge of the feel and texture of true science fiction, as defined in a circular and subjective way from acquaintance with it. The term "science fiction," Damon Knight once wrote, "means what we point to when we say it."

The stories I have collected here fit all of these criteria, especially the fourth. They are what I point to when I say, "This is science fiction."

For me a science-fiction story can be identified primarily by the sort of concepts it contains, but also to a large extent *by the way those concepts are approached.* Ordinarily, for example, I would class a story about werewolves as fantasy (because there's no biological plausibility to the notion that a primate could temporarily transform itself into a howling canine, full moon or no) and a story about space travel as science fiction. But I have read stories about werewolves that were pure science fiction (James Blish's "There Shall Be No Darkness," for one) and stories about space journeys that were not (C.S. Lewis' *Perelandra* or David Lindsay's *A Voyage to Arcturus*).

I know why I feel that way. I know what I think is real science fiction and what I think is fake science fiction; and I know how to distinguish both kinds from what is not science fiction at all. Some of my criteria should be apparent in what lies ahead, as well as some of the principles by which I have gone about constructing my own science-fiction stories. I think you'll learn something about science fiction from the essays here. I did.

—ROBERT SILVERBERG
Oakland, California

SCIENCE FICTION: 101 ROBERT SILVERBERG'S WORLDS OF WONDER

INTRODUCTION

THE MAKING OF A
SCIENCE-FICTION WRITER

I must have been a peculiar little boy. Most people who grow up to be professional science-fiction writers were peculiar little boys, except for those who were peculiar little girls. (Most, not all. I doubt that Robert A. Heinlein was peculiar, for somehow he is our Great Exception in almost everything, and I suspect that Ray Bradbury may have *appeared* normal at a casual glance. But I know that Isaac Asimov seemed like an oddball to his classmates; surely young Jack Williamson felt shy and gangling and utterly out of place; and the mind boggles at the thought of John W. Campbell, Jr., going out to play stickball with the gang after school.) We are not, by and large, a clan who found it easy to get along with other people when we were young. (Imagine Harlan Ellison as a fifth grader and you'll see what I mean.) Which is probably why we became dreamers in the first place, retreating into private worlds of extraordinary vividness; and which may be why, now that we have learned how to turn those dreams into dollars and live successfully in the world of mundane folk, we still prefer the company of our own kind to that of those others.

Perhaps we were maladjusted little brats, but we were smart ones. Certainly, I was. I walked early, I was a precocious talker, I

3

learned to read when I was three. By the time I was five I was in the first grade; after a year I skipped to the third grade, where I founded and edited a school newspaper, most of which I also wrote myself. (I was six.) I collected bugs and stamps and coins and anything else I could think of, became something of an expert on botany, learned all there was to know about dinosaurs, fooled around with a microscope, and knew the names of all the kings of England in order. (I think I still remember them.) Somewhere around that time I began writing short stories, too. I was small, untidy, and very free with my opinions. I must have been an enormous pain in the neck. (The world will never know how many potential science-fiction writers were strangled or pushed off the tops of tall buildings in childhood by irate classmates or enraged siblings. But I was quick enough and agile enough to elude my classmates, and I didn't have to worry about siblings, thank God, which is why I survived and was able to bring you all those wonderful books and stories.)

The one thing I didn't do when I was busy being a child prodigy was read science fiction. That came later, when I was 10 or 11. Instead, I read things like Henrik Van Loon's *The Story of Mankind* and Charles and Mary Lamb's *Tales from Shakespeare*, and A. Hyatt Verrill's *Great Conquerors of South and Central America*. For my fiction I tended at first toward books like *Huckleberry Finn* and *Penrod* and *Tom Sawyer*.

But I also had an insatiable appetite for stranger things. I virtually committed *Alice in Wonderland* and *Through the Looking Glass* to memory. I read *Gulliver's Travels*, not for the political satire but for the exotic civilizations it depicted. I read *The Hobbit*, a decade before *Lord of the Rings* was published. The Dr. Doolittle books, the tales of George MacDonald, Jules Verne's *20,000 Leagues Under the Sea*, and such escapist stuff—I couldn't get enough of it. I was eight, nine, ten years old. (My copy of the Modern Library Lewis Carroll, 1,293 pages long and many times to be read end to end, bears an inscription from my father dated two months before my eighth birthday: "This reminds me of you—a little jabber-*wacky*." I had just entered the fourth grade.) I read fairy tales galore. I gobbled books of mythology, mainly retellings of the Greek and Norse myths, but such esoterica as the Persian *Book of Kings* as well, and the *Thousand and One Nights* in a translation—Sir Richard Burton's—far less expurgated than my parents could have suspected.

Oddly, it never occurred to me, avidly reading and rereading the adventures of Theseus or Thor or Kaikhosro and searching for more of the same, that what I was looking for was fantasy. Not ordinary boyish fantasy ("Let's build a raft and go down the Mississippi") but something spectacular and flamboyant, with frost-giants in it and Scylla and Charybdis and Valhalla and the Nibelungen and dragons and heroes. I didn't then know, or didn't care, that all those things could be categorized as fantasy. But I knew what I wanted, and I found it with singleminded zeal, hauling books home from the library every Saturday and finishing every one before next week's trip.

And though I read such books as *20,000 Leagues Under the Sea* or H. G. Wells' *The Time Machine* or Mark Twain's *Connecticut Yankee at King Arthur's Court*, I certainly had no idea that those books belonged to that branch of fantasy known as science fiction. In fact, that was the sort of fantasy I preferred—the kind that might almost have been real, except that it was built around a fantastic premise. Since I was definitely science-oriented, trying to decide whether I'd be a botanist or a paleontologist when I grew up, but also had a distinct taste for imaginative fantasies, the chances are good that I'd have jumped at the science-fiction magazines of the wartime era if I had only known they existed. Something called "*science* fiction" (and I would have put the accent on *science* then) unquestionably would have appealed to me right away.

But the term wasn't all that commonly used, back then in the 1940s. The New York Public Library classified science-fiction books under the uninviting and vaguely disreputable-sounding heading, "Pseudoscientific Literature." There were eight or nine science-fiction magazines in those days, but with one exception they were flashy-looking, trashy-looking pulp magazines with names like *Startling Stories* and *Thrilling Wonder Stories*. A serious little boy like me wasn't likely to seek out magazines with names like that, nor did anyone happen to leave them where I might find them accidentally. (The only magazine with "science fiction" in its title was also the only one that didn't look like a garish pulp magazine: John Campbell's austere, dignified *Astounding Science Fiction*. Perhaps I would have wrinkled up my nose at that *astounding* in the title, or perhaps I would have tried an issue and found the stories too abstruse for my 10-year-old mind. But I simply didn't run across any copies.)

Then I did stumble upon science fiction that was plainly labeled as science fiction. I think I was eleven, maybe twelve; and after that everything was permanently changed for me.

Since one of the purposes of this book is to reprint the stories that helped shape me into the writer I was to become, I wish I could include in it the entire contents of the first five or six s-f books I discovered. Their impact on me was overwhelming. I can still taste and feel the extraordinary sensations they awakened in me: it was a physiological thing, a distinct excitement, a certain metabolic quickening at the mere thought of handling them, let alone reading them. It must be like that for every new reader—apocalyptic thunderbolts and eerie unfamiliar music accompanying you as you lurch and stagger, awed and shaken, into a bewildering new world of images and ideas, which is exactly the place you've been hoping to find all your life. A different set of stories, of course, provides that moment of apocalypse for each neophyte. The ones that struck my spirit with such stunning force at that first moment of revelation might seem hopelessly old hat to today's readers, which is one reason why I am not filling this book with them. But this I do know, that every day of the week someone who has never read science fiction comes upon an odd-looking book—one of mine, perhaps, or one of Asimov's, or one by some cluck of a writer whom any knowledgeable reader would scorn—and opens it not knowing what to expect, and reads, and reads on, and reads through the night, and is forever transformed.

For me it was Donald A. Wollheim's *Pocket Book of Science Fiction* that did the trick—the first of all paperback s-f anthologies, published in 1943 and discovered by me in the public library three or four years later. In it I found Theodore Sturgeon's "Microcosmic God" and Stribling's "Green Splotches" and Heinlein's "—And He Built a Crooked House" and above all Weinbaum's "A Martian Odyssey," and H. G. Wells was there too, and Don A. Stuart, and John Collier.

From there it was on to Wollheim's *Portable Novels of Science*, which I remember buying at Macy's when I was twelve. This was even a deeper, stronger dose: an incurable infection, in fact. For here was John Taine's *Before the Dawn*, which spoke to my boyhood passion for dinosaurs, and here was Wells' quaint and charming *First Men in the Moon*, and here too was H. P. Lovecraft's powerful *The Shadow out of Time*, which I will remember always for a single chapter, the fourth, in which Lovecraft showed me giant alien beings moving about in a weird library full of "horrible annals of other worlds and other universes, and of stirrings of formless life outside of all universes. There were records of strange orders of beings which had peopled the world in forgotten pasts, and frightful chronicles of grotesque-bodied intelligences which would people it millions of years after the death of the last human being."

I wanted desperately to explore that library myself. I knew I could not; I would know no more of the furry prehuman Hyperborean worshippers of Tsathoggua and the wholly abominable Tcho-Tchos than Lovecraft chose to tell me, nor would I talk with the mind of Yiang-Li, the philosopher from the cruel empire of Tsan-Chan, which is to come in A.D. 5000, nor with the mind of the king of Lomar who ruled that terrible polar land one hundred thousand years before the squat, yellow Inutos came from the west to engulf it. But I read that page of Lovecraft ten thousand times—it is page 429 of Wollheim's anthology—and even now, scanning it this morning, it stirs me with the hunger to find and absorb all the science fiction in the world, every word of it, so that I might begin to know the mysteries of these lost imaginary kingdoms of time past and time future.

There was another novel in the Wollheim collection that stirred me even more profoundly than Lovecraft's, though. It was Olaf Stapledon's *Odd John*, the quintessential peculiar-little-boy book, a haunting and tragic tale of a child prodigy—one far beyond my own attainments, but with whom, nonetheless, I was easily able to identify. You are not alone, Stapledon was saying to me. You will find others of your sort; and if you are lucky you and your peers will withdraw to a safe island far from the cruel and clumsy bullies who clutter your classroom, and do your work in peace, whatever it may be. Even though it all ends badly for John and his friends, *Odd John* must be a powerfully comforting work for any bright, unhappy child. Certainly, it was for me. I was unhappy because of my brightness; through Stapledon I saw a mode, fantastic though it might be, of escaping all of that into a more secure life. If it is a novel that also feeds paranoia, arrogance, and elitist fantasy, so be it. It made me feel better. I think I am not the only one who used it that way.

The book department at Macy's now became my gateway to other worlds. Some time late in 1947 or early in 1948 I brought home the astonishing collection *Adventures in Time and Space*, edited by Raymond J. Healy and J. Francis McComas (which gave me Hasse's "He Who Shrank," Robert Heinlein's "By His Bootstraps," A. E. van Vogt's "The Weapons Shop," Asimov's "Nightfall," and thirty-one others) and the only slightly less dazzling *Treasury of Science Fiction* (C. L. Moore's "No Woman Born" and "Vintage Season," Jack Williamson's "With Folded Hands," Arthur Clarke's "Rescue Party," and many more) that Groff Conklin had assembled. It was an easy leap from there to the science-fiction magazines of the day, gaudy though they might have been. The full commitment was made. I came home each afternoon with *Weird Tales* or *Amazing Stories* or *Super-Science Stories* under my jacket.

Of course I would try to write my own science-fiction stories, then. Of course.

I have the manuscript of my first attempt on my desk beside me. God knows how it has survived all these years. "The Last Days of Saturn" is its name; I was no more than 12 when I wrote it, in collaboration with Saul Diskin, a boyhood friend. We worked on it in class, I recall, whispering details of the plot to each other despite our teacher's scowls. How much of it was my work and how much his I have no way now of telling. I'd like to believe now that most of it was Saul's, but I suspect the truth is that I'm the main guilty party. All but one of the eight pages seem to be in my handwriting, and I have no doubt that I was the one who wrote jubilantly on the final page, "1,948 words. FINIS, THE END, COMPLETED, ALL DONE." This is how it opens:

The following report is an extract from the records of the Western Hemisphere Council of War against the Eastern Hemisphere, Anno Scienti 3012 [in the Year of Science—ed.] (5013 A.D.):

"The chair recognizes Dr. Neil, the Delegate from the Northern Sector."

"Mr. Chairman, I have received a message through the Magnemit Machine [a machine that hurls messages through space by means of gross atomic magnetism of silverite, a substance known only to the Council] from the Council's expedition to Saturn, to seek room for our excess population. I shall read it.

" 'Saturn is slowly but surely being destroyed. A series of meteors have disrupted the gravitational pulls of the tiny particles which make up Saturn's ring. Hence, each is pulling in a separate direction, and chasms of indescribable size are being formed. Three axial rotations ago we saw our abandoned projectile disappear into a huge Saturnian fissure. Our living quarters have already been destroyed. . . . The days of the planet are decidedly numbered. . . . The Saturnians are panic-stricken. . . .' "

No need to continue, is there? The opening two hundred words plainly demonstrate the gifts that would carry me on to a career of scores of published books, hundreds of anthology appearances, and a long shelf of Nebula and Hugo awards. (What? You can't see even a *shred* of ability there? Look again. Look more closely. You see all that dazzling scientific extrapolation ["gross atomic magnetism of silverite, a substance known only to the Council"]? You see the quick and deft establishment of a crisis ["Saturn is slowly but surely being destroyed"]? You see—well, never mind. I was only a little kid. You think Heinlein did any better when *he* was 12?)

Looking at "The Last Days of Saturn" now, I see that one of the real problems with it was that my antiquarian urges had led me to use the wrong models. I hadn't read much contemporary science fiction—indeed, not much contemporary fiction at all. H. G. Wells' *First Men in the Moon,* which surely provided me with the inspiration for silverite, dated from 1901. Wells was a splendid storyteller, but the fictional conventions of 1901 allowed a writer to halt a story at any point for lengthy expository passages. Neither Lovecraft, Taine, nor Stapledon, the other authors in *Portable Novels of Science,* minded expository passages either. They weren't writing for pulp magazines. Neither was I. So I wrote a story that was virtually *all* expository passages. There were about ten lines of dialog, and even they were basically expository. (" 'Dr. Neil—he's just collapsed.' 'No wonder. His brother was up there in that crumbling hell.' ") The rest is stolid, cheerfully stodgy narrative. ("I was impressed with a will to live longer than they did, even for a primitive feeling of satisfaction. We devised a clever scheme for beating them in hand-to-hand combat: we put on hobnailed boots. Since they were balloon-like, filled with that greenish fluid, a puncture would kill them. . . .")

If I had taken a closer look at the stories I was reading in the issues of *Amazing* and *Super-Science Stories* that I had lately begun buying, or those in such anthologies as *Adventures in Time and Space,* I might have noticed that contemporary s-f writers tended to open their stories with a dramatic situation, which they went on to develop through action, dialog, and (to some degree) the interplay of character, until the story reached a climax and a resolution. Maybe I did notice that, and simply decided it was too hard to do. But I was also rooting around in dusty secondhand shops and acquiring antique, even antediluvian s-f magazines, such as *Science Wonder Stories* from 1929 and *Amazing Stories* from 1932. Those magazines were *full* of fiction cast in the form of Reports of this or that futuristic Council and set in the Year of Science 3012, or its equivalent. The primitive technique of many of the authors didn't include such frills as the ability to create characters or write dialog.

I didn't notice, I guess, that that school of fiction was obsolete. No one told me that the editors of the early science-fiction magazines had found it necessary to rely for their material largely on hobbyists with humpty-dumpty narrative skills; the true storytellers were off writing for the other pulp magazines, knocking out westerns or adventure tales with half the effort for twice the pay. So my early attempts at science fiction were imitative of something that hadn't had much craftsmanship or vitality behind it in the first place. No wonder they were so awful.

That didn't stop me from sending them to the s-f magazines of the day. I don't know if I actually submitted "The Last Days of Saturn" anywhere—I hope not—but within a year or so I certainly was sending some stories out, because I have the rejection slips to prove it. On July 18, 1949, for example, kindly Sam Merwin of *Startling* and *Thrilling Wonder* let me know that "Beneath the Ashes"—my sequel to "Last Days of Saturn"—had been "found not quite suitable for any of our science fiction magazines." He was holding the manuscript for my pickup. (I didn't even have enough sense to include return postage.) About the same month I got a printed form from Street & Smith Publications, which put out *Astounding*, thanking me for the opportunity of examining the enclosed material, and regretting that they could not make use of it at this time.

Probably rejection slips of that sort are still in use by magazines today. I still get stories turned down by editors occasionally, you know, and so does every other well-known science-fiction writer I can think of—if God were a science-fiction writer, *he'd* get rejected once in a while too, editors being what they are—but of course I get tactful, apologetic letters now, not impersonal notes or printed forms. That's only to be expected, a courtesy extended to a veteran professional writer. The heartening thing about my early career, though, was that I stopped getting the printed forms, and began getting encouraging little letters, by the time I was seventeen or so. I still wasn't ready for professional publication. But I was learning fast, and the editors could see the speed of my progress. However it may seem to a beginner, most editors really want to help new writers get started. All they ask of them is that they learn how to produce something that's better than "The Last Days of Saturn." Which I did, way back when, and quickly. I have always been a quick learner.

At the time of "The Last Days of Saturn" I still had no notion of making my livelihood by writing. Such vocational ambitions as I had, age 12, were directed vaguely toward the sciences. Somehow my parents had detected the truth even before I knew it, though, and communicated it to one of my teachers. One day in an eighth-grade class we had a vocational-guidance session, during the course of which that teacher said to me, "I understand from your parents that you're thinking of becoming a writer."

That was complete news to me. I stood there stunned, examining and reexamining the thought. A writer? Well, of course, I was writing all sorts of stories, always had, and I was the editor of the school paper, because I was always the editor of the school paper wherever I went to school, and I plainly had a way with words, and won spelling bees—but a *writer?* Someone who wrote for his living? That had never crossed my mind. Honestly. I was going to be a paleontologist, I thought, and spend my days out in Wyoming digging up dinosaurs. Or do something in botany, maybe. A *writer?* Did that make any sense? Well . . . maybe . . .

I think the damage was done, right then and there, that afternoon in the eighth grade. If it seemed obvious to everybody but me that I was going to be a writer, why, maybe I should give the idea a little thought. By such glancing blows are our fates determined.

I thought about the idea and the more I thought, the more I liked it. I imagined what it would feel like if one of the manuscripts I was sending to *Startling* and *Astounding* were to bring me not a printed rejection slip but an actual check, say as much as fifteen or twenty dollars. I thought of taking a copy of *Thrilling Wonder Stories* to school for show-and-tell and pointing out the magical line on the contents page, "By Robert Silverberg." Yes, that would be fine. But if I really intended to be a writer, I knew I was going to have to learn a little more about how it was done. I could see already that nobody was likely to publish the crude little stories I was writing.

I didn't see anything seriously wrong with my basic material—the dumb implausible ideas, the crude cardboard characters. So far as content went, my stories seemed as good as some of the junk then being published, and maybe they were. The problem, I thought, lay in the *way* I was writing them. You couldn't use the 1929 modes of narrative, I realized, and hope to get your stories published in the advanced, sophisticated s-f magazines of 1949. Technique, that's the problem.

Technique. A word that would obsess me for years.

I know exactly when I became aware that such a concept as technique—narrative technique—existed. It was in the autumn of 1949, and the man who told me about it was a 30-year-old American expatriate living in Tecate, Mexico. His name was Clif Bennett, and I know very little more about him than that, though my sense of him now is that he must have been a restless young Greenwich Village intellectual wandering around the warmer parts of the continent with a little library of Kafka, Kierkegaard, and D. H. Lawrence, supporting himself by making sandals or playing the guitar in coffeeshops or whatever. The last contact I had with him was in 1950, and I have no idea what became of him after that.

He was, in 1949, publishing a neatly mimeographed avant-garde magazine called *Catalyst* in association with another American whom he had met in Mexico. Somehow it was mentioned in a column in *Amazing Stories* and I sent for it. What I got was far beyond my barely adolescent level of comprehension, a magazine that quoted St. Augustine and Lewis Mumford, ran essays on Spengler and Toynbee, and published poems, some of which didn't rhyme. It also included a fantasy story by Clif Bennett. I responded with a letter of comment—I'd love to know what I said—and with great chutzpah sent along some of my own stories.

Clif Bennett's reply has vanished somewhere in the archives, and I don't expect to see it again. But the operative sentence that survives in my memory from our brief correspondence went something like this, and I think my recollection of it must be 95 percent accurate:

"Thanks for your stories. Your plots are excellent, but somewhat underfurnished. I recommend you read Thomas Uzzell's *Narrative Technique.*"

My plots were excellent! Look, Clif Bennett said so! But "somewhat underfurnished." What did that mean? Short on dialog? Short on action? What *is* a plot, anyway? Is that the same thing as a story? How can I find out? Why, by reading this Thomas Uzzell book, *Narrative Technique.* Of course! Technique! That's what I need to know: the way it's done. The secret of writing fiction. The mysterious secret that makes stories by Heinlein or Lewis Padgett or A. E. van Vogt so wonderfully engrossing. The secret that obviously I don't know, which is why my stories get sent back by the magazines, with printed rejection forms.

I ran off to the public library and behold! There was Thomas Uzzell's *Narrative Technique,* which I checked out and brought home and read in a feverish frenzy of rising bewilderment.

I don't have a copy of it today. I couldn't have afforded to buy my own in 1949 and by the time I could, it would have had purely sentimental value for me. Probably it went out of print long ago. So my recollection of what I found in it is pretty hazy; but what I do recall is the terror that it inspired in me. Writing stories was far more complicated than I ever suspected. It wasn't just a matter of thinking up some far-out idea ("Meteors are pulling the rings of Saturn apart, and the whole planet is breaking up") and describing its effects on a little group of people. No, there was the whole problem of plot, which Uzzell (I'm sure) distinguished from story.

Story, he must have said, was the total construct: situation, characters, style, everything. Including plot. Plot was just one ingredient of story, one that could be summarized in a sentence or two; and plot, I believe Thomas Uzzell probably said, was *the working out of a conflict*. That was what fiction was, basically: the record of a conflict, its development and its resolution. ("Agamemnon wants Achilles to come out of his tent and get over to the battlefield and fight the Trojans. But Achilles is annoyed because Agamemnon grabbed his favorite slave-girl, and he refuses to stop sulking. So Agamemnon tells Achilles . . .")

Reading Uzzell on plot shook me up plenty. I saw now that a little piece about the unusual nature of life on Mars, or about what it's like to travel six million years in time, is not a story, because it has no plot, meaning that there's no conflict in it. At best it's an incident or an anecdote. It might be nothing more than a simple speculation. Let the Martians invade Earth, or let the time traveler fall in love with one of the Eloi who inhabit the far future, and you've got the makings of a plot. Most of my "stories" were failing because they didn't have plots.

That was news to me. Honestly. And it annoyed me. I didn't like conflict much. (Still don't.) I wanted to read, and to write, visions of strange places and times. Did that mean I had to put in villains, and chase scenes, and violent showdowns, if I hoped to get my stories published? Well, yes, I did. Not in such literal terms, but I began to recognize—age 13, 14, thereabouts—that *a story has to be built around a pattern of oppositions*. If you want anyone else to read it, that is. At first it seemed tremendously limiting to me, an arbitrary and irrelevant rule that had little or no connection with what I had been writing or, I thought, with much of what I was reading. And then I realized that every story I had ever read, myths and fairy tales included, was built on conflict. Perhaps the protagonist is in conflict with the forces of nature, perhaps with villainous human beings, perhaps with his own inner feelings; but some sort of struggle is always present. Theseus is in the Minotaur's maze; he has to find his way out if he wants to win the princess and go home to Athens. Odysseus has to outwit the enchantresses and elude the monsters if he's ever going to see Ithaca again. King Lear has surrendered all his power to his daughters and now they're being nasty to him. The Martians have landed and they're destroying our cities. Don Quixote lives in a world where romance is dead, and he hates that, so he goes out trying to stir up a little, and attacks windmills that he thinks are evil giants. Conflict. Strife. Opposition of needs. If it isn't there, there's no story. Homer knew that almost three thousand years ago. Shakespeare knew it. Robert A. Heinlein knows it.

Uzzell told me much more than that—more, really, than I could absorb or handle. Character, for example, has to be integrated with plot. People get into conflict because they are the sort of people they are; they deal with conflicts in a way that illustrates their individual characters, and they resolve them in a way unique to their own character traits. Hamlet, who had a murder mystery to solve and a kingdom to inherit, was an indecisive man; Odysseus was wily; Lear was impulsive and rash. So was poor Oedipus, who got himself into a terrible mess because he struck first and stopped to think afterward. They weren't anonymous, interchangeable beings like my explorers of Saturn. Put Hamlet in King Lear's position and you'd get a very different story indeed. Odysseus, faced with Oedipus' problems, would certainly have found a more effective way to deal with them. (Hmm. "Hamlet and His Daughters," by Robert Silverberg. "Odysseus and Jocasta." Might be worth fooling around with. Let's see . . . "Othello in Capetown.")

Uzzell's strictures on the role of character development in fiction plunged me into gloom. It wasn't enough to put a professor, a brave newspaper reporter, and the professor's beautiful daughter together in the time machine, the way they used to do it in 1931. Somehow

I would have to give my characters individual traits—make them seem like real people, that is—and make the outcome of my story depend on the nature of those traits. That is so much a part of my method now—of any writer's method—that I've scarcely thought about it consciously in decades. But to me in 1949 it seemed like an impossible juggling-trick.

Then there was stuff about the proportions of dialog to exposition, about finding the right starting-point for a story, about building suspense, about point of view—well, I don't know. There was a lot of it, and it was all intimidating. I don't recall it in detail, but I know what had to have been there, even though it's close to forty years since I last looked at Uzzell's book. A three-hundred-page book on narrative technique had to be full of matters bound to be bewildering to a fledgling writer like me, no matter how clever.

And then there was the homework. I'm pretty sure that each chapter ended with a long list of exercises I was supposed to do, writing little character descriptions and making up story situations and working out an unfinished plot outline. I'm utterly certain that I put the book aside with a sinking feeling in my stomach. The art of fiction seemed as complicated and difficult to master as the art of brain surgery, and plainly, you had to learn all the rules before the editors would let you through the door. Violate even one of Uzzell's commandments and it would be immediately apparent to any editor that the manuscript before him was the work of an incompetent. This was how I proposed to earn my living? I felt I could no more manage to write a proper story than I could walk on water.

There obviously were people who *could* write proper stories—Heinlein, Asimov, Henry Kuttner, Jack Williamson, and dozens more in the science-fiction world alone. They, so it seemed to me, were the elect. They were the ones who had been admitted to the sanctuary, while I stood on the outside glumly peering in. Why? I had thought it was because they knew some special secret, some fundamental trick of the trade, that was unavailable to me. But no, that wasn't it: here were all the secrets laid out in Thomas Uzzell's book for anyone to see. What you needed, I realized, was the ability to make use of the secrets. Anybody could tell you the secret of hitting a home run in Yankee Stadium: you wait until the precise moment when the ball is approaching the plate, and you step into it and whip your wrists around and hit it as hard as you can. Fine. But Joe DiMaggio could do it and I couldn't, and no matter how many books on batting technique I studied I wasn't ever going to hit the ball out of Yankee Stadium, because I didn't have the right muscles, the right reflexes, the right timing. You had to be born with those things, I supposed. You couldn't be a DiMaggio, or a Caruso, or a Picasso, or a Shakespeare, just by wanting to be, or by taking courses in technique. You had to be born with something extra, something special. The people whose stories I loved in the magazines and anthologies had been born knowing the secrets of storytelling already—the Secret, as I thought of it. Obviously, I hadn't been. If I had, I wouldn't find all of Uzzell's stuff about plot and point of view and characterization so intimidating. I'd *know*. Homer hadn't read any books on narrative technique.

(In fact I was both right and wrong. Any special skill requires certain innate abilities *and* the mastery of some degree of technique, but that doesn't mean that it can be practiced only by those whom the gods favor. All it takes to hit a baseball is reasonably good physical coordination and the willingness to learn how to swing a bat. Becoming a major-league player requires a considerably higher level of innate physical ability plus a considerably more intense study of the technique of the game; but there have been plenty of players with mediocre physical skills who overcame that drawback by dedicated work and study. The same is true in painting, in singing, in writing, or anything else. Some people are born with special advantages—keen vision, or perfect pitch, or an unusually retentive memory—and they have head starts as a result, in certain fields; but those who lack such advantages can nevertheless achieve noteworthy things, unless some outright insuperable handicap interferes. There are those who find reading difficult or boring, and they are not likely to be successful as writers; but anyone with normal verbal skills who is willing to study the craft of fiction ought to be able to write an acceptable story. To reach the level of Shakespeare—or Caruso, or Picasso, or DiMaggio—is a different matter. They really *must* have been born with something extra. But achievement of their kind is very rare. Good as they were, the science-fiction writers who were my boyhood heroes were all of sub-Shakespearean caliber, nor had they emerged from their cradles fully equipped to write memorable fiction. What I didn't let myself see, in that moment of adolescent despair, was that hard work rather than superior genetic endowment is the basic component of most writers' success. Maybe that was something I didn't want to see, just then.)

I gave up the fantasy of becoming a professional writer. I guess I was fourteen or fifteen when I decided that it was a hopeless dream. All my stories were being rejected by the editors and now I had managed to convince myself that successful writers were born, not made. Either you had the right stuff or you didn't, and plainly, I didn't.

Still, if I could only sell *one* story, what a glorious thing that would be! How they would admire me at school when word got around that there was a story by me in the latest issue of some gaudy pulp magazine! It wouldn't be a great story—only the favorites of the gods had the knack of writing those, I now believed—but it would at least have been a publishable one. My best shot might just meet the minimal requirements. It wouldn't match Kuttner. It wouldn't equal Heinlein. I was pretty certain that I never could achieve that, and certainly not at the age of fifteen. But once the first spell of despair was past, I resolved to go on trying, at least until I had managed to sell one humble little piece of fiction. It seemed overwhelmingly difficult but not fundamentally impossible. If I kept on swinging the bat, I told myself, I might eventually hit the ball as far as the front row of seats, maybe. Maybe.

Instead of reading dismaying books like Uzzell, I tried to puzzle out the Secret for myself. That seemed a better way to learn; Uzzell was only confusing and frightening me with his hundreds of pages of how-to-do-it manual. Besides, I hated the idea of doing all those end-of-chapter exercises. So I began to study the stories in the current issues of the s-f magazines with passionate intensity. I concentrated on the lesser magazines, the ones that ran simple stories by not-so-famous writers, and I took those stories apart and stared at the pieces, thinking, This is an opening paragraph, This is how dialog works, This is as much exposition as you can get away with before the reader gets bored. And by 1950, just about the time I needed my first shave, I was producing stories that opened this way:

> A beam of red light glinted on the rocks of the cavern. Stretching out for untold miles, a rippling river flowed, strange blind fish playing in its bottomless, inky depths. The torch flickered once, twice in Mara's hand, casting an eery glow in the dark cavern. A serpent rose up, questioningly, to pass before Mara and slither back to its watery home. Struggling through the dim light, he walked on.
>
> He strode forward into the darkness, standing on the mold-encrusted banks of rock bordering the river. Al'p-he, the Sacred River, the great underground mystery of Venus. Mara battled forward.

Not Hugo-quality stuff. But there's struggle, if not exactly conflict. There's scenery. A mystery is hinted at. I sent it off to Jerome Bixby, the editor of *Planet Stories,* who returned it on April 25, 1950, but said, "Great Ghu, keep it up. . . . You're bound to connect sooner or later. Probably later, though, when your collection [of rejection slips] has grown some."

Bound to connect! Sooner or later! Could he mean it?

I kept on studying stories and writing my own. Conflict, they wanted. Hard choices, decisions, resolution. This is the second page of "Vanguard of Tomorrow," later in 1950:

When he saw the four men materialize out of an unoccupied floor space, he took it calmly, in stride, almost as if he had expected it.

Inwardly, he gulped.

He stared at them in mild surprise.

"What in hell are you doing here?" he growled.

He looked directly at the one who seemed to be the eldest. He was totally bald. Bill noted idly that he had no eyebrows, either.

Bill noted with a shock his clothes.

They were strange clothes. Short—knee-length tights, with a healthy bronzed calf below. They were bright-colored, made of some soft and shimmering cloth. Or was it cloth? Bill blinked his eyes.

Hanging at the man's side was a sword.

"What in hell are you doing here?" Bill softly repeated.

The four men silently shifted around, uncomfortably, looking nearly as surprised as Bill himself. Finally the eldest one licked his lips and spoke, in soft, oddly slurred accents. The words gave Bill a jolt.

He said, "We've come to prevent your marriage."

The plot was vaguely adapted from Heinlein's classic "By His Bootstraps," one of my favorites. The bald guys from the future were borrowed from Lewis Padgett. The short, punchy paragraphs were something I had picked up from Clifford D. Simak's "Time Quarry," which was currently running as a serial in the new magazine *Galaxy*. The editor of *Galaxy*, H. L. Gold, had described Simak's novel as "a powerful story of suspense, mystery, and ideas," and I decided that its power was in the punchiness. I can still remember thinking, as I sat there knocking out "Vanguard to Tomorrow" on my old portable typewriter one humid evening in the late summer of 1950, "This is powerful writing."

It was, at least, commercial-looking writing. As I look through the manuscript now, it seems to me not a whole lot worse than some things that were getting published in 1950. But Morton Klass, the associate editor of *Super-Science Stories*, returned it on February 6, 1951, with the observation that "most of the trouble lies with the plot, which—as you probably know yourself—is one of the oldest in science fiction. Well, you say, why can't somebody give an old plot a new twist? Heinlein took this plot and did it. Trouble is, we're not all Heinleins—at least not every day." Klass suggested I write about something I knew from personal experience, like going to high school. "What would high school be like on Mars? Procyon? Another time-stream? Hit 'em with the stories no one is writing, and see what happens. We'd be happy to see more of your work."

Not a bad idea, high school in another time-stream. I wish I had tried it for him. But I suppose I would have messed it up. I was coming close now to figuring out the right mix of storytelling ingredients—a novel background, an interesting character, a tough problem, an ingenious solution. And I was learning, not by studying Thomas Uzzell's book but by writing fiction after school all the time, how to move my story along through dialog and action. But I was still a little pisher, remember. I knew zilch about life and only minimally more than that about the art and craft of fiction. What editor was going to push Ray Bradbury off his pages to make room for my klutzy imitation pulp-magazine stories?

Keep trying, kid, I told myself, nevertheless. Just sell *one* story, and then you can relax and forget this obsession with writing science fiction and go on to do whatever it is you're going to do for the rest of your life.

Strangely, the next thing that happened to me was that I sold one story. I think I was 16. I may have been 15. Certainly I was still in high school. The story was "The Sacred River," which is the one I quoted a little way back about Mara struggling through the cavern on Venus. Lilith Lorraine, the editor of a magazine for amateur poets called *Different*, paid me five dollars for it. (By the time she used it, in 1952, *Different* had gone out of business and it appeared in something called *The Avalonian*.)

Selling a story to *Different*, which was available only by subscription and had an audience of—who knows, eight hundred readers?—was not quite the same thing as selling one to *Startling* or *Astounding*. None of my classmates would ever see the story unless I went out of my way to show it to them, and even then they weren't likely to be impressed, since *Different* (and the later *Avalonian*) looked a lot like high-school poetry magazines. But someone had been willing to pay—even if it was only five dollars—for the privilege of publishing my fiction, all the same. That was the important thing. Instead of letting me off the hook, that trifling first sale inspired me to keep on plugging forward. If it had happened once, it might happen again, and the next time it might be a real magazine that sent me the check.

I went on writing, went on studying the craft. I picked up tips out of thin air. Some book reviewer, discussing I know not what novel, said of its author that "he writes the sort of dialog that doesn't merely fill space but actually advances the plot. Which of course is the only sort of dialog any story should contain." Or words to that effect.

It was a revelation to me. *Everything* was a revelation to me then. Oh, I said. The dialog is there to move the plot along. Dialog is actually a form of exposition. You can't just chatter about the weather or the fact that your shoes hurt, the way people do in real life: whatever the characters say should help to unfold the story. Of course, a lot of dialog reveals character, and revealing character is part of building the unfolding story. But the dialog must be seen as an essential structural unit, not a decoration. The best writers handle dialog in such a way that it simultaneously illuminates character, provides needed information, and advances the plot, with not a word going to waste. You can, naturally, waste plenty of words and still get published. A science-fiction novel I recall from the early 1980s was absolutely bubbling with needless dialog ("Thank you, Doctor.

You've told us what we need to know. I'm sorry we took so much of your time. I'm sure you're doing your best.") and not only got published but won the Hugo and Nebula awards. It was a book of many worthy aspects, which is why it won awards, but effective dialog was not one of them. Still, patterning your work after horrible examples is no way to master a craft. I still think that the role of dialog is to move the story along, and not just to vary the typography of the page by sprinkling it with quotation marks.

Actually, I see by looking through my primitive early stories that I had already figured that much out, at least unconsciously. But I didn't *know* that I had figured it out, which is why it came as such a surprise to me when I saw someone else state it explicitly. A lot of narrative technique is actually something that you figure out unconsciously as you absorb other people's narratives; later you may consciously codify a set of rules, and later on you internalize them again so that they operate without your having to stop to think about them. At that point you're a professional writer.

Though I had made that lone five-dollar sale, I certainly didn't think of myself as a professional writer in 1951. My stories now had begun to look much more like the ones I saw in the magazines, but I didn't even come close to selling one, and the idea that I would someday break through into the ranks of the published was once again beginning to seem unrealistic to me. And now there were more immediate challenges to deal with, such as getting used to my new almost-adult body, and girls, and applying for college. For the next year, perhaps a year and a half, I did little or no writing. But on some level I refused to give up; and all during 1952—my first year of college—I continued to study the science-fiction magazines with crazy intensity, still hoping to discover the Secret.

That was a golden age for the science-fiction short story. The day of the cheap and sleazy pulp magazine was just about over. A flood of new s-f magazines had come into being, and most of them were small, compact, slick-looking publications with serious-sounding names (*Galaxy, Other Worlds, Worlds Beyond, Fantasy &*

Science Fiction). Whereas just a few years before only John Campbell's *Astounding Science Fiction* and then to some degree Sam Merwin's *Startling* and *Thrilling Wonder* had made a point of publishing stories that might be of interest to a reasonably intelligent adult reader, now virtually all the new magazines were looking for material that was clever, original, and well written. Their editors were men who had been outstanding writers themselves—Anthony Boucher, Horace Gold, Damon Knight, Frederik Pohl, Lester del Rey. Many of them had been associated during the formative days of their own writing careers with the brilliant and demanding editor John W. Campbell, and they were determined to live up to Campbell's high standards of performance or even surpass them.

These sparkling new magazines paid relatively high fees for their material, usually two or three cents a word at a time when the going rate had been a cent or a cent and a half. (Fred Pohl's *Star Science Fiction*, a magazine in paperback form, opened up in 1951 by offering *nine* cents a word, which is more than many science-fiction magazines pay even in today's inflated market.) The lively, sophisticated new editors let it be known that they would not be catering to the action-pulp readers. They would be receptive to writing at the highest level of skill; indeed they would publish nothing less than that. And the little community of professional science-fiction writers, overflowing with story ideas and eager to experiment with fresh and startling ways of handling them, responded with astonishing fervor.

Some of the writers who flocked to the new magazines were veterans, five or in some cases ten years into their careers: Theodore Sturgeon, James Blish, Jack Vance, Fritz Leiber, Alfred Bester, C. M. Kornbluth, Poul Anderson, Isaac Asimov, Arthur C. Clarke, Philip Klass ("William Tenn"), Henry Kuttner, and Kuttner's wife, C. L. Moore. They had little interest in writing conventional pulp fiction and most of them had come to have less and less liking for dealing with the increasingly dogmatic and difficult John Campbell. Gold's *Galaxy* and Boucher's *Fantasy & Science Fiction* and Pohl's *Star* paid them well and gave them creative freedom they had never known before. The results were extraordinary.

But there was also a rush of gifted newcomers—writers in their twenties or early thirties, mainly, who had read and loved science fiction for years and who found a ready welcome for their first stories in the suddenly expanded market of 1952 and 1953: Philip K. Dick, Robert Sheckley, Philip José Farmer, Algis Budrys, Chad Oliver, Kris Neville, Jerome Bixby, Walter M. Miller, Jr., Mack Reynolds, Gordon R. Dickson, J. T. McIntosh, Michael Shaara, Katherine Maclean, James Gunn, and many more. Some passed through and went on their way. Others remained for long and splendid careers.

And I? Where was I while all this was going on?

I was up at Morningside Heights, a freshman at Columbia, reading Dante and Aeschylus with one eye and *Galaxy* and *Fantasy & Science Fiction* with the other, and still desperately trying to figure out the Secret. How I envied all those new writers, just five or ten years older than I was, who were rampaging through the pages of the new magazines! How I stared at the tables of contents, imagining my own name there! It's impossible even now for me to look at one of those magazines without feeling a renewed surge of that old envy and yearning. Nor can I ever shake the belief that the stories in those issues were written by demigods and that their quality will be forever beyond my hope of equalling.

Technique. It's all a matter of technique, I told myself. I can come up with ideas for stories that are just as good as these. But I must learn to match their dazzling technique. I looked at Bester or Sheckley: how quick and supple the prose, how sparkling the dialog, how agile the leaps and pirouettes of the plot! I looked at Blish and Asimov and Clarke: how intricate the conceptual underpinning, how fascinating the ideas! I looked at Sturgeon and Farmer: how rich the emotional tone, how full and strange the vision of life! Dick was clever, Budrys seemed to know how everything worked, Vance brought to life a galaxy of colors and textures, Kuttner and Moore produced stories that functioned like beautifully designed machines.

I wanted to be able to do everything that any of them could do, and do all of it in the same story, and more. (I still feel that way.) Chutz-pah? Hubris? Maybe so. I had big ambitions. How to fulfill them? Technique was the answer. Learn the tricks of the trade. And finish growing up, too. Read everything you can. Travel widely. Talk. Listen. Poke into strange dark corners. Eat strange things. Hear strange music. If you mean to tell stories, you must have stories inside you that are worth telling. And you must master the craft of telling them, so that when you say to a reader, "Listen to what I have to relate," he will stand still and listen.

In my pursuit of technique, four names stand out: Blish, Knight, Kitto, Gold. Blish and Knight were outstanding science-fiction writers who, on the side, wrote criticism of the most merciless kind. Kitto was professor of Greek at Bristol University in England. Gold was the infuriating, opinionated editor of *Galaxy*. Much of what I learned about writing fiction I learned from them—not so much in the form of explicit rules, but in what I took from them in an indirect way, through my own process of observation and internalization.

Blish, who died in 1975, was a cool, precise, somewhat waspish man devoted to the music of Richard Wagner and Richard Strauss, the poetry of Ezra Pound, the fiction of James Joyce, and the philosophy of Oswald Spengler. He also wrote science fiction of a cool and precise and intellectual kind, much of which impressed me to the point of awe. Strangely, he won his widest fame, if that is what it can be called, by turning *Star Trek* teleplays by other writers into short stories that were published in a series of hugely successful paperbacks. I met him first when I was about 16, and—based on nothing more than a ten-minute conversation—he seemed to think I had potential, and said so to a mutual friend. A couple of years later I made myself his disciple, without ever telling him so. Later—when I was a successful professional writer—we became close friends, a friendship that endured (with a few bumpy moments) to the end of his life.

Blish took the business of literary technique very, very seriously, and set forth his beliefs on the subject with firmness and ferocity. Listening to him hold forth about the art of fiction, or reading the formidable essays that were collected in 1964 in a volume called *The Issue at Hand*, I had a sense of him as the high priest of an arcane cult in which I was the merest novice. If Thomas Uzzell had intimidated me in 1950 by letting me see how much there was to learn about writing fiction, Blish positively terrified me a few years later by making it seem as though Uzzell had just skimmed the surface of the topic. Through much of my career, I imagined Blish reading my stories as they appeared and shaking his head sadly as he tossed them aside. I don't think he actually did, but the image provided a useful goad to me, driving me ever onward to meet my notion of his standards. At first that seemed an impossible goal. Yet he and I both lived long enough so that in 1973 he could write of one of my books that it was "so unobstrusively, flawlessly written that even at its most puzzling it comes as perilously close to poetic beauty as any contemporary s-f novel I've ever read." If I had had a time machine handy, I would have rushed back twenty years to show that astounding review to my younger self. Who would probably have just shrugged and smiled, the arrogant little bastard, and told me that he knew all along that he'd be capable of writing a book someday that Jim Blish would find flawless. But he would have been lying through his teeth.

In truth I didn't feel arrogant at all, that day in late 1952 when I read the first essay in what eventually would become Blish's *The Issue at Hand*. I felt frightened and overwhelmed.

"We know," he said, "that there is a huge body of available technique in fiction writing, and that the competence of a writer—entirely aside from the degree of his talent—is determined by how much of this body of technique he can use.

"We know (from study, from our own practice, or from both) the essential features of good narrative practice; we expect writers and editors to know no less than we do.

"We also know that at least half of the science fiction writers being published today are, from the point of view of technical competence, taking up our time unnecessarily. . . ."

My God! If half the s-f being published in the golden year of 1952 was technically inept and worthless, what hope was there for me, still an amateur, still collecting rejection slips? In panic I read and reread Blish's essays as they appeared, looking for clues to this mystery of technique. I knew by then that stories were built about conflict, that they had beginnings, middles, and ends, that they needed dialog and exposition in some reasonable mix, that they had to show appealing or at least interesting characters engaged in coping with obstacles and either succeeding or else failing in some way that was revelatory of character. But what else was there? What were the inner secrets that the true writers had learned? What was that "huge body of available technique" that Blish knew, and Sturgeon, and Bester, and the other masters?

Some of the answers were in Blish's essays, which appeared quarterly all through the early 1950s in a mimeographed, "little" magazine called *Skyhook*, and which I studied as though they were scripture. In each issue he reviewed the current crop of s-f magazines, praised a few stories he found praiseworthy, and shredded the rest without mercy. ("This may seem to be heavy artillery to bring to bear upon a story which can be little over a thousand words long, but I can't see why a story should be excused for being bad because it is short." "For this story, with its cuddly animals with the telepathic ears, nausea is not enough. I can only suggest that both authors— not their story, but the authors themselves—be piled in the middle of the floor and set fire to." "The story is one of the worst stinkers ever to have been printed in the field. To begin on the most elementary level, Mr.——'s prose includes more downright bad grammar than any single *Astounding* piece since . . .")

Of course, there was much more to Blish than hatchet-swinging and vitriol-flinging. His praise was intelligent and searching. Discussing Damon Knight's "Four in One," he pointed out that "the major idea in this story is not only as old as Homer, but has been handled before by science fiction writers of stature: the Proteus, the creature which can assume any shape. Knight makes no attempt to surprise anybody with this notion; even had he himself never encountered the idea before outside his own head, he is too good a craftsman to assume that an idea alone is enough. The contrasting idea is that of escape from a totalitarian society, again a piece of common coin. The result is 'Four in One,' which is compelling not because it contains a single new notion but because nobody but Knight ever before showed these two old notions in such an individual light, and because, in addition, the light is individual throughout—the story contains hardly a single stock reaction."

That one paragraph was worth a year of courses in "How to Write" for me. From it I drew an immensely valuable method for constructing science-fiction stories—not simply stories, but *science-fiction stories*—that would go beyond minimal mediocre attainment. (There is a general art of writing fiction, which I had struggled all through my adolescence to learn, and there is a special art of writing science fiction; the second art requires mastery of the first, but has some unusual requirements of its own.)

It was no news to me, of course, that science-fiction stories had to be based on a speculative idea, a what-if hypothesis. ("Suppose the Martians invaded Earth." "Suppose it was possible to travel through time." "Suppose someone invented artificial servants that would do all our work for us.") The problem is that most of the obvious speculations, being obvious, were proposed long ago. H. G. Wells took care of the Martian invasion and the trip through time—and a great many other themes besides—back in the 1890s; the Czech Karel Čapek thoroughly explored the artificial-servant theme in his 1921 play, *R.U.R.*, which gave the world the word *robot*. The ideas that were not obvious and had not been handled before ("Suppose explorers get to the moon and find it made not of green cheese but of bleached salami") had, I suspected, gone unused because they were too dumb to use. What was a young science-fiction writer to do? Helplessly recycle the standard themes of his forebears?

Blish, using Knight's "Four in One" as an example, gave me the clue. Nobody could found a science-fiction career on coming up with dazzling new ideas all the time. You might manage the trick once or twice in a career, if you were lucky; but to pay the rent you needed to produce salable copy day in and day out. At that point in my life I would have been happy to produce something that was merely salable; but I knew that if I intended to make a career out of writing science fiction I would need to get beyond that minimal level and attain some degree of real excellence. It wouldn't be enough just to write the millionth the-martians-are-landing or someday-we-will-have-robots story. One way of getting there, I saw now, was to yoke a couple of familiar themes together so that they illuminated one another and provided new insights. Knight had done that in "Four in One." Jack Williamson's superb "With Folded Hands" had done that for the robot theme by asking whether robots designed to free us from the boredom of menial labor might turn out to be *too* effective in sparing us from toil. John W. Campbell's scary "Who Goes There" had linked the alien-invader theme with the old medieval shape-changer idea. And so on.

Not only did Blish discuss current stories that he thought were unusually fine or unusually awful examples of science fiction, and substantiate his opinions with close analysis of text, but he also scattered little technical tips throughout his essays. It is a good idea, he said, to give your major characters names, and to describe them physically, early in a story. It is a bad idea, he said, to use metaphors of the concrete-is-abstract form ("She was love. . . . She was ache and anguish and doubt. . . .") because such metaphors create wooliness and vagueness where clarity is desired. It is unwise, said Blish, to use synonyms for "said" in writing dialog ("He shouted. . . . He repeated. . . . He instructed. . . . He grunted. . . . He half-whispered. . . . He lipped thinly. . . .") because such tags are redundant at best—the content of the sentence ought to tell the reader right away that something is being shouted or repeated—and at worst they became preposterous. It was permissible sometimes to give a clue—"He whispered," for instance—but all too often the amateur writer, Blish noted, would go on beyond using tags that represent a manner of speaking and substitute ones that represent facial expressions ("He sneered") or adjectives ("He flustered") or verbs ("He pointed"). Worst of all, said Blish, was the complete sentence dropped in between two chunks of dialog as a substitute for "He said," in this manner:

" 'You will never get me to sign that document,' Stanley flung the sheet of paper from him, 'so long as it contains the loathsome Clause Seventeen.' "

To Blish such stuff read "like a freshman translation from the German."

These were only working rules, of course—not absolute commandments. They could be broken from time to time, and some writers could get away with breaking them *all* the time. (One best-selling science-fiction novelist of the 1970s and 1980s scatters dozens of "said" substitutes over every page; but readers love her books anyway, and stand in long lines to buy the new ones when they come out. When another well-known writer used a complete sentence as a "said" substitute and I objected, he showed me where Hemingway had once done the same thing. Well, I said, even if Hemingway did it, it's still a dumb thing to do. Besides, you're not Hemingway.) But though it might be possible to violate such ad-hoc rules and get away with it, Blish made me see that they did have intrinsic underlying value. The idea, after all, is not so much to get away with things as to know what tends to work best—and what does not—in building the bond between the writer and reader that makes him keep on reading with pleasure.

Filling your page of dialog with strings of "She asserted hotly" and "He protested vehemently" and "She cudgelled" and "He parried thoughtfully" may seem to you a good way of enlivening a passage of conversation. But it might well induce a reader with a keen sense of style to begin skipping down the page looking for the next silly substitute for "said" instead of paying attention to the dialog itself.

Failing to describe characters' physical appearances is likewise not a criminal offense, and in certain cases may actually be necessary for the strategy of your plot; but as a rule, readers are drawn into stories more quickly if they have some idea of what the people they're reading about look like. A little landscape painting doesn't hurt either. (Too much description will have the opposite effect, though.) The point is to draw the reader in, not to push him away. Distracting your reader from the narrative material of the story by cluttering the page with extraneous stuff is rarely a useful tactic, unless your story itself is so thin that it's best to hide its failings under a welter of mannerisms.

It was easy enough for me to accept these stylistic dictates. My ear was acute and I had already come to be able to distinguish good writing—that is, direct, effective communication—from bad. I was, remember, a college boy who, when he was not reading *Galaxy* and *Star Science Fiction*, was busy taking courses in Joyce and Faulkner and Shakespeare. But what Blish also showed me was that a story could be well written—*beautifully* written, even—and still be bad science fiction.

For instance, good science fiction ought to be built around some idea (or cluster of ideas) that stimulates thought. A story about little furry long-eared animals called smeerps that go hippity-hop and eat lettuce does not become science fiction because you have called your rabbits smeerps. Telling us that the smeerps live on Mars doesn't change anything if your Mars looks just like Illinois. There are ways to turn such stories into science fiction (the smeerps may have interestingly nefarious reasons for masquerading as rabbits; Mars may look like Illinois because the Martians are playing a trick on the visiting spacemen from Earth) but the would-be writer needs to be aware that what is needed is ingenious speculative thinking, not just a bunch of funny names.

A science-fiction story ought to make sense. An idea that contradicts itself within five pages illuminates nothing and irritates the intelligent reader. Blish cites a Ray Bradbury story that proposes that the Messiah is traveling through the universe one world at a time. Having brought His message to Earth, He is now moving on to Mars. Blish found the idea "a numerical absurdity," pointing out that it would take forever for Jesus to spread the word through the entire galaxy, and that surely an omnipotent God could find some more efficient way of bringing about the Advent in the universe than by "turning His Son into the Wandering Salesman." Similarly, a story that depends for its plot complications on a character's failure to notice some screamingly obvious fact is going to annoy rather than entertain readers, and one with a plot that functions only because everyone acts like a total nincompoop will not arouse much sympathy for, or interest in, the events that stem from all that nincompoopery.

Blish thought that science-fiction writers should know something about science and make use of it in their stories. This notion was beginning to seem old-fashioned thirty years ago and must strike many writers of today as downright odd. What he was saying, though, was not that it is the writer's job to include a wiring diagram for every gadget in his stories or to provide lengthy footnotes describing the underlying astronomical assumptions he is using. It was simply that a science-fiction story ought to be based on some speculative departure from real-world conditions, and in order to do a good job of framing his speculation, the writer first needs to know something about how the real world is put together, or at a bare minimum "that anything one wishes to call a science-fiction story should contain some vestige of some knowledge of some science."

This was another way of saying that a story has to make sense. It will not do to have your hero get from Mars to Venus in a rowboat, or rebuild a flashlight so that a deadly radioactive beam issues from it, or turn a mushroom into a gorilla by applying powerful magnetic forces. A really clever s-f pro probably could make any of those three notions plausible if he put his mind to it, but the fact is that in the ordinary sense of things we know that all three are impossible and pretty silly besides. A story that blithely violates the present body of scientific knowledge—by telling us, say, that ferns have lovely flow-ers or that table salt is made up of equal parts of carbon and potas-sium or that a squid has a skeleton—may in fact get published, if the editor is as ignorant as the writer, but it's going to bother a lot of readers. *Falsus in uno, falsus in omnibus,* as the lawyers say: "False in one thing, false in all." A reader who sees that you believe ferns have nice blossoms is going to suspect the rest of your story of being nonsense too: characters, background, plot, resolution. A knowledge of science not only gives the s-f writer something to work with in coming up with story ideas, but also helps in avoiding blunders of fact in a field where such blunders are more than usually fatal to a writer's aspiration.

So I studied Blish with care, and polished my stories to avoid the infelicities of style and construction that he so acidly deplored in others, and checked the logic of my ideas for hidden nonsense, and pored over *Scientific American* and textbooks of astronomy and physics to fill in the gaps of my education. And went on writing. And sold a few stories, finally, and then some more. They were pretty mediocre, sure. Some of them were less than mediocre. But to my great relief, Jim Blish never found any of them bad in a way that was interesting enough to discuss in his column in *Skyhook.* By the time he did get around to writing about my work a few years later, I was an established pro, doing work that was not wonderful but competent and in no danger of being held up to public scorn. (From other cor-ners, as you will see, would come private scorn—because I seemed willing to settle for being merely competent. Precocious as ever, I had learned my lessons well enough so that no one was likely to poke fun at my stories; but in my youthful zeal to attain technical competence I had forgotten about attaining excellence. I'll get to that in a little while.)

The second of my teenage mentors was Damon Knight—writer, editor, ferocious critic. In person Knight was not much like the dry, astringent Blish; he was and is a gentle man of much charm and playful, oddly goofy wit. But when he turned his hand to the critical analysis of science fiction he proved to be an even more effective demolisher of all that was foolish, technically inadequate, or lazily conceived. Here are a few samples from his remarkable volume of collected essays, *In Search of Wonder* (1956, second edition 1967):

On Robert Sheckley:

Most of the stories in Robert Sheckley's *Citizen in Space* . . . are brief, brightly inventive, and logically unstable. Sheckley's faceless characters chirp, twitter, whirl with captivating grace around an idea, but seldom settle down long enough to exercise ordinary intelligence upon it. . . . Sheckley's heroes weigh in at an I.Q. of about 90, just sufficient to get aboard their shiny machines, but not enough to push all the right levers. . . . Once in a while, when Sheckley bothers to put something under his slick surfaces, his work comes brilliantly and even movingly to life. . . . Like it or not, what Sheckley does is art. But he could use a little less art, and a little more craftsmanship.

On A. E. van Vogt:

John W. Campbell has said editorially more than once that *The World of Null-A* is "one of those once-in-a-decade classics of science fiction." I offer the alternate judgment that, far from being a "classic" by any reasonable standard, *The World of Null-A* is one of the worst allegedly-adult science fiction stories ever published.

I'll try to prove that assertion by an analysis of the story on four levels: Plot, Characterization, Background, and Style. . . .

The World of Null-A abounds in contradictions, misleading clues, and irrelevant action. . . . Van Vogt has not bothered to integrate the gadgets into the technological background of his story; and . . . he has no clear idea of their nature. . . . Examples of bad writing could be multiplied endlessly. It is my personal opinion that the whole of it is written badly, with only minor exceptions; but this is a purely subjective judgment and is not susceptible of proof. . . . By means of his writing style, which is discursive and hard to follow, van Vogt also obscures his plot to such an extent that when it falls to pieces at the end, as it frequently does, the event passes without remark. . . .

On John Wyndham's novel *Re-Birth*:

These first few chapters have the genuine autobiographical sense—that Wellsian retrospective clarity, the torment of writers who can't do it themselves. More's the pity that Wyndham, for once, failed to realize how good a thing he had. The sixth toe was immensely believable, and sufficient: but Wyndham has dragged in a telepathic mutation on top of it; has made David himself one of the nine child telepaths, and hauled the whole plot away from his carefully built background, into just one more damned chase with a rousing cliché at the end of it.

Wyndham's unflaggingly expert writing, all the way through, only proves that there are no exceptions: this error is fatal.

Knight's vigorous, detailed, and total destruction of van Vogt's famous novel was great fun to read for everyone except, I imagine, van Vogt, but it struck me then and now as largely unfair, a mixture of justified criticism and a studied misreading of van Vogt's intentions. Knight's pieces on Sheckley and Wyndham, though—and indeed the bulk of his criticism—began from a position of respect for the writer, and singled out disturbing flaws *within a context of appreciation*. That seemed admirable to me and immensely instructive. And where Knight found nothing at all to criticize, but offered only warm praise (" 'The Census Takers' is a beautifully compact exercise in indirection. Entirely successful on its own terms, it plays one speculative idea . . . against another without wasting a word or a motion," or "When it's all done, the story means something. Harness' theme is the triumph of spirit over flesh. . . . This is the rock under all Harness' hypnotic cat's-cradles of invention—faith in the spirit, the denial of pain, the affirmation of eternal life," or "Jack Vance's *Big Planet* . . . shows this brilliant writer at the top of his form. Big Planet, where most of the action takes place, is as vividly compelling as the dream-world of Eddison's *The Worm Ouroboros*: and that's the highest praise I know"), off I would go like a shot to the story under discussion, and I would read and reread it, trying to locate the qualities that had elicited such praise from Knight so that I could come up with my own equivalents of them in the work I was doing. You will find some of the stories that Knight singled out for such praise in this collection.

Of course it was impossible for me, now age 18 or 19 or so, to match the achievements of other writers that brought forth Knight's warmest encomiums. But by studying them, as also I studied the works praised by Blish, I could at least attain an Idea of the Good as defined by a man whose experience as a reader and a writer went far beyond my own and who had himself written notable fiction. (I don't believe that a good critic of fiction necessarily has to be capable of writing good fiction himself; but for me there is a certain unanswerable plausibility in an analysis of a story's flaws done by someone who has himself demonstrated clear excellence in the form.) The only problem I had with Knight's essays was their occasional tendency to rekindle in me the old Uzzell hopelessness, that sense that the task of constructing a worthwhile work of fiction required arcane skills that would forever be beyond the attainment of a poor mortal like me. Here, for example, is Knight discussing a story by James Blish:

There is a really fantastic body of technique in this short novel [*Beanstalk*], but unless you are looking at it you will never notice it; it's submerged, where it belongs. . . . Not merely embedded in *Beanstalk*, but inseparably united to make one coherent and symmetrical narrative, are whole exemplars or recognizable fragments of the following: a sports story; a love story; a Western story—plus, for good measure, a couple of panels from "Buck Rogers". . . . Wildly incompatible as the above-listed elements are, not one has been dragged in by the hair; every one has been almost unrecognizably altered by the author's inventiveness; every one is essential. The sports fragment is a jet-powered, gimmicked-up Titan football game, necessary to pave the way for the Buck Rogers element, which is itself (a) indispensable and (b) brilliantly rationalized, down to the last silly flange on the flying-belt-borne superman's helmet.

I don't think such a technical stunt would be beyond my skill now; it had better not be, with thirty-odd years of practice behind me. But reading that paragraph in 1953, when it appeared in Knight's review column in *Future Science Fiction*, I felt myself close to tears of helplessness and bitter self-reproach. How, I wondered, for perhaps the thousandth time, could I ever attain such technical proficiency? As Knight himself had said, you couldn't even *see* what Blish was doing in that story: he had submerged it all beyond the notice of anyone but one who was already among the adept.

And then I thought: All right, dummy. Make yourself one of the adept.

H. D. F. Kitto helped me toward that goal, though I don't think he ever intended his studies of Aeschylus, Sophocles, and Euripides to serve as instruction to an ambitious young science-fiction writer. I bought a copy of Kitto's *Greek Tragedy* in 1954, as collateral reading for a course in Greek plays that I was taking during my junior year at Columbia. But 1954 was also the year when I was making the most determined assault of my life on the goal of becoming a professional science-fiction writer. Late in 1953 I had submitted a proposal for a novel for young readers, *Revolt on Alpha C,* to the old-line publishing firm of Thomas Y. Crowell, and on the first day of the new year had come a call from the legendary Crowell juvenile-books editor, Elizabeth M. Riley, telling me that she was offering me a contract for my book, though she would want extensive revisions. Later in January, 1954, "Gorgon Planet," a short story I had sent to the Scottish s-f magazine *Nebula,* was accepted and brought me a check for $12.60. A little while later I finally sold a story to a professional American magazine: my little vignette "The Silent Colony" yielded $13.50 from *Future Science Fiction.* Plainly, I had solved enough of the technical mysteries of story writing to qualify for an entry-level position. Now was the moment to build on the new confidence that these early sales had provided, and produce some ambitious work that would establish me in the ranks of the professionals.

The unwitting Kitto became my most valuable teacher. By his close examination of the works of the great Greek playwrights, he provided me with a deep understanding of the nature of drama, without which it is impossible to construct an effective story plot.

I had already come to see Greek tragedy as a public ritual in which a dramatic situation—that is, a conflict unavoidable by the nature of events—is proposed, displayed, and resolved. The resolution, by demonstrating a return to the natural harmony of the universe, sends the audience home cleansed and calm—purged, as Aristotle said, of pity and fear. To this day I have continued to believe that all fiction, even the sleaziest, is a ritual healing art fundamentally akin to Greek tragedy in its purpose: that by showing the tension of opposite forces (plot, drama, conflict) and by resolving that tension (climax and ending) fiction performs a function of psychic cleansing. It seems to me that there can be no other reason for the universality of the narrative mode: patterns of story development are surprisingly similar everywhere, in cultures as far apart as those of Japan and West Africa, of ancient Sumer and modern America.

Kitto began with the premise that each Greek tragedy was built around a significant dramatic situation designed to create the kind of tension that would provide the desired release for the audience when the tension was resolved. In his *Poetics* Aristotle asserted that that was what Greek tragedy was all about: catharsis, the purging of pity and fear. Aristotle had used as his prime technical example *Oedipus Rex* by Sophocles. But Kitto observed that many other surviving Greek plays failed to follow the technical rules that Aristotle, working from *Oedipus Rex*, had laid down as the fundamental requirements for a Greek tragedy. Did that mean that other Greek playwrights (and sometimes even Sophocles himself) had done a lot of incompetent work?

No, Kitto said. We know that the plays that have come down to us were warmly hailed in their time and evidently had fulfilled the requirements of their audience. Their authors must be regarded as masters of their art, in full technical command. If sometimes their plays seem poorly constructed to us, static and undramatic, it must be because we are failing to find the true dramatic center of them. Instead of dismissing those plays as badly made, Kitto argued, we need to reexamine our own assumptions about their structure.

He begins with Aeschylus, the earliest playwright whose work has survived. "Although Aeschylus was a young man when he wrote the *Supplices*," says Kitto, "he was already Aeschylus, and we may suppose that he built the play as he felt it. Technical difficulties we may allow him, but we will not readily suppose that he got his proportions and his emphasis all wrong. . . . We must be sure that we have made allowance before we call a play undramatic."

He analyzes the *Supplices* scene by scene. It is the story of the flight of the fifty daughters of Danaus from Egypt to Argos to avoid the unwanted suitors who wish to marry them—a difficult play, for it was the first part of a trilogy of which the other two parts are lost, and we do not know where Aeschylus meant the story to go; what remains to us seems at first reading short on action and tension. The maidens and their aged father arrive in Argos; Pelasgus, the king of Argos, is uneasy about granting them sanctuary, because it might bring war to his land if the Egyptian suitors pursue; the people of Argos vote to grant sanctuary anyway, out of fear of the wrath of Zeus if they refuse; and then Egyptian ships arrive. A herald threatens war if the maidens are not returned; Pelasgus angrily refuses to be bullied; old Danaus tells his daughters to be modest and brave and offer prayers to the gods; and the play ends with a hopeful chorus.

"What is it all about?" asks Kitto. "What was Aeschylus thinking at the age of 30? We are not certain how the trilogy went, but at least we can hold fast to what we have.

"The trilogy was not simply a stage-version of the renowned story of the Danaids. What arrests and detains the attention most in the *Supplices* is the tragic dilemma of Pelasgus; this is where Aeschylus was most engaged—not in the running about of Danaus." The center of the play lies elsewhere than in the troubles of Danaus and his daughters; Danaus is offstage most of the time and his daughters are simply a faceless chorus. The plight of the innocent Pelasgus, whose peaceful land is threatened by war over a dispute that has nothing to do with him, is more central. Pelasgus is the real tragic hero, caught inextricably in a situation not of his own making, and we know from the myth on which Aeschylus based his play that he will die in the warfare that engulfs his kingdom. But even this, Kitto demonstrates, is not the true center.

What is? "Through no deficiency of sense, intellect or morality has [Pelasgus] fallen into this awful dilemma. A disharmony in the makeup of things, and a perfectly innocent man is broken. Here, in the earliest of Greek tragedies, we find one of the most purely tragic situations; the Flaw in the Universe, which the philosophers will have none of, is plain enough to Aeschylus." And Kitto shows us—reconstructing, where necessary, the missing two plays of the trilogy—how everything in the play works toward dramatizing the harshness of Zeus' law and the necessity for humans to conform to the workings of a universe beyond comprehension. "If we suppose . . . there must be some middle way out, one which will not involve the innocent, we deceive ourselves. Once the moral balance of things is disturbed in this way there is no telling how far calamity will not spread. . . . The Supplicants, unable to accept injury, involve innocent Argos. They destroy their persecutors—and it serves *them* right—but the disturbance is not at an end until they are made to bring themselves into harmony with Zeus' law. It may be hard, but Aeschylus never pretended that life was easy, or that Zeus was simple, or that only the guilty are tortured."

I was much impressed by Kitto's demonstration that the seemingly undramatic *Supplices* was in fact a carefully constructed examination of the rigors of cosmic law. There is much more to plotting a story, I saw, than pitting a hero against a villain and letting them go at it. Kitto went on, play by play, showing how seeming flaws in dramaturgy were simply flaws in our perception of the play's meaning; and I read on and on in wonder.

When he came to Sophocles, that paragon of playwrights, Kitto faced the problem of dealing with a couple of plays that do not seem at all Sophoclean in their construction: *Ajax* and *The Trachinian Women*. But once in, starting from the assumption that Sophocles was a great artist and must have known what he was doing, Kitto provided stunning illumination.

Ajax, Sophocles' earliest known play, is set during the Trojan War. The great soldier Ajax, having been defeated by Odysseus in the contest for dead Achilles' armor, goes mad with shame and chagrin and commits horrid and outrageous deeds; when he recovers his sanity long enough to see what he has done, he chooses to take his own life rather than endure disgrace. That much might make a satisfactory tragedy, but the problem is that the death of Ajax occurs at line 865 and the play goes on for another 550 lines, mostly devoted to a bitter dispute among the Greek heroes over his burial. This long wrangle, which can make the play seem like a disquisition on Greek funeral customs, has led some critics to speak of the "sense of diminished tragic feeling" or "a disastrous lowering of tone" in the closing scene. No, says Kitto. What we see as an imperfection was to Sophocles and his audience the whole point of *Ajax*. Kitto argues that the play is not really about Ajax or the burial of Ajax at all: it is about the conflict between Ajax and Odysseus and the resolution of that conflict.

The play, Kitto points out, begins and ends not with Ajax, but with wise Odysseus, Ajax' rival and enemy. At the opening Odysseus speaks in horror of Ajax' crimes of madness; in the end he prevails over King Agamemnon and his brother Menelaus and obtains a hero's burial for the dead warrior. "The unifying theme," writes Kitto, "is the antagonism of Ajax and Odysseus, of physical, and we may admit, of spiritual daring against intellectual greatness; an antagonism the more dramatic in that Ajax never understands Odysseus whereas Odysseus always understands Ajax. Ajax, lacking 'wisdom,' brings himself to ruin: Odysseus, rich in wisdom, not only is successful . . . but also attains moral grandeur. . . . In [Agamemnon and Menelaus] there is no resolution of the antagonism; that comes only when the greatness of Odysseus recognizes the greatness of the defeated Ajax and above all the greatness of the fact of Death. The end is rather the triumph of Odysseus than the rehabilitation of Ajax. In the prologue he triumphs over Athena's suggestions of crude force and resentment; by the vote of the army [to give him rather than Ajax the armor of Achilles] his intellectual greatness has already overcome Ajax' soldierly greatness, now he brings the drama to a harmonious close by overcoming the moral violence [of Agamemnon and Menelaus]."

Kitto's controversial interpretations of Greek drama may or may not be "right." But, in the course of showing that if we have trouble finding the dramatic center of a Greek play, it may be because its dramatic center is actually located someplace other than where we are looking for it, he taught me what a dramatic situation really is: a zone of inevitable opposition of powerful forces that emits ever-widening reverberations until it is neutralized somehow in a way that creates understanding, insight, and harmony. Knowing that, I could work backward from my perception of my story's central issue to generate its plot. What created this conflict? What can possibly resolve it? Who is being hurt by it, and why? Those are the questions I learned to ask myself; and out of them came *Thorns, To Live Again, Tower of Glass, Dying Inside, Lord Valentine's Castle*, and all the rest.

But not right away. Though I had read my Kitto, I was not quite as good as Sophocles, yet. Though I had studied Blish and Knight and the stories they found praiseworthy, my own work continued to fall some distance short of their precepts. In fact, I was barely competent at my chosen trade, no longer a novice but only a minimally adept journeyman. But at least I had figured out, with their help, how to construct salable fiction. My basic notions of technique were now in place: find a situation of dissonance growing out of a striking idea or some combination of striking ideas, find the characters affected by that dissonance, write clearly and directly using dialog that moves each scene along and avoiding any clumsiness of style and awkward shifts of viewpoint, and bring matters in the end to a point where the harmony of the universe is restored and Zeus is satisfied.

Having learned and internalized all that, I spent my final year in college writing science fiction as fast as I could, and I sold practically everything I wrote. It was a heady feeling: too heady, perhaps. By the time I took my degree in June of 1956 my name was on the cover of a dozen magazines at once and I was earning a respectable living as a free-lance writer. A few months later the World Science Fiction Convention provided the final blessing by awarding me a Hugo as the most promising new author of the year. And so I lived happily ever after, more or less.

Except that in the course of turning myself from a trembling beginner into a smartass pro I had overlooked the biggest lesson, which is that selling everything you write doesn't mean that you know it all, or even that you know very much. The stuff I was writing, with a few honorable exceptions, was generic boilerplate material designed to help harried editors fill their back pages, not anything likely to live down the ages. Once I had decided that I was missing whatever gene it was that carries literary greatness, I chose to settle merely for learning how to write things that someone, anyone, would publish, and now I had accomplished that.

I had hit on a formula for turning story ideas into cash, and it worked just fine. But the same formula can be applied in many ways, as can be verified by comparing the bouquet and flavor of Château Mouton-Rothschild with that of a bottle of $3.98 Basic Wino Burgundy. Somehow I had failed to realize that my fiercely intense studies of narrative technique during the years of my late adolescence had given me the equipment I needed to construct the very best stories I had within me, and so perhaps in time to equal the work of the writers I idolized. Instead, still telling myself that I was inherently incapable of matching such lofty achievements, I was content to use my hard-won skills for nothing more than supplying a hungry market with routine potboilers by the dozen.

Enter the final and harshest mentor: H. L. Gold, the brooding, irascible, brilliant editor of *Galaxy Science Fiction*. I had begun sending stories to him in 1953. The first one came back with an amiable note: "Aside from a tendency to be overexplicit in spots and repeat in dialog something already stated in narrative, you've told your story well. [He was right. It's a fault I still sometimes slip into.] Trouble is that you don't have an ending. Not, at any rate, one that fantasy readers would be happy with. Anyone who buys a fantasy magazine naturally expects a fantasy payoff, and is understandably put out when he fails to get one. . . ."

That was before I began selling. Later on, after I did, I got to know Gold and eventually sold him some stories. But he rejected as many as he accepted, and the rejection notes were horrendous. Here's one, from early 1956:

> If I had to pick your one biggest fault, I'd say it was your
> not thinking beneath the surface of your stories. It leads to
> almost appalling glibness. But the writing style has grown a
> great deal. Now upgrade the thinking and plotting to the

level of style and you will be far beyond this buttery little item.

And this, a couple of months later:

> You're selling more than you're learning. The fact that you sell is tricking you into believing that your technique is adequate. It is—for now. But project your career twenty years into the future and see where you'll stand if you don't sweat over improving your style, handling of character and conflict, resourcefulness in story development. You'll simply be more facile at what you're doing right now, more glib, more skilled at invariably taking the easiest way out.
>
> If I didn't see a talent there—a potential one, a good way from being fully realized—I wouldn't take the time to point out the greased skidway you're standing on. I wouldn't give a damn. But I'm risking your professional friendship for the sake of a better one.

And this, early in 1957:

> The opening is fine. How you flattened out the balance into its present featurelessness is hard to figure, but I suppose persistence can do it—persistence, in this case, being its own reward.
>
> There's one thing that stands between our doing business: You by God will *not* squeeze the most juice—juice, not wordage—from a setup. That, because I need material, is the selfish view. The unselfish view is that I'm a writer as well as editor, and in both capacities I'm appalled and outraged that a talent should be *encouraged* to stay small, so that the least effort and maximum glibness will sell the most literary yard goods . . . and the hell with whether you grow as a writer. I know I'd have less trouble and fewer enemies

if I bought in the same way, but I've seen too many aged hacks, Bob, and damned if I want to help even one person join that pathetic ragged crowd. The time has come for you to do some real work to learn your craft. If not now, *when?*

Gold's letters upset me, of course. But they also angered me. Hadn't I won a Hugo, the youngest writer ever to do so? (Still true, thirty years later.) Hadn't I sold stories by the dozen to X and Y and Z? (I promptly sold all the stories Gold rejected, too.) What was he saying, time to learn my craft? I *knew* my craft!

Gradually, though, what he was saying sank in—especially when I heard much the same things, in a more oblique and much gentler way, from a couple of other old pros who had become close friends of mine, Frederik Pohl and Lester del Rey. They—along with everyone else in science fiction—were looking at me by this time as some sort of bizarre phenomenon, a kid who could write two short stories a day and a novel in two weeks and sell everything he wrote. They envied me that; but they also knew that my crazy facility and my growing glibness were traps, as deadly as they were profitable, and I shudder to think what they were all saying behind my back. To my face, though, they said plenty, Gold and Blish and Knight, Pohl and del Rey, Algis Budrys and Cyril Kornbluth and Judy Merril and Ted Sturgeon. I got the message. I'm grateful to them all for letting me on to the truth. Which was: You have talent, kid. God knows you have ambition. You have energy beyond belief. Now it's time you start doing something with all those gifts besides showing us how fast you can turn out minimally acceptable stuff that editors can use to fill the back pages of their magazines. Learn your craft, kid.

But I *have* learned my craft, I replied silently.

And indeed I had. Some of it, anyway. But one aspect of a writer's craft is knowing how to put the things you have learned to their best possible use, rather than doing no more than you have to, to get by. Another is realizing how much more there still is to learn—always.

So they just smiled, and waited for time to pass. Which it did; and I changed; and so, thank God, did my work, once I came to understand that a writer who is satisfied just by getting some editor to say yes is a writer who isn't really doing anything that's worth doing at all.

What I wasn't willing to see when I was 21 is that selling stories proves only that you know how to sell stories. That isn't trivial, but it isn't enough. I had been too easy on myself, circa age 15, with the circular argument that the stories I was writing were poor because I hadn't been born with the innate gift of writing good ones. If such a gift exists, very likely I *was* born with it; it certainly seems that way to me now. But what I wouldn't let myself see, back then, is that it takes more than being born with a knack for words to write something worth reading. Those stories I wrote in my teens were poor because I didn't know enough about the craft I wanted to follow and because at that age I didn't know enough about anything to have any worthwhile stories to tell. No point complaining to the gods that they hadn't given me the natural writing skills of Shakespeare, or Dickens, or Heinlein: what I needed to do was what anyone setting out to accomplish anything needs to do, which is to do the best you can with whatever gifts you may have, constantly striving with all your soul to enhance your mastery of your chosen craft. That very well may be how all those great writers whose natural endowments I once envied had had to achieve their greatness: by constant study, practice, and sweaty hard work. Shakespeare's first plays may have been better than anyone else's first plays, but even he didn't turn out *Lear* and *Othello* during his apprentice days.

Mastery of craft is a matter of process, not of a single blinding moment of attainment: you go on working toward it all your life. If you go about things the right way, you get better and better all the time, and that means you may get very good indeed. But the diabolical thing is that you never quite get good enough, ever, so you have to go on learning. Even when you're good enough to please Damon Knight or James Blish or whatever other external authority you've set up for yourself, you still won't be good enough to please yourself—not unless you've established goals for yourself that are contemptibly easy to fulfill.

Of course, there's much more to writing than mastery of technique. Technique is merely a means to an end, and in this case the end is to convey understanding in the guise of entertainment. The storytelling art evolved as a way of interpreting the world—as a way of creating order out of the chaos that the cruel or merely absent-minded gods handed us long ago. To perform that task effectively, the writer must peer into the heart of the chaos; the writer must know something about the world. Even if what you want to write about is a planet a million light-years away, you must have some understanding of this one, or the inhabitants of this world will have little interest in what you have to say.

You are compelled, then, to go on seeking knowledge endlessly, knowledge of your craft and of the world—an eternal apprentice in your own eyes, however you may appear to others. I once believed that there was a single Secret of Writing that all the true writers had managed to learn: an ultimate revelation of the deepest mysteries of the art. I believed that the writers whose books and stories I admired had attained that Secret, and that everything became magically easy for them at that point. Now I'm not so sure. I suspect that that dazzling moment of ultimate revelation never does come. The secret of the Secret is that it doesn't exist. There are many things that you must master if you hope to practice the art and the craft of writing, but they are far from secret, nor do they add up to one single great Secret. You just go on, doing your best, living and reading and thinking and studying and working and searching for answers, using everything that you've learned along the way and hoping that each new story is deeper and richer than the one before.

There you have it: the truth at last, the real Secret. It took me a long time to figure it out, because I had to work it out all by myself, regardless of the things that helpful teachers and editors and fellow writers tried to tell me. The process of becoming a writer involves discovering how to use the accumulated wisdom of our guild, all those tricks of the storytelling trade that have evolved around the campfire over the past five or ten or fifty thousand years. Others can show you what those tricks are. But only you can make a writer out of yourself, by reading, by studying what you have read, and above all by writing. The stories that follow are some of the hundreds that helped me teach myself the things I had to know.

FOUR IN ONE
DAMON KNIGHT

I

George Meister had once seen the nervous system of a man—a display specimen, achieved by coating the smallest of the fibers until they were coarse enough to be seen, then dissolving all the unwanted tissue and replacing it with clear plastic. A marvelous job, that fellow on Torkas III had done it—what was his name? At any rate: having seen the specimen, Meister knew approximately what he himself must look like at the present moment.

Of course, there were distortions: for example, he was almost certain that the neurons between his visual center and his eyes had produced themselves by at least thirty centimeters. Also, no doubt, the system as a whole was curled up and spread out rather oddly, since the musculature it had originally controlled was gone; and he had noticed certain other changes which might or might not be reflected by gross structural differences. The fact remained that he—all that he could still call *himself*—was nothing more than a brain, a pair of eyes, a spinal cord, and a spray of neurons.

George closed his eyes for a second. It was a thing he had learned to do only recently, and he was proud of it. That first long period, when he had had no control whatever, had been very bad. He had decided later that the paralysis had been due to the lingering effects of some anaesthetic—the agent, whatever it was, that had kept him unconscious while his body was being—Well.

Either that, or the neuron branches had simply not yet knitted firmly in their new positions. Perhaps he could verify one or the other supposition at some future time. But at first, when he had only been able to see and not to move, knowing nothing beyond the moment when he had fallen face first into that mottled green and brown puddle of gelatin . . . that had been upsetting.

He wondered how the others were taking it. There were others, he knew, because occasionally he would feel a sudden acute pain down where his legs belonged, and at the same instant the motion of the landscape would stop with a jerk. That could only be some other brain, trapped like his, trying to move their common body in another direction.

Usually the pain stopped immediately, and George could go on sending messages down to the nerve endings which had formerly belonged to his fingers and toes, and the gelatinous body would keep on creeping slowly forward. When the pains continued, there was nothing to do but to stop moving until the other brain quit—in which case George would feel like an unwilling passenger in a very slow vehicle—or try to alter his own movements to coincide, or at least produce a vector with the other brain's.

He wondered who else had fallen in—Vivian Bellis? Major Gumps? Miss McCarty? Or all three of them? There ought to be some way of finding out.

He tried looking down once more, and was rewarded with a blurry view of a long, narrow strip of mottled green and brown, moving very slowly forward along the dry stream bed they had been crossing for the last hour or more. Twigs and shreds of dry vegetable matter were stuck to the dusty, translucent surface.

He was improving; the last time, he had only been able to see the thinnest possible edge of his new body.

When he looked up again, the far edge of the stream bed was perceptibly closer. There was a cluster of stiff-looking, dark-brown vegetable shoots just beyond, on the rocky shoulder; George was aiming slightly to the left of it. It had been a plant very much like that one that he'd been reaching for when he lost his balance and got himself into this condition. He might as well have a good look at it, anyhow.

The plant would probably turn out to be of little interest. It would be out of all reason to expect every new life form to be a startling novelty; and George was convinced that he had already stumbled into the most interesting organism on this planet.

Something *meisterii*, he thought. He had not settled on a species name—he would have to learn more about it before he decided—but *meisterii* certainly. It was his discovery, and nobody could take it away from him. Or—unhappily—him away from it.

It was a really lovely organism, though. Primitive—less structure of its own than a jellyfish, and only on a planet with light surface gravity, like this one, could it ever have hauled itself up out of the sea. No brain, no nervous system at all, apparently. But it had the perfect survival mechanism. It simply let its rivals develop highly organized nervous tissue, sat in one place (looking exactly like a deposit of leaves and other clutter) until one of them fell into it, and then took all the benefit.

It wasn't parasitism, either; it was a true symbiosis, on a higher level than any other planet, so far as George knew, had ever developed. The captive brain was nourished by the captor; wherefore it served the captive's interest to move the captor toward food and away from danger. *You steer me, I feed you.* It was fair.

They were close to the plant now, almost touching it. George inspected it; as he had thought, it was a common grass type, of no particular interest.

Now his body was tilting itself up a ridge he knew to be low, although from his eye level it looked tremendous. He climbed it laboriously and found himself looking down into still another gully. This could go on, no doubt, indefinitely. The question was, did he have any choice?

He looked at the shadows cast by the low-hanging sun. He was heading approximately northwest, or directly away from the encampment. He was only a few hundred meters away; even at a crawl, he could make the distance easily enough . . . if he turned back.

He felt uneasy at the thought, and didn't know why. Then it struck him that his appearance was not obviously that of a human being in distress; the chances were that he looked rather more like a monster which had eaten and partially digested one or more people.

If he crawled into camp in his present condition, it was a certainty that he would be shot at before any questions were asked, and only a minor possibility that narcotic gas would be used instead of a machine rifle.

No, he decided, he was on the right course. The idea was to get away from camp so that he wouldn't be found by the relief party which was probably searching for him now. Get away, bury himself in the forest, and study his new body: find out how it worked and what he could do with it, whether there actually were others in it with him, and if so, if there was any way of opening communications with them.

It would take a long time, he thought, but he could do it.

Limply, like a puddle of mush oozing over the edge of a tablecloth, George started down into the gully.

The circumstances leading up to George's fall into the something *meisterii* were, briefly, as follows:

Until as late as the mid-twenty-first century, a game invented by the ancient Japanese was still played by millions in the eastern hemisphere of Terra. The game was called *go*. Although its rules were almost childishly simple, its strategy included more permutations and was more difficult to master than that of chess.

Go was played, at the height of its development—just before the geological catastrophe that wiped out most of its devotees—on a board with nine hundred shallow holes, using small pill-shaped counters. At each turn, one of the two players placed a counter on the board, wherever he chose, the object being to capture as much territory as possible by surrounding it completely.

There were no other rules; and yet it had taken the Japanese almost a thousand years to work up to that thirty-by-thirty board, adding perhaps one rank and file per century. A hundred years was not too long to explore all the possibilities of that additional rank and file.

At the time George Meister fell into the gelatinous green-and-brown monster, toward the end of the twenty-third century A.D., a kind of *go* was being played in a three-dimensional field which contained more than ten billion positions. The galaxy was the board, the positions were star systems, men were the counters. The loser's penalty was annihilation.

The galaxy was in the process of being colonized by two opposing federations. In the early stages of this conflict, planets had been raided, bombs dropped, and a few battles had even been fought by fleets of spaceships. Later that haphazard sort of warfare became impossible. Robot fighters, carrying enough armament to blow each other into dust, were produced in trillions. In the space around the outer stars of a cluster belonging to one side or the other, they swarmed like minnows.

Within such a screen, planets were utterly safe from attack and from any interference with their commerce . . . unless the enemy succeeded in colonizing enough of the circumambient star systems to set up and maintain a second screen outside the first. It was *go*, played for desperate stakes and under impossible conditions.

Everyone was in a hurry; everyone's ancestors for seven generations had been in a hurry. You got your education in a speeded-up, capsulized form. You mated early and bred frantically. And if you were assigned to an advance ecological team, as George was, you had to work without any decent preparation.

The sensible, the obvious thing to do in opening up a new planet with unknown life forms would have been to begin with at least ten years of immunological study conducted from the inside of a sealed station. After the worst bacteria and viruses had been licked, you might proceed to a little cautious field work and exploration. Finally—total elapsed time fifty years, say—the colonists would be shipped in.

There simply wasn't that much time.

Five hours after the landing, Meister's team had unloaded fabricators and set up barracks enough to house its two thousand, six hundred and twenty-eight members. An hour after that, Meister, Gumbs, Bellis, and McCarty started out across the level cinder and ash left by the transport's tail jets to the nearest living vegetation, six hundred meters away. They were to trace a spiral path outward from the camp site to a distance of a thousand meters, and then return with their specimens—providing nothing too large and hungry to be stopped by a machine rifle had previously eaten them.

Meister, the biologist, was hung with collecting boxes to the point that his slender torso was totally invisible. Major Gumbs had a survival kit, binoculars, and a machine rifle. Vivian Bellis, who knew exactly as much mineralogy as had been contained in the three-month course prescribed for her rating, and no more, carried a light rifle, a hammer, and a specimen sack. Miss McCarty—no one knew her first name— had no scientific function. She was the group's Loyalty Monitor. She wore two squat pistols and a bandolier bristling with cartridges. Her only job was to blow the cranium off any team member caught using an unauthorized communicator, or in any other way behaving oddly.

All of them were heavily gloved and booted, and their heads were covered by globular helmets, sealed to their tunic collars. They breathed through filtered respirators, so finely meshed that—in theory—nothing larger than an oxygen molecule could get through.

On their second circuit of the camp, they had struck a low ridge and a series of short, steep gullies, most of them choked with the dusty-brown stalks of dead vegetation. As they started down into one of these, George, who was third in line—Gumbs leading, then Bellis, and McCarty behind George—stepped out onto a protruding slab of stone to examine a cluster of plant stalks rooted on its far side.

His weight was only a little more than twenty kilograms on this planet, and the slab looked as if it were firmly cemented into the wall of the gully. Just the same, he felt it shift under him as soon as his weight was fully on it. He felt himself falling, shouted, and caught a flashing glimpse of Gumbs and Bellis, standing as if caught by a high-speed camera. He heard a rattling of stones as he went by. Then he saw what looked like a shabby blanket of leaves and dirt floating toward him, and he remembered thinking, *It looks like a soft landing, anyhow....* That was all, until he woke up feeling as if he had been prematurely buried, with no part of him alive but his eyes.

Much later, his frantic efforts to move had resulted in the first fractional success. From then on, his field of vision had moved fairly steadily forward, perhaps a meter in every fifty minutes, not counting the times when someone else's efforts had interfered with his own.

His conviction that nothing remained of the old George Meister except a nervous system was not supported by observation, but the evidence was regrettably strong. To begin with, the anaesthesia of the first hours had worn off, but his body was not reporting the position of the torso, head, and four limbs he had formerly owned. He had, instead, a vague impression of being flattened and spread out over an enormous area. When he tried to move his fingers and toes, the response he got was so multiplied that he felt like a centipede. He had no sense of cramped muscles, such as would normally be expected after a long period of paralysis; and he was not breathing. Yet his brain was evidently being well supplied with food and oxygen; he felt clear-headed, at ease, and healthy.

He wasn't hungry, either, although he had been using energy steadily for a long time. There were, he thought, two possible reasons for that, depending on how you looked at it ... one, that he wasn't hungry because he no longer had any stomach lining to contract; two, that he wasn't hungry because the organism he was riding in had been well nourished by the superfluous tissues George had contributed....

Two hours later, when the sun was setting, it began to rain. George saw the big, slow-falling drops and felt their dull impacts on his "skin." He didn't know whether rain would do him any damage or not, rather thought not, but crawled under a bush with large, fringed leaves just to be on the safe side. When the rain stopped it was dark, and he decided he might as well stay where he was until morning. He did not feel tired, and it occurred to him to wonder whether he still needed to sleep. He composed himself as well as he could to wait for the answer.

He was still wakeful after a long time had passed, but had made no progress toward deciding whether this answered the question or prevented it from being answered, when he saw a pair of dim lights coming slowly and erratically toward him.

George watched them with an attentiveness compounded of professional interest and apprehension. Gradually, as they came closer, he made out that the lights were attached to long, thin stalks which grew from an ambiguous shape below—either light organs, like those of some deep-sea fish, or simply luminescent eyes.

George noted a feeling of tension in himself which seemed to suggest that adrenaline or an equivalent was being released somewhere in his system. He promised himself to follow this lead at the first possible moment; meanwhile he had a more urgent problem to consider. Was this approaching organism the kind which the something *meisterii* ate, or the kind which devoured the something *meisterii*? If the latter, what would he do about it?

For the present, at any rate, sitting where he was seemed to be indicated. The body he inhabited made use of camouflage in its normal, or untenanted state, and was not equipped for speed. So George held still and watched, keeping his eyes half closed, while he considered the possible nature of the approaching animal.

The fact that it was nocturnal, he told himself, meant

nothing. Moths were nocturnal; so were bats—no, the devil with bats, they were carnivores. . . . The light-bearing creature came nearer, and George saw the faint gleam of a pair of long, narrow eyes below the two stalks.

Then the creature opened its mouth.

It had a great many teeth.

George found himself crammed into some kind of crevice in a wall of rock, without any clear recollection of how he had got there. He remembered a flurry of branches as the creature sprang at him, and the moment's furious pain, and then nothing but vague, starlit glimpses of leaves and earth.

The thing was impossible. How had he got away?

He puzzled over it until dawn came, and then, looking down at himself, he saw something that had not been there before. Under the smooth edge of gelatinous flesh three or four projections of some kind were visible. It struck George that his sensation of contact with the stone underneath him had changed, too: he seemed to be standing on a number of tiny points instead of lying flat.

He flexed one of these projections experimentally, then thrust it out straight ahead of him. It was a lumpy, single-jointed caricature of a finger—or a leg.

George lay still for a long time and thought about it with as much coherence as he could muster. Then he waggled the thing again. It was there, and so were all the others, as solid and real as the rest of him.

He moved forward experimentally, sending the same messages down to his finger-and-toe nerve ends as before. His body lurched out of the cranny with a swiftness that very nearly tumbled him down over the edge of a minor precipice.

Where he had crawled like a snail before, he now scuttled like an insect.

But how . . . ? No doubt, in his terror when the thing with

the teeth attacked, he had unconsciously tried to run as if he still had legs. Was that all there was to it?

George thought of the carnivore again, and of the stalks supporting the organs which he had thought might be eyes. That would do as an experiment. He closed his own eyes and imagined them rising outward, imagined the mobile stalks growing, growing. . . . He tried to convince himself that he had eyes like that, had always had them—that everyone who was anyone had eyes on stalks.

Surely, something was happening?

George opened his eyes again, and found himself looking straight down at the ground, getting a view so close up that it was blurred, out of focus. Impatiently, he tried to look up. All that happened was that his field of vision moved forward a matter of ten or twelve centimeters.

It was at this point that a voice shattered the stillness. It sounded like someone trying to shout through half a meter of lard. "Urghh! Lluhh! *Eeraghh!*"

George leaped convulsively, executed a neat turn and swept his eyes around a good two hundred and forty degrees of arc. He saw nothing but rocks and lichens. On a closer inspection, it appeared that a small green-and-orange larva or grub of some kind was moving past him. George regarded it with suspicion for a long moment, until the voice broke out again:

"Ellfff! Ellffneee!"

The voice, somewhat higher this time, came from behind. George whirled again, swept his mobile eyes around—

Around an impossible wide circuit. His eyes *were* on stalks, and they were mobile—whereas a moment ago he had been staring at the ground, unable to look up. George's brain clattered into high gear. He had grown stalks for his eyes, all right, but they'd been limp—just extensions of the jellylike mass of his body, without a stiffened cell structure or muscular tissue to move them. Then, when the voice had startled him, he'd got the stiffening and the muscles in a hurry.

That must have been what had happened the previous night. Probably the process would have been completed, but much more slowly, if he hadn't been frightened. A protective mechanism, obviously. As for the voice—

George rotated once more, slowly, looking all around him. There was no question about it: he was alone. The voice, which had seemed to come from someone or something standing just behind him, must in fact have issued from his own body.

The voice started again, at a less frantic volume. It burbled a few times, then said quite clearly in a high tenor, "Whass happen'? Wheh am I?"

George was floundering in a sea of bewilderment. He was in no condition to adapt quickly to more new circumstances, and when a large, desiccated lump fell from a nearby bush and bounced soundlessly to within a meter of him, he simply stared at it.

He looked at the hard-shelled object, and then at the laden bush from which it had dropped. Slowly, painfully, he worked his way through to a logical conclusion. The dried fruit had fallen without a sound. This was natural, because he had been totally deaf ever since his metamorphosis. But— he had heard a voice!

Ergo, hallucination, or telepathy.

The voice began again. "He-elp. Oh, dear, I wish someone would answer!"

Vivian Bellis. Gumbs, even if he affected that tenor voice, wouldn't say, "Oh, dear." Neither would McCarty.

George's shaken nerves were returning to normal. He thought intently, *I get scared, grow legs. Bellis gets scared, grows a telepathic voice. That's reasonable, I guess—her first and only instinct would be to yell.*

George tried to put himself into a yelling mood. He tried his eyes and imagined himself cooped up in a terrifyingly alien medium, without any control or knowledge of his predicament. He tried to shout: "Vivian!"

He kept on trying, while the girl's voice continued at intervals. Finally she stopped abruptly in the middle of a sentence. George said, "Can you hear me?"

"Who's that—what do you want?"

"This is George Meister, Vivian. Can you understand what I'm saying?"

"What—"

George kept at it. His pseudo-voice, he judged, was a little garbled, just as Bellis's had been at first. At last the girl said, "Oh, George—I mean Mr. Meister! Oh, I've been so frightened. Where are you?"

George explained, apparently not very tactfully, because Bellis shrieked when he was through and then went back to burbling. George sighed, and said, "Is there anyone else on the premises? Major Gumbs? Miss McCarty?"

A few minutes later two sets of weird sounds began almost simultaneously. When they became coherent, it was no trouble to identify the voices. Gumbs, the big, red-faced professional soldier, shouted, "Why the hell don't you watch where you're going, Meister? If you hadn't started that rock slide we wouldn't be in this mess!"

Miss McCarty, who had had a seamed white face, a jutting jaw, and eyes the color of mud, said coldly, "Meister, all of this will be reported. *All* of it."

2

It appeared that only Meister and Gumbs had kept the use of their eyes. All four of them had some muscle control, though

Gumbs was the only one who had made any serious attempt to interfere with George's locomotion. Miss McCarty, not to George's surprise, had managed to retain a pair of functioning ears.

But Bellis had been blind, deaf, and dumb all through the afternoon and night. The only terminal sense organs she had been able to use had been those of the skin—the perceptors of touch, heat and cold, and pain. She had heard nothing, seen nothing, but she had felt every leaf and stalk they had brushed against, the cold impact of every raindrop, and the pain of the toothy monster's bite. George's opinion of her went up several notches when he learned this. She had been terrified, but she hadn't been driven into hysteria or insanity.

It further appeared that nobody was doing any breathing, and nobody was aware of a heartbeat.

George would have liked nothing better than to continue this discussion, but the other three were united in believing that what had happened to them after they got in was of less importance than how they were going to get out.

"We can't get *out*," said George. "At least, I don't see any possibility of it in the present state of our knowledge. If we—"

"But we've got to get out!" said Vivian.

"We'll go back to camp," said McCarty coldly. "Immediately. And you'll explain to the Loyalty Committee why you didn't turn back as soon as you regained consciousness."

"That's right," Gumbs put in self-consciously. "If you can't do anything, Meister, maybe the other technical fellows can."

George patiently explained his theory of their probable reception by the guards at the camp. McCarty's keen mind detected a flaw. "You grew legs, and stalks for your eyes, according to your own testimony. If you weren't lying, you can also grow a mouth. We'll announce ourselves as we approach."

"That may not be easy," George told her. "We couldn't get along with just a mouth, we'd need teeth, tongue, hard and soft palates, lungs or the equivalent, vocal cords, and some kind of substitute for a diaphragm to power the whole business. I'm wondering if it's possible at all, because when Miss Bellis finally succeeded in making herself heard, it was by the method we're using now. She didn't—"

"You talk too much," said McCarty. "Major Gumbs, Miss Bellis, you and I will try to form a speaking apparatus. The first to succeed will receive a credit mark on his record. Commence."

George, being left out of the contest by implication, used his time in trying to restore his hearing. It seemed to him likely that the whatever-it-was *meisterii* had some sort of division-of-labor principle built into it, since Gumbs and he— the first two to fall in—had kept their sight without making any special effort in that direction, while matters like hearing and touch had been left for the latecomers. This was fine in principle, and George approved of it, but he didn't like the idea of Miss McCarty's being the sole custodian of any part of the apparatus.

Even if he were able to persuade the other two to follow his lead—and at the moment this prospect seemed dim— McCarty was certain to be a holdout. And it might easily be vital to all of them, at some time in the near future, to have their hearing hooked into the circuit.

He was distracted at first by muttered comments between Gumbs and Vivian—"Getting anywhere?" "I don't think so. Are you?"—interspersed between yawps, humming sounds, and other irritating noises as they tried unsuccessfully to switch over from mental to vocal communication. Finally McCarty snapped, "Be quiet. Concentrate on forming the necessary organs—don't bray like jackasses."

George settled down to his work, using the same technique he had found effective before. With his eyes shut, he imagined that the thing with all the teeth was approaching in darkness—tap; slither; tap; click. He wished valiantly for ears to catch the faint approaching sounds. After a long time he thought he was beginning to succeed—or were those mental sounds, unconsciously emitted by one of the other three? *Click. Slither. Swish. Scrape.*

George opened his eyes, genuinely alarmed. A hundred meters away, facing him across the shallow slope of rocky ground, was a uniformed man just emerging from a stand of black, bamboolike spears. As George raised his eye stalks, the man paused, stared back at him, then shouted and raised his rifle.

George ran. Instantly there was a babble of voices inside him, and the muscles of his "legs" went into wild spasms. "Run, dammit!" he said frantically. "There's a trooper with—"

The rifle went off with a deafening roar, and George felt a sudden hideous pain aft of his spine. Vivian Bellis screamed. The struggle for possession of their common legs stopped, and they scuttled full speed ahead for the cover of a nearby boulder. The rifle roared again, and George heard rock splinters screeching through the foliage overhead. Then they were plunging down the side of a gully, up the other slope, over a low hummock and into a forest of tall, bare-limbed trees.

George spotted a leaf-filled hollow and headed for it, fighting somebody else's desire to keep on running in a straight line. They plopped into the hollow and stayed there while three running men went past them, and for an hour afterward.

Vivian was moaning steadily. Raising his eye stalks cautiously, George was able to see that several jagged splinters of stone had penetrated the monster's gelatinous flesh near the fat rim.... They had been very lucky. The shot had apparently been a near miss—accountable only on the grounds that the trooper had been shooting downhill at a moving target—and had shattered the boulder behind them.

Looking more closely, George observed something which excited his professional interest. The whole surface of the monster appeared to be in constant slow ferment: tiny pits opening and closing as if the flesh were boiling ... except that here the bubbles of air were not forcing their way outward, but were being engulfed at the surface and pressed down into the interior.

He could also see, deep under the mottled surface of the huge lens-shaped body, four vague clots of darkness which must be the living brains of Gumbs, Bellis, McCarty—and Meister.

Yes, there was one which was radially opposite his own eye stalks. It was an odd thing, George reflected, to be looking at your own brain. No doubt you could get used to it in time.

The four dark spots were arranged close together in an almost perfect square at the center of the lens. The spinal cords, barely visible, crossed between them and rayed outward from the center.

Pattern, George thought. The thing was designed to make use of more than one nervous system. It arranged them in an orderly fashion, with the brains inward for greater protection—and perhaps for another reason. Perhaps there was even a provision for conscious cooperation among the passengers: a matrix that somehow promoted the growth of communication cells between the separate brains.... If that were so, it would account for their ready success with telepathy. George wished most acutely that he could get inside and find out.

Vivian's pain was diminishing. Hers was the brain opposite George's, and she had taken most of the effect of the rock splinters. But the fragments were sinking now, slowly, through the gelid substance of the monster's tissues. Watching carefully, George could see them move. When they got to the bottom, they would be excreted, no doubt—just as the indigestible parts of their clothing and equipment had been.

George wondered idly which of the remaining two brains was McCarty's and which Gumbs's. The answer was easy to find. To George's left, as he looked back toward the center of the mound, was a pair of blue eyes set flush with the surface. They had lids apparently grown from the monster's substance, but thickened and opaque.

To his right, George could make out two tiny openings, extending a few centimeters into the body, which could only be Miss McCarty's ears. George had an impulse to see if he could devise a method of dropping dirt into them.

Anyhow, the question of returning to camp had been settled, at least for the moment. McCarty said nothing more about growing a set of speech organs, although George was sure she herself was determined to keep on trying.

He didn't think she would succeed. Whatever the mechanism was by which these changes in bodily structure were accomplished, it seemed probable that amateurs like themselves could succeed only under the pressure of considerable emotional strain, and then only with comparatively simple tasks which involved one new structure at a time. And as he had already told McCarty, the speech organs in man were extraordinarily diverse and complicated.

It occurred to George that the thing just might be done by creating a thin membrane to serve as a diaphragm, and an air chamber behind it, with a set of muscles to produce the necessary vibrations and modulate them. He kept the notion to himself.

He didn't want to go back. George was a rare bird: a

scientist who was actually fitted for his work and loved it for its own sake. And at the moment he was sitting squarely in the middle of the most powerful research tool that had ever existed in his field: a protean organism, with the observer inside it, able to order its structure and watch the results; able to devise theories of function and test them on the tissues of what was effectively his own body—able to construct new organs, new adaptations to environment!

George saw himself at the point of an enormous cone of new knowledge; and some of the possibilities he glimpsed humbled and awed him.

He *couldn't* go back, even if it were possible to do it without getting killed. If only he had fallen into the damned thing alone—No, then the others would have pulled him out and killed the monster.

There were, he felt, too many problems demanding solutions all at once. It was hard to concentrate; his mind kept slipping maddeningly out of focus.

Vivian, whose pain had stopped some time ago, began to wail again. Gumbs snapped at her. McCarty cursed both of them. George himself felt that he had had very nearly all he could take—cooped up with three idiots who had no more sense than to—

"Wait a minute," he said. "Do you all feel the same way? Irritable? Jumpy? As if you'd been working for sixty hours straight and were too tired to sleep?"

"Stop talking like a video ad," Vivian said angrily. "Haven't we got enough trouble without—"

"We're hungry," George interrupted. "We didn't realize it, because we haven't got the organs that usually signal hunger. But the last thing this body ate was *us*, and that was at least twenty hours ago. We've got to find something to ingest."

"Good Lord, you're right," said Gumbs. "But if this thing only eats people—I mean to say—"

"It never met any people until we landed," George said curtly. "Any protein should do, but the only way we can find out is to try. The sooner we start, the better."

He started off in what he hoped was the direction they had been following all along—directly away from camp. At least, he thought, if they put enough distance behind them, they might get thoroughly lost.

3

They moved out of the trees and down the long slope of a valley, over a wiry carpet of dead grasses, until they reached a watercourse in which a thin trickle was still flowing. Far down the bank, partly screened by clumps of skeletal shrubbery, George saw a group of animals that looked vaguely like miniature pigs. He told the others about it, and started cautiously in that direction.

"Which way is the wind blowing, Vivian?" he asked. "Can you feel it?"

She said, "No. I could before, when we were going downhill, but now I think we're facing into it."

"Good," said George. "We may be able to sneak up on them.

"But—we're not going to eat *animals*, are we?"

"Yes, how about it, Meister?" Gumbs put in. "I don't say I'm a squeamish fellow, but after all—"

George, who felt a little squeamish himself—like all the others, he had been brought up on a diet of yeasts and synthetic protein—said testily, "What else can we do? You've got eyes—you can see that it's autumn here. Autumn after a hot summer, at that. Trees bare, streams dried up. We eat meat, or go without—unless you'd rather hunt for insects?"

Gumbs, shocked to the core, muttered for a while and then gave up.

Seen at closer range, the animals looked less porcine and even less appetizing than before. They had lean, segmented, pinkish-gray bodies, four short legs, flaring ears, and blunt scimitarlike snouts with which they were rooting in the grounds, occasionally turning up something which they gulped, ears flapping.

George counted thirty of them, grouped fairly closely in a little space of clear ground between the bushes and the river. They moved slowly, but their short legs looked powerful; he guessed that they could run when they had to.

He inched forward, keeping his eye stalks low, stopping instantly whenever one of the beasts looked up. Moving with increasing caution, he had got to within ten meters of the nearest when McCarty said abruptly:

"Meister, has it occurred to you to wonder just *how* we are going to eat these animals?"

"Don't be foolish," he said irritably. "We'll—" He stopped.

Wait a minute—did the thing's normal method of assimilation stop as soon as it got a tenant? Were they supposed to grow fangs and a gullet and all the rest of the apparatus? Impossible; they'd starve to death first. But on the other hand—*damn* this fuzzy-headed feeling—wouldn't it have to stop, to prevent the tenant from being digested with his first meal?

"Well?" McCarty demanded.

That was wrong, George knew, but he couldn't say why; and it was a distinctly unpleasant thought. Or—even worse—suppose the meal became the tenant, and the tenant the meal?

The nearest animal's head went up, and four tiny red eyes stared directly at George. The floppy ears snapped to attention.

It was no time for speculation. "He's seen us!" George shouted mentally. *"Run!"*

The scene exploded into motion. One instant they were lying still in the prickly dry grass; the next they were skimming at express-train speed across the ground, with the herd galloping away straight ahead of them. The hams of the nearest beast loomed up closer and closer, bounding furiously; then they had run it down and vaulted over it.

Casting an eye backward, George saw that it was lying motionless in the grass—unconscious or dead.

They ran down another one. *The anaesthetic*, George thought lucidly. *One touch does it.* And another, and another. *Of course we can digest them*, he thought with relief. *It has to be selective to begin with, or it couldn't have separated out our nervous tissue.*

Four down. Six down. Three more together as the herd bunched between the last arm of the thicket and the steep river bank; then two that tried to double back; then four stragglers, one after the other.

The rest of the herd disappeared into the tall grass up the slope; but fifteen bodies were strewn behind them.

Taking no chances, George went back to the beginning of the line and edged the monster's body under the first carcass.

"Crouch down, Gumbs," he said. "We have to slide under it . . . that's far enough. Leave the head hanging over."

"What for?" said the soldier.

"You don't want his brain in here with us, do you? We don't know how many this thing is equipped to take. It might even like this one better than one of ours. But I can't see it bothering to keep the rest of the nervous system, if we make sure not to eat the head—"

"Oh!" said Vivian faintly.

"I beg your pardon, Miss Bellis," George said contritely.

"It shouldn't be too unpleasant, though, if we don't let it bother us. It isn't as if we had taste buds, or—"

"It's all right," she said. "Just please let's not talk about it."

"I should think not," Gumbs put in. "A little more tact, don't you think, Meister?"

Accepting this reproof, George turned his attention to the corpse that lay on the monster's glabrous surface, between his section and Gumbs's. It was sinking, just visibly, into the flesh. A cloud of opacity was spreading around it.

When it was almost gone, and the neck had been severed, they moved on to the next. This time, at George's suggestion, they took aboard two at once. Gradually their irritable mood faded; they began to feel at ease and cheerful, and George found it possible to think consecutively without having vital points slip out of his reach.

They were on their eighth and ninth courses, and George was happily engaged in an intricate chain of speculation as to the monster's circulatory system, when Miss McCarty broke a long silence to announce:

"I have now perfected a method by which we can return to camp safely. We will begin at once."

Startled and dismayed, George turned his eyes toward McCarty's quadrant of the monster. Protruding from the rim was a stringy, jointed something that looked like—yes, it was!—a grotesque but recognizable arm and hand. As he watched, the lumpy fingers fumbled with a blade of grass, tugged, uprooted it.

"Major Gumbs!" said McCarty. "It will be your task to locate the following articles, as quickly as possible. One. A surface suitable for writing. I suggest a large leaf, light in color, dry but not brittle. Or a tree from which a large section of bark can be easily peeled. Two. A pigment. No doubt you will be able to discover berries yielding suitable juice. If not,

74

mud will do. Three. A twig or reed for use as a pen. When you have directed me to all these essential items, I will employ them to write a message outlining our predicament. You will read the result and point out any errors, which I will then correct. When the message is completed, we will return with it to the camp, approaching at night, and deposit it in a conspicuous place. We will retire until daybreak, and when the message has been read we will approach again. Begin, Major."

"Well, yes," said Gumbs, "that ought to work, except—I suppose you've worked out some system for holding the pen, Miss McCarty?"

"Fool," she replied, "I have made a hand, of course."

"Well, in that case, by all means. Let's see, I believe we might try this thicket first—" Their common body gave a lurch in that direction.

George held back. "Wait a minute," he said desperately. "Let's at least have the common sense to finish this meal before we go. There's no telling when we'll get another."

McCarty demanded, "How large are these creatures, Major?"

"Oh—about sixty centimeters long, I should say."

"And we have consumed nine of them, is that correct?"

"Nearer eight," George said. "These two are only half gone."

"In other words," McCarty said, "we have had two apiece. That should be ample. Don't you agree, Major?"

George said earnestly, "You're wrong, Miss McCarty. You're thinking in terms of human food requirements, whereas this organism has a different metabolic rate and at least three times the mass of four human beings. Look at it this way—the four of us together had a mass of about three hundred kilos, and yet twenty hours after this thing absorbed us, it was hungry again. Well, these animals wouldn't weigh much more than twenty kilos apiece at one G—and according to your scheme we've got to hold out until sometime after daybreak tomorrow."

"Something in that," Gumbs said. "Yes, on the whole, Miss McCarty, I think we had better forage while we can. It won't take us more than half an hour longer, at this rate."

"Very well. Be as quick as you can."

They moved on to the next pair of victims. George's brain was working furiously. It was no good arguing with McCarty, and Gumbs was not much better, but he had to try. If he could only convince Gumbs, then Bellis would fall in with the majority—maybe. It was the only hope he had.

"Gumbs," he said, "have you given any thought to what's going to happen to us when we get back?"

"Not quite my line, you know. Leave that to the technical fellows like yourself."

"No, that isn't what I mean. Suppose you were the C.O. of this team, and four other people had fallen into this organism instead of us—"

"What, what? I don't follow."

George patiently repeated it.

"Yes, I see what you mean. And so—"

"What order would you give?"

Gumbs thought a moment. "Turn the thing over to the bio section, I suppose. What else?"

"You don't think you might order it destroyed as a possible menace?"

"Good Lord, I suppose I might. No, but you see, we'll be careful what we say in the note. We'll point out that we're a valuable specimen, and so on. Handle with care."

"All right," George said, "but suppose that works, then what? Since it's out of your line, I'll tell you. Nine chances out of ten, bio section will classify us as a possible enemy weapon. That means, first of all, that we'll go through a full-dress interrogation—and I don't have to tell you what that can be like."

"Major Gumbs," said McCarty stridently, "Meister will be executed for disloyalty at the first opportunity. You are forbidden to talk to him, under the same penalty."

"But she can't stop you from listening to me," George said tensely. "In the second place, Gumbs, they'll take samples. Without anaesthesia. And finally, they'll either destroy us just the same, or they'll send us back to the nearest strong point for more study. We will then be Federation property, Gumbs, in a top-secret category, and since nobody in Intelligence will ever dare to take the responsibility of clearing us, we'll *stay* there.

"Gumbs, this *is* a valuable specimen, but it will never do anybody any good if we go back to camp. Whatever we discover about it, even if it's knowledge that could save billions of lives, that will be top-secret too, and it'll never get past the walls of Intelligence. . . . If you're still hoping that they can get you out of this, you're wrong. This isn't like limb grafts; *your whole body* has been destroyed, Gumbs, everything but your nervous system and your eyes. The only new body we'll get is the one we make ourselves. We've got to stay here and—and work this out ourselves."

"Major Gumbs," said McCarty, "I think we have wasted quite enough time. Begin your search for the materials I need."

For a moment Gumbs was silent, and their collective body did not move.

Then he said: "Yes, that was a leaf, a twig, and a bunch of berries, wasn't it? Or mud. Miss McCarty, unofficially of course, there's one point I'd like your opinion on. Before we begin. That is to say, I daresay they'll be able to patch together some sort of bodies for us, don't you think? I mean, one technical fellow says one thing, another says the opposite. Do you see what I'm driving at?"

George had been watching McCarty's new limb uneasily. It was flexing rhythmically and, he was almost certain, growing minutely larger. The fingers groped occasionally in the dry grass, plucking first a single blade, then two together, finally a whole tuft. Now she said: "I have no opinion, Major. The question is irrelevant. Our duty is to return to camp. That is all we need to know."

"Oh, I quite agree with you there," said Gumbs. "And besides, there really isn't any alternative, is there?"

George, staring down at one of the fingerlike projections visible below the rim of the monster, was passionately willing it to turn into an arm. He had, he suspected, started much too late.

"The alternative," he said, "is simply to keep on going as we are. Even if the Federation holds this planet for a century, there'll be places on it that will never be explored. We'll be safe."

"I mean to say," added Gumbs as if he had only paused for thought, "a fellow can't very well cut himself off from civilization, can he?"

Again George felt a movement toward the thicket; again he resisted it. Then he found himself overpowered, as another set of muscles joined themselves to Gumbs's. Quivering, crabwise, the something *meisterii* moved half a meter. Then it stopped, straining.

And for the second time that day, George was forced to revise his opinion of Vivian Bellis.

"I believe you, Mr. Meister—George," she said. "I don't want to go back. Tell me what you want me to do."

"You're doing beautifully now," George said after a speechless instant. "Except if you can grow an arm, I imagine that will be useful."

The struggle went on.

"Now we know where we are," said McCarty to Gumbs.

"Yes. Quite right."

"Major Gumbs," she said crisply, "you are opposite me, I believe?"

"Am I?" said Gumbs doubtfully.

"Never mind. I believe you are. Now: is Meister to your right or left?"

"Left. I know that, anyhow. Can see his eye stalks out of the corner of my eye."

"Very well." McCarty's arm rose, with a sharp-pointed fragment of rock clutched in the blobby fingers.

Horrified, George watched it bend backward across the curve of the monster's body. The long, knife-sharp point probed tentatively at the surface three centimeters short of the area over his brain. Then the fist made an abrupt up-and-down movement, and a fierce stab of pain shot through him.

"Not quite long enough, I think," McCarty said. She flexed the arm, then brought it back to almost the same spot and stabbed again.

"No," she said thoughtfully. "It will take a little longer," then, "Major Gumbs, after my next attempt you will tell me if you notice any reaction in Meister's eye stalks."

The pain was still throbbing along George's nerves. With one half-blinded eye he watched the embryonic arm that was growing, too slowly, under the rim; with the other, fascinated, he watched McCarty's arm lengthen slowly toward him.

It was growing visibly, he suddenly realized—but it wasn't getting any nearer. In fact, incredibly enough, it seemed to be losing ground.

The monster's flesh was flowing away under it, expanding in both directions.

McCarty stabbed again, with vicious strength. This time the pain was less acute.

"Major?" she said. "Any result?"

"No," said Gumbs, "no, I think not. We seem to be moving forward a bit, though, Miss McCarty."

"A ridiculous error," she replied. "We are being forced *back*. Pay attention, Major."

"No, really," he protested. "That is to say, we're moving toward the thicket. Forward to me, backward to you."

"Major Gumbs, *I* am moving forward, *you* are moving back."

They were both right, George discovered: the monster's body was no longer circular, it was extending itself along the Gumbs-McCarty axis. A suggestion of concavity was becoming visible in the center. Below the surface, too, there was motion.

The four brains now formed an oblong, not a square.

The positions of the spinal cords had shifted. His own and Vivian's seemed to be about where they were, but Gumbs's now passed under McCarty's brain, and vice versa.

Having increased its mass by some two hundred kilos, the something *meisterii* was fissioning into two individuals— and tidily separating its tenants, two to each. Gumbs and Meister in one, McCarty and Bellis in the other.

The next time it happened, he realized, each product of the fission would be reduced to one brain—and the time after that, one of the new individuals out of each pair would be a monster in the primary or untenanted state, quiescent, camouflaged, waiting to be stumbled over.

But that meant that, like the common amoeba, this fascinating organism was immortal. It never died, barring accidents; it simply grew and divided.

Not the tenants, though, unfortunately—their tissues would wear out and die.

Or would they? Human nervous tissue didn't proliferate as George's and Miss McCarty's had done; neither did *any* human tissue build new cells fast enough to account for George's eye stalks or Miss McCarty's arm.

There was no question about it: none of that new tissue could possibly be human; it was all counterfeit, produced by the monster from its own substance according to the structural blueprints in the nearest genuine cells. And it was a perfect counterfeit: the new tissues knit with the old, axones coupled with dendrites, muscles contracted or expanded on command. The imitation *worked*.

And therefore, when nerve cells wore out, they could be replaced. Eventually the last human cell would go, the human tenant would have become totally monster—but "a difference that makes no difference is no difference." Effectively, the tenant would still be human—and he would be immortal.

Barring accidents.

Or murder.

Miss McCarty was saying, "Major Gumbs, you are being ridiculous. The explanation is quite obvious. Unless you are deliberately deceiving me, for what reason I cannot imagine, then our efforts to move in opposite directions must be pulling this creature apart."

McCarty was evidently confused in her geometry. Let her stay that way—it would keep her off balance until the fission was complete. No, that was no good. George himself was out of her reach already, and getting farther away—but how about Bellis? Her brain and McCarty's were, if anything, closer together. . . .

What to do? If he warned the girl, that would only draw McCarty's attention to her sooner. Unless he could misdirect her at the same time—

There wasn't much time left, he realized abruptly. If he

was right in thinking that some physical linkage between the brains had occurred to make communication possible, those cells couldn't hold out much longer; the gap between the two pairs of brains was widening steadily.

"Vivian!" he said.

"Yes, George?"

Relieved, he said rapidly, "Listen, we're not pulling this body apart, it's splitting. That's the way it reproduces. You and I will be in one half, Gumbs and McCarty in the other. If they don't give us any trouble, we can all go where we please—"

"Oh, I'm so glad!"

What a warm voice she had. . . . "Yes," said George nervously, "but we may have to fight them; it's up to them. So *grow an arm*, Vivian."

"I'll try," she said doubtfully. "I don't know—"

McCarty's voice cut across hers. "Ah. Major Gumbs, since you have eyes, it will be your task to see to it that those two do not escape. Meanwhile, I suggest that you, also, grow an arm."

"Doing my best," said Gumbs.

Puzzled, George glanced downward, past his own half-formed arm: there, almost out of sight, was a fleshy bulge under Gumbs's section of the rim! The major had been working on it in secret, keeping it hidden . . . and it was already better developed than George's.

"Oh-oh," said Gumbs abruptly. "Look here, Miss McCarty, Meister's been leading you up the garden path. Look here, I mean, you and I aren't going to be in the same half. How could we be? We're on *opposite sides* of the blasted thing. It's going to be you and Miss Bellis, me and Meister."

The monster was developing a definite waistline. The spinal cords had rotated, now, so that there was clear space between them in the center.

"Yes," said McCarty faintly. "*Thank* you, Major Gumbs."

"George!" came Vivian's frightened voice, distant and weak. "What shall I do?"

"Grow an arm!" he shouted.

There was no reply.

4

Frozen, George watched McCarty's arm, the rock-fragment still clutched at the end of it, rise into view and swing leftward at full stretch over the bubbling surface of the monster. He had time to see it bob up and viciously down again; time to think, *Still short, thank God—that's McCarty's right arm, it's farther from Vivian's brain than it was from mine*; time, finally, to realize that he could not possibly help her before McCarty lengthened the arm the few centimeters more that were necessary. The fission was not more than half complete; and he could no more move to where he wanted to be than a Siamese twin could walk around his brother.

Then his time was up. A flicker of motion warned him, and he looked back to see a lumpy, distorted pseudo-hand clutching for his eye stalks.

Instinctively he brought his own hand up, grasped the other's wrist and hung on desperately. It was half again the size of his, and so strongly muscled that although his leverage was better, he couldn't force it back or hold it away; he could only keep the system oscillating up and down, adding his strength to Gumbs's so that the mark was overshot.

Gumbs began to vary the force and rhythm of his movements, trying to catch him off guard. A thick finger brushed the base of one eye stalk.

"Sorry about this, Meister," said Gumbs's voice. "No hard feelings in it, on my side. Between us (oof) I don't fancy that

McCarty woman much—but (ugh! almost had you that time) beggars can't be choosers. Ah. Way I see it, I've got to look after myself; mean to say (ugh) if I don't, who will? See what I mean?"

George did not reply. Astonishingly enough, he was no longer afraid, either for himself or for Vivian; he was simply overpoweringly, ecstatically, monomaniacally angry. Power from somewhere was surging into his arm; fiercely concentrating, he thought, *Bigger! Stronger! Longer! More arm!*

The arm grew. Visibly it added substance to itself, it lengthened, thickened, bulged with muscle. So did Gumbs's.

He began another arm. So did Gumbs.

All around him the surface of the monster was bubbling violently. And, George realized finally, the lenticular bulk of it was perceptibly shrinking. Its curious breathing system was inadequate; the thing was cannibalizing itself, destroying its own tissues to make up the difference.

How small could it get and still support two human tenants?

And which brain would it dispense with first?

He had no leisure to think about it. Scrabbling in the grass with his second hand, Gumbs had failed to find anything that would serve as a weapon; now, with a sudden lurch, he swung their entire body around.

The fission was complete.

That thought reminded George of Vivian and McCarty. He risked a split second's glance behind him, saw nothing but a featureless avoid mound, and looked back in time to see Gumbs's half-grown right fist pluck a long, sharp-pointed dead branch out of the grass. In the next instant the thing came whipping at his eyes.

The lip of the river bank was a meter away to the left. George made it in one abrupt surge. They slipped, tottered, hesitated, hands clutching wildly—and toppled, end over end, hurtling in a cloud of dust and pebbles down the breakneck slope to a meaty smash at the bottom.

The universe made one more giant turn around them and came to rest. Half blinded, George groped for the hold he had lost, found the wrist and seized it.

"Oh, Lord," said Gumbs's voice, "that's done me. I'm hurt, Meister. Go on, man, finish it, will you? Don't waste time."

George stared at him suspiciously, without relaxing his grip. "What's the matter with you?"

"I tell you I'm done," said Gumbs pettishly. "Paralyzed. I can't move."

They had fallen, George saw, onto a small boulder, one of many with which the river bed was strewn. This one was roughly conical; they were draped over it, and the blunt point was directly under Gumbs's spinal cord, a few centimeters from the brain.

"Gumbs," he said, "that may not be as bad as you think. If I can show you it isn't, will you give up and put yourself under my orders?"

"How do you mean? My spine's crushed."

"Never mind that now. Will you or won't you?"

"Why, yes," said Gumbs. "That's very decent of you, Meister, matter of fact. You have my word, for what it's worth."

"All right," said George. Straining hard, he managed to get their body down off the boulder. Then he stared up at the slope down which they had tumbled. Too steep; he'd have to find an easier way back. He turned and started off to eastward, paralleling the thin stream that still flowed in the center of the watercourse.

"What's up now?" Gumbs asked after a moment.

"We've got to find a way up to the top." George said impatiently. "I may still be able to help Vivian."

"Ah, yes. Afraid I was thinking about myself, Meister. If you don't mind telling me—"

She couldn't still be alive, George was thinking despondently, but if there were any small chance—"You'll be all right," he said. "If you were still in your old body that would be a fatal injury, or permanently disabling, anyhow, but not in this thing. You can repair yourself as easily as you can grow a new limb."

"Good Lord," said Gumbs. "Stupid of me not to think of that. But look here, Meister, does that mean we were simply wasting our time trying to kill one another? I mean to say—"

"No. If you'd crushed my brain, I think the organism would have digested it, and that would be the end of me. But short of anything that drastic, I believe we're immortal."

"Immortal," said Gumbs. "Good Lord. . . . That does rather put another face on it, doesn't it?"

The bank was becoming a little lower, and at one point, where the raw earth was thickly seeded with boulders, there was a talus slope that looked as if it could be climbed. George started up it.

"Meister," said Gumbs after a moment.

"What do you want?"

"You're right, you know—I'm getting some feeling back already. . . . Look here, Meister, is there anything this beast *can't* do? I mean, for instance, do you suppose we could put ourselves back together the way we were, with all the—appendages, and so on?"

"It's possible," George said curtly. It was a thought that had been in the back of his mind, but he didn't feel like discussing it with Gumbs just now.

They were halfway up the slope.

"Well, in that case—" said Gumbs meditatively. "The thing has *military* possibilities, you know. Man who brought a thing like that direct to the War Department could write his own ticket, more or less."

"After we split up," George said, "you can do whatever you please."

"But, dammit," said Gumbs in an irritated tone, "that won't do."

"Why not?"

"Because," said Gumbs, "they might find you." His hands reached up abruptly, grasped a small boulder, and before George could stop him, pried it sideways out of its socket in the earth.

The larger boulder above it trembled, dipped and leaned ponderously outward. George, directly underneath, found that he could move neither forward nor back.

"Sorry again," he heard Gumbs saying, with what sounded like genuine regret. "But you know the Loyalty Committee. I simply can't take the chance."

The boulder seemed to take forever to fall. George tried twice more, with all his strength, to move out of its path. Then, instinctively, he put his arms up straight under it.

At the last possible instant he moved them to the left, away from the center of the toppling gray mass.

It struck.

George felt his arms breaking like twigs, and saw a looming grayness that blotted out the sky; he felt a sledgehammer impact that made the earth shudder beneath him.

He heard a splattering sound.

And he was still alive. That astonishing fact kept him fully occupied for a long time after the boulder had clattered its way down the slope into silence. Then, finally, he looked down to his right.

The resistance of his stiffened arms, even while they broke, had been barely enough to lever the falling body over, a distance of some thirty centimeters. . . . The right half of the monster was a flattened, shattered ruin. He could see a few flecks of pasty gray matter, melting now into green-brown translucence as the mass flowed slowly together again.

In twenty minutes the last remnants of a superfluous spinal cord had been reabsorbed, the monster had collected itself back into its normal lens shape, and George's pain was diminishing. In five minutes more his mended arms were strong enough to use. They were also more convincingly shaped and colored than before—the tendons, the fingernails, even the wrinkles of the skin were in good order. In ordinary circumstances this discovery would have left George happily bemused for hours; now, in his impatience, he barely noticed it. He climbed to the top of the bank.

Thirty meters away a humped green-brown body like his own lay motionless on the dry grass.

It contained, of course, only one brain. Whose?

McCarty's, almost certainly; Vivian hadn't had a chance. But then how did it happen that there was no visible trace of McCarty's arm?

Unnerved, George walked around the creature for a closer inspection.

On the far side he encountered two dark-brown eyes, with an oddly unfinished appearance. They focused on him after an instant, and the whole body quivered slightly, moving toward him.

Vivian's eyes had been brown; George remembered them distinctly. Brown eyes with heavy dark lashes in a tapering slender face. . . . But did that prove anything? What color had McCarty's eyes been? He couldn't remember for certain.

There was only one way to find out. George moved closer, hoping fervently that the something *meisterii* was at least advanced enough to conjugate, instead of trying to devour members of its own species. . . .

The two bodies touched, clung and began to flow together. Watching, George saw the fissioning process reverse itself: from paired lenses the alien flesh melted into a slipper shape, to an ovoid, to lens shape again. His brain and the other drifted closer together, the spinal cords crossing at right angles.

And it was only then that he noticed an oddity about the other brain: it seemed to be lighter and larger than his, the outline a trifle sharper.

"Vivian?" he said doubtfully. "Is that you?"

No answer. He tried again; and again.

Finally:

"George! Oh, dear—I want to cry, but I can't seem to do it."

"No lachrymal glands," George said automatically. "Uh, Vivian?"

"Yes, George." That warm voice again. . . .

"What happened to Miss McCarty? How did you—I mean, what happened?"

"I don't know. She's gone, isn't she? I haven't heard her for a long time."

"Yes," said George, "she's gone. You mean you don't *know*? Tell me what you did."

"Well, I wanted to make an arm, because you told me to, but I didn't think I had time enough. So I made a skull instead. And those things to cover my spine—"

"Vertebrae." *Now why*, he thought dazedly, *didn't I think of that?* "And then?" he said.

"I think I'm crying now," she said. "Yes, I am. It's such a relief. And then, after that, nothing. She was still hurting me, and I just lay here and thought how wonderful it would be if she weren't in here with me. And then, after a while, she wasn't. Then I grew eyes to look for you."

The explanation, it seemed to George, was more perplex-

ing than the enigma. Staring around in a vague search for
enlightenment, he caught sight of something that had escaped his notice before. Two meters to his left, just visible in
the grass, was a damp-looking grayish lump, with a suggestion of a stringy extension trailing off from it. . . .

There must, he decided suddenly, be some mechanism in
the something *meisterii* for disposing of tenants who failed
to adapt themselves—brains that went into catatonia, or hysteria, or suicidal frenzy. An eviction clause.

Somehow, Vivian had managed to stimulate that mechanism—to convince the organism that McCarty's brain was
not only superfluous but dangerous—"poisonous" was the
word.

Miss McCarty—it was the final ignominy—had not been
digested, but excreted.

By sunset, twelve hours later, they had made a good deal of
progress. They had reached an understanding very agreeable
to them both; they had hunted down another herd of the
pseudo-pigs for their noon meal; and, for divergent reasons—
on George's side because the monster's normal metabolism
was grossly inefficient when it had to move quickly, and on
Vivian's because she refused to believe that any man could
be attracted to her in her present condition—they had begun
a serious attempt to reshape themselves.

The first trials were extraordinarily difficult, the rest surprisingly easy. Again and again they had to let themselves
collapse back into amoeboid masses, victims of some omitted
or malfunctioning organ; but each failure smoothed the road;
eventually they were able to stand breathless but breathing,
swaying but erect, face to face—two protean giants in the
fortunate dimness, two sketches of self-created Man.

They had also put thirty kilometers between themselves
and the Federation camp. Standing on the crest of a rise and

looking southward across the shallow valley, George could see a faint funereal glow: the mining machines, chewing out metals to feed the fabricators that would spawn a billion ships.

"We'll never go back, will we?" said Vivian.

"No," said George soberly. "They'll come to us, in time. We have lots of time. We're the future."

And one thing more, a small thing, but important to George; it marked his sense of accomplishment, of one phase ended and a new one begun. He had finally completed the name of his discovery—not, as it turned out, anything *meisterii* at all. *Spes hominis*:

Man's hope.

FOUR IN ONE:
COMPLICATIONS, WITH ELEGANCE

James Blish, discussing the "Baldy" series of stories by Henry Kuttner and C. L. Moore, described the Kuttners' customary method of beginning a story this way:

"The narrative hook, almost always dealing with incipient violence, madness, or both; enough development of the hook to lead the story into a paradox; then a complete suspension of the story while the authors lecture the reader on the background for a short time, seldom more than 1,000 words. The lecture technique is generally taboo for fiction, especially in the hands of new writers, and only two science fiction writers have managed to get away with it and make the reader like it, Heinlein being the other."

Blish might have added Damon Knight to that short list. Knight, always a fluent and *seemingly* effortless writer, generally has avoided the temptations of stopping his stories for background lectures. But when he does it—and the temptation can be irresistible for the science-fiction writer, with so very much unfamiliar background to communicate—he manages the trick neatly and effectively. "Four in One," which first appeared in the February, 1953, issue of *Galaxy*, shows Knight using the Kuttner method to excellent purpose.

The opening sequence is concerned only in the most tangential way with the "incipient madness or violence" of a Kuttner opening gambit. But the potential is there, for George Meister has lost his body and has, like Gregor Samsa in Kafka's "Metamorphosis," been transformed into something unutterably weird and strange. The discovery of his new condition might well be expected to drive Meister out of his mind—except that he, like the author who created him, is a calm and rational man, not much given to emotional frenzy.

See how calmly the story opens: Meister's recollection of a human nervous system that he once had seen on display, dissected out of its body and encased in plastic. But at the end of the first paragraph Knight puts in his hook—"Having seen the specimen, Meister knew approximately what he himself must look like at the present moment"—and sets up the initial dissonance out of which the story is to be generated. (There will be more: this is a long story, some eleven thousand words, and needs not only a main plot—Meister's response to his bizarre predicament—but also several subplots to sustain the length.)

Notice that Knight has his protagonist in terrible trouble right at the start. The first paragraph of a story, or certainly the first page, is the place to do that: if not to show your hero already in a mess, then to imply it in a way that may not be obvious to the reader at first but that, on a second reading, can plainly be seen to have indicated the trouble that lies ahead. This seemingly simpleminded rule is not something that was invented by pulp-magazine hacks in the 1920s. The principle of beginning a story *in medias res*—"in the middle of things"—was already well established in ancient times. See how *The Iliad* begins:

It was Apollo, son of Zeus and Leto, who started the feud.

Or *The Odyssey*:

> All the survivors of the war had reached their homes by now
> and so put the perils of battle and the sea behind them.
> Odysseus alone was prevented from returning to the home
> and wife he longed for by that powerful goddess, the nymph
> Calypso, who wished him to marry her, and kept him in her
> vaulted cave.

Or *Oedipus Rex*:

> Children, new blood of Cadmus' ancient line—
> What is the meaning of this supplication,
> These branches and garlands, the incense filling the city,
> These prayers for the healing of pain, these
> lamentations?

Or Dante's *Inferno*:

> Midway this way of life we're bound upon,
> I woke to find myself in a dark wood,
> Where the right road was wholly lost and gone.

A feud between great chieftains is under way at the outset of *The Iliad*. Homer's other great poem begins with Odysseus held prisoner. Dante is lost in a dark wood. Oedipus is in deep trouble, though he doesn't yet realize it—for *something* is plainly wrong in the city where he is king, and he is in fact responsible for the difficulty; very swiftly we will see him in the most horrible of messes as he presses for explanations of what is going on.

Similarly in "Four in One." George Meister has fallen into some kind of giant carnivorous alien amoeba that has digested all of him except his brain, and he and we know it right away. This could be the stuff of a really dumb upchuck horror story as Meister, crazed with rage, prowls the camp of the Earth exploration team by night, gobbling up his former companions. But Knight has other purposes in mind. His Meister is a scientist. He takes his catastrophe coolly—a lot more coolly than most of us would. And sets out to make the most of it, a very sensible attitude, considering that there's no apparent way he can undo the thing that has happened to him. After all, he points out, he has "stumbled into the most interesting organism on this planet." He will study it from within. He even muses on the scientific name the creature will have to be given. "Something *meisterii*, he thought. He had not settled on a species name—he would have to learn more about it before he decided—but *meisterii* certainly." This bit of pardonable vanity is charming—he has discovered the animal, hasn't he, in the most direct possible way?—but also these early speculations on scientific nomenclature will prove useful to Knight in the final moment of the story. (It's always artistically pleasing when a story's end hearkens back to its beginning.)

But a calm, reasonable protagonist making a calm, reasonable assessment of a grotesque predicament doesn't hold much potential for interesting fiction. A story needs *complication*—annoying problems, mounting difficulties, bothersome jeopardy. Meister was not alone when he fell into the monster. Where are his three companions? Have they been digested also? Perhaps so. If they are in here too, can he make contact with them? (Knight does not suggest at this point that sharing the alien body with the nervous systems of several of his companions may cause trouble for Meister. Meister is not the sort of man who sees conflict as the normal outcome of any human interaction; he is too rational for that. But the reader, knowing something about human nature and perhaps about the storytelling tradition, is likely to guess that 1) the other humans *have* been engulfed also and 2) Meister will find their presence a complication. The reader is apt to keep on reading to see if his guess is correct. Sometimes it's useful in building suspense for a writer to let a reader get a little way ahead of him.)

Meister is as concerned as any of us would be about how to deal with his predicament. One obvious response would be to scuttle back to his home base, a few hundred meters away, and beg his fellow Earthmen to rescue him. But then it occurs to him "that his appearance was not obviously that of a human being in distress; the chances were that he looked rather more like a monster which had eaten and partially digested one or more people." If he returns to camp, he'll probably be shot on sight. Knight has arrived at the Kuttnerian paradox that concludes his opening scene: the one place where Meister might actually secure assistance is the place where he would be in the greatest jeopardy. What he must do instead of returning to camp is "get away, bury himself in the forest, and study his new body: find out how it worked and what he could do with it." Having established the problem, the character of his protagonist, and the first complication of the problem, all in the opening few hundred words, Knight can now allow himself the luxury of halting the story long enough to tell us how Meister got himself into this mess. We are interested in knowing; and Knight does it so smoothly, with so much circumstantial detail ("Meister, Gumbs, Bellis, and McCarty started out across the level cinder and ash left by the transport's tail jets to the nearest living vegetation, six hundred meters away"), that we don't at all object to this lengthy departure from Meister's immediate dilemma.

Complications now ensue. In an elegant way, which you can be sure I studied with intense concentration when I first read this story in 1953, Knight methodically unfolds the consequences of finding yourself devoured by a giant alien amoeba. He is in no hurry: the situation is strange enough to hold the reader's interest a while longer even without interaction with other human beings or dialog of any sort. Meister learns some things about his captor. He makes the first efforts at gaining control of his situation. In the course of these efforts he discovers that he is not alone in the monster. (A good story builds each plot situation from the one preceding it: one event leads naturally to the next. If you can reshuffle the event sequence of a story so that some scene can fit just as easily on page 5, page 15, or page 22, there's probably something wrong with your story.)

Before long the other three members of Meister's expedition have been heard from. Now Knight has the material for the interplay of character that powers most fiction. The characters he brings in are little more than handy types: a genial but blustering military man, a stern and prudish female security officer, and a pleasant but undifferentiated young woman. You can tell one from another simply by what they say and the way they say it—the minimal expectation of workmanlike characterization in a story—but they aren't depicted with any depth. It isn't necessary. We don't need to hear about Major Gumbs' homosexual episode at West Point or Miss McCarty's teenage dalliance with Communism in this story. It's Meister's story. We are told just enough about the other characters to see what problems they pose for Meister. All we know about Meister, really, is that he's sensible and decent and resourceful. Beyond that, we are concerned first with Meister and the monster, then with Meister's struggle to survive against his human antagonists. That's sufficient to sustain interest in a story of this length. Rich characterization can sometimes be an impediment in science fiction, where the focus is often on a unique external problem rather than on a unique human being.

Meister's companions inside the monster are less cool about it all than he is. Vivian Bellis is scared stiff; Gumbs is indignant and annoyed; Miss McCarty, brusque and officious, thinks that proper action will quickly save the day and set everything to rights. (It is worth noting that Knight gave the name "McCarty" to his disagreeable security officer, who is murderously preoccupied with issues of loyalty and conformity to authority, in the very year that the United States was convulsed by the anti-Communist witch-hunt being conducted by Wisconsin's Senator Joseph McCarthy and his unsavory aides. At that time of harsh congressional inquisitions, blacklists, and purges, that was an amazingly courageous act of protest. But of course no one in the government was apt to take notice of anything so unimportant as a crazy science-fiction story.)

As the other three begin reacting to the situation, the tempo of the story picks up—and just in time, for Meister by himself is simply too unflappable to generate an interesting story of this length. But suddenly there is direct conflict—a struggle between Meister and McCarty over whether to guide their monstrous host back to camp. The story becomes exciting, whereas earlier it has only been interesting. Meister prevails for the moment over McCarty, in the course of which he learns even more about the way the monster works. (The humans are able to grow humanlike organs out of the monster's protoplasm whenever they experience emotional strain— a rough analog of the theory that evolution is a response to external stress.) But McCarty is learning about the monster, too. Because she sees Meister not only as a threat to her hope of regaining human form but as disloyal and untrustworthy, she makes more and more trouble for him. Meister seeks allies. Vivian Bellis is useless— still numb with fear. (Her general blankness is one of the story's few weaknesses.) Meister's attempt to enlist the aid of Major Gumbs fails because Gumbs is too slow-witted and too much the stock military man to defy McCarty. And then Meister is in real physical danger. McCarty has decided to *kill* him. There is nothing like placing your protagonist in danger of death to hold your reader's attention, especially if he is in a peculiar and awkward situation, where an attack can come from almost any direction and maximum ingenuity is needed to ward it off.

The physical struggle between Meister and McCarty, with Bellis and Gumbs playing subordinate roles, sets the climax of the story in motion. Because Knight has rigorously remained in Meister's viewpoint throughout, except for the brief historical flashback near the beginning, we have come by now to care very much about him. When McCarty extrudes an armlike organ and waves a knife-sharp sliver of rock three centimeters from Meister's brain, we shiver and shudder, as we are meant to do. A lesser science-fiction writer would have been content to let this death-struggle provide the entire resolution of the tale. But Knight is a purist; he knows that a science-fiction story should have a science-fictional payoff. And so the biology of the monster is brought into play: it begins to divide in amoebalike fission, unexpectedly separating the protagonists, and naturally not separating them in the way most advantageous to Meister. (He lands in the half with Gumbs. If he had landed with Bellis, it would have been too easy; if he had landed with McCarty, the possibility for melodrama would have been too strong.) And so "Four in One" moves on to its finale, Knight telling his story in brisk, clear, unfancy prose: "He heard a splattering sound. . . . Thirty meters away a humped green-brown body like his own lay motionless on the dry grass. It contained, of course, only one brain. Whose?"

Now we see that an odd sort of love story has actually been going on while our attention was elsewhere. Meister's terrible calamity has in fact dumped him into the most intimate kind of marriage imaginable. And, at the end, he and Vivian, having survived their strange ordeal, walk off into the sunset, more or less human again but vastly, unimaginably transformed. Now is the moment for Knight to loop back to the issue of the monster's scientific name; and he does it neatly and prettily in a manner that converts that seemingly dry subject into a note of warmth and optimism on which to end.

"Four in One" is an effective, *efficient* story. It offers no soaringly eloquent prose, no visions of cosmic splendor, no searching analysis of character, no sudden mind-rocking philosophical revelations. What it does do is demonstrate how to go about the job of constructing a science-fiction story. A novel idea—monster eats man but man's mind survives; methodical and exhaustive exploration of the consequences of that idea; suspense generated by conflict growing out of the strange science-fictional predicament of the characters;

resolution of that conflict likewise growing out of the specifically science-fictional situation. Characters individuated, if not depicted in extraordinary depth. Uncluttered, almost transparent prose.

It works. It works very well.

FONDLY FAHRENHEIT
ALFRED BESTER

He doesn't know which of us I am these days, but they know one truth. You must own nothing but yourself. You must make your own life, live your own life and die your own death . . . or else you will die another's.

The rice fields on Paragon III stretch for hundreds of miles like checkerboard tundras, a blue and brown mosaic under a burning sky of orange. In the evening, clouds whip like smoke, and the paddies rustle and murmur.

A long line of men marched across the paddies the evening we escaped from Paragon III. They were silent, armed, intent; a long rank of silhouetted statues looming against the smoking sky. Each man carried a gun. Each man wore a walkie-talkie belt pack, the speaker button in his ear, the microphone bug clipped to his throat, the glowing viewscreen strapped to his wrist like a green-eyed watch. The multitude of screens showed nothing but a multitude of individual paths through the paddies. The annunciators uttered no sound but the rustle and splash of steps. The men spoke infrequently, in heavy grunts, all speaking to all.

"Nothing here."

"Where's here?"

"Jenson's fields."

"You're drifting too far west."

"Close in the line there."

"Anybody covered the Grimson paddy?"

"Yeah. Nothing."

"She couldn't have walked this far."

"Could have been carried."

"Think she's alive?"

"Why should she be dead?"

The slow refrain swept up and down the long line of beaters advancing toward the smoky sunset. The line of beaters wavered like a writhing snake, but never ceased its remorseless advance. One hundred men spaced fifty feet apart. Five thousand feet of ominous search. One mile of angry determination stretching from east to west across a compass of heat. Evening fell. Each man lit his search lamp. The writhing snake was transformed into a necklace of wavering diamonds.

"Clear here. Nothing."

"Nothing here."

"Nothing."

"What about the Allen paddies?"

"Covering them now."

"Think we missed her?"

"Maybe."

"We'll beat back and check."

"This'll be an all-night job."

"Allen paddies clear."

"God damn! We've got to find her!"

"We'll find her."

"Here she is. Sector seven. Tune in."

The line stopped. The diamonds froze in the heat. There was silence. Each man gazed into the glowing green screen on his wrist, tuning to sector seven. All tuned to one. All showed a small nude figure awash in the muddy water of a paddy. Alongside the figure an owner's stake of bronze read: VANDALEUR. The ends of the line converged toward the Vandaleur field. The necklace turned into a cluster of stars. One hundred men gathered around a small nude body, a child dead in a rice paddy. There was no water in her mouth. There were fingermarks on her throat. Her innocent face was battered. Her body was torn. Clotted blood on her skin was crusted and hard.

"Dead three-four hours at least."

"Her mouth is dry."

"She wasn't drowned. Beaten to death."

In the dark evening heat the men swore softly. They picked up the body. One stopped the others and pointed to the child's fingernails. She had fought her murderer. Under the nails were particles of flesh and bright drops of scarlet blood, still liquid, still uncoagulated.

"That blood ought to be clotted, too."

"Funny."

"Not so funny. What kind of blood don't clot?"

"Android."

"Looks like she was killed by one."

"Vandaleur owns an android."

"She couldn't be killed by an android."

"That's android blood under her nails."

"The police better check."

"The police'll prove I'm right."

"But andys can't kill."

"That's android blood, ain't it?"

"Androids can't kill. They're made that way."

"Looks like one android was made wrong."

"Jesus!"

And the thermometer that day registered 92.9° gloriously Fahrenheit.

So there we were aboard the *Paragon Queen* en route for Megaster V, James Vandaleur and his android. James Vandaleur counted his money and wept. In the second-class cabin with him was his android, a magnificent synthetic creature with classic features and wide blue eyes. Raised on its forehead in a cameo of flesh were the letters MA, indicating that this was one of the rare multiple-aptitude androids, worth $57,000 on the current exchange. There we were, weeping and counting and calmly watching.

"Twelve, fourteen, sixteen. Sixteen hundred dollars," Vandaleur wept. "That's all. Sixteen hundred dollars. My house was worth ten thousand. The land was worth five. There was furniture, cars, my paintings, etchings, my plane, my—And nothing to show for everything but sixteen hundred dollars. Christ!"

I leaped up from the table and turned on the android. I pulled a strap from one of the leather bags and beat the android. It didn't move.

"I must remind you," the android said, "that I am worth fifty-seven thousand dollars on the current exchange. I must warn you that you are endangering valuable property."

"You damned crazy machine," Vandaleur shouted.

"I am not a machine," the android answered. "The robot is a machine. The android is a chemical creation of synthetic tissue."

"What got into you?" Vandaleur cried. "Why did you do it? Damn you!" He beat the android savagely.

"I must remind you that I cannot be punished," I said. "The pleasure-pain syndrome is not incorporated in the android synthesis."

"Then why did you kill her?" Vandaleur shouted. "If it wasn't for kicks, why did you—"

"I must remind you," the android said, "that the second-class cabins in these ships are not soundproofed."

Vandaleur dropped the strap and stood panting, staring at the creature he owned.

"Why did you do it? Why did you kill her?" I asked.

"I don't know," I answered.

"First it was malicious mischief. Small things. Petty destruction. I should have known there was something wrong with you then. Androids can't destroy. They can't harm. They—"

"There is no pleasure-pain syndrome incorporated in the android synthesis."

"Then it got to arson. Then serious destruction. Then assault . . . that engineer on Rigel. Each time worse. Each time we had to get out faster. Now it's murder. Christ! What's the matter with you? What's happened?"

"There are no self-check relays incorporated in the android brain."

"Each time we had to get out it was a step downhill. Look at me. In a second-class cabin. Me. James Paleologue Vandaleur. There was a time when my father was the wealthiest— Now, sixteen hundred dollars in the world. That's all I've got. And you. Christ damn you!"

Vandaleur raised the strap to beat the android again, then dropped it and collapsed on a berth, sobbing. At last he pulled himself together.

"Instructions," he said.

The multiple android responded at once. It arose and awaited orders.

"My name is now Valentine. James Valentine. I stopped off on Paragon III for only one day to transfer to this ship for Megaster V. My occupation: Agent for one privately owned MA android which is for hire. Purpose of visit: To settle on Megaster V. Fix the papers."

The android removed Vandaleur's passport and papers from a bag, got pen and ink and sat down at the table. With an accurate, flawless hand—an accomplished hand that could draw, write, paint, carve, engrave, etch, photograph, design, create, and build—it meticulously forged new credentials for Vandaleur. Its owner watched me miserably.

"Create and build," I muttered, "and now destroy. Oh God! What am I going to do? Christ! If I could only get rid of you. If I didn't have to live off you. God! If only I'd inherited some guts instead of you."

Dallas Brady was Megaster's leading jewelry designer. She was short, stocky, amoral, and a nymphomaniac. She hired Vandaleur's multiple-aptitude android and put me to work in her shop. She seduced Vandaleur. In her bed one night, she asked abruptly, "Your name's Vandaleur, isn't it?"

"Yes," I murmured. Then: "No! It's Valentine. James Valentine."

"What happened on Paragon?" Dallas Brady asked. "I thought androids couldn't kill or destroy property. Prime Directives and Inhibitions set up for them when they're synthesized. Every company guarantees they can't."

"Valentine!" Vandaleur insisted.

"Oh come off it," Dallas Brady said. "I've known for a week. I haven't hollered copper, have I?"

"The name is Valentine."

"You want to prove it? You want I should call the cops?" Dallas reached out and picked up the phone.

"For God's sake, Dallas!" Vandaleur leaped up and struggled to take the phone from her. She fended him off, laughing at him, until he collapsed and wept in shame and helplessness.

"How did you find out?" he asked at last.

"The papers are full of it. And Valentine was a little too close to Vandaleur. That wasn't smart, was it?"

"I guess not. I'm not very smart."

"Your android's got quite a record, hasn't it? Assault. Arson. Destruction. What happened on Paragon?"

"It kidnapped a child. Took her out into the rice fields and murdered her."

"Raped her?"

"I don't know."

"They're going to catch up with you."

"Don't I know it? Christ! We've been running for two years now. Seven planets in two years. I must have abandoned fifty thousand dollars' worth of property in two years."

"You better find out what's wrong with it."

"How can I? Can I walk into a repair clinic and ask for an overhaul? What am I going to say? 'My android's just turned killer. Fix it.' They'd call the police right off." I began to shake. "They'd have that android dismantled inside one day. I'd probably be booked as accessory to murder."

"Why didn't you have it repaired before it got to murder?"

"I couldn't take the chance," Vandaleur explained angrily. "If they started fooling around with lobotomies and body chemistry and endocrine surgery, they might have destroyed its aptitudes. What would I have left to hire out? How would I live?"

"You could work yourself. People do."

"Work at what? You know I'm good for nothing. How could I compete with specialist androids and robots? Who can, unless he's got a terrific talent for a particular job?"

"Yeah. That's true."

"I lived off my old man all my life. Damn him! He had

to go bust just before he died. Left me the android and that's all. The only way I can get along is living off what it earns."

"You better sell it before the cops catch up with you. You can live off fifty grand. Invest it."

"At three percent? Fifteen hundred a year? When the android returns fifteen percent on its value? Eight thousand a year. That's what it earns. No, Dallas. I've got to go along with it."

"What are you going to do about its violence kick?"

"I can't do anything . . . except watch it and pray. What are you going to do about it?"

"Nothing. It's none of my business. Only one thing. . . . I ought to get something for keeping my mouth shut."

"What?"

"The android works for me for free. Let somebody else pay you, but I get it for free."

The multiple-aptitude android worked. Vandaleur collected its fees. His expenses were taken care of. His savings began to mount. As the warm spring of Megaster V turned to hot summer, I began investigating farms and properties. It would be possible, within a year or two, for us to settle down permanently, provided Dallas Brady's demands did not become rapacious.

On the first hot day of summer, the android began singing in Dallas Brady's workshop. It hovered over the electric furnace which, along with the weather, was broiling the shop, and sang an ancient tune that had been popular half a century before.

> Oh, it's no feat to beat the heat.
> All reet! All reet!
> So jeet your seat
> Be fleet be fleet

Cool and discreet
Honey . . .

It sang in a strange, halting voice, and its accomplished fingers were clasped behind its back, writhing in a strange rumba all their own. Dallas Brady was surprised.

"You happy or something?" she asked.

"I must remind yóu that the pleasure-pain syndrome is not incorporated in the android synthesis," I answered. "All reet! All reet! Be fleet be fleet, cool and discreet, honey . . ."

Its fingers stopped their writhing and picked up a heavy pair of iron tongs. The android poked them into the glowing heart of the furnace, leaning far forward to peer into the lovely heat.

"Be careful, you damned fool!" Dallas Brady exclaimed. "You want to fall in?"

"I must remind you that I am worth fifty-seven thousand dollars on the current exchange," I said. "It is forbidden to endanger valuable property. All reet! All reet! Honey . . ."

It withdrew a crucible of glowing gold from the electric furnace, turned, capered hideously, sang crazily, and splashed a sluggish gobbet of molten gold over Dallas Brady's head. She screamed and collapsed, her hair and clothes flaming, her skin crackling. The android poured again while it capered and sang.

"Be fleet be fleet, cool and discreet, honey . . ." It sang and slowly poured and poured the molten gold. Then I left the workshop and rejoined James Vandaleur in his hotel suite. The android's charred clothes and squirming fingers warned its owner that something was very much wrong.

Vandaleur rushed to Dallas Brady's workshop, stared once, vomited, and fled. I had enough time to pack one bag and raise nine hundred dollars on portable assets. He took a third-class cabin on the *Megaster Queen*, which left that morning for Lyra Alpha. He took me with him. He wept and counted his money and I beat the android again.

And the thermometer in Dallas Brady's workshop registered 98.1° beautifully Fahrenheit.

On Lyra Alpha we holed up in a small hotel near the university. There, Vandaleur carefully bruised my forehead until the letters MA were obliterated by the swelling and the discoloration. The letters would reappear again, but not for several months, and in the meantime Vandaleur hoped the hue and cry for an MA android would be forgotten. The android was hired out as a common laborer in the university power plant. Vandaleur, as James Venice, eked out life on the android's small earnings.

I wasn't too unhappy. Most of the other residents in the hotel were university students, equally hard-up, but delightfully young and enthusiastic. There was one charming girl with sharp eyes and a quick mind. Her name was Wanda, and she and her beau, Jed Stark, took a tremendous interest in the killing android which was being mentioned in every paper in the galaxy.

"We've been studying the case," she and Jed said at one of the casual student parties which happened to be held this night in Vandaleur's room. "We think we know what's causing it. We're going to do a paper." They were in a high state of excitement.

"Causing what?" somebody wanted to know.

"The android rampage."

"Obviously out of adjustment, isn't it? Body chemistry gone haywire. Maybe a kind of synthetic cancer, yes?"

"No." Wanda gave Jed a look of suppressed triumph.

"Well, what is it?"

"Something specific."

"What?"

"That would be telling."

"Oh come on."

"Nothing doing."

"Won't you tell us?" I asked intently. "I . . . We're very much interested in what could go wrong with an android."

"No, Mr. Venice," Wanda said. "It's a unique idea and we've got to protect it. One thesis like this and we'll be set up for life. We can't take the chance of somebody stealing it."

"Can't you give us a hint?"

"No. Not a hint. Don't say a word, Jed. But I'll tell you this much, Mr. Venice. I'd hate to be the man who owns that android."

"You mean the police?" I asked.

"I mean projection, Mr. Venice. Projection! That's the danger . . . and I won't say any more. I've said too much as is."

I heard steps outside, and a hoarse voice singing softly: "Be fleet be fleet, cool and discreet, honey . . ." My android entered the room, home from its tour of duty at the university power plant. It was not introduced. I motioned to it and I immediately responded to the command and went to the beer keg and took over Vandaleur's job of serving the guests. Its accomplished fingers writhed in a private rumba of their own. Gradually they stopped their squirming, and the strange humming ended.

Androids were not unusual at the university. The wealthier students owned them along with cars and planes. Vandaleur's android provoked no comment, but young Wanda was sharp-eyed and quick-witted. She noted my bruised forehead and she was intent on the history-making thesis she and Jed Stark were going to write. After the party broke up, she consulted with Jed walking upstairs to her room.

"Jed, why'd that android have a bruised forehead?"

"Probably hurt itself, Wanda. It's working in the power plant. They fling a lot of heavy stuff around."

"That all?"

"What else?"

"It could be a convenient bruise."

"Convenient for what?"

"Hiding what's stamped on its forehead."

"No point to that, Wanda. You don't have to see marks on a forehead to recognize an android. You don't have to see a trademark on a car to know it's a car."

"I don't mean it's trying to pass as a human. I mean it's trying to pass as a lower-grade android."

"Why?"

"Suppose it had 'MA' on its forehead."

"Multiple aptitude? Then why in hell would Venice waste it stoking furnaces if it could earn more—Oh. Oh! You mean it's—?"

Wanda nodded.

"Jesus!" Stark pursed his lips. "What do we do? Call the police?"

"No. We don't know if it's an MA for a fact. If it turns out to be an MA and the killing android, our paper comes first anyway. This is our big chance, Jed. If it's *that* android we can run a series of controlled tests and—"

"How do we find out for sure?"

"Easy. Infrared film. That'll show what's under the bruise. Borrow a camera. Buy some film. We'll sneak down to the power plant tomorrow afternoon and take some pictures. Then we'll know."

They stole down into the university power plant the following afternoon. It was a vast cellar, deep under the earth. It was dark, shadowy, luminous with burning light from the furnace doors. Above the roar of the fires they could hear a strange voice shouting and chanting in the echoing vault: "All reet! All reet! So jeet your seat. Be fleet be fleet, cool and discreet, honey . . ." And they could see a capering figure dancing a lunatic rumba in time to the music it shouted. The legs twisted. The arms waved. The fingers writhed.

Jed Stark raised the camera and began shooting his spool of infrared film, aiming the camera sights at that bobbing head. Then Wanda shrieked, for I saw them and came charging down on them, brandishing a polished steel shovel. It smashed the camera. It felled the girl and then the boy. Jed fought me for a desperate hissing moment before he was bludgeoned into helplessness. Then the android dragged them to the furnace and fed them to the flames, slowly, hideously. It capered and sang. Then it returned to my hotel.

The thermometer in the power plant registered 100.9° murderously Fahrenheit. All reet! All reet!

We bought steerage on the *Lyra Queen*, and Vandaleur and the android did odd jobs for their meals. During the night watches, Vandaleur would sit alone in the steerage head with a cardboard portfolio on his lap, puzzling over its contents. That portfolio was all he had managed to bring with him from Lyra Alpha. He had stolen it from Wanda's room. It was labeled ANDROID. It contained the secret of my sickness.

And it contained nothing but newspapers. Scores of newspapers from all over the galaxy, printed, microfilmed, engraved, etched, offset, photostatted . . . Rigel *Star-Banner* . . . Paragon *Picayune* . . . Megaster *Times-Leader* . . . Lalande *Herald* . . . Lacaille *Journal* . . . Indi *Intelligencer* . . . Eridani *Telegram-News*. All reet! All reet!

Nothing but newspapers. Each paper contained an account of one crime in the android's ghastly career. Each paper also contained news, domestic and foreign, sports, society, weather, shipping news, stock exchange quotations, human interest stories, features, contests, puzzles. Somewhere in that mass of uncollated facts was the secret Wanda and Jed Stark had discovered. Vandaleur pored over the papers helplessly. It was beyond him. So jeet your seat!

"I'll sell you," I told the android. "Damn you. When we land on Terra, I'll sell you. I'll settle for three percent on whatever you're worth."

"I am worth fifty-seven thousand dollars on the current exchange," I told him.

"If I can't sell you, I'll turn you in to the police," I said.

"I am valuable property," I answered. "It is forbidden to endanger valuable property. You won't have me destroyed."

"Christ damn you!" Vandaleur cried. "What? Are you arrogant? Do you know you can trust me to protect you? Is that the secret?"

The multiple-aptitude android regarded him with calm accomplished eyes. "Sometimes," it said, "it is a good thing to be property."

It was three below zero when the *Lyra Queen* dropped at Croydon Field. A mixture of ice and snow swept across the field, fizzing and exploding into steam under the *Queen*'s tail jets. The passengers trotted numbly across the blackened concrete to customs inspection, and thence to the airport bus that was to take them to London. Vandaleur and the android were broke. They walked.

By midnight they reached Piccadilly Circus. The December ice storm had not slackened, and the statue of Eros was encrusted with ice. They turned right, walked down to Trafalgar Square and then along the Strand shaking with cold and wet. Just above Fleet Street, Vandaleur saw a solitary figure coming from the direction of St. Paul's. He drew the android into an alley.

"We've got to have money," he whispered. He pointed at the approaching figure. "He has money. Take it from him."

"The order cannot be obeyed," the android said.

"Take it from him," Vandaleur repeated. "By force. Do you understand? We're desperate."

"It is contrary to my prime directive," I said. "I cannot endanger life or property. The order cannot be obeyed."

"For God's sake!" Vandaleur burst out. "You've attacked, destroyed, murdered. Don't gibber about prime directives. You haven't any left. Get his money. Kill him if you have to. I tell you, we're desperate!"

"It is contrary to my prime directive," I said. "I cannot endanger life or property. The order cannot be obeyed."

I thrust the android back and leaped out at the stranger. He was tall, austere, competent. He had an air of hope curdled by cynicism. He carried a cane. I saw he was blind.

"Yes?" he said. "I hear you near me. What is it?"

"Sir . . ." Vandaleur hesitated. "I'm desperate."

"We are all desperate," the stranger replied. "Quietly desperate."

"Sir . . . I've got to have some money."

"Are you begging or stealing?" The sightless eyes passed over Vandaleur and the android.

"I'm prepared for either."

"Ah. So are we all. It is the history of our race." The stranger motioned over his shoulder. "I have been begging at St. Paul's, my friend. What I desire cannot be stolen. What is it you desire that you are lucky enough to be able to steal?"

"Money," Vandaleur said.

"Money for what? Come, my friend, let us exchange confidences. I will tell you why I beg, if you will tell me why you steal. My name is Blenheim."

"My name is . . . Vole."

"I was not begging for sight at St. Paul's, Mr. Vole. I was begging for a number."

"A number?"

"Ah yes. Numbers rational, numbers irrational, numbers imaginary. Positive integers. Negative integers. Fractions, positive and negative. Eh? You have never heard of Blenheim's immortal treatise on Twenty Zeros, or The Differences in Absence of Quantity?" Blenheim smiled bitterly. "I am the wizard of the Theory of Number, Mr. Vole, and I have exhausted the charm of number for myself. After fifty years of wizardry, senility approaches and the appetite vanishes. I have been praying in St. Paul's for inspiration. Dear God, I prayed, if You exist, send me a number."

Vandaleur slowly lifted the cardboard portfolio and touched Blenheim's hand with it. "In here," he said, "is a number. A hidden number. A secret number. The number of a crime. Shall we exchange, Mr. Blenheim? Shelter for a number?"

"Neither begging nor stealing, eh?" Blenheim said. "But a bargain. So all life reduces itself to the banal." The sightless eyes again passed over Vandaleur and the android. "Perhaps the All-Mighty is not God but a merchant. Come home with me."

On the top floor of Blenheim's house we shared a room—two beds, two closets, two washstands, one bathroom. Vandaleur bruised my forehead again and sent me out to find work, and while the android worked, I consulted with Blenheim and read him the papers from the portfolio, one by one. All reet! All reet!

Vandaleur told him so much and no more. He was a student, I said, attempting a thesis on the murdering android. In these papers which he had collected were the facts that would explain the crimes of which Blenheim had heard nothing. There must be a correlation, a number, a statistic, something which would account for my derangement, I explained, and Blenheim was piqued by the mystery, the detective story, the human interest of number.

We examined the papers. As I read them aloud, he listed them and their contents in his blind, meticulous writing. And then I read his notes to him. He listed the papers by type, by typeface, by fact, by fancy, by article, spelling, words, theme, advertising, pictures, subject, politics, prejudices. He analyzed. He studied. He meditated. And we lived together in that top floor, always a little cold, always a little terrified, always a little closer . . . brought together by our fear of it, our hatred between us. Like a wedge driven into a living tree and splitting the trunk, only to be forever incorporated into the scar tissue, we grew together. Vandaleur and the android. Be fleet be fleet!

And one afternoon Blenheim called Vandaleur into his study and displayed his notes. "I think I've found it," he said, "but I can't understand it."

Vandaleur's heart leaped.

"Here are the correlations," Blenheim continued. "In fifty papers there are accounts of the criminal android. What is there, outside the depredations, that is also in fifty papers?"

"I don't know, Mr. Blenheim."

"It was a rhetorical question. Here is the answer. The weather."

"What?"

"The weather." Blenheim nodded. "Each crime was committed on a day when the temperature was above ninety degrees Fahrenheit."

"But that's impossible," Vandaleur exclaimed. "It was cool on Lyra Alpha."

"We have no record of any crime committed on Lyra Alpha. There is no paper."

"No. That's right, I—" Vandaleur was confused. Suddenly he exclaimed, "No. You're right. The furnace room. It was hot there. Hot! Of course. My God, yes! That's the answer. Dallas Brady's electric furnace . . . the rice deltas on Paragon. So jeet your seat. Yes. But why? Why? My God, why?"

I came into the house at that moment, and passing the study, saw Vandaleur and Blenheim. I entered, awaiting commands, my multiple aptitudes devoted to service.

"That's the android, eh?" Blenheim said after a long moment.

"Yes," Vandaleur answered, still confused by the discovery. "And that explains why it refused to attack you that night on the Strand. It wasn't hot enough to break the prime directive. Only in the heat . . . The heat, all reet!" He looked at the android. A silent lunatic command passed from man to android. I refused. It is forbidden to endanger life. Vandaleur gestured furiously, then seized Blenheim's shoulders and yanked him back out of his desk chair to the floor. Blenheim shouted once. Vandaleur leaped on him like a tiger, pinning him to the floor and sealing his mouth with one hand.

"Find a weapon," he called to the android.

"It is forbidden to endanger life."

"This is a fight for self-preservation. Bring me a weapon!" He held the squirming mathematician with all his weight. I went at once to a cupboard where I knew a revolver was kept. I checked it. It was loaded with five cartridges. I handed it to Vandaleur. I took it, rammed the barrel against Blenheim's head and pulled the trigger. He shuddered once.

We had three hours before the cook returned from her day off. We looted the house. We took Blenheim's money and jewels. We packed a bag with clothes. We took Blenheim's notes, destroyed the newspapers; and we left, carefully locking the door behind us. In Blenheim's study we left a pile of crumpled papers under a half inch of burning candle. And we soaked the rug around it with kerosene. No, I did all that.

The android refused. I am forbidden to endanger life or property.

All reet!

They took the tubes to Leicester Square, changed trains, and rode to the British Museum. There they got off and went to a small Georgian house just off Russell Square. A shingle in the window read: NAN WEBB, PSYCHOMETRIC CONSULTANT. Vandaleur had made a note of the address some weeks earlier. They went into the house. The android waited in the foyer with the bag. Vandaleur entered Nan Webb's office.

She was a tall woman with gray shingled hair, very fine English complexion, and very bad English legs. Her features were blunt, her expression acute. She nodded to Vandaleur, finished a letter, sealed it and looked up.

"My name," I said, "is Vanderbilt. James Vanderbilt."

"Quite."

"I'm an exchange student at London University."

"Quite."

"I've been researching on the killing android, and I think I've discovered something very interesting. I'd like your advice on it. What is your fee?"

"What is your college at the University?"

"Why?"

"There is a discount for students."

"Merton College."

"That will be two pounds, please."

Vandaleur placed two pounds on the desk and added to the fee Blenheim's notes. "There is a correlation," he said, "between the crimes of the android and the weather. You will note that each crime was committed when the temperature rose above nintey degrees Fahrenheit. Is there a psychometric answer for this?"

Nan Webb nodded, studied the notes for a moment, put down the sheets of paper, and said: "Synesthesia, obviously."

"What?"

"Synesthesia," she repeated. "When a sensation, Mr. Vanderbilt, is interpreted immediately in terms of a sensation from a different sense organ from the one stimulated, it is called synesthesia. For example: A sound stimulus gives rise to a simultaneous sensation of definite color. Or color gives rise to a sensation of taste. Or a light stimulus gives rise to a sensation of sound. There can be confusion or short circuiting of any sensation of taste, smell, pain, pressure, temperature, and so on. D'you understand?"

"I think so."

"Your research has uncovered the fact that the android most probably reacts to temperature stimulus above the ninety-degree level synesthetically. Most probably there is an endocrine response. Probably a temperature linkage with the android adrenal surrogate. High temperature brings about a response of fear, anger, excitement, and violent physical activity . . . all within the province of the adrenal gland."

"Yes. I see. Then if the android were to be kept in cold climates . . ."

"There would be neither stimulus nor response. There would be no crimes. Quite."

"I see. What is projection?"

"How do you mean?"

"Is there any danger of projection with regard to the owner of the android?"

"Very interesting. Projection is a throwing forward. It is the process of throwing out upon another the ideas or impulses that belong to oneself. The paranoid, for example, projects upon others his conflicts and disturbances in order to externalize them. He accuses, directly or by implication, other men of having the very sicknesses with which he is struggling himself."

"And the danger of projection?"

"It is the danger of believing what is implied. If you live with a psychotic who projects his sickness upon you, there is a danger of falling into his psychotic pattern and becoming virtually psychotic yourself. As, no doubt, is happening to you, Mr. Vandaleur."

Vandaleur leaped to his feet.

"You are an ass," Nan Webb went on crisply. She waved the sheets of notes. "This is no exchange student's writing. It's the unique cursive of the famous Blenheim. Every scholar in England knows this blind writing. There is no Merton College at London University. That was a miserable guess. Merton is one of the Oxford colleges. And you, Mr. Vandaleur, are so obviously infected by association with your deranged android . . . by projection, if you will . . . that I hesitate between calling the Metropolitan Police and the Hospital for the Criminally Insane."

I took out the gun and shot her.

Reet!

"Antares II, Alpha Aurigae, Acrux IV, Pollux IX, Rigel Centaurus," Vandaleur said. "They're all cold. Cold as a witch's kiss. Mean temperatures of forty degrees Fahrenheit. Never gets hotter than seventy. We're in business again. Watch that curve."

The multiple-aptitude android swung the wheel with its accomplished hands. The car took the curve sweetly and sped on through the northern marshes, the reeds stretching for miles, brown and dry, under the cold English sky. The sun was sinking swiftly. Overhead, a lone flight of bustards flapped clumsily eastward. High above the flight, a lone helicopter drifted toward home and warmth.

"No more warmth for us," I said. "No more heat. We're safe when we're cold. We'll hole up in Scotland, make a little money, get across to Norway, build a bankroll, and then ship out. We'll settle on Pollux. We're safe. We've licked it. We can live again."

There was a startling *bleep* from overhead, and then a ragged roar: "ATTENTION JAMES VANDALEUR AND ANDROID. ATTENTION JAMES VANDALEUR AND ANDROID!"

Vandaleur started and looked up. The lone helicopter was floating above them. From its belly came amplified commands: "YOU ARE SURROUNDED. THE ROAD IS BLOCKED. YOU ARE TO STOP YOUR CAR AT ONCE AND SUBMIT TO ARREST. STOP AT ONCE!"

I looked at Vandaleur for orders.

"Keep driving," Vandaleur snapped.

The helicopter dropped lower: "ATTENTION ANDROID. YOU ARE IN CONTROL OF THE VEHICLE. YOU ARE TO STOP AT ONCE. THIS IS A STATE DIRECTIVE SUPERSEDING ALL PRIVATE COMMANDS."

"What the hell are you doing?" I shouted.

"A state directive supersedes all private commands," the android answered. "I must point out to you that—"

"Get the hell away from the wheel," Vandaleur ordered. I clubbed the android, yanked him sideways, and squirmed over him to the wheel. The car veered off the road in that moment and went churning through the frozen mud and dry reeds. Vandaleur regained control and continued westward through the marshes toward a parallel highway five miles distant.

"We'll beat their goddamned block," he grunted.

The car pounded and surged. The helicopter dropped even lower. A searchlight blazed from the belly of the plane.

"ATTENTION JAMES VANDALEUR AND ANDROID.

SUBMIT TO ARREST. THIS IS A STATE DIRECTIVE SUPER-SEDING ALL PRIVATE COMMANDS."

"He can't submit," Vandaleur shouted wildly. "There's no one to submit to. He can't and I won't."

"Christ!" I muttered. "We'll beat them yet. We'll beat the block. We'll beat the heat. We'll—"

"I must point out to you," I said, "that I am required by my prime directive to obey state directives which supersede all private commands. I must submit to arrest."

"Who says it's a state directive?" Vandaleur said. "Them? Up in that plane? They've got to show credentials. They've got to prove it's state authority before you submit. How d'you know they're not crooks trying to trick us?"

Holding the wheel with one arm, he reached into his side pocket to make sure the gun was still in place. The car skidded. The tires squealed on frost and reeds. The wheel was wrenched from his grasp and the car yawed up a small hillock and overturned. The motor roared and the wheels screamed. Vandaleur crawled out and dragged the android with him. For the moment we were outside the circle of light boring down from the helicopter. We blundered off into the marsh, into the blackness, into concealment . . . Vandaleur running with a pounding heart, hauling the android along.

The helicopter circled and soared over the wrecked car, searchlight peering, loudspeaker braying. On the highway we had left, lights appeared as the pursuing and blocking parties gathered and followed radio directions from the plane. Vandaleur and the android continued deeper and deeper into the marsh, working their way toward the parallel road and safety. It was night by now. The sky was a black matte. Not a star showed. The temperature was dropping. A southeast night wind knifed us to the bone.

Far behind there was a dull concussion. Vandaleur turned, gasping. The car's fuel had exploded. A geyser of flame shot up like a lurid fountain. It subsided into a low crater of burning reeds. Whipped by the wind, the distant hem of flame fanned up into a wall, ten feet high. The wall began marching down on us, cracking fiercely. Above it, a pall of oil smoke surged forward. Behind it, Vandaleur could make out the figures of men . . . a mass of beaters searching the marsh.

"Christ!" I cried and searched desperately for safety. He ran, dragging me with him, until their feet crunched through the surface ice of a pool. He trampled the ice furiously, then flung himself down in the numbing water, pulling the android with us.

The wall of flame approached. I could hear the crackle and feel the heat. He could see the searchers clearly. Vandaleur reached into his side pocket for the gun. The pocket was torn. The gun was gone. He groaned and shook with cold and terror. The light from the marsh fire was blinding. Overhead, the helicopter floated helplessly to one side, unable to fly through the smoke and flames and aid the searchers who were beating far to the right of us.

"They'll miss us," Vandaleur whispered. "Keep quiet. That's an order. They'll miss us. We'll beat them. We'll beat the fire. We'll—"

Three distinct shots sounded less than a hundred feet from the fugitives. *Blam! Blam! Blam!* They came from the last three cartridges in my gun as the marsh fire reached it where it had dropped, and exploded the shells. The searchers turned toward the sound and began working directly toward us. Vandaleur cursed hysterically and tried to submerge even deeper to escape the intolerable heat of the fire. The android began to twitch.

The wall of flame surged up to them. Vandaleur took a deep breath and prepared to submerge until the flame passed over them. The android shuddered and burst into an earsplitting scream.

"All reet! All reet!" it shouted. "Be fleet be fleet!"

"Damn you!" I shouted. I tried to drown it.

"Damn you!" I cursed him. I smashed his face.

The android battered Vandaleur, who fought it off until it exploded out of the mud and staggered upright. Before I could return to the attack, the live flames captured it hypnotically. It danced and capered in a lunatic rumba before the wall of fire. Its legs twisted. Its arms waved. The fingers writhed in a private rumba of their own. It shrieked and sang and ran in a crooked waltz before the embrace of the heat, a muddy monster silhouetted against the brilliant sparkling flare.

The searchers shouted. There were shots. The android spun around twice and then continued its horrid dance before the face of the flames. There was a rising gust of wind. The fire swept around the capering figure and enveloped it for a roaring moment. Then the fire swept on, leaving behind it a sobbing mass of synthetic flesh oozing scarlet blood that would never coagulate.

The thermometer would have registered 1200° wondrously Fahrenheit.

Vandaleur didn't die. I got away. They missed him while they watched the android caper and die. But I don't know which of us he is these days. Projection, Wanda warned me. Projection, Nan Webb told him. If you live with a crazy man or a crazy machine long enough, I become crazy too. Reet!

But we know one truth. We know they were wrong. The new robot and Vandaleur know that because the new robot's started twitching too. Reet! Here on cold Pollux, the robot is twitching and singing. No heat, but my fingers writhe. No heat, but it's taken the little Talley girl off for a solitary walk.

A cheap labor robot. A servo-mechanism . . . all I could afford . . . but it's twitching and humming and walking alone with the child somewhere and I can't find them. Christ! Vandaleur can't find me before it's too late. Cool and discreet, honey, in the dancing frost while the thermometer registers 10° fondly Fahrenheit.

FONDLY FAHRENHEIT:
WHO AM I, WHICH ARE YOU?

It is the Persian carpet-weavers, I think, who deliberately introduce one almost imperceptible technical flaw into their intricate patterns, on the grounds that to weave a perfect rug would be dangerously blasphemous. Alfred Bester's breathtaking classic "Fondly Fahrenheit" has, to my great relief, one little technical blemish. I suspect it wasn't deliberate, but maybe so. In any case, its presence has spared Alfie from the anger of the gods ever since the story first appeared in the August, 1954, issue of *Fantasy & Science Fiction*, and by the same token has spared me from feeling really miserable over Bester's awesome performance.

That one technical flaw in this otherwise flawless story occurs right at the outset, as if Bester had decided to disarm the Furies quickly. Here is the magnificent opening paragraph, which beautifully announces the entire crux of the story in the first sentence and elegantly elaborates on it in the next two:

> He doesn't know which of us I am these days, but they know one truth. You must own nothing but yourself. You must make your own life, live your own life and die your own death . . . or else you will die another's.

And this is the equally splendid paragraph that follows:

The rice fields on Paragon III stretch for hundreds of miles like checkerboard tundras, a blue and brown mosaic under a burning sky of orange. In the evening, clouds whip like smoke, and the paddies rustle and murmur.

A flaw, you say? Where? There's no flaw visible anywhere!

Ah, but some technical flaws are flaws of omission: leaving out a piece of a bridge's underpinning, for example. I work on the theory —which I picked up somewhere along the way from Ernest Hemingway—that every paragraph of a story ought to be firmly and inextricably welded to the one that precedes it, except where a scene break is used to create a deliberate discontinuity. Particularly in the opening paragraphs of a story, where the reader is being led step by step into an unfamiliar (and, in this case, bewildering) situation, I think it's vital to forge thematic links connecting every paragraph to its predecessor. Bester's opening paragraph neatly tells us that the story is going to be about a fatal confusion of identity. With superb chutzpah the first sentence lets it be known that the chief technical device by which this confusion of identity will be rendered in the story is the daring one of ambivalence of narrative person ("*He* doesn't know which of *us I* am these days, but *they* know one truth"). Third singular, first plural, first singular, third plural, all within the span of fifteen words. The next sentence switches to the conventional second-person-hypothetical mode ("You must own nothing but yourself") to warn that as a general principle it's a perilous idea to let your identity get tangled with somebody else's.

Fine. The story is off and running. But suddenly we leap to the rice fields of Paragon III. That tells us that we're on another world, and a hot, humid one at that, where rice can be grown. We get a beautiful image, "a blue and brown mosaic under a burning sky of orange." The only thing wrong is that nothing links Bester's second paragraph to the first, which gives the sensitive reader an unnecessary little jolt of displacement and tends to turn the cunningly devised opening paragraph into a stand-alone editorial comment on the action that is to follow, a mere précis instead of a lead-in.

That little glitch is the only mistake, as far as I can see, that Bester makes in this story. The rest of it unfolds with such dazzling assurance that it will make a veteran professional writer weep with envy and certainly made me, as a teenage novice, bow down in homage.

Dazzle has always been Bester's stock-in-trade. His technical command was evident as early in his career as 1942, when he was not yet thirty: in the novella "Hell Is Forever" he manifested the wild narrative vigor, the quick and keen deployment of dialog, and the fondness for piling image on image that would later typify his work. After a prolonged sojourn in radio and then television, he returned to the science-fiction magazines in 1951 with the pyrotechnical novel *The Demolished Man*, instantly famous for the ingenuity of its storytelling method and the cleverness of its minor details. In the years immediately following he amused himself (and disheartened me) with a string of wondrously ingenious short stories—"Hobson's Choice," "Time Is the Traitor," "Star Light, Star Bright," "5,271,009," and "Fondly Fahrenheit"—which handled various familiar themes of science fiction with startling breeziness and astonishing verbal confidence. Of these, "Fondly Fahrenheit" was the one that seemed to me to extend the technical possibilities of the science-fiction short story the farthest, and I studied it the most closely.

Bester himself, in a commentary on the story written years later, tells us of its genesis in an account by Mark Twain of a slave guilty of murder whose owner had smuggled him to another state because the slave was too valuable to surrender to justice. "It seemed to me," Bester wrote, "that there might be an interesting story in this conflict between master and slave; the slave aware of his value and the hold it gives him over his owner, the master constrained by greed to condone criminal acts which he abhors."

It was easy enough to translate Twain's anecdote into superficial science-fictional terms by changing "slave" to "android." But that immediately raised the question: Why would a carefully conditioned android go berserk? "I remembered a note I'd made long before on the statistics of crime, relating crime rate to temperature," Bester wrote. " 'Good,' I said. 'The android breaks his conditioning only when the temperature rises above a certain level.' "

Now Bester had an additional s-f gimmick—the heat level—to use in building suspense as master and android traveled from world to world. But a critical element of plot was missing. What was the bond that held the murderous android and his master together? Mere greed wasn't sufficient: sooner or later the android's crimes would make it more of a liability than an asset to its owner. Bester found his clue in a psychiatric text discussing "cases where disturbed people attribute their own strange behavior to others." He had his final twist. "Temperature may break the android's conditioning," he wrote, "but the master is really the criminal. We'll extrapolate the projection theme. The master unconsciously but actually imposes his own insanity on the slave."

To a technician of Bester's level, theme dictates form. A story must have a point of view: a node of perception through which the events are seen. The point of view may be the author's, standing omnisciently above the action and telling us first what this character, then that, is doing and perhaps thinking. (This is a particularly useful method when working on a large scale. The chief thing to avoid is jumping around from one character's mind to another within the same scene, which readers find disconcerting. Frank Herbert ignored that rule entirely in his *Dune* and many other books and made ten or fifteen million dollars from his writing, but I still think it's a bad idea.) Or one of the characters may be the sole viewpoint figure throughout, which is usually the most effective method in a short story. He may tell the story in his own words, or it may be told for him in third person by the author. Writers employing this method need to guard against trying to slip in information that the viewpoint character couldn't possibly know. That's hard to do in a first-person story, but beginners often lapse when using third person, drifting briefly into the author-omniscient mode to tell us about something that happens while the protagonist is asleep, or looking the other way. Getting outside a viewpoint character's awareness like that can be useful when employed sparingly or used for comic purposes, but generally it flattens or disrupts the reader's involvement with the story. A third-person story written tightly from the protagonist's viewpoint ("Tensely Sheriff Barnes walked down the main street, looking warily in all directions") ought not to jump beyond the central character's range of perception ("Unknown to him, Pecos Mike was crouching behind Banker Thomas' desk, coolly aiming his Colt .45"). Doing that punctures the illusion that the protagonist is a camera viewing the events of the story, and costs the writer something in overall impact. Bester, having conceived a story in which two characters have interlocking consciousnesses and overlapping identities, chose a novel and daring viewpoint stance: a first-person story, but a multiple viewpoint; two different "I" characters narrating the tale in an interwoven way, slipping now and then into an inextricable "we."

Which is how the story begins, with that astoundingly ambiguous opening, "He doesn't know which of us I am these days." In first person plural that verges on author-omniscient narrative we see the two protagonists fleeing for their lives, a scene enlivened by Bester's stunning sequence of images: the pursuers form a line "like a writhing snake," but when they light their lamps the snake is "transformed into a necklace of wavering diamonds," and when the line comes to a halt "the diamonds froze in the heat"—a startling paradox, but legitimate. Later in the story, when the plot is established and can carry the narrative, Bester becomes less concerned with creating such intricate patterns of image: by the middle of the story they would simply get in the way, since by then the reader is more involved with what's going on than with the way things look.

Now Bester introduces the first of his paradoxes: the pursuers find the body of a murder victim with android blood under her fingernails. But androids are conditioned against murder. Is the killer a defective android? We don't know yet. "And the thermometer that day registered 92.9° gloriously Fahrenheit," Bester tells us, finishing the opening scene with what will be a refrain in the story.

The second scene opens in first person plural, shifts quickly to third, then to first plural again. When "I" finally appears in the narrative it is the "I" of Vandaleur, the owner of the android, but only for a moment; the android and Vandaleur have an angry argument related in third person (" 'You damned crazy machine,' Vandaleur shouted. 'I am not a machine,' the android answered") and when "I" reappears it is clearly the android speaking. A moment later Vandaleur and the android are back in third person, shouting at each other; then Vandaleur as "I" asks a question and the android, also as "I," replies to it. This is violating writing-school teachings on viewpoint with a vengeance. The unsophisticated reader, expecting some sort of consistent point of view, is flung about mercilessly, unable to find anything firm to grasp. The professional writer, even though he may already be aware that Bester is implying some linkage of identities between his two characters, will also have a distinct feeling of seasickness.

The basic situation is now established, both by what has been told and by the way it has been told: the murderous android, the feckless master, locked in some unfathomable relationship. Now Bester unfolds the development. The story, as science fiction, offers nothing very startling. The stars have been colonized; humans move freely about from world to world; androids and robots, artificial human beings, do most of the labor. All old stuff. The androids are conditioned against violence toward humans: nothing new there either. Gradually it appears that extreme heat can undo that conditioning: an interesting plot angle, but once again not a remarkable or intellectually stimulating idea. The quick views of the extraterrestrial planets that Bester gives us reveal no noteworthy qualities of imagination. Everything is vivid and glossy and has that indefinable science-fictional feel to it, but Bester has not chosen to load his story with fresh inventions, though he leaves us with no doubt that he could do it if he cared to. It isn't necessary here. Although the speculative content of the story is slight, that doesn't matter at all. What does matter is the suspense, which operates on two levels: What the *hell* is going on here? and Why has the writer chosen to tell the story in this crazy way? And it will turn out that the two questions have the same answer.

The murders continue. The second one is again associated with heat—"98.1° beautifully Fahrenheit"—and now a second motif is introduced, an old popular song with the lines *Oh, it's no feat to beat the heat. All reet! All reet! So jeet your seat* and so forth. There can be no doubt that the android is the murderer; we watch the crime in third-person narration, and just before it happens we see the android's fingers writhing uncontrollably, which is to be the third of the story's three thematic motifs. Then it is back to the game of shifting from third person to first, and from one first-person narrator to the other, often within a single paragraph. We begin to see a certain instability in Vandaleur, even a self-destructiveness: on each new planet where he takes refuge he chooses a name with initials identical to his own, and he talks compulsively about the android murders wherever he goes.

At the midpoint of the story Bester tips his hand, but only to the close student of literary technique. This is in the scene of the killing of Jeff and Wanda ("100.9° murderously Fahrenheit. All reet! All reet!"). The android, fingers writhing, is present at the scene; Vandaleur is not; yet the passage describing the murder is told successively in first-person android ("I saw them and came charging down on them"), third-person omniscient ("Then the android dragged them to the furnace"), and first-person Vandaleur ("Then it returned to my hotel"). Yes, the android is the actual murderer; but Vandaleur's consciousness is present somehow in the android's mind, so that Vandaleur himself is often not certain which of the two he is; and so the story's viewpoint wavers constantly from one to the other. This becomes more obvious a few pages later with a memorably involuted figure of speech: "Like a wedge driven into a living tree and splitting the trunk, only to be forever incorporated into the scar tissue, we grew together. Vandaleur and the android. Be fleet be fleet!" Then Vandaleur, finally drawing the connection between heat and the breakdown of the android's conditioning, unexpectedly interjects a bit of the android's silly jingle ("So jeet your seat") into an otherwise rational speech. A moment later he orders the android to commit a murder. But now they are in chilly England; the conditioning holds; Vandaleur has to carry out the crime himself. ("All reet!") It is the master who is insane. We are reading a study in psychopathology in which the clues lie in the narrative point of view.

At the climax of the story the initial image of a line of pursuers reappears. Vandaleur and the android are again fleeing from police. Their car explodes; the android is caught in the flame. "All reet! All reet!" it cries. "Be fleet be fleet!" Its fingers writhe as it dies. "The temperature would have registered 1200° wondrously Fahrenheit." All three recurrent motifs come together at the end.

And now Bester can be explicit at last. In two final paragraphs Vandaleur lets us know, still obsessively switching narrative person, "Vandaleur didn't die. I got away. They missed him while they watched the android caper and die. But I don't know which of us he is these days." Was the android insane, and did he become insane from living with it? Vandaleur may want us to believe that; but there is no way of knowing. What is certain is that his madness can be projected onto artificial humans. For at the very end Vandaleur, living now on a cold planet, has bought a cheap robot, a simple mechanical laborer; and the robot has gone off for a sinister stroll with a little girl. "It's twitching and humming and walking alone with the child somewhere and I can't find them. Christ! Vandaleur can't find me before it's too late. Cool and discreet, honey, in the dancing frost while the thermometer registers 10° fondly Fahrenheit."

A bravura finish. The story is circular; it will all happen over again, with a robot and low temperatures instead of an android and high temperatures. Vandaleur has been the only narrator throughout, and he stands condemned by his own words. (The unknowingly self-condemning narrator is a familiar fictional device; I doubt that it has ever been handled better than here.) "Fondly Fahrenheit" is not only a strikingly vivid depiction of insanity from the madman's point of view, but it provides a humbling lesson in the art of narrative construction.

NO WOMAN BORN
C. L. MOORE

She had been the loveliest creature whose image ever moved along the airways. John Harris, who was once her manager, remembered doggedly how beautiful she had been as he rose in the silent elevator toward the room where Deirdre sat waiting for him.

Since the theater fire that had destroyed her a year ago, he had never been quite able to let himself remember her beauty clearly, except when some old poster, half in tatters, flaunted her face at him, or a maudlin memorial program flashed her image unexpectedly across the television screen. But now he had to remember.

The elevator came to a sighing stop and the door slid open. John Harris hesitated. He knew in his mind that he had to go on, but his reluctant muscles almost refused him. He was thinking helplessly, as he had not allowed himself to think until this moment, of the fabulous grace that had poured through her wonderful dancer's body, remembering her soft and husky voice with the little burr in it that had fascinated the audiences of the whole world.

There had never been anyone so beautiful.

In times before her, other actresses had been lovely and adulated, but never before Deirdre's day had the entire world been able to take one woman so wholly to its heart. So few outside the capitals had ever seen Bernhardt or the fabulous Jersey Lily. And the beauties of the movie screen had had to limit their audiences to those who could reach the theaters. But Deirdre's image had once moved glowingly across the television screens of every home in the civilized world. And in many outside the bounds of civilization. Her soft, husky songs had sounded in the depths of jungles, her lovely, languorous body had woven its patterns of rhythm in desert tents and polar huts. The whole world knew every smooth motion of her body and every cadence of her voice, and the way a subtle radiance had seemed to go on behind her features when she smiled.

And the whole world had mourned her when she died in the theater fire.

Harris could not quite think of her as other than dead, though he knew what sat awaiting him in the room ahead. He kept remembering the old words James Stephens wrote long ago for another Deirdre, also lovely and beloved and unforgotten after two thousand years.

> *The time comes when our hearts sink utterly,*
> *When we remember Deirdre and her tale,*
> *And that her lips are dust. . . .*
> *There has been again no woman born*
> *Who was so beautiful; not one so beautiful*
> *Of all the women born—*

That wasn't quite true, of course—there had been one. Or maybe, after all, this Deirdre who died only a year ago had not been beautiful in the sense of perfection. He thought the other one might not have been either, for there are always women with perfection of feature in the world, and they are not the ones that legend remembers. It was the light within, shining through her charming, imperfect features, that had made this Deirdre's face so lovely. No one else he had ever seen had anything like the magic of the lost Deirdre.

> *Let all men go apart and mourn together—*
> *No man can ever love her. Not a man*
> *Can dream to be her lover. . . . No man say—*
> *What could one say to her? There are no words*
> *That one could say to her.*

No, no words at all. And it was going to be impossible to go through with this. Harris knew it overwhelmingly just as his finger touched the buzzer. But the door opened almost instantly, and then it was too late.

Maltzer stood just inside, peering out through his heavy spectacles. You could see how tensely he had been waiting. Harris was a little shocked to see that the man was trembling. It was hard to think of the confident and imperturbable Maltzer, whom he had known briefly a year ago, as shaken like this. He wondered if Deirdre herself were as tremulous with sheer nerves—but it was not time yet to let himself think of that.

"Come in, come in," Maltzer said irritably. There was no reason for irritation. The year's work, so much of it in secrecy and solitude, must have tried him physically and mentally to the very breaking point.

"She all right?" Harris asked inanely, stepping inside.

"Oh yes . . . yes, *she's* all right." Maltzer bit his thumbnail and glanced over his shoulder at an inner door, where Harris guessed she would be waiting.

"No," Maltzer said, as he took an involuntary step toward

it. "We'd better have a talk first. Come over and sit down. Drink?"

Harris nodded, and watched Maltzer's hands tremble as he tilted the decanter. The man was clearly on the very verge of collapse, and Harris felt a sudden cold uncertainty open up in him in the one place where until now he had been oddly confident.

"She *is* all right?" he demanded, taking the glass.

"Oh yes, she's perfect. She's so confident it scares me." Maltzer gulped his drink and poured another before he sat down.

"What's wrong, then?"

"Nothing, I guess. Or . . . well, I don't know. I'm not sure any more. I've worked toward this meeting for nearly a year, but now—well, I'm not sure it's time yet. I'm just not sure."

He stared at Harris, his eyes large and indistinguishable behind the lenses. He was a thin, wire-taut man with all the bone and sinew showing plainly beneath the dark skin of his face. Thinner, now, than he had been a year ago when Harris saw him last.

"I've been too close to her," he said now. "I have no perspective any more. All I can see is my own work. And I'm just not sure that's ready yet for you or anyone to see."

"She thinks so?"

"I never saw a woman so confident." Maltzer drank, the glass clicking on his teeth. He looked up suddenly through the distorting lenses. "Of course a failure now would mean—well, absolute collapse," he said.

Harris nodded. He was thinking of the year of incredibly painstaking work that lay behind this meeting, the immense fund of knowledge, of infinite patience, the secret collaboration of artists, sculptors, designers, scientists, and the genius of Maltzer governing them all as an orchestra conductor governs his players.

He was thinking too, with a certain unreasoning jealousy, of the strange, cold, passionless intimacy between Maltzer and Deirdre in that year, a closer intimacy than any two humans can ever have shared before. In a sense the Deirdre whom he saw in a few minutes would *be* Maltzer, just as he thought he detected in Maltzer now and then small mannerisms of inflection and motion that had been Deirdre's own. There had been between them a sort of unimaginable marriage stranger than anything that could ever have taken place before.

"—so many complications," Maltzer was saying in his worried voice with its faintest possible echo of Deirdre's lovely, cadenced rhythm. (The sweet, soft huskiness he would never hear again.) "There was shock, of course. Terrible shock. And a great fear of fire. We had to conquer that before we could take the first steps. But we did it. When you go in you'll probably find her sitting before the fire." He caught the startled question in Harris' eyes and smiled. "No, she can't feel the warmth now, of course. But she likes to watch the flames. She's mastered any abnormal fear of them quite beautifully."

"She can—" Harris hesitated. "Her eyesight's normal now?"

"Perfect," Maltzer said. "Perfect vision was fairly simple to provide. After all, that sort of thing has already been worked out, in other connections. I might even say her vision's a little better than perfect, from our own standpoint." He shook his head irritably. "I'm not worried about the mechanics of the thing. Luckily they got to her before the brain was touched at all. Shock was the only danger to her sensory centers, and we took care of all that first of all, as soon as communication could be established. Even so, it needed great courage on her part. Great courage." He was silent for a moment, staring into his empty glass.

"Harris," he said suddenly, without looking up, "have I made a mistake? Should we have let her die?"

Harris shook his head helplessly. It was an unanswerable question. It had tormented the whole world for a year now. There had been hundreds of answers and thousands of words written on the subject. Has anyone the right to preserve a brain alive when its body is destroyed? Even if a new body can be provided, necessarily so very unlike the old?

"It's not that she's—ugly—now," Maltzer went on hurriedly, as if afraid of an answer. "Metal isn't ugly. And Deirdre . . . well, you'll see. I tell you, I can't see myself. I know the whole mechanism so well—it's just mechanics to me. Maybe she's—grotesque. I don't know. Often I've wished I hadn't been on the spot, with all my ideas, just when the fire broke out. Or that it could have been anyone but Deirdre. She was so beautiful—Still, if it had been someone else I think the whole thing might have failed completely. It takes more than just an uninjured brain. It takes strength and courage beyond common, and—well, something more. Something—unquenchable. Deirdre has it. She's still Deirdre. In a way she's still beautiful. But I'm not sure anybody but myself could see that. And you know what she plans?"

"No—what?"

"She's going back on the air-screen."

Harris looked at him in stunned disbelief.

"She *is* still beautiful," Maltzer told him fiercely. "She's got courage, and a serenity that amazes me. And she isn't in the least worried or resentful about what's happened. Or afraid what the verdict of the public will be. But I am, Harris. I'm terrified."

They looked at each other for a moment more, neither speaking. Then Maltzer shrugged and stood up.

"She's in there," he said, gesturing with his glass.

Harris turned without a word, not giving himself time to hesitate. He crossed toward the inner door.

The room was full of a soft, clear, indirect light that climaxed in the fire cracking on a white tiled hearth. Harris paused inside the door, his heart beating thickly. He did not see her for a moment. It was a perfectly commonplace room, bright, light, with pleasant furniture, and flowers on the tables. Their perfume was sweet on the clear air. He did not see Deirdre.

Then a chair by the fire creaked as she shifted her weight in it. The high back hid her, but she spoke. And for one dreadful moment it was the voice of an automaton that sounded in the room, metallic, without inflection.

"Hel-lo—" said the voice. Then she laughed and tried again. And it was the old, familiar, sweet huskiness he had not hoped to hear again as long as he lived.

In spite of himself he said, "Deirdre!" and her image rose before him as if she herself had risen unchanged from the chair, tall, golden, swaying a little with her wonderful dancer's poise, the lovely, imperfect features lighted by the glow that made them beautiful. It was the cruelest thing his memory could have done to him. And yet the voice—after that one lapse, the voice was perfect.

"Come and look at me, John," she said.

He crossed the floor slowly, forcing himself to move. That instant's flash of vivid recollection had nearly wrecked his hard-won poise. He tried to keep his mind perfectly blank as he came at last to the verge of seeing what no one but Maltzer had so far seen or known about in its entirety. No one at all had known what shape would be forged to clothe the most beautiful woman on Earth, now that her beauty was gone.

He had envisioned many shapes. Great, lurching robot forms, cylindrical, with hinged arms and legs. A glass case with the brain floating in it and appendages to serve its needs. Grotesque visions, like nightmares come nearly true. And each more inadequate than the last, for what metal shape could possibly do more than house ungraciously the mind and brain that had once enchanted a whole world?

Then he came around the wing of the chair, and saw her.

The human brain is often too complicated a mechanism to function perfectly. Harris' brain was called upon now to perform a very elaborate series of shifting impressions. First, incongruously, he remembered a curious inhuman figure he had once glimpsed leaning over the fence rail outside a farm-house. For an instant the shape had stood up integrated, un-gainly, impossibly human, before the glancing eye resolved it into an arrangement of brooms and buckets. What the eye had found only roughly humanoid, the suggestible brain had accepted fully formed. It was thus now, with Deirdre.

The first impression that his eyes and mind took from sight of her was shocked and incredulous, for his brain said to him unbelievingly, *"This is Deirdre! She hasn't changed at all!"*

Then the shift of perspective took over, and even more shockingly, eye and brain said, "No, not Deirdre—not human. Nothing but metal coils. Not Deirdre at all—" And that was the worst. It was like walking from a dream of someone be-loved and lost, and facing anew, after that heartbreaking re-assurance of sleep, the inflexible fact that nothing can bring the lost to life again. Deirdre was gone, and this was only machinery heaped in a flowered chair.

Then the machinery moved, exquisitely, smoothly, with a grace as familiar as the swaying poise he remembered. The sweet, husky voice of Deirdre said,

"It's me, John darling. It really is, you know."

And it was.

That was the third metamorphosis, and the final one. Illusion steadied and became factual, real. It was Deirdre.

He sat down bonelessly. He had no muscles. He looked at her speechless and unthinking, letting his senses take in the sight of her without trying to rationalize what he saw.

She was golden still. They had kept that much of her, the first impression of warmth and color which had once belonged to her sleek hair and the apricot tints of her skin. But they had had the good sense to go no farther. They had not tried to make a wax image of the lost Deirdre. (*No woman born who was so beautiful—Not one so beautiful, of all the women born—*)

And so she had no face. She had only a smooth, delicately modeled ovoid for her head, with a . . . a sort of crescent-shaped mask across the frontal area where her eyes would have been if she had needed eyes. A narrow, curved quarter-moon, with the horns turned upward. It was filled in with something translucent, like cloudy crystal, and tinted the aquamarine of the eyes Deirdre used to have. Through that, then, she saw the world. Through that she looked without eyes, and behind it, as behind the eyes of a human—she was.

Except for that, she had no features. And it had been wise of those who designed her, he realized now. Subconsciously he had been dreading some clumsy attempt at human features that might creak like a marionette's in parodies of animation. The eyes, perhaps, had had to open in the same place upon her head, and at the same distance apart, to make easy for her an adjustment to the stereoscopic vision she used to have. But he was glad they had not given her two eye-shaped openings with glass marbles inside them. The mask was better.

(Oddly enough, he did not once think of the naked brain that must lie inside the metal. The mask was symbol enough for the woman within. It was enigmatic; you did not know if her gaze was on you searchingly, or wholly withdrawn. And it had no variations of brilliance such as once had played across the incomparable mobility of Deirdre's face. But eyes, even human eyes, are as a matter of fact enigmatic enough. They have no expression except what the lids impart; they take all animation from the features. We automatically watch the eyes of the friend we speak with, but if he happens to be lying down so that he speaks across his shoulder and his face is upside down to us, quite as automatically we watch the mouth. The gaze keeps shifting nervously between mouth and eyes in their reversed order, for it is the position in the face, not the feature itself, which we are accustomed to accept as the seat of the soul. Deirdre's mask was in that proper place; it was easy to accept it as a mask over eyes.)

She had, Harris realized as the first shock quieted, a very beautifully shaped head—a bare, golden skull. She turned it a little, gracefully upon her neck of metal, and he saw that the artist who shaped it had given her the most delicate suggestion of cheekbones, narrowing in the blankness below the mask to the hint of a human face. Not too much. Just enough so that when the head turned you saw by its modeling that it had moved, lending perspective and foreshortening to the expressionless golden helmet. Light did not slip uninterrupted as if over the surface of a golden egg. Brancusi himself had never made anything more simple or more subtle than the modeling of Deirdre's head.

But all expression, of course, was gone. All expression had gone up in the smoke of the theater fire, with the lovely, mobile, radiant features which had meant Deirdre.

As for her body, he could not see its shape. A garment hid her. But they had made no incongruous attempt to give her back the clothing that once had made her famous. Even the softness of cloth would have called the mind too sharply to the remembrance that no human body lay beneath the folds, nor does metal need the incongruity of cloth for its protection. Yet without garments, he realized, she would have looked oddly naked, since her new body was humanoid, not angular machinery.

The designer had solved his paradox by giving her a robe of very fine metal mesh. It hung from the gentle slope of her shoulders in straight, pliant folds like a longer Grecian chlamys, flexible, yet with weight enough of its own not to cling too revealingly to whatever metal shape lay beneath.

The arms they had given her were left bare, and the feet and ankles. And Maltzer had performed his greatest miracle in the limbs of the new Deirdre. It was a mechanical miracle basically, but the eye appreciated first that he had also showed supreme artistry and understanding.

Her arms were pale shining gold, tapered smoothly, without modeling, and flexible their whole length in diminishing metal bracelets fitting one inside the other clear down to the slim, round wrists. The hands were more nearly human than any other feature about her, though they, too, were fitted together in delicate, small sections that slid upon one another with the flexibility almost of flesh. The fingers' bases were solider than human, and the fingers themselves tapered to longer tips.

Her feet, too, beneath the tapering broader rings of the metal ankles, had been constructed upon the model of human feet. Their finely tooled sliding segments gave her an arch and a heel and a flexible forward section formed almost like the *sollerets* of medieval armor.

She looked, indeed, very much like a creature in armor, with her delicately plated limbs and her featureless head like a helmet with a visor of glass, and her robe of chain-mail. But no knight in armor ever moved as Deirdre moved, or wore his armor upon a body of such inhumanly fine proportions. Only a knight from another world, or a knight of Oberon's court, might have shared that delicate likeness.

Briefly he had been surprised at the smallness and exquisite proportions of her. He had been expecting the ponderous mass of such robots as he had seen, wholly automatons. And then he realized that for them, much of the space had to be devoted to the inadequate mechanical brains that guided them about their duties. Deirdre's brain still preserved and proved the craftsmanship of an artisan far defter than man. Only the body was of metal, and it did not seem complex, though he had not yet been told how it was motivated.

Harris had no idea how long he sat staring at the figure in the cushioned chair. She was still lovely—indeed, she was still Deirdre—and as he looked he let the careful schooling of his face relax. There was no need to hide his thoughts from her.

She stirred upon the cushions, the long, flexible arms moving with a litheness that was not quite human. The motion disturbed him as the body itself had not, and in spite of himself his face froze a little. He had the feeling that from behind the crescent mask she was watching him very closely.

Slowly she rose.

The motion was very smooth. Also it was serpentine, as if the body beneath the coat of mail were made in the same interlocking sections as her limbs. He had expected and feared mechanical rigidity; nothing had prepared him for this more than human suppleness.

She stood quietly, letting the heavy mailed folds of her garment settle about her. They fell together with a faint ringing sound, like small bells far off, and hung beautifully in pale golden, sculptured folds. He had risen automatically as she did. Now he faced her, staring. He had never seen her stand perfectly still, and she was not doing it now. She swayed just a bit, vitality burning inextinguishably in her brain as once it had burned in her body, and stolid immobility was as impossible to her as it had always been. The golden garment caught points of light from the fire and glimmered at him with tiny reflections as she moved.

Then she put her featureless helmeted head a little to one side, and he heard her laughter as familiar in its small, throaty, intimate sound as he had ever heard it from her living throat. And every gesture, every attitude, every flowing of motion into motion was so utterly Deirdre that the overwhelming illusion swept his mind again and this was the flesh-and-blood woman as clearly as if he saw her standing there whole once more, like Phoenix from the fire.

"Well, John," she said in the soft, husky, amused voice he remembered perfectly. "Well, John, is it I?" She knew it was. Perfect assurance sounded in the voice. "The shock will wear off, you know. It'll be easier and easier as time goes on. I'm quite used to myself now. See?"

She turned away from him and crossed the room smoothly, with the old, poised, dancer's glide, to the mirror that paneled one side of the room. And before it, as he had so often seen her preen before, he watched her preening now, running flexible metallic hands down the folds of her metal garment, turning to admire herself over one metal shoulder, making the mailed folds tinkle and sway as she struck an arabesque position before the glass.

His knees let him down into the chair she had vacated. Mingled shock and relief loosened all his muscles in him, and she was more poised and confident than he.

"It's a miracle," he said with conviction. "It's *you*. But I don't see how—" He had meant, "—how, without face or body—" but clearly he could not finish that sentence.

She finished it for him in her own mind, and answered

without self-consciousness. "It's motion, mostly," she said, still admiring her own suppleness in the mirror. "See?" And very lightly on her springy, armored feet she flashed through an enchaînement of brilliant steps, swinging round with a pirouette to face him. "That was what Maltzer and I worked out between us, after I began to get myself under control again." Her voice was somber for a moment, remembering a dark time in the past. Then she went on, "It wasn't easy, of course, but it was fascinating. You'll never guess how fascinating, John! We knew we couldn't work out anything like a facsimile of the way I used to look, so we had to find some other basis to build on. And motion is the other basis of recognition, after actual physical likeness."

She moved lightly across the carpet toward the window and stood looking down, her featureless face averted a little and the light shining across the delicately hinted curves of the cheekbones.

"Luckily," she said, her voice amused, "I never was beautiful. It was all—well, vivacity, I suppose, and muscular coordination. Years and years of training, and all of it engraved here"—she struck her golden helmet a light, ringing blow with golden knuckles—"in the habit patterns grooved into my brain. So this body ... did he tell you? ... works entirely through the brain. Electromagnetic currents flowing along from ring to ring, like this." She rippled a boneless arm at him with a motion like flowing water. "Nothing holds me together—nothing!—except muscles of magnetic currents. And if I'd been somebody else—somebody who moved differently, why the flexible rings would have moved differently too, guided by the impulse from another brain. I'm not conscious of doing anything I haven't always done. The same impulses that used to go out to my muscles go out now to—this." And she made a shuddering, serpentine motion of both arms at him, like a Cambodian dancer, and then laughed wholeheartedly, the sound of it ringing through the room with such full-throated merriment that he could not help seeing again the familiar face crinkled with pleasure, the white teeth shining. "It's all perfectly subconscious now," she told him. "It took lots of practice at first, of course, but now even my signature looks just as it always did—the co-ordination is duplicated that delicately." She rippled her arms at him again and chuckled.

"But the voice, too," Harris protested inadequately. "It's *your* voice, Deirdre."

"The voice isn't only a matter of throat construction and breath control, my darling Johnnie! At least, so Professor Maltzer assured me a year ago, and I certainly haven't any reason to doubt him!" She laughed again. She was laughing a little too much, with a touch of the bright, hysteric overexcitement he remembered so well. But if any woman ever had reason for mild hysteria, surely Deirdre had it now.

The laughter rippled and ended, and she went on, her voice eager. "He says voice control is almost wholly a matter of hearing what you produce, once you've got adequate mechanism, of course. That's why deaf people, with the same vocal cords as ever, let their voices change completely and lose all inflection when they've been deaf long enough. And luckily, you see, I'm not deaf!"

She swung around to him, the folds of her robe twinkling and ringing, and rippled up and up a clear, true scale to a lovely high note, and then cascaded down again like water over a falls. But she left him no time for applause. "Perfectly simple, you see. All it took was a little matter of genius from the professor to get it worked out for me! He started with a new variation of the old Voder you must remember hearing about, years ago. Originally, of course, the thing was ponderous. You know how it worked—speech broken down to a few basic sounds and built up again in combinations produced from a keyboard. I think originally the sounds were a sort of *ktch* and a *shooshing* noise, but we've got it all worked to a flexibility and range quite as good as human now. All I do is—well, mentally play on the keyboard of my ... my sound-unit, I suppose it's called. It's much more complicated than that, of course, but I've learned to do it unconsciously. And I regulate it by ear, quite automatically now. If you were—*here*—instead of me, and you'd had the same practice, your own voice would be coming out of the same keyboard and diaphragm instead of mine. It's all a matter of the brain patterns that operated the body and now operate the machinery. They send out very strong impulses that are stepped up as much as necessary somewhere or other in here—" Her hands waved vaguely over the mesh-robed body.

She was silent a moment, looking out the window. Then she turned away and crossed the floor to the fire, sinking again into the flowered chair. Her helmet-skull turned its mask to face him and he could feel a quiet scrutiny behind the aquamarine of its gaze.

"It's—odd," she said, "being here in this ... this ... instead of a body. But not as odd or as alien as you might think. I've thought about it a lot—I've had plenty of time to think—and I've begun to realize what a tremendous force the human ego really is. I'm not sure I want to suggest it has any mystical power it can impress on mechanical things, but it does seem to have a power of some sort. It does instill its own force into inanimate objects, and they take on a personality of their own. People do impress their personalities on the houses they live in, you know. I've noticed that often. Even empty rooms. And it happens with other things too, especially, I think, with inanimate things that men depend on for their lives. Ships, for instance—they always have personalities of their own.

"And planes—in wars you always hear of planes crippled

too badly to fly, but struggling back anyhow with their crews. Even guns acquire a sort of ego. Ships and guns and planes are 'she' to the men who operate them and depend on them for their lives. It's as if machinery with complicated moving parts almost simulates life, and does acquire from the men who used it—well, not exactly life, of course—but a personality. I don't know what. Maybe it absorbs some of the actual electrical impulses their brains throw off, especially in times of stress.

"Well, after a while I began to accept the idea that this new body of mine could behave at least as responsively as a ship or a plane. Quite apart from the fact that my own brain controls its 'muscles.' I believe there's an affinity between men and the machines they make. They make them out of their own brains, really, a sort of mental conception and gestation, and the result responds to the minds that created them, and to all human minds that understand and manipulate them."

She stirred uneasily and smoothed a flexible hand along her mesh-robed metal thigh. "So this is myself," she said. "Metal—but me. And it grows more and more myself the longer I live in it. It's my house and the machine my life depends on, but much more intimately in each case than any real house or machine ever was before to any other human. And you know, I wonder, I wonder if in time I'll forget what flesh felt like—my own flesh, when I touched it like this—and the metal against the metal will be so much the same I'll never even notice?"

Harris did not try to answer her. He sat without moving, watching her expressionless face. In a moment she went on.

"I'll tell you the best thing, John," she said, her voice softening to the old intimacy he remembered so well that he could see superimposed upon the blank skull the warm, intent look that belonged with the voice. "I'm not going to live forever. It may not sound like a—best thing—but it is, John. You know, for a while that was the worst of all, after I knew I was—after I woke up again. The thought of living on and on in a body that wasn't mine, seeing everyone I knew grow old and die, and not being able to stop—

"But Maltzer says my brain will probably wear out quite normally—except, of course, that I won't have to worry about looking old!—and when it gets tired and stops, the body I'm in won't be any longer. The magnetic muscles that hold it into my own shape and motions will let go when the brain lets go, and there'll be nothing but a . . . a pile of disconnected rings. If they ever assemble it again, it won't be me." She hesitated. "I like that, John," she said, and he felt from behind the mask a searching of his face.

He knew and understood that somber satisfaction. He could not put it into words; neither of them wanted to do that. But he understood. It was the conviction of mortality, in spite of her immortal body. She was not cut off from the rest of her race in the essence of their humanity, for though she wore a body of steel and they perishable flesh, yet she must perish too, and the same fears and faiths still united her to mortals and humans, though she wore the body of Oberon's inhuman knight. Even in her death she must be unique—dissolution in a shower of tinkling and clashing rings, he thought, and almost envied her the finality and beauty of that particular death—but afterward, oneness with humanity in however much or little awaited them all. So she could feel that this exile in metal was only temporary, in spite of everything.

(And providing, of course, that the mind inside the metal did not veer from its inherited humanity as the years went by. A dweller in a house may impress his personality upon the walls, but subtly the walls, too, may impress their own shape upon the ego of the man. Neither of them thought of that, at the time.)

Deirdre sat a moment longer in silence. Then the mood vanished and she rose again, spinning so that the robe belled out ringing about her ankles. She rippled another scale up and down, faultlessly and with the same familiar sweetness of tone that had made her famous.

"So I'm going right back on the stage, John," she said serenely. "I can still sing. I can still dance. I'm still myself in everything that matters, and I can't imagine doing anything else for the rest of my life."

He could not answer without stammering a little. "Do you think . . . will they accept you, Deirdre? After all—"

"They'll accept me," she said in that confident voice. "Oh, they'll come to see a freak at first, of course, but they'll stay to watch—Deirdre. And come back again and again just as they always did. You'll see, my dear."

But hearing her sureness, suddenly Harris himself was unsure. Maltzer had not been, either. She was so regally confident, and disappointment would be so deadly a blow at all that remained of her—

She was so delicate a being now, really. Nothing but a glowing and radiant mind poised in metal, dominating it, bending the steel to the illusion of her lost loveliness with a sheer self-confidence that gleamed through the metal body. But the brain sat delicately on its poise of reason. She had been through intolerable stresses already, perhaps more terrible depths of despair and self-knowledge than any human brain had yet endured before her, for—since Lazarus himself— who had come back from the dead?

But if the world did not accept her as beautiful, what then? If they laughed, or pitied her, or came only to watch a jointed freak performing as if on strings where the loveliness of Deirdre had once enchanted them, what then? And he could not be perfectly sure they would not. He had known her too well in the flesh to see her objectively even now, in metal. Every inflection of her voice called up the vivid memory of the face that had flashed its evanescent beauty in some look to match the tone. She was Deirdre to Harris simply because she had been so intimately familiar in every poise and attitude, through so many years. But people who knew her only slightly, or saw her for the first time in metal—what would they see?

A marionette? Or the real grace and loveliness shining through?

He had no possible way of knowing. He saw her too clearly as she had been to see her now at all, except so linked with the past that she was not wholly metal. And he knew what Maltzer feared, for Maltzer's psychic blindness toward her lay at the other extreme. He had never known Deirdre except as a machine, and he could not see her objectively any more than Harris could. To Maltzer she was pure metal, a robot his own hands and brain had devised, mysteriously animated by the mind of Deirdre, to be sure, but to all outward seeming a thing of metal solely. He had worked so long over each intricate part of her body, he knew so well how every jointure in it was put together, that he could not see the whole. He had studied many film records of her, of course, as she used to be, in order to gauge the accuracy of his facsimile, but this thing he had made was a copy only. He was too close to Deirdre to see her. And Harris, in a way, was too far. The indomitable Deirdre herself shone so vividly through the metal that his mind kept superimposing one upon the other.

How would an audience react to her? Where in the scale between these two extremes would their verdict fall?

For Deirdre, there was only one possible answer.

"I'm not worried," Deirdre said serenely, and spread her

golden hands to the fire to watch lights dancing in reflection upon their shining surfaces. "I'm still myself. I've always had ... well, power over my audiences. Any good performer knows when he's got it. Mine isn't gone. I can still give them what I always gave, only now with greater variations and more depths than I'd ever have done before. Why, look—" She gave a little wriggle of excitement.

"You know the arabesque principle—getting the longest possible distance from fingertip to toetip with a long, slow curve through the whole length? And the brace of the other leg and arm giving contrast? Well, look at me. I don't work on hinges now. I can make every motion a long curve if I want to. My body's different enough now to work out a whole new school of dancing. Of course there'll be things I used to do that I won't attempt now—no more dancing *sur les pointes*, for instance—but the new things will more than balance the loss. I've been practicing. Do you know I can turn a hundred *fouettés* now without a flaw? And I think I could go right on and turn a thousand, if I wanted."

She made the firelight flash on her hands, and her robe rang musically as she moved her shoulders a little. "I've already worked out one new dance for myself," she said. "God knows I'm no choreographer, but I did want to experiment first. Later, you know, really creative men like Massanchine or Fokhileff may want to do something entirely new for me— a whole new sequence of movements based on a new technique. And music—that could be quite different, too. Oh, there's no end to the possibilities! Even my voice has more range and power. Luckily I'm not an actress—it would be silly to try to play Camille or Juliet with a cast of ordinary people. Not that I couldn't, you know." She turned her head to stare at Harris through the mask of glass. "I honestly think I could. But it isn't necessary. There's too much else. Oh, I'm not worried!"

"Maltzer's worried," Harris reminded her.

She swung away from the fire, her metal robe ringing, and into her voice came the old note of distress that went with a furrowing of her forehead and a sidewise tilt of the head. The head went sidewise as it had always done, and he could see the furrowed brow almost as clearly as if flesh still clothed her.

"I know. And I'm worried about him, John. He's worked so awfully hard over me. This is the doldrums now, the let-down period, I suppose. I know what's on his mind. He's afraid I'll look just the same to the world as I look to him. Tooled metal. He's in a position no one ever quite achieved before, isn't he? Rather like God." Her voice rippled a little with amusement. "I suppose to God we must look like a col-lection of cells and corpuscles ourselves. But Maltzer lacks a god's detached viewpoint."

"He can't see you as I do, anyhow." Harris was choosing his words with difficulty. "I wonder, though—would it help him any if you postponed your debut awhile? You've been with him too closely, I think. You don't quite realize how near a breakdown he is. I was shocked when I saw him just now."

The golden head shook. "No. He's close to a breaking point, maybe, but I think the only cure's action. He wants me to retire and stay out of sight, John. Always. He's afraid for anyone to see me except a few old friends who remember me as I was. People he can trust to be—kind." She laughed. It was very strange to hear that ripple of mirth from the blank, unfeatured skull. Harris was seized with sudden panic at the thought of what reaction it might evoke in an audience of strangers. As if he had spoken the fear aloud, her voice denied it. "I don't need kindness. And it's no kindness to Maltzer to hide me under a bushel. He *has* worked too hard, I know. He's driven himself to a breaking point. But it'll be a complete negation of all he's worked for if I hide myself now. You don't know what a tremendous lot of geniuses and artistry went into me, John. The whole idea from the start was to re-create what I'd lost so that it could be proved that beauty and talent need not be sacrificed by the destruction of parts or all the body.

"It wasn't only for me that we meant to prove that. There'll be others who suffer injuries that once might have ruined them. This was to end all suffering like that forever. It was Maltzer's gift to the whole race as well as to me. He's really a humanitarian, John, like most great men. He'd never have given up a year of his life to this work if it had been for any one individual alone. He was seeing thousands of others beyond me as he worked. And I won't let him ruin all he's achieved because he's afraid to prove it now he's got it. The whole wonderful achievement will be worthless if I don't take the final step. I think his breakdown, in the end, would be worse and more final if I never tried than if I tried and failed."

Harris sat in silence. There was no answer he could make to that. He hoped the little twinge of shamefaced jealousy he suddenly felt did not show, as he was reminded anew of the intimacy closer than marriage which had of necessity bound these two together. And he knew that any reaction of his would in its way be almost as prejudiced as Maltzer's, for a reason at once the same and entirely opposite. Except that he himself came fresh to the problem, while Maltzer's viewpoint was colored by a year of overwork and physical and mental exhaustion.

"What are you going to do?" he asked.

She was standing before the fire when he spoke, swaying just a little so that highlights danced all along her golden body. Now she turned with a serpentine grace and sank into the cushioned chair beside her. It came to him suddenly that she was much more than humanly graceful—quite as much as he had once feared she would be less than human.

"I've already arranged for a performance," she told him, her voice a little shaken with a familiar mixture of excitement and defiance.

Harris sat up with a start. "How? Where? There hasn't been any publicity at all yet, has there? I didn't know—"

"Now, now, Johnnie," her amused voice soothed him. "You'll be handling everything just as usual once I get started back to work—that is, if you still want to. But this I've arranged for myself. It's going to be a surprise. I . . . I felt it had to be a surprise." She wriggled a little among the cushions. "Audience psychology is something I've always felt rather than known, and I do feel this is the way it ought to be done. There's no precedent. Nothing like this ever happened before. I'll have to go by my own intuition."

"You mean it's to be a complete surprise?"

"I think it must be. I don't want the audience coming in with preconceived ideas. I want them to see me exactly as I am now *first*, before they know who or what they're seeing. They must realize I can still give as good a performance as ever before they remember and compare it with my past performances. I don't want them to come ready to pity my handicaps—I haven't got any!—or full of morbid curiosity. So I'm going on the air after the regular eight-o'clock telecast of the feature from Teleo City. I'm just going to do one specialty in the usual vaude program. It's all been arranged. They'll build up to it, of course, as the highlight of the evening, but they aren't to say who I am until the end of the performance—if the audience hasn't recognized me already, by then."

"Audience?"

"Of course. Surely you haven't forgotten they still play to a theater audience at Teleo City? That's why I want to make my debut there. I've always played better when there were people in the studio, so I could gauge reactions. I think most performers do. Anyhow, it's all arranged."

"Does Maltzer know?"

She wriggled uncomfortably. "Not yet."

"But he'll have to give his permission too, won't he? I mean—"

"Now look, John! That's another idea you and Maltzer will have to get out of your minds. I don't belong to him. In a way he's just been my doctor through a long illness, but I'm free to discharge him whenever I choose. If there were ever any legal disagreement, I suppose he'd be entitled to quite a lot of money for the work he's done on my new body—for the body itself, really, since it's his own machine, in one sense. But he doesn't own it, or me. I'm not sure just how the question would be decided by the courts—there again, we've got a problem without precedent. The body may be his work, but the brain that makes it something more than a collection of metal rings is *me*, and he couldn't restrain me against my will even if he wanted to. Not legally, and not—" She hesitated oddly and looked away. For the first time Harris was aware of something beneath the surface of her mind which was quite strange to him.

"Well, anyhow," she went on, "that question won't come up. Maltzer and I have been much too close in the past year to clash over anything as essential as this. He knows in his heart that I'm right, and he won't try to restrain me. His work won't be completed until I do what I was built to do. And I intend to do it."

That strange little quiver of something—something un-Deirdre—which had so briefly trembled beneath the surface of familiarity stuck in Harris' mind as something he must recall and examine later. Now he said only,

"All right. I suppose I agree with you. How soon are you going to do it?"

She turned her head so that even the glass mask through which she looked out at the world was foreshortened away from him, and the golden helmet with its hint of sculptured cheekbone was entirely enigmatic.

"Tonight," she said.

Maltzer's thin hand shook so badly that he could not turn the dial. He tried twice and then laughed nervously and shrugged at Harris.

"You get her," he said.

Harris glanced at his watch. "It isn't time yet. She won't be on for half an hour."

Maltzer made a gesture of violent impatience. "Get it, get it!"

Harris shrugged a little in turn and twisted the dial. On the tilted screen above them shadows and sound blurred together and then clarified into a somber medieval hall, vast, vaulted, people in bright costume moving like pygmies through its dimness. Since the play concerned Mary of Scotland, the actors were dressed in something approximating Elizabethan garb, but as every era tends to translate costume into terms of the current fashions, the women's hair was dressed in a style that would have startled Elizabeth, and their footgear was entirely anachronistic.

The hall dissolved and a face swam up into soft focus upon the screen. The dark, lush beauty of the actress who was playing the Stuart queen glowed at them in velvety perfection from the clouds of her pearl-strewn hair. Maltzer groaned.

"She's competing with *that*," he said hollowly.

"You think she can't?"

Maltzer slapped the chair arms with angry palms. Then the quivering of his fingers seemed suddenly to strike him, and he muttered to himself, "Look at 'em! I'm not even fit to handle a hammer and saw." But the mutter was an aside. "Of course she can't compete," he cried irritably. "She hasn't any sex. She isn't female any more. She doesn't know that yet, but she'll learn."

Harris stared at him, feeling a little stunned. Somehow the thought had not occurred to him before at all, so vividly had the illusion of the old Deirdre hung about the new one.

"She's an abstraction now," Maltzer went on, drumming his palms upon the chair in quick, nervous rhythms. "I don't know what it'll do to her, but there'll be change. Remember Abelard? She's lost everything that made her essentially what the public wanted, and she's going to find it out the hard way. After that—" He grimaced savagely and was silent.

"She hasn't lost everything," Harris defended. "She can dance and sing as well as ever, maybe better. She still has grace and charm and—"

"Yes, but where did the grace and charm come from? Not out of the habit patterns in her brain. No, out of human contacts, out of all the things that stimulate sensitive minds to creativeness. And she's lost three of her five senses. Everything she can't see and hear is gone. One of the strongest stimuli to a woman of her type was the knowledge of sex competition. You know how she sparkled when a man came into the room? All that's gone, and it was an essential. You know how liquor stimulated her? She's lost that. She couldn't taste food or drink even if she needed it. Perfume, flowers, all the odors we respond to mean nothing to her now. She can't feel anything with tactual delicacy any more. She used to surround herself with luxuries—she drew her stimuli from them—and that's all gone too. She's withdrawn from all physical contacts."

He squinted at the screen, not seeing it, his face drawn into lines like the lines of a skull. All flesh seemed to have dissolved off his bones in the past year, and Harris thought almost jealously that even in that way he seemed to be drawing nearer Deirdre in her fleshlessness with every passing week.

"Sight," Maltzer said, "is the most highly civilized of the senses. It was the last to come. The other senses tie us in closely with the very roots of life; I think we perceive with them more keenly than we know. The things we realize through taste and smell and feeling stimulate directly, without a detour through the centers of conscious thought. You know how often a taste or odor will recall a memory to you so subtly you don't know exactly what caused it? We need those primitive senses to tie us in with nature and the race. Through those ties Deirdre drew her vitality without realizing it. Sight is a cold, intellectual thing compared with the other senses. But it's all she has to draw on now. She isn't a human being any more, and I think what humanity is left in her will drain out little by little and never be replaced. Abelard, in a way, was a prototype. But Deirdre's loss is complete."

"She isn't human," Harris agreed slowly. "But she isn't pure robot either. She's something somewhere between the two, and I think it's a mistake to try to guess just where, or what the outcome will be."

"I don't have to guess," Maltzer said in a grim voice. "I know. I wish I'd let her die. I've done something to her a thousand times worse than the fire ever could. I should have let her die in it."

"Wait," said Harris. "Wait and see. I think you're wrong."

On the television screen Mary of Scotland climbed the scaffold to her doom, the gown of traditional scarlet clinging warmly to supple young curves as anachronistic in their way as the slippers beneath the gown, for—as everyone but playwrights knows—Mary was well into middle age before she died. Gracefully this latter-day Mary bent her head, sweeping the long hair aside, kneeling to the block.

Maltzer watched stonily, seeing another woman entirely.

"I shouldn't have let her," he was muttering. "I shouldn't have let her do it."

"Do you really think you'd have stopped her if you could?" Harris asked quietly. And the other man after a moment's pause shook his head jerkily.

"No, I suppose not. I keep thinking if I worked and waited a little longer maybe I could make it easier for her, but—no, I suppose not. She's got to face them sooner or later, being herself." He stood up abruptly, shoving back his chair. "If she only weren't so . . . so frail. She doesn't realize how delicately poised her very sanity is. We gave her what we could—the artists and the designers and I, all gave our very best—but she's so pitifully handicapped even with all we could do. She'll always be an abstraction and a . . . a freak, cut off from the world by handicaps worse in their way than anything any human being ever suffered before. Sooner or later she'll realize it. And then—" He began to pace up and down with quick, uneven steps, striking his hands together. His face was twitching with a little *tic* that drew up one eye to a squint and released it again at irregular intervals. Harris could see how very near collapse the man was.

"Can you imagine what it's like?" Maltzer demanded fiercely. "Penned into a mechanical body like that, shut out from all human contacts except what leaks in by way of sight and sound? To know you aren't human any longer? She's been through shocks enough already. When that shock fully hits her—"

"Shut up," said Harris roughly. "You won't do her any good if you break down yourself. Look—the vaude's starting."

Great golden curtains had swept together over the unhappy Queen of Scotland and were parting again now, all sorrow and frustration wiped away once more as cleanly as the passing centuries had already expunged them. Now a line of tiny dancers under the tremendous arch of the stage kicked and pranced with the precision of little mechanical dolls too small and perfect to be real. Vision rushed down upon them and swept along the row, face after stiffly smiling face racketing by like fence pickets. Then the sight rose into the rafters and looked down upon them from a great height, the grotesquely foreshortened figures still prancing in perfect rhythm even from this inhuman angle.

There was applause from an invisible audience. Then someone came out and did a dance with lighted torches that streamed long, weaving ribbons of fire among clouds of what looked like cotton wool but was most probably asbestos. Then a company in gorgeous pseudo-period costumes postured its way through the new singing ballet form of dance, roughly following a plot which had been announced as *Les Sylphides*, but had little in common with it. Afterward the precision dancers came on again, solemn and charming as performing dolls.

Maltzer began to show signs of dangerous tension as act succeeded act. Deirdre's was to be the last, of course. It seemed very long indeed before a face in close-up blotted out the stage, and a master of ceremonies with features like an amiable marionette's announced a very special number as the finale. His voice was almost cracking with excitement—perhaps he, too, had not been told until a moment before what lay in store for the audience.

Neither of the listening men heard what it was he said, but both were conscious of a certain indefinable excitement rising among the audience, murmurs and rustlings and a mounting anticipation as if time had run backward here and knowledge of the great surprise had already broken upon them.

Then the golden curtains appeared again. They quivered and swept apart on long upward arcs, and between them the stage was full of a shimmering golden haze. It was, Harris realized in a moment, simply a series of gauze curtains, but the effect was one of strange and wonderful anticipation, as if something very splendid must be hidden in the haze. The world might have looked like this on the first morning of creation, before heaven and earth took form in the mind of God. It was a singularly fortunate choice of stage-set in its symbolism, though Harris wondered how much necessity had figured in its selection, for there could not have been much time to prepare an elaborate set.

The audience sat perfectly silent, and the air was tense. This was no ordinary pause before an act. No one had been told, surely, and yet they seemed to guess—

The shimmering haze trembled and began to thin, veil by veil. Beyond was darkness, and what looked like a row of shining pillars set in a balustrade that began gradually to take shape as the haze drew back in shining folds. Now they could see that the balustrade curved up from left and right to the head of a sweep of stairs. Stage and stairs were carpeted in black velvet; black velvet draperies hung just ajar behind the balcony, with a glimpse of dark sky beyond them trembling with dim synthetic stars.

The last curtain of golden gauze withdrew. The stage was empty. Or it seemed empty. But even through the aerial distances between this screen and the place it mirrored, Harris thought that the audience was not waiting for the performer to come on from the wings. There was no rustling, no coughing, no sense of impatience. A presence upon the stage was in command from the first drawing of the curtains; it filled the theater with its calm domination. It gauged its timing, holding the audience as a conductor with lifted baton gathers and holds the eyes of his orchestra.

For a moment everything was motionless upon the stage. Then, at the head of the stairs, where the two curves of the pillared balustrade swept together, a figure stirred.

Until that moment she had seemed another shining column in the row. Now she swayed deliberately, light catching
and winking and running molten along her limbs and her
robe of metal mesh. She swayed just enough to show that
she was there. Then, with every eye upon her, she stood quietly to let them look their fill. The screen did not swoop to
a close-up upon her. Her enigma remained inviolate and the
television watchers saw her no more clearly than the audience in the theater.

Many must have thought her at first some wonderfully
animate robot, hung perhaps from wires invisible against the
velvet, for certainly she was no woman dressed in metal—her
proportions were too thin and fine for that. And perhaps the
impression of robotism was what she meant to convey at
first. She stood quiet, swaying just a little, a masked and
inscrutable figure, faceless, very slender in her robe that
hung in folds as pure as a Grecian chlamys, though she did
not look Grecian at all. In the visored golden helmet and the
robe of mail that odd likeness to knighthood was there again,
with its implications of medieval richness behind the simple
lines. Except that in her exquisite slimness she called to mind
no human figure in armor, not even the comparative delicacy
of a St. Joan. It was the chivalry and delicacy of some other
world implicit in her outlines.

A breath of surprise had rippled over the audience when
she moved. Now they were tensely silent again, waiting. And
the tension, the anticipation, was far deeper than the surface
importance of the scene could ever have evoked. Even those
who thought her a manikin seemed to feel the forerunning
of greater revelations.

Now she swayed and came slowly down the steps, moving with a suppleness just a little better than human. The
swaying strengthened. By the time she reached the stage
floor she was dancing. But it was no dance that any human

creature could ever have performed. The long, slow, languorous rhythms of her body would have been impossible to a figure hinged at its joints as human figures hinge. (Harris remembered incredulously that he had feared once to find her jointed like a mechanical robot. But it was humanity that seemed, by contrast, jointed and mechanical now.)

The languor and the rhythm of her patterns looked impromptu, as all good dances should, but Harris knew what hours of composition and rehearsal must lie behind it, what laborious graving into her brain of strange new pathways, the first to replace the old ones and govern the mastery of metal limbs.

To and fro over the velvet carpet, against the velvet background, she wove the intricacies of her serpentine dance, leisurely and yet with such hypnotic effect that the air seemed full of looping rhythms, as if her long, tapering limbs had left their own replicas hanging upon the air and fading only slowly as she moved away. In her mind, Harris knew, the stage was a whole, a background to be filled in completely with the measured patterns of her dance, and she seemed almost to project that complete pattern to her audience so that they saw her everywhere at once, her golden rhythms fading upon the air long after she had gone.

Now there was music, looping and hanging in echoes after her like the shining festoons she wove with her body. But it was no orchestral music. She was humming, deep and sweet and wordlessly, as she glided her easy, intricate path about the stage. And the volume of the music was amazing. It seemed to fill the theater, and it was not amplified by hidden loudspeakers. You could tell that. Somehow, until you heard the music she made, you had never realized before the subtle distortions that amplification puts into music. This was utterly pure and true as perhaps no ear in all her audience had ever heard music before.

While she danced the audience did not seem to breathe. Perhaps they were beginning already to suspect who and what it was that moved before them without any fanfare of the publicity they had been half-expecting for weeks now. And yet, without the publicity, it was not easy to believe the dancer they watched was not some cunningly motivated manikin swinging on unseen wires about the stage.

Nothing she had done yet had been human. The dance was no dance a human being could have performed. The music she hummed came from a throat without vocal cords. But now the long, slow rhythms were drawing to their close, the pattern tightening in to a finale. And she ended as inhumanly as she had danced, willing them not to interrupt her with applause, dominating them now as she had always done. For her implication here was that a machine might have performed the dance, and a machine expects no applause. If they thought unseen operators had put her through those wonderful paces, they would wait for the operators to appear for their bows. But the audience was obedient. It sat silently, waiting for what came next. But its silence was tense and breathless.

The dance ended as it had begun. Slowly, almost carelessly, she swung up the velvet stairs, moving with rhythms as perfect as her music. But when she reached the head of the stairs she turned to face her audience, and for a moment stood motionless, like a creature of metal, without volition, the hands of the operator slack upon its strings.

Then, startlingly, she laughed.

It was lovely laughter, low and sweet and full-throated. She threw her head back and let her body sway and her shoulders shake, and the laughter, like the music, filled the theater, gaining volume from the great hollow of the roof and sounding in the ears of every listener, not loud, but as intimately as if each sat alone with the woman who laughed.

And she was a woman now. Humanity had dropped over her like a tangible garment. No one who had ever heard that laughter before could mistake it here. But before the reality of who she was had quite time to dawn upon her listeners she let the laughter deepen into music, as no human voice could have done. She was humming a familiar refrain close in the ear of every hearer. And the humming in turn swung into words. She sang in her clear, light, lovely voice:

"The yellow rose of Eden, is blooming in my heart—"

It was Deirdre's song. She had sung it first upon the airways a month before the theater fire that had consumed her. It was a commonplace little melody, simple enough to take first place in the fancy of a nation that had always liked its songs simple. But it had a certain sincerity too, and no taint of the vulgarity of tune and rhythm that foredooms so many popular songs to oblivion after their novelty fades.

No one else was ever able to sing it quite as Deirdre did. It had been identified with her so closely that though for a while after her accident singers tried to make it a memorial for her, they failed so conspicuously to give it her unmistakable flair that the song died from their sheer inability to sing it. No one ever hummed the tune without thinking of her and the pleasant, nostalgic sadness of something lovely and lost.

But it was not a sad song now. If anyone had doubted whose brain and ego motivated this shining metal suppleness, they could doubt no longer. For the voice was Deirdre, and the song. And the lovely, poised grace of her mannerisms that made up recognition as certainly as sight of a familiar face.

She had not finished the first line of her song before the audience knew her.

And they did not let her finish. The accolade of their

interruption was a tribute more eloquent than polite waiting could ever have been. First a breath of incredulity rippled over the theater, and a long sighing gasp that reminded Harris irrelevantly as he listened to the gasp which still goes up from matinee audiences at the first glimpse of the fabulous Valentino, so many generations dead. But this gasp did not sigh itself away and vanish. Tremendous tension lay behind it, and the rising tide of excitement rippled up in little murmurs and spatterings of applause that ran together into one overwhelming roar. It shook the theater. The television screen trembled and blurred a little to the volume of that transmitted applause.

Silenced before it, Deirdre stood gesturing on the stage, bowing and bowing as the noise rolled up about her, shaking perceptibly with the triumph of her own emotion.

Harris had an intolerable feeling that she was smiling radiantly and that the tears were pouring down her cheeks. He even thought, just as Maltzer leaned forward to switch off the screen, that she was blowing kisses over the audience in the time-honored gesture of the grateful actress, her golden arms shining as she scattered kisses abroad from the featureless helmet, the face that had no mouth.

"Well?" Harris said, not without triumph.

Maltzer shook his head jerkily, the glasses unsteady on his nose so that the blurred eyes behind them seemed to shift.

"Of course they applauded, you fool," he said in a savage voice. "I might have known they would under this set-up. It doesn't prove anything. Oh, she was smart to surprise them—I admit that. But they were applauding themselves as much as her. Excitement, gratitude for letting them in on a historic performance, mass hysteria—*you* know. It's from now on the test will come, and this hasn't helped any to prepare her for it. Morbid curiosity when the news gets out—people laughing when she forgets she isn't human. And they will, you know.

There are always those who will. And the novelty wearing off. The slow draining away of humanity for lack of contact with any human stimuli any more—"

Harris remembered suddenly and reluctantly the moment that afternoon which he had shunted aside mentally, to consider later. The sense of something unfamiliar beneath the surface of Deirdre's speech. Was Maltzer right? Was the drainage already at work? Or was there something deeper than this obvious answer to the question? Certainly she had been through experiences too terrible for ordinary people to comprehend. Scars might still remain. Or, with her body, had she put on a strange, metallic something of the mind, that spoke to no sense which human minds could answer?

For a few minutes neither of them spoke. Then Maltzer rose abruptly and stood looking down at Harris with an abstract scowl.

"I wish you'd go now," he said.

Harris glanced up at him, startled. Maltzer began to pace again, his steps quick and uneven. Over his shoulder he said,

"I've made up my mind, Harris. I've got to put a stop to this."

Harris rose. "Listen," he said. "Tell me one thing. What makes you so certain you're right? Can you deny that most of it's speculation—hearsay evidence? Remember, I talked to Deirdre, and she was just as sure as you are in the opposite direction. Have you any real reason for what you think?"

Maltzer took his glasses off and rubbed his nose carefully, taking a long time about it. He seemed reluctant to answer. But when he did, at last, there was a confidence in his voice Harris had not expected.

"I have a reason," he said. "But you won't believe it. Nobody would."

"Try me."

Maltzer shook his head. "Nobody *could* believe it. No two

people were ever in quite the same relationship before as Deirdre and I have been. I helped her come back out of complete—oblivion. I knew her before she had voice or hearing. She was only a frantic mind when I first made contact with her, half insane with all that had happened and fear of what would happen next. In a very literal sense she was reborn out of that condition, and I had to guide her through every step of the way. I came to know her thoughts before she thought them. And once you've been that close to another mind, you don't lose the contact easily." He put the glasses back on and looked blurrily at Harris through the heavy lenses. "Deirdre is worried," he said. "I know it. You won't believe me, but I can—well, sense it. I tell you, I've been too close to her very mind itself to make any mistake. You don't see it, maybe. Maybe even she doesn't know it yet. But the worry's there. When I'm with her, I feel it. And I don't want it to come any nearer the surface of her mind than it's come already. I'm going to put a stop to this before it's too late."

Harris had no comment for that. It was too entirely outside his own experience. He said nothing for a moment. Then he asked simply, "How?"

"I'm not sure yet. I've got to decide before she comes back. And I want to see her alone."

"I think you're wrong," Harris told him quietly. "I think you're imagining things. I don't think you *can* stop her."

Maltzer gave him a slanted glance. "I can stop her," he said, in a curious voice. He went on quickly, "She has enough already—she's nearly human. She can live normally as other people live, without going back on the screen. Maybe this taste of it will be enough. I've got to convince her it is. If she retires now, she'll never guess how cruel her own audiences could be, and maybe that deep sense of—distress, uneasiness, whatever it is—won't come to the surface. It mustn't. She's too fragile to stand that." He slapped his hands together sharply. "I've got to stop her. For her own sake I've got to do it!" He swung round again to face Harris. "Will you go now?"

Never in his life had Harris wanted less to leave a place. Briefly he thought of saying simply, "No I won't." But he had to admit in his own mind that Maltzer was at least partly right. This was a matter between Deirdre and her creator, the culmination, perhaps, of that year's long intimacy so like marriage that this final trial for supremacy was a need he recognized.

He would not, he thought, forbid the showdown if he could. Perhaps the whole year had been building up to this one moment between them in which one or the other must prove himself victor. Neither was very well stable just now, after the long strain of the year past. It might very well be that the mental salvation of one or both hinged upon the outcome of the clash. But because each was so strongly motivated not by selfish concern but by solicitude for the other in this strange combat, Harris knew he must leave them to settle the thing alone.

He was in the street and hailing a taxi before the full significance of something Maltzer had said came to him. *"I can stop her,"* he had declared, with an odd inflection in his voice.

Suddenly Harris felt cold. Maltzer had made her—of course he could stop her if he chose. Was there some key in that supple golden body that could immobilize it at its maker's will? Could she be imprisoned in the cage of her own body? No body before in all history, he thought, could have been designed more truly to be a prison for its mind than Deirdre's, if Maltzer chose to turn the key that locked her in. There must be many ways to do it. He could simply withhold whatever source of nourishment kept her brain alive, if that were the way he chose.

But Harris could not believe he would do it. The man wasn't insane. He would not defeat his own purpose. His determination rose from his solicitude for Deirdre; he would not even in the last extremity try to save her by imprisoning her in the jail of her own skull.

For a moment Harris hesitated on the curb, almost turning back. But what could he do? Even granting that Maltzer would resort to such tactics, self-defeating in their very nature, how could any man on earth prevent him if he did it subtly enough? But he never would. Harris knew he never would. He got into his cab slowly, frowning. He would see them both tomorrow.

He did not. Harris was swamped with excited calls about yesterday's performance, but the message he was awaiting did not come. The day went by very slowly. Toward evening he surrendered and called Maltzer's apartment.

It was Deirdre's face that answered, and for once he saw no remembered features superimposed upon the blankness of her helmet. Masked and faceless, she looked at him inscrutably.

"Is everything all right?" he asked, a little uncomfortable.

"Yes, of course," she said, and her voice was a bit metallic for the first time, as if she were thinking so deeply of some other matter that she did not trouble to pitch it properly. "I had a long talk with Maltzer last night, if that's what you mean. You know what he wants. But nothing's been decided yet."

Harris felt oddly rebuffed by the sudden realization of the metal of her. It was impossible to read anything from face or voice. Each had its mask.

"What are you going to do?" he asked.

"Exactly as I'd planned," she told him, without inflection.

Harris floundered a little. Then, with an effort at practicality, he said, "Do you want me to go to work on bookings, then?"

She shook the delicately modeled skull. "Not yet. You saw the reviews today, of course. They—*did* like me." It was an understatement, and for the first time a note of warmth sounded in her voice. But the preoccupation was still there, too. "I'd already planned to make them wait awhile after my first performance," she went on. "A couple of weeks, anyhow. You remember that little farm of mine in Jersey, John? I'm going over today. I won't see anyone except the servants there. Not even Maltzer. Not even you. I've got a lot to think about. Maltzer has agreed to let everything go until we've both thought things over. He's taking a rest, too. I'll see you the moment I get back, John. Is that all right?"

She blanked out almost before he had time to nod and while the beginning of a stammered argument was still on his lips. He sat there staring at the screen.

The two weeks that went by before Maltzer called him again were the longest Harris had ever spent. He thought of many things in the interval. He believed he could sense in that last talk with Deirdre something of the inner unrest that Maltzer had spoken of—more an abstraction than a distress, but some thought had occupied her mind which she would not—or was it that she could not?—share even with her closest confidants. He even wondered whether, if her mind was as delicately poised as Maltzer feared, one would ever know whether or not it had slipped. There was so little evidence one way or the other in the unchanging outward form of her.

Most of all he wondered what two weeks in a new environment would do to her untried body and newly patterned brain. If Maltzer were right, then there might be some perceptible—drainage—by the time they met again. He tried not to think of that.

Maltzer televised him on the morning set for her return. He looked very bad. The rest must have been no rest at all.

His face was almost a skull now, and the blurred eyes behind their lenses burned. But he seemed curiously at peace, in spite of his appearance. Harris thought he had reached some decision, but whatever it was had not stopped his hands from shaking or the nervous *tic* that drew his face sidewise into a grimace at intervals.

"Come over," he said briefly, without preamble. "She'll be here in half an hour." And he blanked out without waiting for an answer.

When Harris arrived, he was standing by the window looking down and steadying his trembling hands on the sill.

"I can't stop her," he said in a monotone, and again without preamble. Harris had the impression that for the two weeks his thoughts must have run over and over the same track, until any spoken word was simply a vocal interlude in the circling of his mind. "I couldn't do it. I even tried threats, but she knew I didn't mean them. There's only one way out, Harris." He glanced up briefly, hollow-eyed behind the lenses. "Never mind. I'll tell you later."

"Did you explain everything to her that you did to me?"

"Nearly all. I even taxed her with that . . . that sense of distress I *know* she feels. She denied it. She was lying. We both knew. It was worse after the performance than before. When I saw her that night, I tell you I *knew*—she senses something wrong, but she won't admit it." He shrugged. "Well—"

Faintly in the silence they heard the humming of the elevator descending from the helicopter platform on the roof. Both men turned to the door.

She had not changed at all. Foolishly, Harris was a little surprised. Then he caught himself and remembered that she would never change—never, until she died. He himself might grow white-haired and senile; she would move before him then as she moved now, supple, golden, enigmatic.

Still, he thought she caught her breath a little when she saw Maltzer and the depths of his swift degeneration. She had no breath to catch, but her voice was shaken as she greeted them.

"I'm glad you're both here," she said, a slight hesitation in her speech. "It's a wonderful day outside. Jersey was glorious. I'd forgotten how lovely it is in summer. Was the sanitarium any good, Maltzer?"

He jerked his head irritably and did not answer. She went on talking in a light voice, skimming the surface, saying nothing important.

This time Harris saw her as he supposed her audiences would, eventually, when the surprise had worn off and the image of the living Deirdre faded from memory. She was all metal now, the Deirdre they would know from today on. And she was not less lovely. She was not even less human—yet. Her motion was a miracle of flexible grace, a pouring of suppleness along every limb. (From now on, Harris realized suddenly, it was her body and not her face that would have mobility to express emotion; she must act with her limbs and her lithe, robed torso.)

But there was something wrong. Harris sensed it almost tangibly in her inflections, her elusiveness, the way she fenced with words. This was what Maltzer had meant, this was what Harris himself had felt just before she left for the country. Only now it was strong—certain. Between them and the old Deirdre whose voice still spoke to them a veil of—detachment—had been drawn. Behind it she was in distress. Somehow, somewhere, she had made some discovery that affected her profoundly. And Harris was terribly afraid that he knew what the discovery must be. Maltzer was right.

He was still leaning against the window, staring out unseeingly over the vast panorama of New York, webbed with traffic bridges, winking with sunlit glass, its vertiginous distances plunging downward into the blue shadows of Earthlevel. He said now, breaking into the light-voiced chatter, "Are you all right, Deirdre?"

She laughed. It was lovely laughter. She moved lithely across the room, sunlight glinting on her musical mailed robe, and stooped to a cigarette box on a table. Her fingers were deft.

"Have one?" she said, and carried the box to Maltzer. He let her put the brown cylinder between his lips and hold a light to it, but he did not seem to be noticing what he did. She replaced the box and then crossed to a mirror on the far wall and began experimenting with a series of gliding ripples that wove patterns of pale gold in the glass. "Of course I'm all right," she said.

"You're lying."

Deirdre did not turn. She was watching him in the mirror, but the ripple of her motion went on slowly, languorously, undisturbed.

"No," she told them both.

Maltzer drew deeply on his cigarette. Then with a hard pull he unsealed the window and tossed the smoking stub far out over the gulfs below. He said,

"You can't deceive me, Deirdre." His voice, suddenly, was quite calm. "I created you, my dear. I know. I've sensed that uneasiness in you growing and growing for a long while now. It's much stronger today than it was two weeks ago. Something happened to you in the country. I don't know what it was, but you've changed. Will you admit to yourself what it is, Deirdre? Have you realized yet that you must not go back on the screen?"

"Why, no," said Deirdre, still not looking at him except

obliquely, in the glass. Her gestures were slower now, weaving lazy patterns in the air. "No, I haven't changed my mind."

She was all metal—outwardly. She was taking unfair advantage of her own metal-hood. She had withdrawn far within, behind the mask of her voice and her facelessness. Even her body, whose involuntary motions might have betrayed what she was feeling, in the only way she could be subject to betrayal now, she was putting through ritual motions that disguised it completely. As long as these looping, weaving patterns occupied her, no one had any way of guessing even from her motion what went on in the hidden brain inside her helmet.

Harris was struck suddenly and for the first time with the completeness of her withdrawal. When he had seen her last in this apartment she had been wholly Deirdre, not masked at all, overflowing the metal with the warmth and ardor of the woman he had known so well. Since then—since the performance on the stage—he had not seen the familiar Deirdre again. Passionately he wondered why. Had she begun to suspect even in her moment of triumph what a fickle master an audience could be? Had she caught, perhaps, the sound of whispers and laughter among some small portion of her watchers, though the great majority praised her?

Or was Maltzer right? Perhaps Harris' first interview with her had been the last bright burning of the lost Deirdre, animated by excitement and the pleasure of meeting after so long a time, animation summoned up in a last strong effort to convince him. Now she was gone, but whether in self-protection against the possible cruelties of human beings, or whether in withdrawal to metal-hood, he could not guess. Humanity might be draining out of her fast, and the brassy taint of metal permeating the brain it housed.

Maltzer laid his trembling hand on the edge of the

opened window and looked out. He said in a deepened voice, the querulous note gone for the first time:

"I've made a terrible mistake, Deirdre. I've done you irreparable harm." He paused a moment, but Deirdre said nothing. Harris dared not speak. In a moment Maltzer went on. "I've made you vulnerable, and given you no weapons to fight your enemies with. And the human race is your enemy, my dear, whether you admit it now or later. I think you know that. I think it's why you're so silent. I think you must have suspected it on the stage two weeks ago, and verified it in Jersey while you were gone. They're going to hate you, after a while, because you are still beautiful, and they're going to persecute you because you are different—and helpless. Once the novelty wears off, my dear, your audience will be simply a mob."

He was not looking at her. He had bent forward a little, looking out the window and down. His hair stirred in the wind that blew very strongly up this high, and whined thinly around the open edge of the glass.

"I meant what I did for you," he said, "to be for everyone who meets with accidents that might have ruined them. I should have known my gift would mean worse ruin than any mutilation could be. I know now that there's only one legitimate way a human being can create life. When he tries another way, as I did, he has a lesson to learn. Remember the lesson of the student Frankenstein? He learned, too. In a way, he was lucky—the way he learned. He didn't have to watch what happened afterward. Maybe he wouldn't have had the courage—I know I haven't."

Harris found himself standing without remembering that he rose. He knew suddenly what was about to happen. He understood Maltzer's air of resolution, his new, unnatural calm. He knew, even, why Maltzer had asked him here today, so that Deirdre might not be left alone. For he remembered that Frankenstein, too, had paid with his life for the unlawful creation of life.

Maltzer was leaning head and shoulders from the window now, looking down with almost hypnotized fascination. His voice came back to them remotely in the breeze, as if a barrier already lay between them.

Deirdre had not moved. Her expressionless mask, in the mirror, watched him calmly. She *must* have understood. Yet she gave no sign, except that the weaving of her arms had almost stopped now, she moved so slowly. Like a dance seen in a nightmare, under water.

It was impossible, of course, for her to express any emotion. The fact that her face showed none now should not, in fairness, be held against her. But she watched so wholly without feeling—Neither of them moved toward the window. A false step, now, might send him over. They were quiet, listening to his voice.

"We who bring life into the world unlawfully," said Maltzer, almost thoughtfully, "must make room for it by withdrawing our own. That seems to be an inflexible rule. It works automatically. The thing we create makes living unbearable. No, it's nothing you can help, my dear. I've asked you to do something I created you incapable of doing. I made you to perform a function, and I've been asking you to forgo the one thing you were made to do. I believe that if you do it, it will destroy you, but the whole guilt is mine; not yours. I'm not even asking you to give up the screen, any more. I know you can't, and live. But I can't live and watch you. I put all my skill and all my love in one final masterpiece, and I can't bear to watch it destroyed. I can't live and watch you do only what I made you to do, and ruin yourself because you must do it.

"But before I go, I have to make sure you understand." He leaned a little farther, looking down, and his voice grew more remote as the glass came between them. He was saying almost unbearable things now, but very distantly, in a cool, passionless tone filtered through wind and glass, and with the distant humming of the city mingled with it, so that the words were curiously robbed of poignancy. "I can be a coward," he said, "and escape the consequences of what I've done, but I can't go and leave you—not understanding. It would be even worse than the thought of your failure, to think of you bewildered and confused when the mob turns on you. What I'm telling you, my dear, won't be any real news—I think you sense it already, though you may not admit it to yourself. We've been too close to lie to each other, Deirdre—I know when you aren't telling the truth. I know the distress that's been growing in your mind. You are not wholly human, my dear. I think you know that. In so many ways, in spite of all I could do, you must always be less than human. You've lost the senses of perception that kept you in touch with humanity. Sight and hearing are all that remain, and sight, as I've said before, was the last and coldest of the senses to develop. And you're so delicately poised on a sort of thin edge of reason. You're only a clear, glowing mind animating a metal body, like a candle flame in a glass. And as precariously vulnerable to the wind."

He paused. "Try not to let them ruin you completely," he said after a while. "When they turn against you, when they find out you're more helpless than they—I wish I could have made you stronger, Deirdre. But I couldn't. I had too much skill for your good and mine, but not quite enough skill for that."

He was silent again, briefly, looking down. He was balanced precariously now, more than halfway over the sill and supported only by one hand on the glass. Harris watched with an agonized uncertainty, not sure whether a sudden leap might catch him in time or send him over. Deirdre was still weaving her golden patterns, slowly and unchangingly, watching the mirror and its reflection, her face and masked eyes enigmatic.

"I wish one thing, though," Maltzer said in his remote voice. "I wish—before I finish—that you'd tell me the truth, Deirdre. I'd be happier if I were sure I'd—reached you. Do you understand what I've said? Do you believe me? Because if you don't, then I know you're lost beyond all hope. If you'll admit your own doubt—and I know you do doubt—I can think there may be a chance for you after all. Were you lying to me, Deirdre? Do you know how . . . how wrong I've made you?"

There was silence. Then very softly, a breath of sound, Deirdre answered. The voice seemed to hang in midair, because she had no lips to move and localize it for the imagination.

"Will you listen, Maltzer?" she asked.

"I'll wait," he said. "Go on. Yes or no?"

Slowly she let her arms drop to her sides. Very smoothly and quietly she turned from the mirror and faced him. She swayed a little, making her metal robe ring.

"I'll answer you," she said. "But I don't think I'll answer that. Not with yes or no, anyhow. I'm going to walk a little, Maltzer. I have something to tell you, and I can't talk standing still. Will you let me move about without—going over?"

He nodded distantly. "You can't interfere from that distance," he said. "But keep the distance. What do you want to say?"

She began to pace a little way up and down her end of the room, moving with liquid ease. The table with the cigarette box was in her way, and she pushed it aside carefully, watching Maltzer and making no swift motions to startle him.

"I'm not—well, sub-human," she said, a faint note of

indignation in her voice. "I'll prove it in a minute, but I want to say something else first. You must promise to wait and listen. There's a flaw in your argument, and I resent it. I'm not a Frankenstein monster made out of dead flesh. I'm myself—alive. You didn't create my life, you only preserved it. I'm not a robot, with compulsions built into me that I have to obey. I'm free-willed and independent, and, Maltzer—I'm human."

Harris had relaxed a little. She knew what she was doing. He had no idea what she planned, but he was willing to wait now. She was not the indifferent automaton he had thought. He watched her come to the table again in a lap of her pacing, and stoop over it, her eyeless mask turned to Maltzer to make sure variation of her movement did not startle him.

"I'm human," she repeated, her voice humming faintly and very sweetly. "Do you think I'm not?" she asked, straightening and facing them both. And then suddenly, almost overwhelmingly, the warmth and the old ardent charm were radiant all around her. She was robot no longer, enigmatic no longer. Harris could see as clearly as in their first meeting the remembered flesh still gracious and beautiful as her voice evoked his memory. She stood swaying a little, as she had always swayed, her head on one side, and she was chuckling at them both. It was such a soft and lovely sound, so warmly familiar.

"Of course I'm myself," she told them, and as the words sounded in their ears neither of them could doubt it. There was hypnosis in her voice. She turned away and began to pace again, and so powerful was the human personality which she had called up about her that it beat out at them in deep pulses, as if her body were a furnace to send out those comforting waves of warmth. "I have handicaps, I know," she said. "But my audiences will never know. I won't let them know. I think you'll believe me, both of you, when

I say I could play Juliet just as I am now, with a cast of ordinary people, and make the world accept it. Do you think I could, John? Maltzer, don't you believe I could?"

She paused at the far end of her pacing path and turned to face them, and they both stared at her without speaking. To Harris she was the Deirdre he had always known, pale gold, exquisitely graceful in remembered postures, the inner radiance of her shining through metal as brilliantly as it had ever shone through flesh. He did not wonder, now, if it were real. Later he would think again that it might be only a disguise, something like a garment she had put off with her lost body, to wear again only when she chose. Now the spell of her compelling charm was too strong for wonder. He watched, convinced for the moment that she was all she seemed to be. She could play Juliet if she said she could. She could sway a whole audience as easily as she swayed himself. Indeed, there was something about her just now more convincingly human than anything he had noticed before. He realized that in a split second of awareness before he saw what it was.

She was looking at Maltzer. He, too, watched, spellbound in spite of himself, not dissenting. She glanced from one to the other. Then she put back her head and laughter came welling and choking from her in a great, full-throated tide. She shook in the strength of it. Harris could almost see her round throat pulsing with the sweet low-pitched waves of laughter that were shaking her. Honest mirth, with a little derision in it.

Then she lifted one arm and tossed her cigarette into the empty fireplace.

Harris choked, and his mind went blank for one moment of blind denial. He had not sat here watching a robot smoke and accepting it as normal. He could not! And yet he had. That had been the final touch of conviction which swayed his hypnotized mind into accepting her humanity. And she had done it so deftly, so naturally, wearing her radiant humanity with such rightness, that his watching mind had not even questioned what she did.

He glanced at Maltzer. The man was still halfway over the window ledge, but through the opening of the window he, too, was staring in stupefied disbelief and Harris knew they had shared the same delusion.

Deirdre was still shaking a little with laughter. "Well," she demanded, the rich chuckling making her voice quiver, "am I all robot, after all?"

Harris opened his mouth to speak, but he did not utter a word. This was not his show. The byplay lay wholly between Deirdre and Maltzer; he must not interfere. He turned his head to the window and waited.

And Maltzer for a moment seemed shaken in his conviction.

"You . . . you *are* an actress," he admitted slowly. "But . . . I'm not convinced I'm wrong. I think—" He paused. The querulous note was in his voice again, and he seemed racked once more by the old doubts and dismay. Then Harris saw him stiffen. He saw the resolution come back, and understood why it had come. Maltzer had gone too far already upon the cold and lonely path he had chosen to turn back, even for stronger evidence than this. He had reached his conclusions only after mental turmoil too terrible to face again. Safety and peace lay in the course he had steeled himself to follow. He was too tired, too exhausted by months of conflict, to retrace his path and begin all over. Harris could see him groping for a way out, and in a moment he saw him find it.

"That was a trick," he said hollowly. "Maybe you could play it on a larger audience, too. Maybe you have more tricks to use. I might be wrong. But Deirdre"—his voice grew urgent—"you haven't answered the one thing I've got to know.

You can't answer it. You *do* feel—dismay. You've learned your own inadequacy, however well you can hide it from us—even from us. I *know*. Can you deny that, Deirdre?"

She was not laughing now. She let her arms fall, and the flexible golden body seemed to droop a little all over, as if the brain that a moment before had been sending out strong, sure waves of confidence had slackened its power, and the intangible muscles of her limbs slackened with it. Some of the glowing humanity began to fade. It receded within her and was gone, as if the fire in the furnace of her body were sinking and cooling.

"Maltzer," she said uncertainly, "I can't answer that—yet. I can't—"

And then, while they waited in anxiety for her to finish the sentence, she *blazed*. She ceased to be a figure in stasis—she *blazed*.

It was something no eyes could watch and translate into terms the brain could follow; her motion was too swift. Maltzer in the window was a whole long room-length away. He had thought himself safe at such a distance, knowing no normal human being could reach him before he moved. But Deirdre was neither normal nor human.

In the same instant she stood drooping by the mirror she was simultaneously at Maltzer's side. Her motion negated time and destroyed space. And as a glowing cigarette tip in the dark describes closed circles before the eye when the holder moves it swiftly, so Deirdre blazed in one continuous flash of golden motion across the room.

But curiously, she was not blurred. Harris, watching, felt his mind go blank again, but less in surprise than because no normal eyes and brain could perceive what it was he looked at.

(In that moment of intolerable suspense his complex human brain paused suddenly, annihilating time in its own way, and withdrew to a cool corner of its own to analyze in a flashing second what it was he had just seen. The brain could do it timelessly; words are slow. But he knew he had watched a sort of tesseract of human motion, a parable of fourth-dimensional activity. A one-dimensional point, moved through space, creates a two-dimensional line, which in motion creates a three-dimensional cube. Theoretically the cube, in motion, would produce a fourth-dimensional figure. No human creature had ever seen a figure of three dimensions moved through space and time before—until this moment. She had not blurred; every motion she made was distinct, but not like moving figures on a strip of film. Not like anything that those who use our language had ever seen before, or created words to express. The mind saw, but without perceiving. Neither words nor thoughts could resolve what happened into terms for human brains. And perhaps she had not actually and literally moved through the fourth dimension. Perhaps—since Harris was able to see her—it had been almost and not quite that unimaginable thing. But it was close enough.)

While to the slow mind's eye she was still standing at the far end of the room, she was already at Maltzer's side, her long, flexible fingers gentle but very firm upon his arms. She waited—

The room shimmered. There was sudden violent heat beating upon Harris' face. Then the air steadied again and Deirdre was saying softly, in a mournful whisper:

"I'm sorry—I had to do it. I'm sorry—I didn't mean you to know—" Time caught up with Harris. He saw it overtake Maltzer too, saw the man jerk convulsively away from the grasping hands, in a ludicrously futile effort to forestall what had already happened. Even thought was slow, compared with Deirdre's swiftness.

The sharp outward jerk was strong. It was strong enough

to break the grasp of human hands and catapult Maltzer out and down into the swimming gulfs of New York. The mind leaped ahead to a logical conclusion and saw him twisting and turning and diminishing with dreadful rapidity to a tiny point of darkness that dropped away through sunlight toward the shadows near the earth. The mind even conjured up a shrill, thin cry that plummeted away with the falling body and hung behind it in the shaken air.

But the mind was reckoning on human factors.

Very gently and smoothly Deirdre lifted Maltzer from the window sill and with effortless ease carried him well back into the safety of the room. She set him down before a sofa and her golden fingers unwrapped themselves from his arms slowly, so that he could regain control of his own body before she released him.

He sank to the sofa without a word. Nobody spoke for an unmeasurable length of time. Harris could not. Deirdre waited patiently. It was Maltzer who regained speech first, and it came back on the old track, as if his mind had not yet relinquished the rut it had worn so deep.

"All right," he said breathlessly. "All right, you can stop me this time. But I know, you see. I know! You can't hide your feeling from me, Deirdre. I know the trouble you feel. And next time—next time I won't wait to talk!"

Deirdre made the sound of a sigh. She had no lungs to expel the breath she was imitating, but it was hard to realize that. It was hard to understand why she was not panting heavily from the terrible exertion of the past minutes; the mind knew why, but could not accept the reason. She was still too human.

"You still don't see," she said. "Think, Maltzer, think!"

There was a hassock beside the sofa. She sank upon it gracefully, clasping her robed knees. Her head tilted back to watch Maltzer's face. She saw only stunned stupidity on it now; he had passed through too much emotional storm to think at all.

"All right," she told him. "Listen—I'll admit it. You're right. I *am* unhappy. I do know what you said was true—but not for the reason you think. Humanity and I are far apart, and drawing farther. The gap will be hard to bridge. Do you hear me, Maltzer?"

Harris saw the tremendous effort that went into Maltzer's wakening. He saw the man pull his mind back into focus and sit up on the sofa with weary stiffness.

"You . . . you do admit it, then?" he asked in a bewildered voice. Deirdre shook her head sharply.

"Do you still think of me as delicate?" she demanded. "Do you know I carried you here at arm's length halfway across the room? Do you realize you weigh *nothing* to me? I could"—she glanced around the room and gestured with sudden, rather appalling violence—"tear this building down," she said quietly. "I could tear my way through these walls, I think. I've found no limit yet to the strength I can put forth if I try." She held up her golden hands and looked at them. "The metal would break, perhaps," she said reflectively, "but then, I have no feeling—"

Maltzer gasped, "*Deirdre—*"

She looked up with what must have been a smile. It sounded clearly in her voice. "Oh, I won't. I wouldn't have to do it with my hands, if I wanted. Look—listen!"

She put her head back and a deep, vibrating hum gathered and grew in what one still thought of as her throat. It deepened swiftly and the ears began to ring. It was deeper, and the furniture vibrated. The walls began almost imperceptibly to shake. The room was full and bursting with a sound that shook every atom upon its neighbor with a terrible, disrupting force.

The sound ceased. The humming died. Then Deirdre

laughed and made another and quite differently pitched sound. It seemed to reach out like an arm in one straight direction—toward the window. The opened panel shook. Deirdre intensified her hum, and slowly, with imperceptible jolts that merged into smoothness, the window jarred itself shut.

"You see?" Deirdre said. "You see?"

But still Maltzer could only stare. Harris was staring too, his mind beginning slowly to accept what she implied. Both were too stunned to leap ahead to any conclusions yet.

Deirdre rose impatiently and began to pace again, in a ringing of metal robe and a twinkling of reflected lights. She was pantherlike in her suppleness. They could see the power behind that lithe motion now; they no longer thought of her as helpless, but they were far still from grasping the truth.

"You were wrong about me, Maltzer," she said with an effort at patience in her voice. "But you were right too, in a way you didn't guess. I'm not afraid of humanity. I haven't anything to fear from them. Why"—her voice took on a tinge of contempt—"already I've set a fashion in women's clothing. By next week you won't see a woman on the street without a mask like mine, and every dress that isn't cut like a chlamys will be out of style. I'm not afraid of humanity! I won't lose touch with them unless I want to. I've learned a lot—I've learned too much already."

Her voice faded for a moment, and Harris had a quick and appalling vision of her experimenting in the solitude of her farm, testing the range of her voice, testing her eyesight—could she see microscopically and telescopically?—and was her hearing as abnormally flexible as her voice?

"You were afraid I had lost feeling and scent and taste," she went on, still pacing with that powerful, tigerish tread. "Hearing and sight would not be enough, you think? But why do you think sight is the last of the senses? It may be the latest, Maltzer—Harris—*but why do you think it's the last?*"

She may not have whispered that. Perhaps it was only their hearing that made it seem thin and distant, as the brain contracted and would not let the thought come through in its stunning entirety.

"No," Deirdre said, "I haven't lost contact with the human race. I never will, unless I want to. It's too easy . . . too easy."

She was watching her shining feet as she paced, and her masked face was averted. Sorrow sounded in her soft voice now.

"I didn't mean to let you know," she said. "I never would have, if this hadn't happened. But I couldn't let you go believing you'd failed. You made a perfect machine, Maltzer. More perfect than you knew."

"But Deirdre—" breathed Maltzer, his eyes fascinated and still incredulous upon her, "but Deirdre, if we did succeed— what's wrong? I can feel it now—I've felt it all along. You're so unhappy—you still are. Why, Deirdre?"

She lifted her head and looked at him, eyelessly, but with a piercing stare.

"Why are you so sure of that?" she asked gently.

"You think I could be mistaken, knowing you as I do? But I'm not Frankenstein . . . you say my creation's flawless. Then what—"

"Could you ever duplicate this body?" she asked.

Maltzer glanced down at his shaking hands. "I don't know. I doubt it. I—"

"Could anyone else?"

He was silent. Deirdre answered for him. "I don't believe anyone could. I think I was an accident. A sort of mutation halfway between flesh and metal. Something accidental and . . . and unnatural, turning off on a wrong course of evolution that never reaches a dead end. Another brain in a body like this might die or go mad, as you thought I would. The synapses are too delicate. You were—

call it lucky—with me. From what I know now, I don't think a . . . a baroque like me could happen again." She paused a moment. "What you did was kindle the fire for the Phoenix, in a way. And the Phoenix rises perfect and renewed from its own ashes. Do you remember why it had to reproduce itself that way?"

Maltzer shook his head.

"I'll tell you," she said. "It was because there was only one Phoenix. Only one in the whole world."

They looked at each other in silence. Then Deirdre shrugged a little.

"He always came out of the fire perfect, of course. I'm not weak, Maltzer. You needn't let that thought bother you any more. I'm not vulnerable and helpless. I'm not sub-human." She laughed dryly. "I suppose," she said, "that I'm—superhuman."

"But—not happy."

"I'm afraid. It isn't unhappiness, Maltzer—it's fear. I don't want to draw so far away from the human race. I wish I needn't. That's why I'm going back on the stage—to keep in touch with them while I can. But I wish there could be others like me. I'm . . . I'm lonely, Maltzer."

Silence again. Then Maltzer said, in a voice as distant as when he had spoken to them through glass, over gulfs as deep as oblivion:

"Then I am Frankenstein, after all."

"Perhaps you are," Deirdre said very softly. "I don't know. Perhaps you are."

She turned away and moved smoothly, powerfully, down the room to the window. Now that Harris knew, he could almost hear the sheer power purring along her limbs as she walked. She leaned the golden forehead against the glass—it clinked faintly, with a musical sound—and looked down into the depths Maltzer had hung above. Her voice was reflective as she looked into those dizzy spaces which had offered oblivion to her creator.

"There's one limit I can think of," she said, almost inaudibly. "Only one. My brain will wear out in another forty years or so. Between now and then I'll learn . . . I'll change . . . I'll know more than I can guess today. I'll change—That's frightening. I don't like to think about that." She laid a curved golden hand on the latch and pushed the window open a little, very easily. Wind whined around its edge. "I could put a stop to it now, if I wanted," she said. "If I wanted. But I can't, really. There's so much still untried. My brain's human, and no human brain could leave such possibilities untested. I wonder, though . . . I do wonder—"

Her voice was soft and familiar in Harris' ears, the voice Deirdre had spoken and sung with, sweetly enough to enchant a world. But as preoccupation came over her a certain flatness crept into the sound. When she was not listening to her own voice, it did not keep quite to the pitch of trueness. It sounded as if she spoke in a room of brass, and echoes from the walls resounded in the tones that spoke there.

"I wonder," she repeated, the distant taint of metal already in her voice.

NO WOMAN BORN:
FLOWING FROM RING TO RING

The ideal science-fiction story begins with a strikingly original speculative premise, which is rigorously developed to the limit of its probable consequences while the story's plot, or pattern of human conflicts, is moving through a series of ingeniously devised complications toward its resolution. That resolution should provide a satisfying conclusion not only to the problems of the protagonists but to the speculative thesis that the story is meant to propound. And, of course, the story should be written with grace, elegance, a deep understanding of human (or, if necessary, nonhuman) psychology, a keen eye for imagery, and a sharp ear for the rhythms of dialog and prose exposition.

Or so I believe. Certainly that's what I set out to do every time I begin a story; and if I keep after it long enough, maybe I'll achieve it sooner or later. In the real world it's usually necessary to settle for less. There's only so much that a writer can accomplish in five or ten thousand words. The speculative premise, if it's developed with real rigor, is apt to crowd out characterization. Conversely, to delve deep into the souls of a story's characters may cut into the space available for the exposition of the premise; or else close attention to character development will require some reduction of subplot development. And so on and so on. The beginning writer—me, for instance, circa 1953—often wants to tackle everything at once, and cram whole novels into five thousand words. The professional understands the limitations of the form, and works toward a single primary effect in each story.

Thus we've already seen how Damon Knight was able to turn an old-hat idea (monster eats man) into a fresh one by the careful working out of the consequences of that idea, and so to write an admirable story using characters who aren't much more than clusters of broadly differentiated standard traits. Deep penetration of personality profiles would have been beside the point. We've seen Alfred Bester generate something unforgettable out of another old idea (artificial human being turns killer), some dazzling imagery, a few haunting repetitive tag lines, and the wondrous manipulation of point of view. Decorating the story with elaborate extrapolative subplot material dramatizing the changes in human society that the development of androids and robots had caused might have been a good strategy if Bester had been writing a novel, but it probably would have fatally cluttered "Fondly Fahrenheit"; likewise dragging in a vengeful detective who had a score to settle with Vandaleur, or providing us with extensive detail about Vandaleur's three failed marriages.

And now we come to C. L. Moore's masterpiece "No Woman Born," a story notable neither for originality of idea nor complexity of plot, which nevertheless succeeds magnificently by achieving extraordinary richness of vision and emotion, conveyed through supple, beautifully modulated prose. Where Knight and Bester overwhelm you (in very different ways) with sheer cleverness, Moore charms and captivates you with a sensitivity of perception that reflects itself in the sensitivity of her writing.

Her writing, yes. Moore is actually Catherine Lucile Moore, the first significant female science-fiction writer of the twentieth century, and a figure of immense historical importance in the development of modern American science fiction.

Until fairly recent times women were not a visible presence on the science-fiction scene. Mary Shelley's *Frankenstein* of 1818 can legitimately be considered the first true science-fiction novel of the modern era, but few women followed her lead. When science fiction emerged as a popular commercial form early in the twentieth century, it was written and edited almost entirely by men, for a largely male audience. This was, I suspect, partly the effect of sexual stereotyping: since science was not considered a proper field for study for young women, fiction about science was not likely to attract the interest of many female writers or readers. But there was also a self-fulfilling aspect to this exclusionary principle. Because science fiction in the first half of the twentieth century was written mainly by and for male readers, most of what was published tended to be either male-oriented action fiction or the bloodless, emotionless, wiring-diagram fiction of the Hugo Gernsback school. Either way, women weren't likely to be attracted to such stuff. In general, women seem to prefer fiction of some emotional depth, so the stories in Gernsback's *Amazing Stories* and *Wonder Stories* of fifty years ago would have bored them silly. The men in those stories were either slab-jawed heroes or else stiff-jointed puppets who delivered scientific lectures, and the women, when there were any, were fluttery little things who ran about shrieking and screaming to be rescued from monsters.

When 22-year-old Catherine Moore began writing professionally in 1933, she chose to conceal her sex behind those impersonal initials, perhaps because she thought she stood a better chance of getting published that way. Nor did what she write bear much resemblance to the magazine s-f of her day. Her first few stories, which starred the rugged soldier of fortune Northwest Smith, appeared at first glance to make use of the modes of male adventure fiction. But Smith's adventures on other worlds, rich in color and romantic mystery, had more in common with the tales of Poe or Lovecraft than they did with the dry, mechanical fiction of the science-fiction magazines of that period. Nor did Moore appear often in those magazines; most of her early work was published not in *Wonder* or *Amazing* but in *Weird Tales*, a magazine that included some science fiction but that embraced all other branches of fantasy fiction as well. And soon she moved away from Northwest Smith toward eerie fantasy with a female protagonist, using the Amazonlike Jirel of Joiry as her heroine.

Moore's work was surprisingly popular with the science-fiction audience, which seems to have had little or no inkling of her true sex. As late as 1938, when the gifted young s-f writer Henry Kuttner began writing to her, he addressed his letters to *Mr.* C. L. Moore. But Kuttner soon was set straight on that score, and in 1940 he and Moore were married, inaugurating one of the most fruitful husband-and-wife collaborations in literary history.

Kuttner was prolific, versatile, clever, and technically adept. His stories were tightly constructed, but most of them prior to his marriage to Moore tended to be little more than facile pulp-magazine stuff. Moore's early work depended more on emotional intensity and evocative coloration than on intricacy of plot or swiftness of action; her stories were long and moody and slow, and often culminated in a swirl of powerful but impenetrable strangeness that defied rational analysis. Each writer thus complemented the other; and when they worked as collaborators they were triumphantly able to merge their strongest talents and produce fiction superior to anything either had done alone. That their work is largely out of print today is both saddening and perplexing to me. There were no science-fiction writers I studied more closely, in that enormously formative period of my late teens, than C. L. Moore and Henry Kuttner. In everything they wrote—even the stories that Kuttner seemed to have tossed off in an hour or two before lunch to pay the rent—they seemed supremely in command of their craft. I still feel that way about them; and I still go back often to read with pleasure, and to ponder, the myriad stories they produced singly and in collaboration.

It is difficult and dangerous to try to figure out who wrote what in the Kuttner-Moore canon. Apparently, virtually everything that either one published from the time of their marriage until Kuttner's early death in 1958 was to some extent a joint work. The byline is no clue. Most of their work was published under pseudonyms—Lawrence O'Donnell, Lewis Padgett, Keith Hammond, and a dozen more. It is easy enough to say that the richer, warmer stories are Moore's and the quick, clever ones are Kuttner's, but it seems more probable that scarcely any story left their household without having been jointly planned, written, and revised. Trying to identify distinctive Kuttner or Moore traits is almost hopeless. *Fury*, a novel that bore the O'Donnell pseudonym when it was serialized in a magazine, is thought by students of this remarkable team to be largely Kuttner's work, and was published under Kuttner's name alone when it appeared in book form. It is a sequel to the O'Donnell story "Clash by Night," which is thought to have been written mainly by Moore. Yet *Fury* has more of a Moore tone to it than the earlier story. Had he so fully absorbed her style by then that he could speak in her voice, or did she have a hand in the story? We'll probably never know. Even the stories published under Kuttner's name alone may well have been collaborations, though it seems somewhat more likely that those published after 1940 that carried Moore's byline alone were primarily her work. Byline credit seems to have been a matter of little importance to them for most of the eighteen years they worked together. Toward the end, though, it created in them what they called the "who-am-I?" syndrome, and they resolved to abandon pseudonyms entirely and to identify all new stories either as individually written or as by Kuttner and Moore. One last book of short stories appeared under the double byline; after Kuttner's death Moore published no further books or stories, turning her efforts instead entirely to writing television scripts.

Despite all these problems, there seems little doubt that "No Woman Born" is essentially or totally Moore's work. The superficial evidence indicates that: it is one of only six stories published under her own name during her years with Kuttner, and she included it in the 1975 collection, *The Best of C. L. Moore*. The internal evidence is convincing also. Kuttner may have had a role in its planning, may even—as I will note—have written a paragraph or two. But in pace and structure the story seems fundamentally Moore's work. And in its underlying theme—the emergence of a powerful female protagonist who in her struggle for survival comes to threaten and even dominate the male characters—it hearkens back to such prototypical Moore figures as Jirel and the vampire Shambleau of the early fantasies.

Science fiction in 1944, when "No Woman Born" was first published in John Campbell's *Astounding Science Fiction*, still was deeply rooted in pulp-magazine narrative traditions. The typical pulp story began fast, with the hero in deep trouble, and zipped along in a series of quick scenes constructed out of physical action and a great deal of dialog until it reached its climax and resolution. For instance:

> Kent Mason stumbled to the top of the ridge, staring about him with sun-swollen eyes. His cracked lips twisted wryly as he viewed the endless wilderness of rock, the death-trap of the Arabian desert, dimmed now by driving gusts of icy

rain. In the valley below him two pinnacles of rock towered, and as Mason stared at them a curious expression crept over his sunburned face. He recognized those great obelisks, and, recognizing them, knew that his search and his life would end almost simultaneously. For before him lay the fabulous twin towers of the lost city of Al Bekr, ancient metropolis of lost wisdom, City of Science!

Or this:

"You say you come from the future," Mason whispered, gripping the woman's wrists. "How do I know what—creatures may exist then?"

She caught the implication. Fury blazed in the jet eyes. She tore free, sprang back, shrilled an angry command.

"Slay him, Bokya—*slay!*"

That's 24-year-old Henry Kuttner, paying the rent with a potboiler called "The Time Trap" in the November, 1938, issue of a minor and short-lived pulp magazine, *Marvel Science Stories.* Once magazine science fiction had emerged in the mid-1930s from the stiltedness of the Gernsback era, much of it sounded like that. Campbell's *Astounding*, whose chief contributors were such talented young writers as Robert A. Heinlein, Isaac Asimov, Theodore Sturgeon, L. Ron Hubbard, and L. Sprague de Camp, was an honorable exception: Campbell despised the idiocies of pulp fiction and urged his writers to produce the sort of mature copy that such slick magazines as *The Saturday Evening Post* or *The New Yorker* might want to publish in the year 2150. (Kuttner's work appeared frequently in *Astounding*, but he would never have dared to offer Campbell anything as absurd as "The Time Trap.") Yet the stories Campbell published, though far beyond the standard pulp item in concept and technique, generally still made use, in disguised and improved form, of the melodramatic conflicts and stock reactions of the pulp magazines, and the writing, though clean and efficient, rarely rose far above the level of simple functional prose.

But there's little about "No Woman Born" to connect it to the pulp-magazine tradition. It must have seemed something of an oddity to the readers of *Astounding* then, as it did to me a few years later when I encountered it in an anthology: a story that paid little heed to the requirements of plot and pace typical of the science fiction of the day, but concentrated instead, in a leisurely and sensuous way, on the analysis of the transformation of a woman's character under the stress of a uniquely science-fictional situation.

Though it is a long story, perhaps ten thousand words, it is strikingly simple in its construction: there is no overt conflict, no banging together of opposing forces to generate action, only the steadily growing awareness that something has gone wrong with Deirdre's resurrection. The nominal protagonist, John Harris, is merely an observer, a point of view through which the events are filtered: he is almost invisible. Harris is stunned and dismayed by what he sees of the new Deirdre, but he is not in any significant way altered by it, since we don't see enough of him to register change in him. The true protagonist, the one who suffers and changes, is Deirdre; but Moore keeps her at a distance. And both her suffering and her changing have taken place *before* the actual story; the story is the revelation of what has already happened. That is the antithesis of pulp fiction, which thrives on immediacy.

Moore might have chosen to generate an orthodox plot by setting up conflict between Deirdre and Harris: he is deeply shocked by what he sees, let us say, and he tries to prevent her from revealing herself on stage, but at the last moment he is defeated in that by her superior cunning. Or he succeeds in thwarting her stage debut and must live thereafter with guilt and doubt. Or perhaps Deirdre is the one unwilling to go on stage, and Harris, motivated by greed or the lust for fame, pushes her forward into a fiasco. Any of those would have worked, more or less, in a conventional magazine story. But Moore has other purposes in mind. Her goal is to create mood, to leave us with a sense of the utter strangeness and isolation of the resurrected Deirdre ("The time comes when our hearts sink utterly/ When we remember Deirdre and her tale," she tells us, quoting James Stephens, seven paragraphs into her story) rather than spin a quick, bouncy tale of show-biz razzmatazz. With slow, subtle touches she will build her portrait of her artificial woman; and to have opted for a complicated plot would have made it difficult for her to achieve the story's voluptuous psychological richness as well except by working on a much larger scale.

Still, "No Woman Born" is twice as long as the average magazine story, and at that length it needs some sort of subplot to support its own voluptuousness. The Maltzer theme—the scientist aghast at what he has done—serves that function for Moore. (Learning the art of subplotting is one of the most difficult aspects of mastering the craft. Certainly, I found it so. But it's hard to sustain any work of fiction longer than the short story without one or more subordinate story lines that illuminate and comment on the main story line while providing necessary distraction from it. Ideally, subplot and main plot should converge at the climax, each resolving the other; but that's easier to prescribe than to achieve.) Because the main plot itself is so deeply submerged, the Maltzer element must be handled similarly, and so we see him only as a figure reacting to the Deirdre events; as in the case of Harris, the story's only other character, Maltzer is never seen engaging in action that seems in any way unrelated to Deirdre. (One perfectly valid way to tell a story is to show independent characters engaged in apparently unrelated actions that gradually converge. But not this story.)

When I say "action," incidentally, I don't mean physical action of the kind dear to the pulp magazines—chases, hand-to-hand combat, desperate swims across turbulent rivers. I use "action" here in a more technical sense, to indicate the working out of a pattern of events. Maltzer's being called before a committee of doctors to be censured for his work on Deirdre would be an "action" in that sense; but there is nothing like it in "No Woman Born."

There's virtually nothing in the way of simple physical action, either—a full choreography of gestures, yes, but no more than that. The main events of the story are interior ones: psychological transitions, changes in ways of seeing the situation. The one exception is the moment when Deirdre interferes with Maltzer's suicide attempt, when we comprehend her at last in her full superhuman condition. Those five or six pages in which the troubled scientist stands by the open window, plainly preparing to jump, represent Moore's lone concession to the requirements for conventional narrative suspense, too. Rereading the story now, I'm not entirely comfortable with that scene; I suspect that the tense and jangled Maltzer, once he had resolved to commit suicide, would probably have done it in a quick impulsive leap when he was alone, rather than sticking around to deliver a farewell oration to Deirdre and Harris. But sometimes even a writer as good as C. L. Moore needs to manipulate psychological probabilities a little for story purposes. The story—for a newsstand magazine of 1944—could not have been left wholly without conventional action or suspense. Maltzer had to have an opportunity to make his reasons for suicide explicit. ("I can't live and watch you. I put all my skill and all my love in one final masterpiece, and I can't bear to watch it destroyed.") And Moore had to have some way of demonstrating the full alienness of Deirdre's new body. So he will threaten to jump, and then he *will* jump, and she will pull him back; and the story will have its climax. Deirdre, who has just said, "I'm human. Do you think I'm not?" is revealed as something not at all human. And then comes the descent into the acceptance by Maltzer that he has created a monster, and the culminating perception by Harris that what little of humanity there is left in Deirdre may well be absorbed by the metal house in which she lives.

What carries the story, then, is neither the intricacy of its plot nor the swiftness of its events. Moore's psychological insight, manifested in supple and graceful writing, is what holds the reader's interest. One cannot separate the beauty of the prose from the complexity of what is told; the one grows inevitably out of the other.

There is no way that Deirdre's story could have been conveyed in the brisk pulp style ("Fear gripped Mason. He sprang forward, tried to reach the valve. If he could manage to stuff it closed—but it was too high. . . .") of Kuttner's cheerful hackwork for *Marvel Science Stories*.

The level of writing in "No Woman Born" had never, I think, been reached in a science-fiction magazine before. It marks Moore not only as a distinguished artist but as a great innovator within her field, willing to take risks with her audience. Consider the range of emotional depth, the breadth of vocabulary, the command of extended metaphor, and the rhythmic control of lengthy sentences in this passage from "No Woman Born":

> Oddly enough, he did not once think of the naked brain that must be inside the metal. The mask was symbol enough for the woman within. It was enigmatic; you did not know if her gaze was on you searchingly, or wholly withdrawn. And it had no variations of brilliance such as once had played across the incomparable mobility of Deirdre's face. But eyes, even human eyes, are as a matter of fact enigmatic enough. They have no expression except what the lids impart; they take all animation from the features. We automatically watch the eyes of the friend we speak with, but if he happens to be lying down so that he speaks across the shoulder and his face is upside-down to us, quite as automatically we watch the mouth. The gaze keeps shifting nervously between mouth and eyes in their reversed order, for it is the position in the face, not the feature itself, which we are accustomed to accept as the seat of the soul. Deirdre's mask was in that proper place; it was easy to accept it as a mask over eyes.

The fluency of Moore's writing is extraordinary. Here she displays it in a passage that at once defines Deirdre's character, offers

a novel and pleasing technological rationale to explain the new body
that has been created for her, and delights the demanding reader with
a series of quick, vivid images:

> "Luckily," she said, her voice amused, "I never was beau-
> tiful. It was all—well, vivacity, I suppose, and muscular co-
> ordination. Years and years of training, and all of it engraved
> here"—she struck her golden helmet a light, ringing blow
> with golden knuckles—"in the habit patterns grooved into
> my brain. So this body . . . did he tell you? . . . works en-
> tirely through the brain. Electromagnetic currents flowing
> along from ring to ring, like this." She rippled a boneless
> arm at him with a motion like flowing water. "Nothing holds
> me together—nothing!—except muscles of magnetic cur-
> rents. And if I'd been somebody else—somebody who
> moved differently, why the flexible rings would have moved
> differently too, guided by the impulse from another brain.
> I'm not conscious of doing anything I haven't always done.
> The same impulses that used to go out to my muscles go
> out now to—this!" And she made a shuttering, serpentine
> motion of both arms at him, like a Cambodian dancer, and
> then laughed wholeheartedly, the sound of it ringing
> through the room with such full-throated merriment that he
> could not help seeing again the familiar face crinkled with
> pleasure, the white teeth shining.

How I admire that paragraph! How I envy it! The little sensory
details: the golden helmet, the golden knuckles, the light, *ringing*
blow. The *boneless* arm that ripples *like flowing water*. She makes
us see Deirdre; and she makes us feel the force and presence of her
personality, too, in everything that she says or does.

The story opens calmly, in underplayed fashion. Some horror
may await Harris, but he can think only of her lost beauty as he
prepares to see the rebuilt Deirdre for the first time. Moore uses the

memory of that beauty—and the James Stephens poem—to weave a spell for us that will hold us throughout the story.

Then Maltzer enters, and at once there is dissonance. We don't know who Maltzer is or what his role in the story might be, but we feel, after one paragraph of description, that we know *him*. The tension in Maltzer travels first to Harris and then to us.

After an unhurried buildup—the opening scene of the story is enormously long, longer than most complete short stories, one gigantic fluid demonstration of the art of exposition—Deirdre appears. "She had no face. She had only a smooth, delicately modeled ovoid for her head." It is a brilliant stroke to make her unhuman but beautiful. How much more obvious it would have been for Maltzer—and Moore—to have put her into some lovely android replica of her former self; but how much less powerful. This way she is both strange and even more beautiful than she had been, and the story springs from that. The other way, she would have been a mere museum reproduction of herself, and once Harris had regretted the unreality of the reproduction, what would have been left to say that would be of any interest?

The proportions of the story are unconventional. The opening scene occupies nearly half the story's length, and hardly anything "happens" in it; for a writer that is a great gamble, but Moore holds us by the force of her writing and by the close focus on the fascinating, eerie Deirdre as she gradually manifests herself to the observer-protagonist Harris. An orthodox magazine story would have given us plot and counterplot, three or four changes of scene, and half a dozen characters in that span. None of that matters to Moore, nor does it to us. The story moves onward toward the new Deirdre's debut, the anguish of Maltzer, and the culminating revelation, with its hint of the fate that will overcome Deirdre eventually. Science (that is, the speculative idea of a humanoid reconstruction of a damaged body) and fiction are perfectly blended here: the fascinating and charming Deirdre has been transformed into something much more fascinating and rather less charming, and Moore has generated a powerful story *that could have been told in no other medium but science fiction.* There is no way to translate "No Woman Born" into mundane fiction; its effect is inseparable from its speculative theme.

There are, I feel almost abashed to point out, a few small areas of imperfection in "No Woman Born." I say this in fear and trembling, since this is a story I revere, and the supreme technical mastery of both Moore and Kuttner has been an article of faith for me for decades. But reading it for the fifth or sixth time almost forty years after first encountering it, I found some little things that bothered me. I cite them here not for the sake of showing how clever I am but simply because I think it's unwise to let examples of bad practice go without comment, even when they turn up in the work of so adept a practitioner as C. L. Moore.

For example, there is the parenthetical paragraph about a third of the way through the story: "(And providing, of course, that the mind inside the metal did not veer from its inherited humanity as the years went by. A dweller in a house may impress his personality upon the walls, but subtly the walls, too, may impress their own shape upon the ego of the man. Neither of them thought of that, at the time.)"

It is a passage intended to foreshadow the control that Deirdre's new body will ultimately exert over her mind. I'm not at all convinced that that point needs to be foreshadowed so bluntly. Better, perhaps, merely to have allowed it to emerge from the behavior of the characters as the story goes along, and not to underscore it like this. But the real technical sin of that paragraph is the last sentence, "Neither of them thought of that, at the time." The story is told from Harris' viewpoint throughout: Harris realizes this, Harris is surprised at that, Harris hesitates, Harris looks, Harris looks away. Every event is filtered through Harris' perceptions; every shade of meaning is conveyed to us by showing it registering on Harris. That is what viewpoint means. When Maltzer is shown reacting, we never get his inner feelings but only Harris' speculations about those feelings: "Maltzer for a moment *seemed* shaken in his conviction," or "[Harris] saw the man pull his mind back into focus," or "Maltzer went on hurriedly, as *if* afraid of an answer."

This rigorous adherence to a single point of view, though the reader may be wholly unaware of it, helps greatly to build the power and intensity of a story. As I noted in discussing Bester's "Fondly Fahrenheit," it is common to shift from one point of view to another as a story goes along, but few experienced writers will do it within any one scene, and most will stick to the same viewpoint throughout a short story. A sudden viewpoint shift can jar a reader—even one unaware of the technical aspects of what he is reading—and puncture the illusion of reality that the writer is trying to weave. Moore was aware of that, of course, and all those "as ifs" and "seemeds" are her way of letting us know what is probably going on in Maltzer's mind or in Deirdre's without overtly leaving Harris' point of view. Which makes it all the more puzzling when she suddenly leaps out of Harris' mind to nudge us in the ribs with a comment of her own, telling us something that Harris does not yet realize, *and telling us that he doesn't realize it.* From any writer that would be a needless intrusion; from Moore it seems mystifying.

A second troublesome point comes two thirds of the way through, when Harris, just after Deirdre's performance, asks himself if she has "put on a strange, metallic something of the mind," and the next day, when speaking to her, notes that "her voice was a bit metallic for the first time." This, I think, badly undermines the impact of the story's superb final sentence when it finally arrives many pages later. There's no need to emphasize in so overt a way Deirdre's gradual robotification: every event of the story is designed to show us what is happening. We can see her changing without needing to be told explicitly that Maltzer's remarkable contrivance is invading her soul. When Moore shows us at the end "the distant taint of metal already in her voice," that sinister infiltration of humanity by the machine in which she lives is rendered less powerful because we've encountered the same metaphor two or three times already. Instead of closing the story with an inexorable clang, it merely reiterates what we've previously heard.

Finally, I wonder about another intrusive parenthetical paragraph, the bit of gobbledygook about the fourth dimension in the moment before Deirdre rescues Maltzer. It is my guess, substantiated by nothing at all, that Henry Kuttner must have inserted that paragraph while Moore was occupied elsewhere, thinking to add a bit of extra science-fictional effect to keep John Campbell and his readers happy and perhaps to heighten the suspense of the moment. Whoever wrote it, though, I wish Moore had cut it from the final draft. It doesn't do much for the suspense, which is already extreme, and it drops an impenetrable lump of jargony speculation into the story that is quite unlikely to have passed through John Harris' mind just at the moment that Maltzer was gearing up to jump out the window.

So this magnificent story has, for me, a couple of little flaws. The hypothesis I offered about "Fondly Fahrenheit" 's one very minor technical glitch applies here too: perhaps it's necessary to placate the gods by weaving a few imperfections into any pattern. They aren't significant to anyone's appreciation of the story, and I cite them here only as a way of making certain points about the technique of story construction as I understand it. Certainly, I didn't notice them on my first reading of "No Woman Born" in 1948, and I doubt that they troubled me much on subsequent readings.

There was much that I learned from poring over "No Woman Born" and other C. L. Moore stories, but it wasn't anything that I could put to direct use in the early years of my career. She simply wrote too well. Those noble rhythms of speech and that strong command of language sprang not only from years of practice that I had not had, but also from a far richer experience of life. I think it's valuable practice for a very young writer to imitate writers he respects, but I would have looked silly trying to imitate C. L. Moore: her sensibility was too far removed from my own. I wrote dozens of imitations of Kuttner stories, though—"The Iron Chancellor," about a robot that imposes a near-fatal crash diet on the family it serves, is the first to spring to mind—and I learned plenty from the exercise. Moore was beyond my range. I could only admire her work and use it as a glowing example. I still do.

HOME IS THE HUNTER
HENRY KUTTNER

There's nobody I can talk to except myself. I stand here at the head of the great waterfall of marble steps dropping into the reception hall below, and all my wives in all their jewels are waiting, for this is a Hunter's Triumph—my Triumph, Honest Roger Bellamy, Hunter. The light glitters on the glass cases down there with the hundreds of dried heads that I have taken in fair combat, and I'm one of the most powerful men in New York. The heads make me powerful.

But there's nobody I can talk to. Except myself? Inside me, listening, is there another Honest Roger Bellamy? I don't know. Maybe he's the only real part of me. I go along the best I can, and it doesn't do any good. Maybe the Bellamy inside of me doesn't like what I do. But I have to do it. I can't stop. I was born a Head-Hunter. It's a great heritage to be born to. Who doesn't envy me? Who wouldn't change with me, if they could?

But it doesn't do any good at all.

I'm no good.

Listen to me, Bellamy, listen to me, if you're there at all, deep inside my head. You've got to listen—you've got to understand. You there inside the skull. You can turn up in a glass case in some other Head-Hunter's reception hall any day now, any day, with the crowds of populi outside pressing against the view-windows and the guests coming in to see and envy and all the wives standing by in satin and jewels.

Maybe you don't understand, Bellamy. You should feel fine now. It must be that you don't know this real world I have to go on living in. A hundred years ago, or a thousand, it might have been different. But this is the twenty-first century. It's today, it's now, and there's no turning back.

I don't think you understand.

You see, there isn't any choice. Either you end up in another Head-Hunter's glass case, along with your whole collection, while your wives and children are turned out to be populi, or else you die naturally (suicide is one way) and your eldest son inherits your collection, and you become immortal, in a plastic monument. You stand forever in transparent plastic on a pedestal along the edge of Central Park, like Renway and old Falconer and Brennan and all the others. Everyone remembers and admires and envies you.

Will you keep on thinking then, Bellamy, inside the plastic? Will I?

Falconer was a great Hunter. He never slowed down, and he lived to be fifty-two. For a Head-Hunter, that is a great old age. There are stories that he killed himself. I don't know. The wonder is that he kept his head on his shoulders for fifty-two years. The competition is growing harder, and there are more and more younger men these days.

Listen to me, Bellamy, the Bellamy within. Have you ever really understood? Do you still think this is the wonderful young time, the boyhood time when life is easy? Were you ever with me in the long, merciless years while my body and mind learned to be a Head-Hunter? I'm still young and strong. My training has never stopped. But the early years were the hardest.

Before then, there was the wonderful time. It lasted for six years only, six years of happiness and warmth and love with my mother in the harem, and the foster mothers and the other children. My father was very kind then. But when I was six, it stopped. They shouldn't have taught us love at all, if it had to end so soon. Is it that you remember, Bellamy within? If it is, it can never come back. You know that. Surely you know it.

The roots of the training were obedience and discipline. My father was not kind any more. I did not see my mother often, and when I did she was changed, too. Still, there was praise. There were the parades when the populi cheered me and my father. He and the trainers praised me, too, when I showed I had special skill in the duel, or in marksmanship or judo-stalking.

It was forbidden, but my brothers and I sometimes tried to kill each other. The trainers watched us carefully. I was not the heir, then. But I became the heir when my elder brother's neck was broken in a judo-fall. It seemed an accident, but of course it wasn't, and then I had to be more careful than ever. I had to become very skillful.

All that time, all that painful time, learning to kill. It was natural. They kept telling us how natural it was. We had to learn. And there could be only one heir. . . .

We lived under a cloud of fear, even then. If my father's head had been taken, we would all have been turned out of the mansion. Oh, we wouldn't have gone hungry or unsheltered. Not in this age of science. But not to be a Head-Hunter! Not to become immortal, in a plastic monument standing by Central Park!

Sometimes I dream that I am one of the populi. It seems strange, but in the dream I am hungry. And that is impossible. The great power plants supply all the world needs. Machines synthesize food and build houses and give us all the necessities of life. I could never be one of the populi, but if I were I would go into a restaurant and take whatever food I wished out of the little glass-fronted cubbyholes. I would eat well—far better than I eat now. And yet, in my dream, I am hungry.

Perhaps the food I eat does not satisfy you, Bellamy within me. It does not satisfy me, but it is not meant to. It is nutritious. Its taste is unpleasant, but all the necessary proteins and minerals and vitamins are in it to keep my brain and body at their highest pitch. And it should not be pleasant. It is not pleasure that leads a man to immortality in plastic. Pleasure is a weakening and an evil thing.

Bellamy within—do you hate me?

My life has not been easy. It isn't easy now. The stubborn flesh fights against the immortal future, urging a man to be weak. But if you are weak, how long can you hope to keep your head on your shoulders?

The populi sleep with their wives. I have never even kissed any of mine. (Is it you who have sent me dreams?) My children?—yes, they are mine; artificial insemination is the answer. I sleep on a hard bed. Sometimes I wear a hair shirt. I drink only water. My food is tasteless. With my trainers I exercise every day, until I am very tired. The life is hard—but in the end we shall stand forever in a plastic monument, you and I, while the world envies and admires. I shall die a Head-Hunter, and I shall be immortal.

The proof is in the glass cases down there in my reception hall. The heads, the heads—look, Bellamy, so many heads. Stratton, my first. I killed him in Central Park with a machete. This is the scar on my temple that he gave me that night. I learned to be defter. I had to.

Each time I went into Central Park, fear and hate helped

me. Sometimes it is dreadful in the Park. We go there only at night, and sometimes we stalk for many nights before we take a head. The Park is forbidden, you know, to all but Head-Hunters. It is our hunting ground.

I have been shrewd and cunning and skillful. I have shown great courage. I have stopped my fears and nursed my hate, there in the Park's shadows, listening, waiting, stalking, never knowing when I might feel sharp steel burning through my throat. There are no rules in the Park. Guns or clubs or knives—once I was caught in a mantrap, all steel and cables and sharp teeth. But I had moved in time, and fast enough, so I kept my right hand free and shot Miller between the eyes when he came to take me. There is Miller's head down there. You would never know a bullet had gone through his forehead. The thanatologists are clever. But usually we try not to spoil the heads.

What is it that troubles you so, Bellamy within? I am one of the greatest Hunters in New York. But a man must be cunning. He must lay traps and snares a long way in advance, and not only in Central Park. He must keep his spies active and his lines of contact taut in every mansion in the city. He must know who is powerful and who is not worth taking. What good would it do to win against a Hunter with only a dozen heads in his hall?

I have hundreds. Until yesterday, I stood ahead of every man in my age group. Until yesterday I was the envy of all I knew, the idol of the populi, the acknowledged master of half New York. Half New York! Do you know how much that meant to me? That my rivals loathed me and acknowledged me their better? You do know, Bellamy. It was the breath of life that True Jonathan Hull and Good Ben Griswold ground their teeth when they thought of me, and that Black Bill Lindman and Whistler Cowles counted their trophies and then called me on the TV phone and begged me with tears of hate and fury in their eyes to meet them in the Park and give them the chance they craved.

I laughed at them. I laughed Black Bill Lindman into a berserker rage and then half-envied him, because I have not been berserker myself for a long while now. I like that wild unloosening of all my awarenesses but one—the killing instinct, blind and without reason. I could forget even you then, Bellamy within.

But that was yesterday.

And yesterday night, Good Ben Griswold took a head. Do you remember how we felt when we learned of it, you and I? First I wanted to die, Bellamy. Then I hated Ben as I have never hated anyone before, and I have known much hate. I would not believe he had done it. I would not believe *which* head he took.

I said it was a mistake, that he took a head from the populi. But I know I lied. No one takes a common head. They have no value. Then I said to myself, it can't be the head of True Jonathan Hull. It can't be. It must not be. For Hull was powerful. His hall held almost as many heads as mine. If Griswold were to have them all he would be far more powerful than I. The thought was a thing I could not endure.

I put on my status cap, with as many bells on it as the heads I have taken, and I went out to see. It was true, Bellamy.

The mansion of Jonathan Hull was being emptied. The mob was surging in and out, Hull's wives and children were leaving in little, quiet groups. The wives did not seem unhappy, but the boys did. (Girls are sent to the populi at birth; they are worthless.) I watched the boys for a while. They were all wretched and angry. One was nearly sixteen, a big, agile lad who must have nearly finished his training. Someday I might meet him in the Park.

The other boys were all too young. Now that their training had been interrupted, they would never dare enter the Park. That, of course, is why none of the populi ever become Hunters. It takes long years of arduous training to turn a child from a rabbit to a tiger. In Central Park only the tigers survive.

I looked through True Jonathan's view-windows. I saw that the glass cases in his reception hall were empty. So it was not a nightmare or a lie. Griswold did have them, I told myself, them and True Jonathan's head besides. I went into a doorway and clenched my fists and beat my head against the brownstone and groaned with self-contempt.

I was no good at all. I hated myself, and I hated Griswold too. Presently it was only that second hate that remained. So I knew what I had to do. Today, I thought, he stands where I stood yesterday. Desperate men will be talking to him, begging him, challenging him, trying every means they know to get him into the Park tonight.

But I am crafty. I make my plans far ahead. I have networks that stretch into the mansions of every Hunter in the city, crossing their own webs.

One of my wives, Nelda, was the key here. Long ago I realized that she was beginning to dislike me. I never knew why. I fostered that dislike until it became hate. I saw to it that Griswold would learn the story. It is by stratagems like this that I became as powerful as I was then—and will be again, will surely be again.

I put a special glove on my hand (you could not tell it was a glove) and I went to my TV phone and called Good Ben Griswold. He came grinning to the screen.

"I challenge you, Ben," I said. "Tonight at nine, in the Park, by the carousel site."

He laughed at me. He was a tall, heavily muscled man with a thick neck. I looked at his neck.

"I was waiting to hear from you, Roger," he said.

"Tonight at nine," I repeated.

He laughed again. "Oh no, Roger," he said. "Why should I risk my head?"

"You're a coward."

"Certainly I'm a coward," he said, still grinning, "when there's nothing to gain and everything to lose. Was I a coward last night, when I took Hull's head? I've had my eye on him a long time, Roger. I'll admit I was afraid you'd get him first. Why didn't you, anyway?"

"It's your head I'm after, Ben."

"Not tonight," he said. "Not for quite a while. I'm not going back to the Park for a long time. I'll be too busy. You're out of the running now, Roger, anyhow. How many heads have you?"

He knew, God damn him, how far in advance of me he was—now. I let the hate show in my face.

"The Park at nine tonight," I said. "The carousel site. Or else I'll know you're afraid."

"Eat your heart out, Roger," he mocked me. "Tonight I lead a parade. Watch me. Or don't—but you'll be thinking about me. You can't help that."

"You swine, you rotten cowardly swine."

He laughed; he derided me, he goaded me, as I had done so many times to others. I did not have to pretend anger. I wanted to reach into the screen and sink my fingers in his throat. The furious rage was good to feel. It was very good. I let it build until it seemed high enough. I let him laugh and enjoy it.

Then at last I did what I had been planning. At the right moment, when it looked convincing, I let myself lose all control and I smashed my fist into the TV screen. It shattered. Griswold's face flew apart; I liked that.

The connection was broken, of course. But I knew he would check quickly back. I slipped the protective glove from my right hand and called a servant I knew I could trust. (He is a criminal; I protect him. If I die he will die and he knows it.) He bandaged my unharmed right hand and I told him what to say to the other servants. I knew the word would reach Nelda quickly, in the harem, and I knew that Griswold would hear within an hour.

I fed my anger. All day, in the gymnasium I practiced with my trainers, machete and pistol in my left hand only. I made it seem that I was approaching the berserker stage, the killing madness that overcomes us when we feel we have failed too greatly.

That kind of failure can have one of two results only. Suicide is the other. You risk nothing then, and you know your body will stand by the Park in its plastic monument. But sometimes the hate turns outward and there is no fear left. Then the Hunter is berserker, and while this makes him very dangerous, he is also good quarry then—he forgets his cunning.

It was dangerous to me, too, for that kind of forgetfulness is very tempting. The next best thing to oblivion itself.

Well, I had set the lure for Griswold. But it would take more than a lure to bring him out when he thought he had nothing to gain by such a risk. So I set rumors loose. They were very plausible rumors. I let it be whispered that Black Bill Lindman and Whistler Cowles, as desperate as I at Griswold's triumph over us all, had challenged each other to a meeting in the Park that night. Only one could come out alive, but that one would be master of New York so far as our age group counted power. (There was, of course, Old Murdoch with his fabulous collection accumulated over a lifetime. It was only among ourselves that the rivalry ran so high.)

With that rumor abroad, I thought Griswold would act. There is no way to check such news. A man seldom an-

nounces openly that he is going into the Park. It could even
be the truth, for all I knew. And for all Griswold knew, his
supremacy was in deadly peril before he had even enjoyed
his Triumph. There would be danger, of course, if he went
out to defend his victory. Lindman and Cowles are both good
Hunters. But Griswold, if he did not suspect my trap, had a
chance at one sure victory—myself, Honest Roger Bellamy,
waiting in berserker fury at a known rendezvous and with a
right hand useless for fighting. Did it seem too obvious? Ah,
but you don't know Griswold.

When it was dark I put on my hunting clothes. They are
bulletproof, black, close-fitting but very easy with every motion. I blacked my face and hands. I took gun, knife and
machete with me, the metal treated so that it will not catch
or reflect the light. I like a machete especially. I have strong
arms. I was careful not to use my bandaged hand at all, even
when I thought no one watched me. And I remembered that
I must seem on the verge of berserker rage, because I knew
Griswold's spies would be reporting every motion.

I went toward Central Park, the entrance nearest the carousel site. That far Griswold's men could track me. But no
farther.

At the gate I lingered for a moment—do you remember
this, Bellamy within me? Do you remember the plastic mon-
uments we passed on the edge of the Park? Falconer and
Brennan and the others, forever immortal, standing proud
and godlike in the clear, eternal blocks. All passion spent, all
fighting done, their glory assured forever. Did you envy them
too, Bellamy?

I remember how old Falconer's eyes seemed to look
through me contemptuously. The number of heads he had
taken is engraved on the base of his monument, and he was
a very great man. Wait, I thought. I'll stand in plastic too.

I'll take more heads than even you, Falconer, and the day that I do it will be the day I can lay this burden down. . . .

Just inside the gate, in the deep shadows, I slipped the bandage from my right hand. I drew my black knife and close against the wall I began to work my way rapidly toward the little gate which is nearest Griswold's mansion. I had, of course, no intention of going anywhere near the carousel site. Griswold would be in a hurry to get to me and out again and he might not stop to think. Griswold was not a thinker. I gambled on his taking the closest route.

I waited, feeling very solitary and liking the solitude. It was hard to stay angry. The trees whispered in the darkness. The moon was rising from the Atlantic beyond Long Island. I thought of it shining on the Sound and on the city. It would rise like this long after I was dead. It would glitter on the plastic of my monument and bathe my face with cold light long after you and I, Bellamy, are at peace, our long war with each other ended.

Then I heard Griswold coming. I tried to empty my mind of everything except killing. It was for this that my body and mind had been trained so painfully ever since I was six years old. I breathed deeply a few times. As always, the deep, shrinking fear tried to rise in me. Fear, and something more. Something within me—is it you, Bellamy?—that says I do not really want to kill.

Then Griswold came into sight, and the familiar, hungry hatred made everything all right again.

I do not remember very much about the fight. It all seemed to happen within a single timeless interval, though I suppose it went on for quite a long while. He was suspicious, even as he entered the gate. I thought I had made no sound, but his ears were very sharp and he moved in time to avoid my first shot that should have finished the thing then and there.

It was not a stalk this time. It was a hard, fast, skillful fight. We both wore bulletproof clothing, but we were both wounded before we got close enough to try for each other's heads with steel. He favored a saber and it was longer than my machete. Still, it was an even battle. We had to fight fast, because the noise might draw other Hunters, if there were any in the Park tonight.

But in the end, I killed him.

I took his head. The moon was not yet clear of the high buildings on the other side of the Park and the night was young. I looked up at the calm, proud faces of the immortals along the edge of the Park as I came out with Griswold's head.

I summoned a car. Within minutes I was back in my mansion, with my trophy. Before I would let the surgeons treat me I saw that the head was taken to the laboratory for a quick treatment, a very quick preparation. And I sent out orders for a midnight Triumph.

While I lay on the table and the surgeons washed and dressed my wounds, the news was flashing through the city already. My servants were in Griswold's mansion, transferring his collections to my reception hall, setting up extra cases that would hold all my trophies, all True Jonathan Hull's and all of Griswold's too. I would be the most powerful man in New York, under such masters as old Murdoch and one or two more. All my age group and the one above it would be wild with envy and hate. I thought of Lindman and Cowles and laughed with triumph.

I thought it was triumph—then.

I stand now at the head of the staircase, looking down at the lights and the brilliance, the row upon row of trophies, my wives in all their jewels. Servants are moving to the great bronze doors to swing them ponderously open. What will be revealed? The throng of guests, the great Hunters coming to give homage to a greater Hunter? Or—suppose no one has come to my Triumph after all?

The bronze doors are beginning to open. But there'll be no one outside. I can't be sure yet, but I know it, I'm certain of it. The fear that never leaves a Hunter, except in his last and greatest Triumph, is with me now. Suppose, while I stalked Griswold tonight, some other Hunter has lain in wait for bigger game? Suppose someone has taken old Murdoch's head? Suppose someone else is having a Triumph in New York tonight, a greater Triumph than mine?

The fear is choking me. I've failed. Some other Hunter has beaten me. I'm no good. . . .

No. *No!* Listen. Listen to them shouting my name! Look, look at them pouring in through the opened doors, all the great Hunters and their jewel-flashing women, thronging in to fill the bright hall beneath me. I feared too soon. I was the only Hunter in the Park tonight, after all. So I have won, and this is my Triumph. There they stand among the glittering glass cases, their faces turned up to me, admiring, envious. There's Lindman. There's Cowles. I can read their expressions very, very easily. They can't wait to get me alone tonight and challenge me to a duel in the Park.

They all raise their arms toward me in salute. They shout my name.

Bellamy within—listen! This is our Triumph. It shall never be taken away from us.

I beckon to a servant. He hands me the filled glass that is ready. Now I look down at the Hunters of New York—I look down from the height of my Triumph—and I raise my glass to them.

I drink.

Hunters—you cannot rob me now.

I shall stand proud in plastic, godlike in the eternal block that holds me, all passion spent, all fighting done, my glory assured forever.

The poison works quickly.

This is triumph.

HOME IS THE HUNTER: THE TRIUMPH OF HONEST ROGER BELLAMY

And some Kuttner now. To exclude him from this book is unthinkable; from the beginning I regarded him as the master of the science-fiction short story, the man who knew which parts were essential and where they belonged. But *which* Kuttner story? The wonderfully gimmicky time-twister story "Line to Tomorrow"? The somber future-detective story "Private Eye," with that utterly perfect and inevitable final paragraph? "The Twonky"? "Time Locker"? "Absalom"? One of the "Baldy" stories? "Two-Handed Engine"? Would that I could have used them all; but then this would simply have become *Robert Silverberg Selects His Favorite Kuttner Stories*, which would be a worthwhile book of its own sort but not quite the one I had set out to do.

And so in the end I settled on just one Kuttner story, and not a particularly well-known one at that, nor one from the fertile pseudonymous "Lewis Padgett" period of the wartime years when he was astonishing everyone with his fertility of invention and cleverness of execution. This one comes from a later time, 1953, which was a relatively unproductive period for Kuttner. In 1950, when he was 36 years old, he had enrolled as a freshman at the University of Southern California to fill in what he perceived as gaps in his knowledge of the world, particularly in his knowledge of science, psychology, and English literature. After securing his B.A. in 1954 he went on to seek a master's degree in literature, a project still incomplete when a heart attack took him in February of 1958. During those years he published only a handful of science-fiction stories.

But those were precisely the years when I was frantically taking apart stories to see what made them tick; and, since Kuttner's stories under all his various pseudonyms had struck resounding chords in me during my formative years (1947–50) as a science-fiction reader, his newer work got particularly close attention from me now that I was consciously striving to take up writing s-f as my profession. "Home is the Hunter," which appeared in the July, 1953, issue of *Galaxy*, came at the peak of that time for me—just as I had reached marginal professional quality as a writer, but before I had actually made my first sale. Its impact on me, like the impact of almost every outstanding story I read during that highly sensitized year, was extraordinary; and so I think it belongs here as the Kuttner representative.

There is, as with all of this writer's stories after 1940, the question of whether it is pure Kuttner, or a Kuttner-Moore collaboration. The bibliographical evidence is inconclusive. For its magazine appearance it bore the byline "C. L. Moore and Henry Kuttner," but that may have been mere pro forma acknowledgement that every story leaving their workshop had in some way been touched by both partners. Later the same year it was reprinted in a collection of stories, *Ahead of Time*, that bore Kuttner's name alone. I think this is its first publication since then. It is too short to have required more than one person at the typewriter, and my guess—purely intuitive, but not casual—is that Kuttner did the work, with any Moore participation being nothing more than minor retouching. If I am wrong, so be it: let this still stand as the Kuttner contribution to this book. One way or another he deserves to be in here.

"Home is the Hunter" is a story told in the first person—a difficult and treacherous form, precisely because it seems to be so easy. In the first-person story the writer totally assumes the identity of the protagonist and tries to establish the pretense that the protagonist is telling his story directly to the reader without the presence of any intermediary. When it works, it works so well that it can seem like actual autobiography, and the reader has a hard time remembering that it's merely an invented story. But most of the time first-person narrative doesn't work, particularly in the hands of an inexperienced writer.

The first-person form invites the writer to forget that he must give shape to his material if it is to have effective dramatic impact. Instead, the writer—totally identified in his own mind with his narrator— tends to run on and on in an unfocused drone of events: "And then this happened, and then that happened, and then this, and then that." He feels perfectly free to stop the flow of incident for pages at a time so that his protagonist can discuss the background of the story, or his own sensitive nature, or anything else he feels like talking about. If the protagonist is a fascinating and compelling character, the reader may sit still to listen to all that. More often than not, he won't. (I have frequently suggested to beginning writers using the first-person form that they try rewriting a given story in third person and take a good look at the results. They're often startled to see how slow, congested, and lame the narrative seems. When writing in third person, even beginners seem to realize that the most effective way to tell a story is through incident and dialog; but somehow that awareness goes out the window once "I" starts talking.)

So the first trap for the first-person writer is garrulousness. His long-winded, rambling narrative isn't really a story: it's a monolog delivered to a captive audience. But even if the writer manages not to fall into that trap, he still must contend with the fact that he's asking the reader to hold still for a torrent of egocentricity. "I did this," the narrator says, "and I did that, and I committed the following highly admirable deed, and then I was guilty of the following oversight," and on and on and on. If the narrator is a bore or a braggart or a whiner or a fool, the captive audience is likely to throw off its shackles in a hurry and head for a different story. (If the *writer* is a bore or a braggart or a fool, it's going to be very hard for him to keep his narrator from having the same flaws, though I have seen it done.)

It's essential for the writer of first-person narratives to know how to build sympathy for his protagonist, even if the protagonist is a louse, and to make the reader care about what the protagonist is saying about himself. Once that's achieved, the reader's consciousness fuses with that of the protagonist and the writer has no further problems of holding his audience's attention. Bringing about that fusion, though, requires something more than technique: it requires passion, conviction, confidence, human depth. Which is why I suggest to most beginners that they leave first-person narrative alone.

Most first-person stories are autobiographical in form: the narrator explaining himself to the reader. Here's how Heinlein's *Have Space Suit—Will Travel* begins:

> You see, I had this space suit. How it happened was this way:
>
> "Dad," I said, "I want to go to the Moon."
> "Certainly," he answered and looked back at his book. It was Jerome K. Jerome's *Three Men in a Boat*, which he must know by heart.
> I said, "Dad, please! I'm serious."

Kuttner's approach is slightly different: the interior monolog, in which the protagonist pretends to be addressing *himself*. ("Inside me, listening, is there another Honest Roger Bellamy? I don't know. . . . Listen to me, Bellamy, listen to me, if you're there at all, deep inside my head.") It's a tricky and cumbersome approach, which has even more pitfalls than conventional first person, because when done wrong it will load a story with a lot of self-conscious clutter. Kuttner gets away with it mainly because this story is very short, and because he's Henry Kuttner. But even he doesn't sustain it with any consistency. Bellamy talking to the Bellamy inside would not have bothered telling himself that he is a man with powerful arms or describing his feelings for his parents or pointing out that the character named Nelda is one of his own wives. So the notion that Bellamy is "really" talking to his inner self is very feeble indeed. He is talking to us, and we both know it; the inner Bellamy is a device that not even Bellamy takes seriously. Bellamy may be pretending to be talking to himself, but in fact he is trying to justify his life to us, and in particular—at the end, in what is no longer an interior monolog but a defiant top-of-the-lungs bellow—he is trying to justify his death as well.

With typical economy Kuttner states the story's problem in his first sentence: "There's nobody I can talk to except myself." Bellamy is a great man, an aristocrat, a member of the Head-Hunter elite. For him the world consists of a vast horde of plebeians with which he has nothing in common and a small group of men of his own kind who would like nothing more than to cut off his head and mount it in their trophy rooms. Bellamy is almost incomprehensibly isolated and lonely: that is one level of the story, the one that accounts for the choice of first-person-interior form. Who else can Bellamy talk to but himself? Other Head-Hunters? Hardly. His wives? They're just harem inmates. *Us?* Don't be silly. We don't even exist.

But the story addresses a second problem that Bellamy faces, and a more serious one: the ephemeral nature of success. No matter how great your past achievements, you're still only as good as your last book, your last film, your last game—or, in Bellamy's case, your last duel. Sooner or later you slip from your peak and then what you have accomplished in the past loses its meaning—and you, if you're Bellamy, lose not only your glory but your head. It is the paradox of greatness. The great athlete pathetically still swinging his bat when his reflexes are gone, the great novelist sadly churning out unintentional self-parody during his sober moments, the defeated politician issuing desperate memoirs and manifestos from his retirement headquarters—we see it again and again. Bellamy must keep on hunting: it is the breath of life to him. He cannot stop, for he must not let any other hunter surpass him in the number of heads taken ("The thought was a thing I could not endure"). If he continues to duel, though, he must in time fall to some faster blade and become a mere trophy in someone else's hall. Yet to retire from the field while his neck is still intact would be to concede cowardice. The only fortunate Hunters are those who die of natural causes before they can be defeated. Kuttner tells us that at the outset. "You see, there isn't any choice," Bellamy declares, and the end of the story becomes inevitable. Nevertheless we read on anyway, perhaps because we want to see how well Bellamy will cope with his impossible dilemma, or perhaps because the first-person form tricks us into thinking he will somehow be able to escape his fate.

The story is about 3,500 words long. In the world of magazine fiction, that is one of the shorter lengths, indeed just about the shortest length that can include all the ingredients (plot, character, setting) of the short story in proper measure. (Most magazine short stories come in four standard sizes. There are the fillers, up to 1,500 words long, which customarily depend for their effect on a twist ending rather than on depth of characterization or intricacy of plot: one-punch stories. This category also includes brief mood piece and plotless vignettes. Then there are the 3,000–4,000-word stories, generally built around a single simply developed situation that is resolved in sudden and surprising fashion. Beginners usually find this length easier to handle than the shorter or longer ones. The 5,000–7,500-word range, in which most magazine stories fall, requires some extended character development and at least a simple subplot. Above 7,500 words—about thirty manuscript pages—are the complex, richly worked out stories in which characters cope with many obstacles and setbacks on their way to their goals. This is normally the territory of professional writers only.)

Kuttner, working within the limits of the shortest true short story, gets immediately to the task of limning the bizarre society in which Honest Roger Bellamy operates. Killing, of a particular ritual nature, is legal. There is an aristocracy of the duello. We hear how the wives and children of defeated Hunters "are turned out to be populi," and we know without the need for further explanation that that society has a two-caste system. There are harems. Successful Hunters wear "status caps" with bells on them to proclaim their victories.

All this is conveyed by quick offhand references that Bellamy tosses off in the course of telling us about himself. A less experienced writer who has chosen the first-person form might well have felt it necessary to throw in a solid page or two of exposition that would provide the historical or sociological background for his head-hunting society. Kuttner doesn't bother, in part because he was too shrewd to impede so short a story by putting such lectures in Bellamy's mouth and in part possibly because he sensed that the more such detail he provided, the less plausible such a society would start to look. Instead, he adopts a take-it-or-leave-it approach. This is how it is, he says. I have come up with a fanciful metaphor for the competitiveness of twentieth-century man, not a seriously intended vision of a probable future. Kuttner asks us simply to take his head-hunting society as a given, and goes on from that point to investigate the psychology of one who lives within that society. What matters is internal consistency, not the real-world likelihood of the fundamental situation. Science fiction is a branch of fantasy, after all. Few of those who write it intend their stories to be taken as literal prophecy, and those who do usually find that their work seems woefully quaint after a very few years.

So Bellamy's anguish, not the sociology of head-hunting, is the focus of the story. Bellamy has told us of his loneliness, of his ferocious will to mastery, and of his crushing realization that the path he has chosen will lead only to humiliation unless he can contrive to die before he is killed by another. Of these three traits, the will to mastery is preeminent, or else he would never have become a Head-Hunter in the first place. Thus, the story centers around his rivalry with Good Ben Griswold. But we know, since it is a first-person story, that Bellamy can't perish at Griswold's hands. (Kuttner would not have been above revealing that his narrator was a ghost, if he had needed to, but in this one he's already shown us Bellamy presiding over a Triumph in the first paragraph, from which everything else is a flashback.) So Bellamy will kill Griswold. What concerns us, though, is not so much how he will accomplish that as what will happen afterward, when he must confront the awareness that victory is hollow and that he is condemned to an unending sequence of further duels—a sequence that can never be halted by victory but only by death.

If he had been writing a longer story, Kuttner might well have built up the climactic duel with Good Ben Griswold (this use of the honorific epithets, "Good Ben," "True Jonathan," is a fine little touch, denoting upper caste in a novel way) into an extended action scene, with many a grunt and groan and reversal of jeopardy. Certainly Kuttner knew how to write such scenes. But that would have been irrelevant to the theme of the story, and he had little room for such embroidery: the true climax of the story lies not in the duel but in the events of the celebration of Triumph that will follow it. A huge battle scene would have overloaded the little story with a double climax; instead Kuttner handles the killing of Griswold in a synoptic, even perfunctory, way—"But in the end, I killed him"—and moves on to his real finale.

The structure of the closing scene repays careful study. As the surgeons patch up the victorious Bellamy, word of his victory is flashed through the city and the aristocracy begins to assemble for a midnight Triumph. The other Hunters, Bellamy declares (once again forgetting that he is talking to his own inner self), "would be wild with envy and hate." The curve is upward, for the moment. He stands "at the head of the staircase, looking down at the lights and the brilliance, the row upon row of trophies, my wives in all their jewels."

But the curve of the formal Triumph must not be allowed to rise beyond that point. This is not a story about Honest Roger Bellamy's wonderful victory over Good Ben Griswold. If Kuttner had been writing for readers living in Bellamy's society, such a victory might well have provided a fine upbeat way to end the story. But he is writing for twentieth-century folk, most of whom are likely to find the idea of founding an aristocracy on hand-to-hand duels in Central Park as repugnant if not simply absurd, and they will see no reason to cheer as the curtain falls on the once-again-triumphant Bellamy. So in the moment of his Triumph Kuttner must show us the disintegration of Bellamy's moment of triumphant ecstasy, and he does it in one quick paragraph of wild paranoid leaps:

> The bronze doors are beginning to open. But there'll be no one outside. I can't be sure yet, but I know it. I'm certain of it. The fear that never leaves a Hunter, except in his last and greatest Triumph, is with me now. Suppose, while I stalked Griswold tonight, some other Hunter has lain in wait for bigger game? Suppose someone has taken old Murdoch's head? Suppose someone else is having a Triumph in New York tonight, a greater Triumph than mine?

The rising curve of the climax, having flattened out, now has turned downward, and Bellamy plunges toward a point I like to call the All-Is-Lost of a story, when it seems as if all the protagonist's striving has been in vain: "The fear is choking me. I've failed. Some other Hunter has beaten me. I'm no good. . . ."

The All-Is-Lost may actually be the final moment of the story, if depicting the downfall of the protagonist is the writer's intention (as in Christopher Marlowe's *Dr. Faustus*, where Faust is dragged off to hell as he utters his final lines). But the majority of stories end on some sort of redemptive note, in which case the All-Is-Lost serves as a pivot point for the final reversal and the last upward turn of the curve.* So it is here. Bellamy's gloomy fantasy that no one has come to his triumph is unfounded: "Look at them pouring in through the opened doors, all the great Hunters and their jewel-flashing women, thronging in to fill the bright hall beneath me." It will be a great Triumph after all. And its very greatness will be the measure of its

---

*A story that ends at a point where all really *is* lost needs a reversal in the other direction: a moment of false or short-lived hope just before the final cataclysm, as in *Dr. Faustus* when Faust belatedly talks of repentance and prays to be forgiven.

hollowness for Bellamy. He will not be deluded by the glitter and the applause into believing that those things are going to give him the peace he seeks. And we, knowing by now that the story is about Bellamy's dissatisfaction with the rewards of his profession, expect something further, which Kuttner provides: the suicide that was fore-shadowed from the beginning, but which we, thinking we understood Bellamy's fiercely self-centered nature, had somehow ruled out as a likely solution to the problem. He reaches for the poisoned drink. No one can defeat him now.

If this were a mainstream story, we might feel that it has ended with the highest sort of victory, victory over self, Bellamy's withdrawing of his own free will from the ignoble rat race of head-hunting. But this is science fiction. Kuttner is writing of a society alien to ours, and Bellamy's mind does not work as does yours or mine. Victory over self? Hardly. What Bellamy has accomplished—within the context of his society's values, not ours—is a final and irrevocable victory over the other Hunters. The theme is the difficulty of attaining true triumph; the resolution of the problem is Bellamy's achievement of the only fulfillment available to him on his own terms. That it costs him his life may seem extreme to us, but not to him. Kuttner has brought his story home within the assumptions of its speculative construct. It is, perhaps, a minor piece; but a minor piece by a master, nevertheless.

THE MONSTERS
ROBERT SHECKLEY

Cordovir and Hum stood on the rocky mountaintop, watching the new thing happen. Both felt rather good about it. It was undoubtedly the newest thing that had happened for some time.

"By the way the sunlight glints from it," Hum said, "I'd say it is made of metal."

"I'll accept that," Cordovir said. "But what holds it up in the air?"

They both stared intently down to the valley where the new thing was happening. A pointed object was hovering over the ground. From one end of it poured a substance resembling fire.

"It's balancing on the fire," Hum said. "That should be apparent even to your old eyes."

Cordovir lifted himself higher on his thick tail, to get a better look. The object settled to the ground and the fire stopped.

"Shall we go down and have a closer look?" Hum asked.

"All right. I think we have time—wait! What day is this?"

Hum calculated silently, then said, "The fifth day of Lug-gat."

"Damn," Cordovir said. "I have to go home and kill my wife."

"It's a few hours before sunset," Hum said. "I think you have time to do both."

Cordovir wasn't sure. "I'd hate to be late."

"Well, then. You know how fast I am," Hum said. "If it gets late, I'll hurry back and kill her myself. How about that?"

"That's very decent of you." Cordovir thanked the younger man and together they slithered down the steep mountainside.

In front of the metal object both men halted and stood up on their tails.

"Rather bigger than I thought," Cordovir said, measuring the metal object with his eye. He estimated that it was slightly longer than their village, and almost half as wide. They crawled a circle around it, observing that the metal was tooled, presumably by human tentacles.

In the distance the smaller sun had set.

"I think we had better get back," Cordovir said, noting the cessation of light.

"*I* still have plenty of time." Hum flexed his muscles complacently.

"Yes, but a man likes to kill his own wife."

"As you wish." They started off to the village at a brisk pace.

In his house, Cordovir's wife was finishing supper. She had her back to the door, as etiquette required. Cordovir killed her with a single flying slash of his tail, dragged her body outside, and sat down to eat.

After meal and meditation he went to the Gathering. Hum, with the impatience of youth, was already there, telling of the metal object. He probably bolted his supper, Cordovir thought with mild distaste.

After the youngster had finished, Cordovir gave his own observations. The only thing he added to Hum's account was an idea: that the metal object might contain intelligent beings.

"What makes you think so?" Mishill, another elder, asked.

"The fact that there was fire from the object as it came down," Cordovir said, "joined to the fact that the fire stopped after the object was on the ground. Some being, I contend, was responsible for turning it off."

"Not necessarily," Mishill said. The village men talked about it late into the night. Then they broke up the meeting, buried the various murdered wives, and went to their homes.

Lying in the darkness, Cordovir discovered that he hadn't made up his mind as yet about the new thing. Presuming it contained intelligent beings, would they be moral? Would they have a sense of right and wrong? Cordovir doubted it, and went to sleep.

The next morning every male in the village went to the metal object. This was proper, since the functions of males were to examine new things and to limit the female population. They formed a circle around it, speculating on what might be inside.

"I believe they will be human beings," Hum's elder brother Esktel said. Cordovir shook his entire body in disagreement.

"Monsters, more likely," he said. "If you take in account—"

"Not necessarily," Esktel said. "Consider the logic of our physical development. A single focusing eye—"

"But in the great Outside," Cordovir said, "there may be many strange races, most of them non-human. In the infinitude—"

"Still," Esktel put in, "the logic of our—"

"As I was saying," Cordovir went on, "the chance is infinitesimal that they would resemble us. Their vehicle, for example. Would we build—"

"But on strictly logical grounds," Esktel said, "you can see—"

That was the third time Cordovir had been interrupted. With a single movement of his tail he smashed Esktel against the metal object. Esktel fell to the ground, dead.

"I have often considered my brother a boor," Hum said. "What were you saying?"

But Cordovir was interrupted again. A piece of metal set in the greater piece of metal squeaked, turned and lifted, and a creature came out.

Cordovir saw at once that he had been right. The thing that crawled out of the hole was twin-tailed. It was covered to its top with something partially metal and partially hide. And its color! Cordovir shuddered.

The thing was the color of wet, flayed flesh.

All the villagers had backed away, waiting to see what the thing would do. At first it didn't do anything. It stood on the metal surface, and a bulbous object that topped its body moved from side to side. But there were no accompanying body movements to give the gesture meaning. Finally, the thing raised both tentacles and made noises.

"Do you think it's trying to communicate?" Mishill asked softly.

Three more creatures appeared in the metal hole, carrying metal sticks in their tentacles. The things made noises at each other.

"They are decidedly not human," Cordovir said firmly. "The next question is, are they moral beings?" One of the things crawled down the metal side and stood on the ground.

The rest pointed their metal sticks at the ground. It seemed to be some sort of religious ceremony.

"Could anything so hideous be moral?" Cordovir asked, his hide twitching with distaste. Upon closer inspection, the creatures were more horrible than could be dreamed. The bulbous object on their bodies just might be a head, Cordovir decided, even though it was unlike any head he had ever seen. But in the middle of that head! Instead of a smooth, characterful surface was a raised ridge. Two round indentures were on either side of it, and two more knobs on either side of that. And in the lower half of the head—if such it was—a pale, reddish slash ran across. Cordovir supposed this might be considered a mouth, with some stretching of the imagination.

Nor was this all, Cordovir observed. The things were so constructed as to show the presence of bone! When they moved their limbs, it wasn't a smooth, flowing gesture, the fluid motion of human beings. Rather, it was the jerky snap of a tree limb.

"God above," Gilrig, an intermediate-age male, gasped. "We should kill them and put them out of their misery!" Other men seemed to feel the same way, and the villagers flowed forward.

"Wait!" one of the youngsters shouted. "Let's communicate with them, if such is possible. They might still be moral beings. The Outside is wide, remember, and anything is possible."

Cordovir argued for immediate extermination, but the villagers stopped and discussed it among themselves. Hum, with characteristic bravado, flowed up to the thing on the ground.

"Hello," Hum said.

The thing said something.

"I can't understand it," Hum said, and started to crawl back. The creature waved its jointed tentacles—if they were tentacles—and motioned at one of the suns. He made a sound.

"Yes, it is warm, isn't it?" Hum said cheerfully.

The creature pointed at the ground, and made another sound.

"We haven't had especially good crops this year," Hum said conversationally.

The creature pointed at itself and made a sound.

"I agree," Hum said. "You're as ugly as sin."

Presently the villagers grew hungry and crawled back to the village. Hum stayed and listened to the things making noises at him, and Cordovir waited nervously for Hum.

"You know," Hum said, after he rejoined Cordovir, "I think they want to learn our language. Or want me to learn theirs."

"Don't do it," Cordovir said, glimpsing the misty edge of a great evil.

"I believe I will," Hum murmured. Together they climbed the cliffs back to the village.

That afternoon Cordovir went to the surplus female pen and formally asked a young woman if she would reign in his house for twenty-five days. Naturally, the woman accepted gratefully.

On the way home, Cordovir met Hum, going to the pen.

"Just killed my wife," Hum said, superflously, since why else would he be going to the surplus female stock?

"Are you going back to the creatures tomorrow?" Cordovir asked.

"I might," Hum answered, "if nothing new presents itself."

"The thing to find out is if they are moral beings or monsters."

"Right," Hum said, and slithered on.

There was a Gathering that evening, after supper. All the villagers agreed that the things were non-human. Cordovir argued strenuously that their very appearance belied any possibility of humanity. Nothing so hideous could have moral standards, a sense of right and wrong, and above all, a notion of truth.

The young men didn't agree, probably because there had been a dearth of new things recently. They pointed out that the metal object was obviously a product of intelligence. Intelligence axiomatically means standards of differentiation. Differentiation implies right and wrong.

It was a delicious argument. Olgolel contradicted Arast and was killed by him. Mavrt, in an unusual fit of anger for so placid an individual, killed the three Holian brothers and was himself killed by Hum, who was feeling pettish. Even the surplus females could be heard arguing about it, in their pen in a corner of the village.

Weary and happy, the villagers went to sleep.

The next few weeks saw no end of the argument. Life went on much as usual, though. The women went out in the morning, gathered food, prepared it, and laid eggs. The eggs were taken to the surplus females to be hatched. As usual, about eight females were hatched to every male. On the twenty-fifth day of each marriage, or a little earlier, each man killed his woman and took another.

The males went down to the ship to listen to Hum learning the language; then, when that grew boring, they returned to their customary wandering through hills and forests, looking for new things.

The alien monsters stayed close to their ship, coming out only when Hum was there.

Twenty-four days after the arrival of the non-humans, Hum announced that he could communicate with them, after a fashion.

"They say they come from far away," Hum told the village that evening. "They say that they are bisexual, like us, and that they are humans, like us. They say there are reasons for their different appearance, but I couldn't understand that part of it."

"If we accept them as humans," Mishill said, "then everything they say is true."

The rest of the villagers shook in agreement.

"They say that they don't want to disturb our life, but would be very interested in observing it. They want to come to the village and look around."

"I see no reason why not," one of the younger men said.

"No!" Cordovir shouted. "You are letting in evil. These monsters are insidious. I believe that they are capable of— telling an untruth!" The other elders agreed, but when pressed, Cordovir had no proof to back up this vicious accusation.

"After all," Sil pointed out, "just because they look like monsters, you can't take it for granted that they think like monsters as well."

"I can," Cordovir said, but he was outvoted.

Hum went on. "They have offered me—or us, I'm not sure which, various metal objects which they say will do various things. I ignored this breach of etiquette, since I considered they didn't know any better."

Cordovir nodded. The youngster was growing up. He was showing, at long last, that he had some manners.

"They want to come to the village tomorrow."

"No!" Cordovir shouted, but the vote was against him.

"Oh, by the way," Hum said, as the meeting was breaking up. "They have several females among them. The ones with the very red mouths are females. It will be interesting to see how the males kill them. Tomorrow is the twenty-fifth day since they came."

The next day the things came to the village, crawling slowly and laboriously over the cliffs. The villagers were able to observe the extreme brittleness of their limbs, the terrible awkwardness of their motions.

"No beauty whatsoever," Cordovir muttered. "And they all look alike."

In the village the things acted without any decency. They crawled into huts and out of huts. They jabbered at the surplus female pen. They picked up eggs and examined them. They peered at the villagers through black things and shiny things.

In midafternoon, Rantan, an elder, decided it was about time he killed his woman. So he pushed the thing who was examining his hut aside and smashed his female to death.

Instantly, two of the things started jabbering at each other, hurrying out of the hut.

One had the red mouth of a female.

"He must have remembered it was time to kill his own woman," Hum observed. The villagers waited, but nothing happened.

"Perhaps," Rantan said, "perhaps he would like someone to kill her for him. It might be the custom of their land."

Without further ado Rantan slashed down the female with his tail.

The male creature made a terrible noise and pointed a metal stick at Rantan. Rantan collapsed, dead.

"That's odd," Mishill said. "I wonder if that denotes disapproval?"

The things from the metal object—eight of them—were in a tight little circle. One was holding the dead female, and the rest were pointing the metal sticks on all sides. Hum went up and asked them what was wrong.

"I don't understand," Hum said, after he spoke with them.

"They used words I haven't learned. But I gather that their emotion is one of reproach."

The monsters were backing away. Another villager, deciding it was about time, killed his wife who was standing in a doorway. The group of monsters stopped and jabbered at each other. Then they motioned to Hum.

Hum's body motion was incredulous after he had talked with them.

"If I understood right," Hum said, "they are ordering us not to kill any more of our women!"

"What!" Cordovir and a dozen others shouted.

"I'll ask them again." Hum went back into conference with the monsters who were waving metal sticks in their tentacles.

"That's right," Hum said. Without further preamble he flipped his tail, throwing one of the monsters across the village square. Immediately the others began to point their sticks while retreating rapidly.

After they were gone, the villagers found that seventeen males were dead. Hum, for some reason, had been missed.

"Now will you believe me!" Cordovir shouted. "The creatures told *a deliberate untruth!* They said they wouldn't molest us and then they proceed to kill seventeen of us! Not only an amoral act—but a *concerted death effort!*"

It was almost past human understanding.

"A deliberate untruth!" Cordovir shouted the blasphemy, sick with loathing. Men rarely discussed the possibility of anyone telling an untruth.

The villagers were beside themselves with anger and revulsion, once they realized the full concept of an *untruthful* creature. And, added to that was the monsters' concerted death effort!

It was like the most horrible nightmare come true. Sud-

denly it became apparent that these creatures didn't kill females. Undoubtedly they allowed them to spawn unhampered.
The thought of that was enough to make a strong man retch.

The surplus females broke out of their pens and, joined
by the wives, demanded to know what was happening. When
they were told, they were twice as indignant as the men, such
being the nature of women.

"Kill them!" the surplus females roared. "Don't let them
change our ways. Don't let them introduce immorality!"

"It's true," Hum said sadly. "I should have guessed it."

"They must be killed at once!" a female shouted. Being
surplus, she had no name at present, but she made up for
that in blazing personality.

"We women desire only to live moral, decent lives,
hatching eggs in the pen until our time of marriage comes.
And then twenty-five ecstatic days! How could we desire
more? These monsters will destroy our way of life. They will
make us as terrible as they!"

"Now do you understand?" Cordovir screamed at the
men. "I warned you, I presented it to you, and you ignored
me! Young men must listen to old men in time of crisis!" In
his rage he killed two youngsters with a blow of his tail. The
villagers applauded.

"Drive them out," Cordovir shouted. "Before they corrupt
us!"

All the females rushed off to kill the monsters.

"They have death-sticks," Hum observed. "Do the females
know?"

"I don't believe so," Cordovir said. He was completely
calm now. "You'd better go and tell them."

"I'm tired," Hum said sulkily. "I've been translating. Why
don't you go?"

"Oh, let's both go," Cordovir said, bored with the young-

ster's adolescent moodiness. Accompanied by half the villagers they hurried off after the females.

They overtook them on the edge of the cliff that overlooked the object. Hum explained the death-sticks while Cordovir considered the problem.

"Roll stones on them," he told the females. "Perhaps you
can break the metal of the object."

The females started rolling stones down the cliffs with
great energy. Some bounced off the metal of the object. Immediately, lines of red fire came from the object and females
were killed. The ground shook.

"Let's move back," Cordovir said. "The females have it
well in hand, and this shaky ground makes me giddy."

Together with the rest of the males they moved to a safe
distance and watched the action.

Women were dying right and left, but they were reinforced by women of other villages who had heard of the
menace. They were fighting for their homes now, their rights,
and they were fiercer than a man could ever be. The object
was throwing fire all over the cliff, but the fire helped dislodge more stones which rained down on the thing. Finally,
big fires came out of one end of the metal object.

A landslide started, and the object got into the air just
in time. It barely missed a mountain; then it climbed steadily,
until it was a little black speck against the larger sun. And
then it was gone.

That evening, it was discovered that fifty-three females
had been killed. This was fortunate since it helped keep down
the surplus female population. The problem would become
even more acute now, since seventeen males were gone in a
single lump.

Cordovir was feeling exceedingly proud of himself. His
wife had been gloriously killed in the fighting, but he took
another at once.

"We had better kill our wives sooner than every twenty-five days for a while," he said at the evening Gathering. "Just until things get back to normal."

The surviving females, back in the pen, heard him and applauded wildly.

"I wonder where the things have gone," Hum said, offering the question to the Gathering.

"Probably away to enslave some defenseless race," Cordovir said.

"Not necessarily," Mishill put in and the evening argument was on.

THE MONSTERS:
DON'T FORGET TO KILL YOUR WIFE

Bob Sheckley and I are friends of some thirty years' standing, and I doubt that either of us feels much awe for the other. Respect, yes. We have been through the wars together, doggedly dealing with much the same wobbly publishers and marginal magazines and cantankerous editors through all those three decades, and that inspires the admiration that one longtime survivor engenders in another, along with camaraderie, warm sentiment, and other such fine things. Not awe.

But there was a time when I looked upon Sheckley as a demi-god, and I'll never forget it. The year was 1953; the scene was the vast and stately Bellevue-Stratford Hotel in Philadelphia; the event was the Eleventh World Science Fiction Convention. I was in my late teens, about to begin my sophomore year at Columbia, and frantically eager to break through into the ranks of professional writers. Indeed, I was just on the verge of selling my first science-fiction stories that year, but verges are uncomfortable places, and I had no assurance I'd ever get beyond that awkward point.

Midway through that convention weekend I found myself standing at one side of the Bellevue-Stratford's immense lobby, staring at the crowd of science-fiction people. With me were a couple of boys about my own age—a brash kid named Harlan Ellison and one or two others whose names would be less significant here. Suddenly, there was a little stir in the lobby as a group of older men passed through it, heading briskly toward the elevator bank. One was a slender, graceful man with a little goatee, who was holding a huge guitar. Ellison nudged me.

"That's Ted Sturgeon," he said, and I nodded. He pointed to another. "And Jim Blish. And the stocky one is Willy Ley."

"And who's the other one?" I asked.

Another slender man, considerably younger than the rest, walked at Sturgeon's side. He was carrying a guitar too, and grinning broadly.

"That one's Sheckley," Ellison said. "God, I'd give anything to be in his place now!"

As would I. Seeing the buoyant, confident young Sheckley crossing the lobby in the company of those great writers, I felt a surge of complicated emotions: what I suppose was envy, and admiration, and respect, and even hope. Sheckley was just 25 years old, the hottest new writer in the field. All the editors were courting him, his name was on every contents page from *Galaxy* and *Astounding* to *Colliers* and *Esquire*, and Ballantine Books had just paid some enormous amount of money for the rights to his first collection of short stories, *Untouched by Human Hands*. And there he was, at the World Convention, so young and already one of the elite, moving freely in the charmed circle of the top writers, heading off to some private party upstairs where he and Theodore Sturgeon would amuse their colleagues with a little guitar demonstration. You can bet I envied him.

And studied his stories with very, very close attention.

I had half a dozen different role-models in that critical year of 1953, but Sheckley certainly was one of the most important, for three main reasons. His instant rise to fame while still so very young was something I craved to emulate. Secondly, he was tremendously prolific. I have great respect for overachievers. (All during my early years as a writer I kept at my side a mimeographed pamphlet that listed all the science-fiction stories published in 1953, tabulated by author. I used it as a yardstick to measure my own progress. Sheckley had an astonishing twenty-four stories on that list. Only Philip K. Dick had more than that: twenty-eight. They were my idols.) The third thing about Sheckley that appealed to me was that he made it all look so easy. His stories were quick, light, bright, deft. None of the flamboyant special effects characteristic of Alfred Bester, none of the rich emotional depth of C. L. Moore, none of the complex scientific understructure of James Blish. Just grace, agility, ingenuity.

I knew I couldn't hope to match Bester or Moore or Blish at their specialties. But Sheckley—like Henry Kuttner, a writer who surely must have been one of *his* models—constructed his stories out of the simplest materials, and made them work through sheer cleverness of invention and delicacy of touch. It seemed to me that the sort of thing that Sheckley did was within my own capacity. With luck and persistence I too might be publishing twenty-four stories a year and walking through the convention lobby trading jokes with my fellow celebrities.

Sheckley made it *look* easy, yes. But that doesn't mean that it *was* easy, as I found out when I got a little deeper into my own writing career. I suspect that no story worth reading ever was easy to write. And I discovered, as I came to know Sheckley, that those stories that I imagined he had dashed off blithely in a couple of hours were in fact the product of days of anguished revision. Most really prolific writers are people who have the discipline to keep at the job day in and day out; they aren't necessarily people who write with unusual swiftness or ease. Each page may be a bloody battle, but they add up steadily even if you can produce no more than five hundred or a thousand words a day.

Selecting just one story to represent Sheckley's *Wunderjahr* of

1953 in this book was a tough task for me. I hesitated among "Specialist" and "Keep Your Shape" and "Warm" and "Seventh Victim" and three or four others. "The Monsters" commended itself to me finally above the others, not only because it's an outstanding example of the breezy Sheckley manner but also because in its scant four thousand words it provides a textbook demonstration of a basic technique for generating science-fiction ideas: it creates the unfamiliar by turning the familiar upside down.

The speed with which Sheckley gets the story going is wondrous. The very first sentence signals the dissonance that gives rise to plot: "Cordovir and Hum stood on the rocky mountaintop, watching the new thing happen." The second sentence tells us that the tone of the story will be light, even comic: "Both felt rather good about it." The third sentence adds a further note of playfulness: "It was undoubtedly the newest thing that had happened for some time." Off and running in just thirty-one words.

Now comes some quick dialog and a bit of exposition. The style is compact, uncluttered, efficient. The experienced science-fiction reader is rapidly able to figure out that the "new thing" that is happening is the landing of a spaceship. ("A pointed object was hovering over the ground. From one end of it poured a substance resembling fire.") One sentence more and we know that Cordovir and Hum must be alien beings. ("Cordovir lifted himself higher on his thick tail, to get a better look.") Then—it is still the first page, hardly 150 words into the story—Sheckley plants an astonishing hook. Cordovir asks what day it is. Hum tells him. "Damn," Cordovir says. "I have to go home and kill my wife." They discuss whether he has time to do it before sunset. Hum volunteers to take care of it if Cordovir can't get back to town before dark. "That's very decent of you," Cordovir says, and they slither down the mountainside together.

What is this? A murder mystery? No, not at all. An ugly sexist fable certain to arouse the fury of feminists? Well, not that, either. It's a science-fiction story. The protagonists are aliens. They live in a society where it's absolutely all right—not merely permissible, but legitimate and socially desirable—for men to kill their wives. Common morality requires it of them. Sheckley will work all this out and make it convincing. And he will need only four thousand words to do the job.

Brief though the story is, its plot unfolds on two levels. The aliens are puzzled by the intentions from the visitors from space, and *we* wonder what all this bland and complacent wife-killing can possibly mean. Thus Sheckley arouses suspense, which even a comic story must have. The first thing a writer must know how to accomplish—without which, all other skill is irrelevant—is holding his reader's interest. Here the double plotting pays off. We may feel only mild interest in what the intruding spaceship will bring: after all, we've encountered that situation in a million other stories. But the ritual slaughter of wives, regarded by both sexes as entirely unexceptionable ("She had her back to the door, as etiquette required. Cordovir killed her with a single flying slash of his tail, dragged her body outside, and sat down to eat") is something new and strange and perplexing. The story is called "The Monsters," and most of us here on Earth would readily agree that killing one's wife is a monstrous thing to do, whether before dinner or after. Does Sheckley merely want us to deplore the odious behavior of these brutish alien beings? No, that's too simple. He must be up to something else. But what? What?

Once the killing of wives is out of the way, the men of the village settle down to discuss the arrival of the spaceship in a calm, serious manner. Are there intelligent beings on board? If so, Cordovir wonders, are they moral? Do they have a sense of right and wrong? He doubts it.

This from a "man" who has just killed his wife. We begin to glimpse Sheckley's satiric intent. The debate continues in the morning and Cordovir finds it necessary to kill another male who insists on interrupting him, an act that causes no fuss at all among the other debaters. The picture is becoming clearer.

Now creatures start to emerge from the spaceship. To Cordovir they are hideous aliens, decidedly not human. And surely they are not moral. Morality is very important to Cordovir. "Could anything so hideous be moral?" he asks. The visitors are so repellent that it is hard to see how they can stand themselves; a few villagers suggest killing them to put them out of their misery. Cordovir is of that faction; but Hum wins a delay so he can attempt to communicate with the strangers. Sheckley conveys all this with the simplest of means: brief paragraphs, dialog that rarely runs to more than one or two sentences per speech, and a lean, sparse style that employs a minimum of adjectives and adverbs.

Communication with the visitors fails. Cordovir goes to the surplus-female pen and acquires another wife. We are told that she will live with him only for the next twenty-five days. That seems to be the normal span of a marriage; then she will be killed. Encountering Hum, Cordovir says that the important thing to find out about the strange creatures that have arrived is if they are moral beings or monsters. If it hasn't become apparent yet, the central ironic inversion of the story is revealed here: the wife-killing aliens are the moral beings, the human spacefarers who have arrived on their planet are the monsters. We are back with Gulliver in the land of the Houyhnhnms, where the wise and kindly horses are the dominant beings and the Yahoos, or humans, are bestial creatures lacking any civilized trait.

A satirist like the misanthropic Swift need only turn things upside down and call the horses the masters and the humans the beasts of burden to score the points against our species that he wishes to make. Sheckley is writing science fiction, though. Simply standing the natural order of things on its head would be too easy. In Swift's fable, plausibility was not an issue; it's beside the point to object that there's no way in the world that horses could reduce humans to servitude, because we have cunning brains and useful hands with opposable thumbs, and they don't, which is why we are the riders and they are the steeds. But a science-fiction writer can't simply doodle up any old setup in the name of satire and expect us to suspend our disbelief.

Sheckley knows that he must give his world of wife-killers some kind of plausibility, some convincing rationale, or his story will fall apart.

And he does. At midpoint in "The Monsters" he tells us, in one of his few sections of pure exposition, that on Cordovir's world married females lay eggs every day, and eight females are hatched for every male. Sheckley doesn't tell us *why* that should happen, and doesn't need to. It's simply a fact of biology there.

Killing one's wives after twenty-five-day marriages is not the only way, of course, that the problem of surplus women could have been dealt with on Cordovir's world. The extra female infants could simply have been destroyed as soon as they hatched; or polygamy could have become the rule, or, if that social arrangement proved too intricate, as it generally does, the extra women might have been sent off to live in great nunnerylike assemblages far away. But nature is not required to arrive at the gentlest possible solution for such problems, especially among alien cultures. And there is a kind of genetic wisdom behind the grotesque solution Sheckley propounds. The wives who have been killed have had a chance to lay fertile eggs first. The gene pool of the species is constantly enlarged by the serial polygamy of the men, which would not be the case if seven-eighths of the females were killed at birth or otherwise excluded from the mating process.

What looks like sheer whimsy on Sheckley's part or else like casual and unthinking sexism turns out to have a solid Darwinian rationale. The surplus women are allowed to reach maturity; while they are unmarried they work at gathering food, performing manual tasks, and hatching the eggs of their married sisters. Once a month the most desirable ones are chosen to become the next group of wives; thus they get a chance to pass their useful traits to the new generation. (Culling the females at birth would make this selection process impossible.) Meanwhile a different Darwinian process is going on among the men, who have the leisure to spend their time in philosophical debate. There is no taboo against murder: one philosopher may readily kill another if he finds him discourteous, boring, or annoyingly deficient in logic. Thus the evolution of the race is furthered. The weak, the slow-witted, and the unmannerly are eliminated. Those who survive the nightly disputes and duels are strong, quick, and have a highly developed moral sense. It's a splendidly logical system. Its only apparent failing is that overenthusiastic slaughter among the males will aggravate the problem of the surplus unmarried females; but we can assume that some cultural check is built into the system to keep things in equilibrium. For example, there doesn't appear to be any formal warfare among these people, since the males release their needs for aggression in other ways. Stress-related disease is probably at a minimum, too. So a satisfactory number of males probably do survive past mating age despite the high incidence of mortal combat among them.

A splendidly logical system, yes, but not one that we Earthlings are likely to applaud. (At least not we who subscribe to the morality of Western industrial civilizations. Plenty of earlier civilizations on Earth have tolerated hand-to-hand combat among males; and in modern India today there seems to be a startlingly laissez-faire attitude toward wife-murder.) However, Cordovir and his friends aren't looking for our applause. By their own standards their behavior is perfectly acceptable; indeed it is governed by high moral imperatives. The alien visitors from space, who shamelessly refuse to kill their wives every twenty-five days, are the true monsters. They seem to be capable of telling untruths, also, difficult as that is for the villagers to believe, and beyond much doubt they have a host of other evil customs. If they are allowed to remain, one of the women in the surplus-female pen cries, they "will destroy our way of life. They will make us as terrible as they!" To which Cordovir adds, "Drive them out. Before they corrupt us!" Which is promptly done, and the villagers return to their decent and righteous customs.

Exactly so. Aliens, by definition, are alien: and we are just as alien to them as they are to us. Because Sheckley has so elegantly constructed his satirical inversion, he forces us to examine the meaning of morality and righteousness in a new light. And because he has set forth his parable so deftly, with such admirable craftsmanship, he has amused us as well as caused us to think. The story works as satire, as fanciful scientific speculation, and as light entertainment. No wonder Bob Sheckley was moving in the ranks of the high and mighty at the 1953 World Science Fiction Convention, inspiring esteem and envy in the likes of such callow onlookers as myself. At the age of 25 he was already a master of his craft.

COMMON TIME
JAMES BLISH

... the days went slowly round and round, endless
and uneventful as cycles in space. Time, and time-
pieces! How many centuries did my hammock tell,
as pendulumlike it swung to the ship's dull roll, and
ticked the hours and ages.

Herman Melville, in *Mardi*

I

Don't move.

It was the first thought that came into Garrard's
mind when he awoke, and perhaps it saved his life. He
lay where he was, strapped against the padding, listening to
the round hum of the engines. That in itself was wrong; he
should be unable to hear the overdrive at all.

He thought to himself: *Has it begun already?*

Otherwise everything seemed normal. The DFC-3 had
crossed over into interstellar velocity, and he was still alive,

and the ship was still functioning. The ship should at this moment be traveling at 22.4 times the speed of light—a neat 4,157,000 miles per second.

Somehow Garrard did not doubt that it was. On both previous tries, the ships had whiffed away toward Alpha Centauri at the proper moment when the overdrive should have cut in; and the split second of residual image after they had vanished, subjected to spectroscopy, showed a Doppler shift which tallied with the acceleration predicted for that moment by Haertel.

The trouble was not that Brown and Cellini hadn't gotten away in good order. It was simply that neither of them had ever been heard from again.

Very slowly, he opened his eyes. His eyelids felt terrifically heavy. As far as he could judge from the pressure of the couch against his skin, the gravity was normal; nevertheless, moving his eyelids seemed almost an impossible job.

After long concentration, he got them fully open. The instrument chassis was directly before him, extended over his diaphragm on its elbow joint. Still without moving anything but his eyes—and those only with the utmost patience—he checked each of the meters. Velocity: 22.4 c. Operating temperature: normal. Ship temperature: 37° C. Air pressure: 778 mm. Fuel: No. 1 tank full, No. 2 tank full, No. 3 tank full, No. 4 tank nine-tenths full. Gravity: 1 g. Calendar: stopped.

He looked at it closely, though his eyes seemed to focus very slowly, too. It was, of course, something more than a calendar—it was an all-purpose clock, designed to show him the passage of seconds, as well as of the ten months his trip was supposed to take to the double star. But there was no doubt about it: the second hand was motionless.

That was the second abnormality. Garrard felt an impulse to get up and see if he could start the clock again. Perhaps the trouble had been temporary and safely in the past. Immediately there sounded in his head the injunction he had drilled into himself for a full month before the trip had begun—

Don't move!

Don't move until you know the situation as far as it can be known without moving. Whatever it was that had snatched Brown and Cellini irretrievably beyond human ken was potent, and totally beyond anticipation. They had both been excellent men, intelligent, resourceful, trained to the point of diminishing returns and not a micron beyond that point—the best men in the Project. Preparations for every knowable kind of trouble had been built into their ships, as they had been built into the DFC-3. Therefore, if there was something wrong nevertheless, it would be something that might strike from some commonplace quarter—and strike only once.

He listened to the humming. It was even and placid, and not very loud, but it disturbed him deeply. The overdrive was supposed to be inaudible, and the tapes from the first un-manned test vehicles had recorded no such hum. The noise did not appear to interfere with the overdrive's operation, or to indicate any failure in it. It was just an irrelevancy for which he could find no reason.

But the reason existed. Garrard did not intend to do so much as draw another breath until he found out what it was.

Incredibly, he realized for the first time that he had not in fact drawn one single breath since he had first come to. Though he felt not the slightest discomfort, the discovery called up so overwhelming a flash of panic that he very nearly sat bolt upright on the couch. Luckily—or so it seemed, after the panic had begun to ebb—the curious lethargy which had affected his eyelids appeared to involve his whole body, for the impulse was gone before he could summon the energy to answer it. And the panic, poignant though it had been for an instant, turned out to be wholly intellectual. In a moment, he was observing that his failure to breathe in no way discommoded him as far as he could tell—it was just there, waiting to be explained. . . .

Or to kill him. But it hadn't, yet.

Engines humming; eyelids heavy; breathing absent; calendar stopped. The four facts added up to nothing. The temptation to move something—even if it were only a big toe—was strong, but Garrard fought it back. He had been awake only a short while—half an hour at most—and already had noticed four abnormalities. There were bound to be more, anomalies more subtle than these four; but available to close examination before he had to move. Nor was there anything in particular that he had to do, aside from caring for his own wants; the Project, on the chance that Brown's and Cellini's failure to return had resulted from some tampering with the overdrive, had made everything in the DFC-3 subject only to the computer. In a very real sense, Garrard was just along for the ride. Only when the overdrive was off could he adjust—

Pock.

It was a soft, low-pitched noise, rather like a cork coming out of a wine bottle. It seemed to have come just from the right of the control chassis. He halted a sudden jerk of his head on the cushions toward it with a flat fiat of will. Slowly, he moved his eyes in that direction.

He could see nothing that might have caused the sound. The ship's temperature dial showed no change, which ruled out a heat noise from differential contraction or expansion— the only possible explanation he could bring to mind.

He closed his eyes—a process which turned out to be just as difficult as opening them had been—and tried to visualize what the calendar had looked like when he had first come out of anesthesia. After he got a clear and—he was almost sure—accurate picture, Garrard opened his eyes again.

The sound had been the calendar, advancing one second. It was now motionless again, apparently stopped.

He did not know how long it took the second hand to make that jump, normally; the question had never come up. Certainly the jump, when it came at the end of each second, had been too fast for the eye to follow.

Belatedly, he realized what all this cogitation was costing him in terms of essential information. The calendar had moved. Above all and before anything else, he *must* know exactly how long it took it to move again. . . .

He began to count, allowing an arbitrary five seconds lost. *One-and-a-six, one-and-a-seven, one-and-an-eight—*

Garrard had gotten only that far when he found himself plunged into hell.

First, and utterly without reason, a sickening fear flooded swiftly through his veins, becoming more and more intense. His bowels began to knot, with infinite slowness. His whole body became a field of small, slow pulses—not so much shaking him as putting his limbs into contrary joggling motions, and making his skin ripple gently under his clothing. Against the hum another sound became audible, a nearly subsonic thunder which seemed to be inside his head. Still the fear mounted, and with it came the pain, and the tenesmus—a boardlike stiffening of his muscles, particularly across his abdomen and his shoulders, but affecting his forearms almost as grievously. He felt himself beginning, very gradually, to double at the middle, a motion about which he could do precisely nothing—a terrifying kind of dynamic paralysis. . . .

It lasted for hours. At the height of it, Garrard's mind, even his very personality, was washed out utterly; he was only a vessel of horror. When some few trickles of reason began to return over that burning desert of reasonless emotion, he found that he was sitting up on the cushions, and that with one arm he had thrust the control chassis back on its elbow so that it no longer jutted over his body. His clothing was wet with perspiration, which stubbornly refused to evaporate or to cool him. And his lungs ached a little, although he could still detect no breathing.

What under God had happened? Was it this that had killed Brown and Cellini? For it would kill Garrard, too—of that he was sure, if it happened often. It would kill him even if it happened only twice more, if the next two such things followed the first one closely. At the very best it would make a slobbering idiot of him; and though the computer might bring Garrard and the ship back to Earth, it would not be able to tell the Project about this tornado of senseless fear.

The calendar said that the eternity in hell had taken three seconds. As he looked at it in academic indignation, it said *pock* and condescended to make the total seizure four seconds long. With grim determination, Garrard began to count again.

He took care to establish the counting as an absolutely even, automatic process which would not stop at the back of his mind no matter what other problem he tackled along with it, or what emotional typhoons should interrupt him. Really compulsive counting cannot be stopped by any thing—not the transports of love nor the agonies of empires. Garrard knew the dangers in deliberately setting up such a mechanism in his mind, but he also knew how desperately he needed to time that clock tick. He was beginning to understand what had happened to him—but he needed exact measurement before he could put that understanding to use.

Of course there had been plenty of speculation on the possible effect of the overdrive on the subjective time of the pilot, but none of it had come to much. At any speed below the velocity of light, subjective and objective time were exactly the same as far as the pilot was concerned. For an observer on Earth, time aboard the ship would appear to be vastly slowed at near-light speeds; but for the pilot himself there would be no apparent change.

Since flight beyond the speed of light was impossible—although for slightly differing reasons—by both the current theories of relativity, neither theory had offered any clue as to what would happen on board a translight ship. They would not allow that any such ship could even exist. The Haertel transformation, on which, in effect, the DFC-3 flew, was non-relativistic: it showed that the apparent elapsed time of a translight journey should be identical in ship-time, and in the time of observers at both ends of the trip.

But since ship and pilot were part of the same system, both covered by the same expression in Haertel's equation, it had never occurred to anyone that the pilot and the ship might keep different times. The notion was ridiculous.

One-and-a-sevenhundredone, one-and-a-sevenhundredtwo, one-and-a-sevenhundredthree, one-and-a-sevenhundredfour . . .

The ship was keeping ship-time, which was identical with observer-time. It would arrive at the Alpha Centauri system in ten months. But the pilot was keeping Garrard-time, and it was beginning to look as though he wasn't going to arrive at all.

It was impossible, but there it was. Something—almost certainly an unsuspected physiological side effect of the overdrive field on human metabolism, an effect which naturally could not have been detected in the preliminary, robot-piloted tests of the overdrive—had speeded up Garrard's subjective apprehension of time, and had done a thorough job of it.

The second hand began a slow, preliminary quivering as the calendar's innards began to apply power to it. *Seventy-*

hundred-forty-one, seventy-hundred-forty-two, seventy-hundred-forty-three . . .

At the count of 7,058 the second hand began to jump to the next graduation. It took it several apparent minutes to get across the tiny distance, and several more to come completely to rest. Later still, the sound came to him:

Pock.

In a fever of thought, but without any real physical agitation, his mind began to manipulate the figures. Since it took him longer to count an individual number as the number became larger, the interval between the two calendar ticks probably was closer to 7,200 seconds than to 7,058. Figuring backward brought him quickly to the equivalence he wanted:

One second in ship-time was two hours in Garrard-time.

Had he really been counting for what was, for him, two whole hours? There seemed to be no doubt about it. It looked like a long trip ahead.

Just how long it was going to be struck him with stunning force. Time had been slowed for him by a factor of 7200. He would get to Alpha Centauri in just 72,000 months.

Which was—

Six thousand years!

2

Garrard sat motionless for a long time after that, the Nessus-shirt of warm sweat swathing him persistently, refusing even to cool. There was, after all, no hurry.

Six thousand years. There would be food and water and air for all that time, or for sixty or six hundred thousand years; the ship would synthesize his needs, as a matter of course, for as long as the fuel lasted, and the fuel bred itself.

Even if Garrard ate a meal every three seconds of objective, or ship, time (which, he realized suddenly, he wouldn't be able to do, for it took the ship several seconds of objective time to prepare and serve up a meal once it was ordered; he'd be lucky if he ate once a day, Garrard-time), there would be no reason to fear any shortage of supplies. That had been one of the earliest of the possibilities for disaster that the Project engineers had ruled out in the design of the DFC-3.

But nobody had thought to provide a mechanism which would indefinitely refurbish Garrard. After six thousand years, there would be nothing left of him but a faint film of dust on the DFC-3's dully gleaming horizontal surfaces. His corpse might outlast him a while, since the ship itself was sterile—but eventually he would be consumed by the bacteria which he carried in his own digestive tract. He needed those bacteria to synthesize part of his B-vitamin needs while he lived, but they would consume him without compunction once he had ceased to be as complicated and delicately balanced a thing as a pilot—or as any other kind of life.

Garrard was, in short, to die before the DFC-3 had gotten fairly away from Sol; and when, after twelve thousand apparent years, the DFC-3 returned to Earth, not even his mummy would be still aboard.

The chill that went through him at that seemed almost unrelated to the way he thought he felt about the discovery; it lasted an enormously long time, and insofar as he could characterize it at all, it seemed to be a chill of urgency and excitement—not at all the kind of chill he should be feeling at a virtual death sentence. Luckily it was not as intolerably violent as the last such emotional convulsion; and when it was over, two clock ticks later, it left behind a residuum of doubt.

Suppose that this effect of time-stretching was only mental? The rest of his bodily processes might still be keeping ship-time; Garrard had no immediate reason to believe otherwise. If so, he would be able to move about only on ship-time, too; it would take many apparent months to complete the simplest task.

But he would live, if that were the case. His mind would arrive at Alpha Centauri six thousand years older, and perhaps madder, than his body, but he would live.

If, on the other hand, his bodily movements were going to be as fast as his mental processes, he would have to be enormously careful. He would have to move slowly and exert as little force as possible. The normal human hand movement, in such a task as lifting a pencil, took the pencil from a state of rest to another state of rest by imparting to it an acceleration of about two feet per second per second—and, of course, decelerated it by the same amount. If Garrard were to attempt to impart to a two-pound weight, which was keeping ship-time, an acceleration of 14,440 ft/sec^2 in his time, he'd have to exert a force of nine hundred pounds on it.

The point was not that it couldn't be done—but that it would take as much effort as pushing a stalled jeep. He'd never be able to lift that pencil with his forearm muscles alone; he'd have to put his back into the task.

And the human body wasn't engineered to maintain stresses of that magnitude indefinitely. Not even the most powerful professional weight-lifter is forced to show his prowess throughout every minute of every day.

Pock.

That was the calendar again; another second had gone by. Or another two hours. It had certainly seemed longer than a second, but less than two hours, too. Evidently subjective time was an intensively recomplicated measure. Even in this world of micro-time—in which Garrard's mind, at least, seemed to be operating—he could make the lapses between calendar ticks seem a little shorter by becoming actively interested in some problem or other. That would help, during the waking hours, but it would help only if the rest of his body were *not* keeping the same time as his mind. If it were not, then he would lead an incredibly active, but perhaps not intolerable, mental life during the many centuries of his awake-time, and would be mercifully asleep for nearly as long.

Both problems—that of how much force he could exert with his body, and how long he could hope to be asleep in his mind—emerged simultaneously into the forefront of his consciousness while he still sat inertly on the hammock, their terms still much muddled together. After the single tick of the calendar, the ship—or the part of it that Garrard could see from here—settled back into complete rigidity. The sound of the engines, too, did not seem to vary in frequency or amplitude, at least as far as his ears could tell. He was still not breathing. Nothing moved, nothing changed.

It was the fact that he could still detect no motion of his diaphragm or his rib-cage that decided him at last. His body had to be keeping ship-time, otherwise he would have blacked out from oxygen starvation long before now. That assumption explained, too, those two incredibly prolonged, seemingly sourceless saturnalias of emotion through which he had suffered: they had been nothing more nor less than the response of his endocrine glands to the purely intellectual reactions he had experienced earlier. He had discovered that he was not breathing, had felt a flash of panic and had tried to sit up. Long after his mind had forgotten those two impulses, they had inched their way from his brain down his nerves to the glands and muscles involved, and actual, *physical* panic had supervened. When that was over, he actually *was* sitting up, though the flood of adrenaline had prevented his noticing the motion as he had made it. The later chill—less violent, and apparently associated with the discovery that he might die long before the trip was completed—actually had been his body's response to a much earlier mental command—the abstract fever of interest he had felt while computing the time differential had been responsible for it.

Obviously, he was going to have to be very careful with apparently cold and intellectual impulses of any kind—or he would pay for them later with a prolonged and agonizing glandular reaction. Nevertheless, the discovery gave him considerable satisfaction, and Garrard allowed it free play; it certainly could not hurt him to feel pleased for a few hours, and the glandular pleasure might even prove helpful if it caught him at a moment of mental depression. Six thousand years, after all, provided a considerable number of opportunities for feeling down in the mouth; so it would be best to encourage all pleasure moments, and let the after-reaction last as long as it might. It would be the instants of panic, of fear, of gloom, which he would have to regulate sternly the moment they came into his mind; it would be those which would otherwise plunge him into four, five, six, perhaps even ten, Garrard-hours of emotional inferno.

Pock.

There now, that was very good: there had been two Garrard-hours which he had passed with virtually no difficulty of any kind, and without being especially conscious of their passage. If he could really settle down and become used to this kind of scheduling, the trip might not be as bad as he had at first feared. Sleep would take immense bites out of it; and during the waking periods he could put in one hell of a lot of creative thinking. During a single day of ship-time, Garrard could get in more thinking than any philosopher of Earth could have managed during an entire lifetime. Garrard could, if he disciplined himself sufficiently, devote his mind for a century to running down the consequences of a single thought, down to the last detail, and still have millennia left to go on to the next thought. What panoplies of pure reason could he not have assembled by the time six thousand years had gone by? With sufficient concentration, he might come up with the solution to the Problem of Evil between breakfast and dinner of a single ship's day, and in a ship's month might put his finger on the First Cause!

Pock.

Not that Garrard was sanguine enough to expect that he would remain logical or even sane throughout the trip. The vista was still grim, in much of its detail. But the opportunities, too, were there. He felt a momentary regret that it hadn't been Haertel, rather than himself, who had been given such an opportunity—

Pock.

—for the old man could certainly have made better use of it than Garrard could. The situation demanded someone trained in the highest rigors of mathematics to be put to the best conceivable use. Still and all Garrard began to feel—

Pock.

—that he would give a good account of himself, and it tickled him to realize that (as long as he held on to his essential sanity) he would return—

Pock.

—to Earth after ten Earth months with knowledge centuries advanced beyond anything—

Pock.

—that Haertel knew, or that anyone could know—

Pock.

—who had to work within a normal lifetime. *Pck.* The whole prospect tickled him. *Pck.* Even the clock tick seemed more cheerful. *Pck.* He felt fairly safe now *Pck* in disregarding his drilled-in command *Pck* against moving *Pck*, since in any *Pck* event he *Pck* had already *Pck* moved *Pck* without

Pck being *Pck* harmed *Pck* *Pck* *Pck* *Pck* *Pck* *Pckpckpckpckpckpckpck.* . . .

He yawned, stretched, and got up. It wouldn't do to be too pleased, after all. There were certainly many problems that still needed coping with, such as how to keep the impulse toward getting a ship-time task performed going, while his higher centers were following the ramifications of some purely philosophical point. And besides—

And besides, he had just moved.

More than that; he had just performed a complicated maneuver with his body *in normal time!*

Before Garrard looked at the calendar itself, the message it had been ticking away at him had penetrated. While he had been enjoying the protracted, glandular backwash of his earlier feeling of satisfaction, he had failed to notice, at least consciously, that the calendar was accelerating.

Good-bye, vast ethical systems which would dwarf the Greeks. Good-bye, calculuses aeons advanced beyond the spinor calculus of Dirac. Good-bye, cosmologies by Garrard which would allot the Almighty a job as third-assistant-waterboy in an n-dimensional backfield.

Good-bye, also, to a project he had once tried to undertake in college—to describe and count the positions of love, of which, according to under-the-counter myth, there were supposed to be at least forty-eight. Garrard had never been able to carry his tally beyond twenty, and he had just lost what was probably his last opportunity to try again.

The micro-time in which he had been living had worn off, only a few objective minutes after the ship had gone into overdrive and he had come out of the anesthetic. The long intellectual agony, with its glandular counterpoint, had come to nothing. Garrard was now keeping ship-time.

Garrard sat back down on the hammock, uncertain whether to be bitter or relieved. Neither emotion satisfied him in the end; he simply felt unsatisfied. Micro-time had been bad enough while it lasted; but now it was gone, and everything seemed normal. How could so transient a thing have killed Brown and Cellini? They were stable men, more stable, by his own private estimation, than Garrard himself. Yet he had come through it. Was there more to it than this?

And if there was—what, conceivably, could it be?

There was no answer. At his elbow, on the control chassis which he had thrust aside during that first moment of infinitely protracted panic, the calendar continued to tick. The engine noise was gone. His breath came and went in natural rhythm. He felt light and strong. The ship was quiet, calm, unchanging.

The calendar ticked, faster and faster. It reached and passed the first hour, ship-time, of flight in overdrive.

Pock.

Garrard looked up in surprise. The familiar noise, this time, had been the hour hand jumping one unit. The minute hand was already sweeping past the past half-hour. The second hand was whirling like a propellor—and while he watched it, it speeded up to complete invisibility—

Pock.

Another hour. The half-hour already passed. *Pock.* Another hour. *Pock.* Another. *Pock. Pock. Pock, Pock, Pock, Pock, pck-pck-pck-pck-pckpckpckpck....*

The hands of the calendar swirled toward invisibility as time ran away with Garrard. Yet the ship did not change. It stayed there, rigid, inviolate, invulnerable. When the date tumblers reached a speed at which Garrard could no longer read them, he discovered that once more he could not move— and that, although his whole body seemed to be aflutter like that of a hummingbird, nothing coherent was coming to him through his senses. The room was dimming, becoming redder; or no, it was—

But he never saw the end of the process, never was allowed to look from the pinnacle of macro-time toward which the Haertel overdrive was taking him.

Pseudo-death took him first.

3

That Garrard did not die completely, and within a comparatively short time after the DFC-3 had gone into overdrive, was due to the purest of accidents; but Garrard did not know that. In fact, he knew nothing at all for an indefinite period, sitting rigid and staring, his metabolism slowed down to next to nothing, his mind almost utterly inactive. From time to time, a single wave of low-level metabolic activity passed through him—what an electrician might have termed a "maintenance turnover"—in response to the urgings of some occult survival urge; but these were of so basic a nature as to reach his consciousness not at all. This was the pseudo-death.

When the observer actually arrived, however, Garrard woke. He could make very little sense out of what he saw or felt even now; but one fact was clear: the overdrive was off—and with it the crazy alterations in time rates—and there was strong light coming through one of the ports. The first leg of the trip was over. It had been these two changes in his environment which had restored him to life.

The thing (or things) which had restored him to consciousness, however, was—it was what? It made no sense. It was a construction, a rather fragile one, which completely surrounded his hammock. No, it wasn't a construction, but evidently something alive—a living being, organized horizontally, that had arranged itself in a circle about him. No, it was a number of beings. Or a combination of all of these things.

How it had gotten into the ship was a mystery, but there it was. Or there they were.

"How do you hear?" the creature said abruptly. Its voice, or their voices, came at equal volume from every point in the circle, but not from any particular point in it. Garrard could think of no reason why that should be unusual.

"I—" he said. "Or we—we hear with our ears. Here."

His answer, with its unintentionally long chain of open vowel sounds, rang ridiculously. He wondered why he was speaking such an odd language.

"We-they wooed to pitch you-yours thiswise," the creature said. With a thump, a book from the DFC-3's ample library fell to the deck beside the hammock. "We wooed there and there and there for a many. You are the being-Garrard. We-they are the clinesterton beademung, with all of love."

"With all of love," Garrard echoed. The beademung's use of the language they both were speaking was odd; but again Garrard could find no logical reason why the beademung's usage should be considered wrong.

"Are—are you-they from Alpha Centauri?" he said hesitantly.

"Yes, we hear the twin radioceles, that show there beyond the gift-orifices. We-they pitched that the being-Garrard with most adoration these twins and had mind to them, soft and loud alike. How do you hear?"

This time the being-Garrard understood the question. "I hear Earth," he said. "But that is very soft, and does not show."

"Yes," said the beademung. "It is a harmony, not a first, as ours. The All-Devouring listens to lovers there, not on the radioceles. Let me-mine pitch you-yours so to have mind of the rodalent beademung and other brothers and lovers, along the channel which is fragrant to the being-Garrard."

Garrard found that he understood the speech without difficulty. The thought occurred to him that to understand a language on its own terms—without having to put it back into English in one's own mind—is an ability that is won only with difficulty and long practice. Yet, instantly his mind said, "But it *is* English," which of course it was. The offer the clinesterton beademung had just made was enormously hearted, and he in turn was much minded and of love, to his own delighting as well as to the beademungen; that almost went without saying.

There were many matings of ships after that, and the being-Garrard pitched the harmonies of the beademungen, leaving his ship with the many gift orifices in harmonic for the All-Devouring to love, while the beademungen made show of they-theirs.

He tried, also, to tell how he was out of love with the overdrive, which wooed only spaces and times, and made featurelings. The rodalent beademung wooed the overdrive, but it did not pitch he-them.

Then the being-Garrard knew that all the time was devoured, and he must hear Earth again.

"I pitch you-them to fullest love," he told the beademungen, "I shall adore the radioceles of Alpha and Proxima Centauri, 'on Earth, as it is in Heaven.' Now the overdrive my-other must woo and win me, and make me adore a featureling much like silence."

"But you will be pitched again," the clinesterton beademung said. "After you have adored Earth. You are much loved by Time, the All-Devouring. We-they shall wait for this othering."

Privately Garrard did not faith as much, but he said, "Yes,

we-they will make a new wooing of the beademungen at some other radiant. With all of love."

On this the beademungen made and pitched adorations, and in the midst the overdrive cut in. The ship with the many gift-orifices and the being-Garrard him-other saw the twin radioceles sundered away.

Then, once more, came the pseudo-death.

4

When the small candle lit in the endless cavern of Garrard's pseudo-dead mind, the DFC-3 was well inside the orbit of Uranus. Since the sun was still very small and distant, it made no spectacular display through the nearby port, and nothing called him from the post-death sleep for nearly two days.

The computers waited patiently for him. They were no longer immune to his control; he could now tool the ship back to Earth himself if he so desired. But the computers were also designed to take into account the fact that he might be truly dead by the time the DFC-3 got back. After giving him a solid week, during which time he did nothing but sleep, they took over again. Radio signals began to go out, tuned to a special channel.

An hour later, a very weak signal came back. It was only a directional signal, and it made no sound inside the DFC-3— but it was sufficient to put the big ship in motion again.

It was that which woke Garrard. His conscious mind was still glazed over with the icy spume of the pseudo-death; and as far as he could see, the interior of the cabin had not changed one whit, except for the book on the deck—

The book. The clinesterton beademung had dropped it there. But what under God was a clinesterton beademung?

And what was he, Garrard, crying about? It didn't make sense. He remembered dimly some kind of experience out there by the Centauri twins—

—the twin radioceles—

There was another one of those words. It seemed to have Greek roots, but he knew no Greek—and besides, why would Centaurians speak Greek?

He leaned forward and actuated the switch which would roll the shutter off the front port, actually a telescope with a translucent viewing screen. It showed a few stars, and a faint nimbus off on one edge which might be the Sun. At about one o'clock on the screen was a planet about the size of a pea which had tiny projections, like teacup handles, on each side. The DFC-3 hadn't passed Saturn on its way out; at that time it had been on the other side of the Sun from the route the starship had had to follow. But the planet was certainly difficult to mistake.

Garrard was on his way home—and he was still alive and sane. Or was he still sane? These fantasies about Centaurians —which still seemed to have such a profound emotional effect upon him—did not argue very well for the stability of his mind.

But they were fading rapidly. When he discovered, clutching at the handiest fragments of the "memories," that the plural of *beademung* was *beademungen*, he stopped taking the problem seriously. Obviously a race of Centaurians who spoke Greek wouldn't also be forming weak German plurals. The whole business had obviously been thrown up by his unconscious.

But what *had* he found by the Centaurus stars?

There was no answer to that question but that incomprehensible garble about love, the All-Devouring, and beademungen. Possibly he had never seen the Centaurus stars at all, but had been lying here, cold as a mackerel, for the entire twenty months.

Or had it been twelve thousand years? After the tricks the overdrive had played with time, there was no way to tell what the objective date actually was. Frantically Garrard put the telescope into action. Where was the Earth? After twelve thousand years—

The Earth was there. Which, he realized swiftly, proved nothing. The Earth had lasted for many millions of years; twelve thousand years was nothing to a planet. The Moon was there, too; both were plainly visible, on the far side of the Sun—but not too far to pick them out clearly, with the telescope at highest power. Garrard could even see a clear sun-highlight on the Atlantic Ocean, not far east of Greenland; evidently the computers were bringing the DFC-3 in on the Earth from about 23° north of the plane of the ecliptic.

The Moon, too, had not changed. He could even see on its face the huge splash of white, mimicking the sun-highlight on Earth's ocean, which was the magnesium hydroxide landing beacon, which had been dusted over the Mare Vaporum in the earliest days of space flight, with a dark spot on its southern edge which could only be the crater Monilius.

But that again proved nothing. The Moon never changed. A film of dust laid down by modern man on its face would last for millennia—what, after all, existed on the Moon to blow it away? The Mare Vaporum beacon covered more than four thousand square miles; age would not dim it, nor could man himself undo it—either accidentally, or on purpose—in anything under a century. When you dust an area that large on a world without atmosphere, it stays dusted.

He checked the stars against his charts. They hadn't moved; why should they have, in only twelve thousand years? The pointer stars in the Dipper still pointed to Polaris.

Draco, like a fantastic bit of tape, wound between the two Bears, and Cepheus and Cassiopeia, as it always had done. These constellations told him only that it was spring in the northern hemisphere of Earth.

But spring of what year?

Then, suddenly, it occurred to Garrard that he had a method of finding the answer. The Moon causes tides in the Earth, and action and reaction are always equal and opposite. The Moon cannot move things on Earth without itself being affected—and that effect shows up in the moon's angular momentum. The Moon's distance from the Earth increases steadily by 0.6 inches every year. At the end of 12,000 years, it should be six hundred feet farther away from the Earth.

Was it possible to measure? Garrard doubted it, but he got out his ephemeris and his dividers anyhow, and took pictures. While he worked, the Earth grew nearer. By the time he had finished his first calculation—which was indecisive, because it allowed a margin for error greater than the distances he was trying to check—Earth and Moon were close enough in the telescope to permit much more accurate measurements.

Which were, he realized wryly, quite unnecessary. The computer had brought the DFC-3 back, not to an observed sun or planet, but simply to a calculated point. That Earth and Moon would not be near that point when the DFC-3 returned was not an assumption that the computer could make. That the Earth was visible from here was already good and sufficient proof that no more time had elapsed than had been calculated for from the beginning.

This was hardly new to Garrard; it had simply been retired to the back of his mind. Actually he had been doing all this figuring for one reason, and one reason only: because deep in his brain, set to work by himself, there was a mechanism that demanded counting. Long ago, while he was still trying to time the ship's calendar, he had initiated compulsive counting—and it appeared that he had been counting ever since. That had been one of the known dangers of deliberately starting such a mental mechanism; and now it was bearing fruit in these perfectly useless astronomical exercises.

The insight was healing. He finished the figures roughly, and that unheard moron deep inside his brain stopped counting at last. It had been pawing its abacus for twenty months now, and Garrard imagined that it was as glad to be retired as he was to feel it go.

His radio squawked, and said anxiously, "DFC-3, DFC-3. Garrard, do you hear me? Are you still alive? Everybody's going wild down here. Garrard, if you hear me, call us!"

It was Haertel's voice. Garrard closed the dividers so convulsively that one of the points nipped into the heel of his hand. "Haertel, I'm here. DFC-3 to the Project. This is Garrard." And then, without knowing quite why, he added: "With all of love."

Haertel, after all the hoopla was over, was more than interested in the time effects. "It certainly enlarges the manifold in which I was working," he said. "But I think we can account for it in the transformation. Perhaps even factor it out, which would eliminate it as far as the pilot is concerned. We'll see, anyhow."

Garrard swirled his highball reflectively. In Haertel's cramped old office, in the Project's administration shack, he felt both strange and as old, as compressed, constricted. He said, "I don't think I'd do that, Adolph. I think it saved my life."

"How?"

"I told you that I seemed to die after a while. Since I got home, I've been reading; and I've discovered that the psychologists take far less stock in the individuality of the human psyche than you and I do. You and I are physical scientists, so we think about the world as being all outside our skins—something which is to be observed, but which doesn't alter the essential *I*. But evidently, that old solipsistic position isn't quite true. Our very personalities, really, depend in large part upon *all* the things in our environment, large and small, that exist outside our skins. If by some means you could cut a human being off from every sense impression that comes to him from outside, he would cease to exist as a personality within two or three minutes. Probably he would die."

"Unquote: Harry Stack Sullivan," Haertel said, dryly. "So?"

"So," Garrard said, "think of what a monotonous environment the inside of a spaceship is. It's perfectly rigid, still, unchanging, lifeless. In ordinary interplanetary flight, in such an environment, even the most hardened spaceman may go off his rocker now and then. You know the typical spaceman's psychosis as well as I do, I suppose. The man's personality goes rigid, just like his surroundings. Usually he recovers as soon as he makes port, and makes contact with a more-or-less normal world again.

"But in the DFC-3, I was cut off from the world around me much more severely. I couldn't look outside the ports—I was in overdrive, and there was nothing to see. I couldn't communicate with home, because I was going faster than light. And then I found I couldn't move either, for an enormous long while; and that even the instruments that are in constant change for the usual spaceman wouldn't be in motion for me. Even those were fixed.

"After the time rate began to pick up, I found myself in an even more impossible box. The instruments moved, all right, but then they moved too *fast* for me to read them. The whole situation was now utterly rigid—and, in effect, I died.

I froze as solid as the ship around me, and stayed that way as long as the overdrive was on."

"By that showing," Haertel said dryly, "the time effects were hardly your friends."

"But they were, Adolph. Look. Your engines act on subjective time; they keep it varying along continuous curves—from far-too-slow to far-too-fast—and, I suppose, back down again. Now, this is a *situation of continuous change*. It wasn't marked enough, in the long run, to keep me out of pseudo-death; but it was sufficient to protect me from being obliterated altogether, which I think is what happened to Brown and Cellini. Those men knew that they could shut down the overdrive if they could just get to it, and they killed themselves trying. But I knew that I just had to sit and take it—and, by my great good luck, your sine-curve time variation made it possible for me to survive."

"Ah, ah," Haertel said. "A point worth considering—though I doubt that it will make interstellar travel very popular!"

He dropped back into silence, his thin mouth pursed. Garrard took a grateful pull at his drink.

At last Haertel said: "Why are you in trouble over these Centaurians? It seems to me that you have done a good job. It was nothing that you were a hero—any fool can be brave—but I see also that you *thought*, where Brown and Cellini evidently only reacted. Is there some secret about what you found when you reached those two stars?"

Garrard said, "Yes, there is. But I've already told you what it is. When I came out of the pseudo-death, I was just a sort of plastic palimpsest upon which anybody could have made a mark. My own environment, my ordinary Earth environment, was a hell of a long way off. My present surroundings were nearly as rigid as they had ever been. When I met the Centaurians—if I did, and I'm not at all sure of that—*they* became the most important thing in my world, and my personality changed to accommodate and understand them. That was a change about which I couldn't do a thing.

"Possibly I did understand them. But the man who understood them wasn't the same man you're talking to now, Adolph. Now that I'm back on Earth, I don't understand that man. He even spoke English in a way that's gibberish to me. If I can't understand myself during that period—and I can't; I don't even believe that that man was the Garrard I know—what hope have I of telling you or the Project about the Centaurians? They found me in a controlled environment, and they altered me by entering it. Now that they're gone, nothing comes through; I don't even understand why I think they spoke English!"

"Did they have a name for themselves?"

"Sure," Garrard said. "They were the beademungen."

"What did they look like?"

"I never saw them."

Haertel leaned forward. "Then . . ."

"I heard them. I think." Garrard shrugged, and tasted his Scotch again. He was home, and on the whole he was pleased.

But in his malleable mind he heard someone say, *On Earth, as it is in Heaven*; and then, in another voice, which might also have been his own (why had he thought "him-other"?), *It is later than you think*.

"Adolph," he said, "is this all there is to it? Or are we going to go on with it from here? How long will it take to make a better starship, a DFC-4?"

"Many years," Haertel said, smiling kindly. "Don't be anxious, Garrard. You've come back, which is more than the others managed to do, and nobody will ask you to go out again. I really think that it's hardly likely that we'll get another ship built during your lifetime; and even if we do, we'll be slow to launch it. We really have very little information about what kind of playground you found out there."

"I'll go," Garrard said. "I'm not afraid to go back—I'd like to go. Now that I know how the DFC-3 behaves, I could take it out again, bring you back proper maps, tapes, photos."

"Do you really think," Haertel said, his face suddenly serious, "that we could let the DFC-3 go out again? Garrard, we're going to take that ship apart practically molecule by molecule; that's preliminary to the building of any DFC-4. And no more can we let you go. I don't mean to be cruel, but has it occurred to you that this desire to go back may be the result of some kind of post-hypnotic suggestion? If so, the more badly you want to go back, the more dangerous to us all you may be. We are going to have to examine you just as thoroughly as we do the ship. If these beademungen wanted you to come back, they must have had a reason—and we have to know that reason."

Garrard nodded, but he knew that Haertel could see the slight movement of his eyebrows and the wrinkles forming in his forehead, the contractions of the small muscles which stop the flow of tears only to make grief patent on the rest of the face.

"In short," he said, *"don't move."*

Haertel looked politely puzzled. Garrard, however, could say nothing more. He had returned to humanity's common time, and would never leave it again.

Not even, for all his dimly remembered promise, with all there was left in him of love.

COMMON TIME:
WITH ALL OF LOVE

his is a marvelous story. I have thought so for more than thirty years, and since 1970 I have included it in no less than five of the anthologies I have edited, which is one way of putting my money where my mouth is. It is built around the startling and uniquely science-fictional predicament of a space voyager traveling faster than light, and handles that theoretically impossible situation with as much scientific plausibility as anyone could; it is told in an effective and dramatically moving manner; and at the proper moment it leaps into a passage of (completely legitimate) linguistic fantasy that continues to haunt me a generation after I first came upon it in that year—so memorable for me—of 1953.

I happen to know, because I was a close friend both of James Blish and of the editor (Robert A. W. Lowndes) who commissioned the story, how "Common Time" came into being: and a very curious genesis it was indeed. Those who wonder how story ideas are born are likely to find the tale instructive.

There was, in the olden days, a custom among fiction magazines of printing four magazine covers at a time. Evidently, it was cheaper to do it that way; and the old pulp magazines were nothing if they weren't cheap. Magazines then, as they usually do now, preferred their cover illustrations to depict some scene from one of the stories within. But sometimes the press date for the latest batch of covers would approach and the editor would have no story on hand for the next issue that contained an appropriately illustratable scene. Printers' schedules are notoriously inflexible and writers' schedules are notoriously haphazard, which led some editors finally to come up with this ingenious solution to the problem: have the cover painted *first*, find the story that it illustrated afterward. Since commercial artists are generally more reliable about deadlines than most short-story writers, the editor and his art director could work well in advance, keeping a backlog of paintings on hand and asking certain dependable writers to produce stories written around the scenes shown. That way there would always be "cover stories" waiting to be included in the issues whose covers were being printed in those batches of four. (I did a good many such stories myself, from 1956 until about 1963, and one final one in 1968. The custom seems to be extinct now.)

Blish, early in 1953, was handed a photostat of a painting that showed a draftsman's compasses with their points extended to pierce two planets, one of them the Earth and the other a cratered globe that might have been the Moon. A line of yellow string also connected the two worlds. In the background were two star-charts and the swirling arms of a spiral nebula. Blish later recalled that the pair of planets and their connecting yellow string reminded him on some unconscious level of a pair of testicles and the vas deferens, which is the long tube through which sperm passes during the act of ejaculation. And out of that—by the tortuous and always mysterious process of manipulation of initial material that is the way stories come into being—he somehow conjured up the strange and unforgettable voyage of "Common Time," which duly appeared as the cover story on the August, 1953, issue of *Science Fiction Quarterly*, where I encountered it, and read it with deep astonishment, one hot summer afternoon early in the Eisenhower Administration.

I failed to notice, I ought to admit, anything in the story suggesting that it was about the passage of sperm through the vas deferens and onward to the uterus. To me in my innocence it was nothing more than an ingenious tale of the perils of faster-than-light travel between stars. Damon Knight, in a famous essay published in 1957, demonstrated that the voyage of the sperm was what the story was "really" about, extracting from it a long series of puns and other figures of speech that exemplified the underlying sexual symbolism of everything that happens: the repeated phrase *"Don't move"* indicates the moment of orgasm, and so forth. Blish himself was fascinated by that interpretation of his story and added a host of embellishments to Knight's theory in a subsequent letter to him. All of which called forth some hostility from other well-known science-fiction writers, and for months a lively controversy ran through the s-f community. Lester del Rey, for example, had no use for any symbolist interpretations of fiction. "A story, after all, is not a guessing game," del Rey said. "We write for entertainment, which means primarily for casual reading. Now even Knight has to pore through a story carefully and deliberately to get all the symbols, so we can't really communicate readily and reliably by them. To the casual reader, the conscious material on the surface must be enough. Hence we have to construct a story to be a complete and satisfying thing, even without the symbols. . . . If we get off on a binge of writing symbols for our own satisfaction, there's entirely too much temptation to feel that we don't have to make our points explicitly, but to feel a smug glow of satisfaction in burying them so they only appear to those who look for symbols."

It seems to me, looking back at the controversy across nearly thirty years, that everyone was addressing a slightly different issue. Knight's point about symbols was that nearly every story—Blish's was simply an extreme example—has an underlying symbolic content, scarcely apparent to the reader *and perhaps not even to the writer*, which operated on the reader on the unconscious level to enhance the story's power. Nowhere was Knight suggesting that a writer should begin with the pattern of symbols and fill in the plot, the character, and the setting afterward, although some of his opponents seemed to interpret his essay that way. Del Rey, of course, was right to insist that the writer must attend to the surface level of his story: unless it makes sense as narrative to a casual but not inattentive reader, it isn't likely to *have* any readers who will appreciate its amazing symbolic substructure. But that isn't to say that a story doesn't have such a substructure, whether the author meant it to be there or not. Blish, who supplied additional symbolic details to buttress Knight's clever analysis and went searching for more in all his previous stories, could have been construed as having been converted by Knight to the notion that the symbols are more important than the story; but I don't think that that was the case. Having written "Common Time" as a response to someone else's set of images, Blish now was looking with much fascination at the set of images his own unconscious mind apparently had thrust up into the narrative levels of his story, and to his own surprise found many of the same images in his earlier works.

My own position lay somewhere in the middle, and still does. I think every story is probably full of unconscious symbols, but Knight's idea that there are grand archetypes that can be relied on to affect a reader's response seems untrustworthy, because to my way of thinking there is no universally shared language of symbols: a burning barn may "mean" *sexual excitement* to one reader and *famine and hardship* to another. So *spaceship = penis* or *flowing water = eternal life* are not likely to evoke the automatic and universal response that the writer may be hoping to achieve. But it can be tremendously effective for a writer to bury a private symbol-set in the deeper layers of a story. A coherent and coherently evolving group of internally consistent images and correlations that works in the depths of a story to amplify and intensify the events of the narrative can certainly lend additional structural integrity to that narrative, I believe. But the surface narrative, as del Rey insists, must come first; the writer, if he is so inclined, may experiment with building in a symbolic substructure, which may or may not have much effect on the reader; and the writer's own unconscious will surely add its own additional level of symbology, which will probably have a strong but indeterminable effect on the power of the story but which is best detected after the fact by someone other than the writer. (And the writer himself would be well advised to pay no attention, lest he wind up paralyzing himself with a self-conscious scramble for bigger and better symbols.)

All that having been said, what do we have in "Common Time"? Again, the fast opening. *Don't move*, we read, and we know that something must be wrong. Garrard is in trouble, but he may have saved his life by keeping still.

What sort of trouble? Blish tells us. The exposition is quick and clear. An experimental faster-than-light voyage is under way. There have been two previous such flights. The pilots of both—each traveling solo—were never heard from again. Good: the science-fictional situation has been established, and the protagonist is in jeopardy. He is awakening on schedule into a strange situation that turns out to be even stranger than expected, for time, it seems, is standing still for him.

Garrard comes to that realization in stages. He has to struggle to move his eyelids. Then he notices that the clock isn't running. And then it occurs to him that he isn't breathing. Such use of transitions and gradual processes are valuable in developing a story: they build reader involvement, they create suspense. Where an amateur might baldly say, "Time had apparently stopped," Blish takes a couple of pages to make us *feel* Garrard's discovery of that fact, step by step. (The trick can be abused; we might have been buried under ten pages of tiny transitions, thus hiding the forest behind the trees. A sense of proportion is essential in every aspect of constructing a story.)

In fact, time hasn't stopped—only slowed enormously, so far as Garrard can tell. It becomes his task to figure out what is really going on. He suspects that his two predecessors must have perished because they failed at that task. His survival, then, is at stake. The problem of the story is established. Now Garrard must struggle for his life, undergoing an agony that is the main body of the tale. (I'm using agony in its classical meaning here: not necessarily pain or grief, but simply a struggle or a contest. It comes from the Greek word *agon*, which referred originally to such contests as those of the Olympic Games. The word protagonist, meaning the chief personage or personages in a drama, comes from the same root: the protagonists are the ones who enact the agon, or struggle, that lies at the heart of every dramatic situation.)

Garrard's agony is indeed an agonizing one. It brings him periods of prolonged emotional and physical distress, which gradually he learns to understand and even use to his own advantage. Blish relates it in a dry, concise way. The tone of the story is controlled, the texture is austere; that is one of its fascinations. Hysteria would not have enhanced anything here. The situation itself is weird enough; no need to hype it up with heavy breathing, only to tell what happens simply, clearly, and straightforwardly. (Or, at any rate, *apparently* straightforwardly, I ought to add, considering that Damon Knight would have us believe that what we are really reading is a description of the process of fertilization and not an account of the problems of a space farer.) Tension is created by the absolutely clear delineation of the absolutely incomprehensible, and by a few technical devices such as the use of italicized words: the initial *Don't move*, and then the repeated *pocks* of the calendar.

Thus Blish guides us deeper and deeper into the mysteries of the flight of the DFC-3, maintaining tight control as he draws us along. One way he does this is by making the unreal as real as he can: by giving us the air-pressure readings, for instance, or by his brief and masterly discussion of the relativistic effects, or by such incidental bits of erudition as the reference to tenesmus—followed immediately by its definition to keep the reader from feeling baffled and hostile. Blish does beautiful detail-work, down to calculating the force Garrard must exert to move a pencil. (Is the calculation correct? Most readers, including this one, won't bother to check. Best not to fake it, though. God will check, and so will a few readers of a certain disposition, and they'll tell everybody. Besides, a writer who gets into the habit of faking what doesn't need to be faked is sure to forfeit his credibility somewhere along the line: everybody needs to fake a little here and there, and you will be able to fool even a smart reader on many things, but the limit is all too easily reached.)

The detail-work is part of the job of creating and maintaining the illusion. The author, by demonstrating a fund of competence and experience deeper than the reader's, exerts his authority. (The pun is no accident.) One necessary thing any writer must do is make the reader believe at least for the time it takes to read it that this made-up chunk of events and conversations is actually a report on a segment of reality; and a good way to achieve this is to tell the story in a calm, confident way, so that it seems as though one is operating from a position of complete knowledge. Genuinely holding such a position is a great help in accomplishing this, which is why the best writers try to learn everything they can about the universe and how it works. Nobody learns it all, but if you learn enough you can feel safe in adopting an air of omniscience and make it seem convincing. Nervous and apologetic writers, like nervous and apologetic lovers, are rarely successful. And the skillful writer, like the skillful lover, knows how to move deftly around his own areas of inadequacy so that he gives the illusion that he is without any.

Having made us believe that Garrard really is out there somewhere in the DFC-3, Blish now begins to pull the rabbits out of his hat. Garrard, by methodical counting, manages to discover that he will experience six thousand subjective years while the ship is making its ten-month journey to Alpha Centauri. We feel the horror of that revelation. Then comes the elegant and ironic return to normal time, denoted by the cascade of pocks just as Garrard has begun to come to terms with the problem of how he will usefully spend his vastly extended life span aboard ship. Which leads to the next surprise: having figured out how to cope with slowing down, Garrard suddenly finds himself speeding up. Which leads into the "pseudo-death" and the beautifully dreamlike scene of the clinesterton beademung.

Here Blish's cool, precise style pays off. He has been setting us up for a sudden wild departure into the utterly alien; and when it comes, we can handle it, more or less, because it is embedded in an otherwise unflamboyant narrative texture. The clinesterton beademung! The twin radioceles! What wonderful gibberish! Only it isn't really gibberish. When he constructed the words of this section, Blish's Joycean studies stood him in good stead. That word "radioceles" is derived from a medical term suggested to Blish by the original image of testicles that he thought he saw on the cover painting and used as his starting point; "beademung" is a sort of Latin-German dream-language hybrid meant to mean "the Blessed," and so on. None of this really matters to the reader, though it surely amused Blish. What does matter is that the scene gradually and brilliantly drops into the syntax of the beademung ("The offer the clinesterton beademung had just made was enormously hearted," Blish tells us *in exposition*, "and he in turn was much minded and of love, to his own delighting as well to the beademungen; that almost went without saying"). The miracle of the scene is that we often come close to understanding what is going on, and where we fail we can still take pleasure in our perplexity. It is a lovely passage, charmingly mysterious.

The awakening from pseudo-death is almost comic. Garrard notices a fallen book, and remembers that the clinesterton beademung had dropped it. "But what under God was a clinesterton beademung?" Garrard asks himself—a beautifully-handled double take. And the rest of the story is devoted to answering that question, with uncertain results. Garrard returns to Earth; he assesses his experience; the structure of the story is reinforced now by references hearkening back to the voyage, such as the unwinding of the counting mechanism. Then come the explanations, such as they are. The *Don't move* of the first sentence proves to have been the solution to the story's basic problem, that of surviving a faster-than-light voyage. Blish recapitulates that by reusing the phrase, in a wryly altered context, at the very end—along with an echo of the beademung's wondrous dreamlike "with all of love" phrase.

Garrard has had a strange voyage that comes to a revelatory conclusion; and so have we, which is why the story is so satisfying. It works on many levels. It is a pleasing exploration of a classic science-fiction theme, the problem of what might happen if we violate the accepted relativistic laws and attain velocities faster than that of light. It is constructed deftly, each situation introduced at the proper moment and tied together by a neat circularity of phrase linking the beginning and the end. It is written in crisp, efficient prose, vivid without being flashy, which admirably communicates what it intends to tell us. And, if we are to go along with Damon Knight's symbolic analysis, it provides us not only with an interesting s-f tale but with a subterranean narrative carrying us through the fundamental adventure with which human life begins. The only aspect of short-story technique that is neglected is character development, but not, I think, because Blish was incapable of telling us more about Garrard, only that he saw it as unnecessary. It must have seemed sufficient to Blish to depict him as a competent and resilient man. Filling the story with details of Garrard's unhappy marriage, his yearning for the stamp collection he left behind on Earth, or his fierce abhorrence of Chinese food would probably not have added to its impact. (Though at least one amplification of Garrard's character would have been useful, I think. I'll get to that in a little while.)

I found "Common Time" particularly valuable, encountering it as I did in 1953 while my own ideas of how to construct a story were still in the formative stages, because it keyed right in to a structural formulation that I had encountered at about that time in my college studies, and which has remained important to me ever since: Kenneth Burke's notion of "the tragic rhythm," which for him underlies all dramatic art.

Burke, one of the most profound of the great American literary critics of the first half of the twentieth century, sought in a number of fertile, stimulating books (*A Grammar of Motives, A Rhetoric of Motives, The Philosophy of Literary Form,* and many others) to arrive at a set of generalizations that would explain the fundamental structure of any literary work, be it a novel, a poem, or a play, of any era and any culture. This brought him some derision from other literary critics: R. P. Blackmur, for instance, charged that Burke's method "could be applied with equal fruitfulness to Shakespeare, Dashiell Hammett, or Marie Corelli." Burke, upon consideration of Blackmur's attack, saw nothing really wrong with that. "You can't properly put Marie Corelli and Shakespeare apart until you have first put them together," he replied. Which was a fair statement of my own position. For there I was with H. D. F. Kifto under one arm and the new issue of *Astounding Science Fiction* under the other, trying to derive for myself a set of structural principles that would apply equally well to pulp-magazine fiction and to the plays of Sophocles and Euripides.

What Burke called the tragic rhythm could be encapsulated in a three-word formula, which I still keep somewhere in the back of my mind as I plan a story: *"Purpose, passion, perception."* In his 1943 essay, "The Tactics of Motivation," he provided this explanation: "Out of the agent's action there grows a corresponding passion, and from the sufferance of this passion there arises a knowledge of his act, a knowledge that also to a degree transcends his act." All the structural formulations for fiction that I know say approximately the same thing—what it all boils down to is that Odysseus wants to get home to his wife, runs into all sorts of problems during the voyage, and is rewarded in the end by his discovery of her constancy—but Burke's version, because it identifies the components with one-word tags, seems to me the most basic.

Purpose. Easy enough. The main character has a goal in mind. Odysseus wants to get home; Hamlet wants to know who murdered his father; Raskolnikov wants to demonstrate his innate superiority by knocking off a nasty old pawnbroker and getting away with it. Garrard wants to survive his voyage in the DFC-3 and come back home with an explanation of what happened to his two predecessors.

In a simple adventure story the protagonist's purpose is the center of the narrative, and the whole point of the story is how he goes about achieving (or failing to achieve) what he has set out to do. In deeper, richer stories there is some larger, underlying purpose. What goes on in *Hamlet* is not only a detective story but a rite of purification for an entire troubled kingdom. ("Something is rotten in the state of Denmark.") *Crime and Punishment,* too, is about larger things than the murder of one pawnbroker and the efforts of the local police to bring the killer to justice. Garrard wants to figure out some way of outlasting the relativistic effects that are complicating his starship voyage, but there are issues in "Common Time" also having to do with the relationship of the human species to the rest of the galaxy.

Passion. In our day this word has come to mean nothing more than romantic ardor, or even simply the acting out of physical desire. But it has an older cluster of meanings having to do with pain, suffering, and being acted upon, and that is the sense Burke uses. The love of Romeo and Juliet involves passion not only in the physical sense but in the sense of real torment: what those two go through for their love is harrowing indeed and brings them to a terrible calamity. Theologians speak of the passion of Christ on the Cross, by which they mean His agony during the crucifixion. (And remember the discussion of the underlying meaning of "agony," a few pages back.)

So passion, in Burke's sense of the word, is the central action of a story: the struggle of the protagonist, against whatever obstacles may arise, to achieve his purpose. The protagonist, be it noted, is not the only character in a story with a purpose; others have them too, and some have purposes that are diametrically opposed to that of the protagonist. Such characters are called *antagonists*, and it is the struggle or *agon* of protagonist and antagonist from which springs the conflict that gives a story its plot. In "Common Time" there is no concrete antagonist: as is frequently seen in science fiction, the antagonist is the universe itself. Garrard must wrestle with the inexorable laws of relativistic travel. The sufferings he undergoes aboard the DFC-3—the passion at the heart of the story—are unique, and uniquely fascinating. (It was the great science-fiction writer C. M. Kornbluth who pointed out during the 1957 debate over the symbolic content of "Common Time" that the initials of Garrard's ship, DFC, also stand for Distinguished Flying Cross, a deliberate or perhaps unconscious pun. Kornbluth thought this might be construed as a reference to Christ's agony on the Cross; for surely Garrard's experiences aboard the DFC-3 are a kind of crucifixion.)

Perception. The culmination of the story; the outcome of the passion of the protagonist. All that turmoil is not without result. Some fundamental change must come about, or the story leaves us with a sense of incompletion. Hamlet avenges his father's death, perishing himself in the process; but he sees at the end that the commonwealth has been purged of its ills ("I do prophesy the election lights on Fortinbras: he has my dying voice") and moments later the new king enters to begin the process of repair. Raskolnikov, having been convicted of his crime and shipped off to Siberia, contemplates at leisure his relationship to the rest of humanity and undergoes renewal and regeneration. Odysseus, after sweeping his wife's rascally suitors to destruction, achieves peace and reconciliation within the polity of Ithaca. Garrard not only figures out how to keep himself alive aboard his starship ("Don't move") but encounters alien beings of a superior kind and indicates to them that the people of Earth may be worthy of being taken into the community of worlds. And perceives his own human limitations thereby; for although he tells the clinesterton beademung that he hopes to return to them someday ("Yes, we they will make a new wooing of the beademungen at some other radiant. With all of love") he realizes, once he is safely back on Earth, that he will not go, "Not even, for all his dimly remembered promise, with all there was left in him of love." (Here, perhaps, is the story's one technical failing: for if Garrard had been explicitly defined at the outset, even with a single, quick stroke, as a man whose urge toward exploration is insatiable, then his renunciation of star travel at the end would have more power. Virtually every story is built about some sort of explicit or implicit change of character; but the more profound that change of character is, the greater the story's impact. Blish tells us so little about Garrard's nature that we are left largely unmoved by its change at the end.)

Purpose, passion, perception. Of all the formulas for constructing fiction that I have heard, this seems the most useful. Like all formulas it is a simplification, but not, I think, an oversimplification, any more than the chemical formula for water or table salt or carbon dioxide can be called an oversimplification. Chemical formulas tell us which elements are contained in a molecule, and in what proportions. They provide useful reality-checks. ("If this stuff has carbon in it, it isn't salt, and it isn't water.") Not that writing stories is a great deal like doing chemistry, but there are some similarities. Burke's little schematic gives me a good way of testing the plan for a story to see if the essential elements are all there. If the story doesn't lead toward some culminating perception as a result of the chain of events that the fulfillment of the protagonist's purpose sets in motion, something seems missing to me. A story isn't a random bunch of happenings. It's a carefully orchestrated pattern—an *action*, in the technical sense of that word—designed to carry the protagonist, and the reader along with him, through to some new and deeper understanding of one aspect of the universe. At least, so I think, and so I have tried to do for more than thirty years, with all there is in me of love.

SCANNERS LIVE IN VAIN
CORDWAINER SMITH

Martel was angry. He did not even adjust his blood away from anger. He stamped across the room by judgment, not by sight. When he saw the table hit the floor, and could tell by the expression on Luci's face that the table must have made a loud crash, he looked down to see if his leg was broken. It was not. Scanner to the core, he had to scan himself. The action was reflex and automatic. The inventory included his legs, abdomen, chestbox of instruments, hands, arms, face and back with the mirror. Only then did Martel go back to being angry. He talked with his voice, even though he knew that his wife hated its blare and preferred to have him write.

"I tell you, I must cranch. I have to cranch. It's my worry, isn't it?"

When Luci answered, he saw only a part of her words as he read her lips: "Darling . . . you're my husband . . . right to love you . . . dangerous . . . do it . . . dangerous . . . wait . . ."

He faced her, but put sound in his voice, letting the blare hurt her again: "I tell you, I'm going to cranch."

Catching her expression, he became rueful and a little

tender: "Can't you understand what it means to me? To get out of this horrible prison in my own head? To be a man again—hearing your voice, smelling smoke? To *feel* again—to feel my feet on the ground, to feel the air move against my face? Don't you know what it means?"

Her wide-eyed worrisome concern thrust him back into pure annoyance. He read only a few words as her lips moved: ". . . love you . . . your own good . . . don't you think I want you to be human? . . . your own good . . . too much . . . he said . . . they said . . ."

When he roared at her, he realized that his voice must be particularly bad. He knew that the sound hurt her no less than did the words: "Do you think I wanted you to marry a scanner? Didn't I tell you we're almost as low as the habermans? We're dead, I tell you. We've got to be dead to do our work. How can anybody go to the up-and-out? Can you dream what raw space is? I warned you. But you married me. All right, you married a man. Please, darling, let me be a man. Let me hear your voice, let me feel the warmth of being alive, of being human. Let me!"

He saw by her look of stricken assent that he had won the argument. He did not use his voice again. Instead, he pulled his tablet up from where it hung against his chest. He wrote on it, using the pointed fingernail of his right forefinger—the talking nail of a scanner—in quick cleancut script: *Pls, drlng, whrs crnching wire?*

She pulled the long gold-sheathed wire out of the pocket of her apron. She let its field sphere fall to the carpeted floor. Swiftly, dutifully, with the deft obedience of a scanner's wife, she wound the cranching wire around his head, spirally around his neck and chest. She avoided the instruments set in his chest. She even avoided the radiating scars around the instruments, the stigmata of men who had gone up and into the out. Mechanically he lifted a foot as she slipped the wire between his feet. She drew the wire taut. She snapped the small plug into the high-burden control next to his heart-reader. She helped him to sit down, arranging his hands for him, pushing his head back into the cup at the top of the chair. She turned then, full-face toward him, so that he could read her lips easily. Her expression was composed.

She knelt, scooped up the sphere at the other end of the wire, stood erect calmly, her back to him. He scanned her, and saw nothing in her posture but grief which would have escaped the eye of anyone but a scanner. She spoke: he could see her chest-muscles moving. She realized that she was not facing him, and turned so that he could see her lips.

"Ready at last?"

He smiled a *yes*.

She turned her back to him again. (Luci could never bear to watch him go under the wire.) She tossed the wire-sphere into the air. It caught in the force-field, and hung there. Suddenly it glowed. That was all. All—except for the sudden red stinking roar of coming back to his senses. Coming back, across the wild threshold of pain.

When he awakened, under the wire, he did not feel as though he had just cranched. Even though it was the second cranching within the week, he felt fit. He lay in the chair. His ears drank in the sound of air touching things in the room. He heard Luci breathing in the next room, where she was hanging up the wire to cool. He smelt the thousand and one smells that are in anybody's room: the crisp freshness of the germ-burner, the sour-sweet tang of the humidifier, the odor of the dinner they had just eaten, the smells of clothes, furniture, of people themselves. All these were pure delight. He sang a phrase or two of his favorite song:

> "Here's to the haberman, up-and-out!
> Up—oh!—and out—oh!—up-and-out! . . ."

He heard Luci chuckle in the next room. He gloated over the sounds of her dress as she swished to the doorway.

She gave him her crooked little smile. "You sound all right. Are you all right, really?"

Even with this luxury of senses, he scanned. He took the flash-quick inventory which constituted his professional skill. His eyes swept in the news of the instruments. Nothing showed off scale, beyond the nerve compression hanging in the edge of *Danger*. But he could not worry about the nervebox. That always came through cranching. You couldn't get under the wire without having it show on the nervebox. Some day the box would go to *Overload* and drop back down to *Dead*. That was the way a haberman ended. But you couldn't have everything. People who went to the up-and-out had to pay the price for space.

Anyhow, he should worry! He was a scanner. A good one, and he knew it. If he couldn't scan himself, who could? This cranching wasn't too dangerous. Dangerous, but not too dangerous.

Luci put out her hand and ruffled his hair as if she had been reading his thoughts, instead of just following them: "But you know you shouldn't have! You shouldn't!"

"But I did!" He grinned at her.

Her gaiety still forced, she said: "Come on, darling, let's have a good time. I have almost everything there is in the icebox—all your favorite tastes. And I have two new records just full of smells. I tried them out myself, and even I liked them. And you know me—"

"Which?"

"Which what, you old darling?"

He slipped his hand over her shoulders as he limped out of the room. He could never go back to feeling the floor beneath his feet, feeling the air against his face, without being bewildered and clumsy. As if cranching was real, and being a haberman was a bad dream. But he *was* a haberman, and a scanner. "You know what I meant, Luci . . . the smells, which you have. Which one did you like, on the record?"

"Well-l-l," said she, judiciously, "there were some lamb chops that were the strangest things—"

He interrupted: "What are lambtchots?"

"Wait till you smell them. Then guess. I'll tell you this much. It's a smell hundreds and hundreds of years old. They found out about it in the old books."

"Is a lambtchot a beast?"

"I won't tell you. You've got to wait," she laughed, as she helped him sit down and spread his tasting dishes before him. He wanted to go back over the dinner first, sampling all the pretty things he had eaten, and savoring them this time with his now-living lips and tongue.

When Luci had found the music wire and had thrown its sphere up into the force-field, he reminded her of the new smells. She took out the long glass records and set the first one into a transmitter.

"Now sniff!"

A queer, frightening, exciting smell came over the room. It seemed like nothing in this world, nor like anything from the up-and-out. Yet it was familiar. His mouth watered. His pulse beat a little faster; he scanned his heartbox. (Faster, sure enough.) But that smell, what was it? In mock perplexity, he grabbed her hands, looked into her eyes, and growled:

"Tell me, darling! Tell me, or I'll eat you up!"

"That's just right!"

"What?"

"You're right. It should make you want to eat me. It's meat."

"Meat. Who?"

"Not a person," said she, knowledgeably, "a Beast. A

Beast which people used to eat. A lamb was a small sheep—you've seen sheep out in the Wild, haven't you?—and a chop is part of its middle-here!" She pointed at her chest.

Martel did not hear her. All his boxes had swung over toward *Alarm*, some to *Danger*. He fought against the roar of his own mind, forcing his body into excess excitement. How easy it was to be a scanner when you really stood outside your own body, haberman-fashion, and looked back into it with your eyes alone. Then you could manage the body, rule it coldly even in the enduring agony of space. But to realize that you *were* a body, that this thing was ruling you, that the mind could kick the flesh and send it roaring off into panic! That was bad.

He tried to remember the days before he had gone into the haberman device, before he had been cut apart for the up-and-out. Had he always been subject to the rush of his emotions from his mind to his body, from his body back to his mind, confounding him so that he couldn't scan? But he hadn't been a scanner then.

He knew what had hit him. Amid the roar of his own pulse, he knew. In the nightmare of the up-and-out, that smell had forced its way through to him, while their ship burned off Venus and the habermans fought the collapsing metal with their bare hands. He had scanned then: all were in *Danger*. Chestboxes went up to *Overload* and dropped to *Dead* all around him as he had moved from man to man, shoving the drifting corpses out of his way as he fought to scan each man in turn, to clamp vises on unnoticed broken legs, to snap the sleeping valve on men whose instruments showed they were hopelessly near *Overload*. With men trying to work and cursing him for a scanner while he, professional zeal aroused, fought to do his job and keep them alive in the great pain of space, he had smelled that smell. It had fought its way along his rebuilt nerves, past the haberman cuts, past all the safeguards of physical and mental discipline. In the wildest hour of tragedy, he had smelled aloud. He remembered it was like a bad cranching, connected with the fury and nightmare all around him. He had even stopped his work to scan himself, fearful that the first effect might come, breaking past all haberman cuts and ruining him with the pain of space. But he had come through. His own instruments stayed and stayed at *Danger*, without nearing *Overload*. He had done his job, and won a commendation for it. He had even forgotten the burning ship.

All except the smell.

And here the smell was all over again—the smell of meat-with-fire . . .

Luci looked at him with wifely concern. She obviously thought he had cranched too much, and was about to haberman back. She tried to be cheerful: "You'd better rest, honey."

He whispered to her: "Cut—off—that—smell."

She did not question his word. She cut the transmitter. She even crossed the room and stepped up the room controls until a small breeze flitted across the floor and drove the smells up to the ceiling.

He rose, tired and stiff. (His instruments were normal, except that heart was fast and nerves still hanging on the edge of *Danger*.) He spoke sadly:

"Forgive me, Luci. I suppose I shouldn't have cranched. Not so soon again. But darling, I have to get out from being a haberman. How can I ever be near you? How can I be a man—not hearing my own voice, not even feeling my own life as it goes through my veins? I love you, darling. Can't I ever be near you?"

Her pride was disciplined and automatic: "But you're a scanner!"

"I know I'm a scanner. But so what?"

She went over the words, like a tale told a thousand times to reassure herself: "You are the bravest of the brave, the most skillful of the skilled. All mankind owes most honor to the scanner, who unites the Earths of mankind. Scanners are the protectors of the habermans. They are the judges in the up-and-out. They make men live in the place where men need desperately to die. They are the most honored of mankind, and even the chiefs of the instrumentality are delighted to pay them homage!"

With obstinate sorrow he demurred: "Luci, we've heard that all before. But does it pay us back—"

" 'Scanners work for more than pay. They are the strong guards of mankind.' Don't you remember that?"

"But our lives, Luci. What can you get out of being the wife of a scanner? Why did you marry me? I'm human only when I cranch. The rest of the time—you know what I am. A machine. A man turned into a machine. A man who has been killed and kept alive for duty. Don't you realize what I miss?"

"Of course, darling, of course—"

He went on: "Don't you think I remember my childhood? Don't you think I remember what it is to be a man and not a haberman? To walk and feel my feet on the ground? To feel a decent clean pain instead of watching my body every minute to see if I'm alive? How will I know if I'm dead? Did you ever think of that, Luci? How will I know if I'm dead?"

She ignored the unreasonableness of his outburst. Pacifyingly, she said:

"Sit down, darling. Let me make you some kind of a drink. You're overwrought."

Automatically, he scanned. "No I'm not! Listen to me. How do you think it feels to be in the up-and-out with the crew tied-for-space all around you? How do you think it feels to watch them sleep? How do you think I like scanning, scanning, scanning month after month, when I can feel the pain of space beating against every part of my body, trying to get past my haberman blocks? How do you think I like to wake the men when I have to, and have them hate me for it? Have you ever seen habermans fight—strong men fighting, and neither knowing pain, fighting until one touches *Overload*? Do you think about that, Luci?" Triumphantly he added: "Can you blame me if I cranch, and come back to being a man, just two days a month?"

"I'm not blaming you, darling. Let's enjoy your cranch. Sit down now, and have a drink."

He was sitting down, resting his face in his hands, while she fixed the drink, using natural fruits out of bottles in addition to the secure alkaloids. He watched her restlessly and pitied her for marrying a scanner; and then, though it was unjust, resented having to pity her.

Just as she turned to hand him the drink, they both jumped a little as the phone rang. It should not have rung. They had turned it off. It rang again, obviously on the emergency circuit. Stepping ahead of Luci, Martel strode over to the phone and looked into it. Vomact was looking at him.

The custom of scanners entitled him to be brusque, even with a senior scanner, on certain given occasions. This was one.

Before Vomact could speak, Martel spoke two words into the plate, not caring whether the old man could read lips or not:

"Cranching. Busy."

He cut the switch and went back to Luci.

The phone rang again.

Luci said, gently, "I can find out what it is, darling. Here, take your drink and sit down."

"Leave it alone," said her husband. "No one has a right to call when I'm cranching. He knows that. He ought to know that."

The phone rang again. In a fury, Martel rose and went to the plate. He cut it back on. Vomact was on the screen. Before Martel could speak, Vomact held up his talking nail in line with his heartbox. Martel reverted to discipline:

"Scanner Martel present and waiting, sir."

The lips moved solemnly: "Top emergency."

"Sir, I am under the wire."

"Top emergency."

"Sir, don't you understand?" Martel mouthed his words, so he could be sure that Vomact followed. "I . . . am . . . under . . . the . . . wire. Unfit . . . for . . . Space!"

Vomact repeated: "Top emergency. Report to Central Tie-in."

"But, sir, no emergency like this—"

"Right, Martel. No emergency like this, ever before. Report to Tie-in." With a faint glint of kindliness, Vomact added: "No need to de-cranch. Report as you are."

This time it was Martel whose phone was cut out. The screen went gray. He turned to Luci. The temper had gone out of his voice. She came to him. She kissed him, and rumpled his hair. All she could say was, "I'm sorry."

She kissed him again, knowing his disappointment. "Take good care of yourself, darling. I'll wait."

He scanned, and slipped into his transparent aircoat. At the window he paused, and waved. She called, "Good luck!" As the air flowed past him he said to himself,

"This is the first time I've felt flight in—eleven years. Lord, but it's easy to fly if you can feel yourself live!"

Central Tie-in lowed white and austere far ahead. Martel peered. He saw no glare of incoming ships from the up-and-out, no shuddering flare of space-fire out of control. Everything was quiet, as it should be on an off-duty night.

And yet Vomact had called. He had called an emergency

higher than space. There was no such thing. But Vomact had called it.

When Martel got there, he found about half the scanners present, two dozen or so of them. He lifted the talking finger. Most of the scanners were standing face to face, talking in pairs as they read lips. A few of the old, impatient ones were scribbling on their tablets and then thrusting the tablets into other people's faces. All the faces wore the dull dead relaxed look of a haberman. When Martel entered the room, he knew that most of the others laughed in the deep isolated privacy of their own minds, each thinking things it would be useless to express in formal words. It had been a long time since a scanner showed up at a meeting cranched.

Vomact was not there: probably, thought Martel, he was still on the phone calling others. The light of the phone flashed on and off; the bell rang. Martel felt odd when he realized that of all those present, he was the only one to hear that loud bell. It made him realize why ordinary people did not like to be around groups of habermans or scanners. Martel looked around for company.

His friend Chang was there, busy explaining to some old and testy scanner that he did not know why Vomact had called. Martel looked farther and saw Parizianski. He walked over, threading his way past the others with a dexterity that showed he could feel his feet from the inside, and did not have to watch them. Several of the others stared at him with their dead faces, and tried to smile. But they lacked full muscular control and their faces twisted into horrid masks. (Scanners usually knew better than to show expression on faces which they could no longer govern. Martel added to himself, *I swear I'll never smile again unless I'm cranched.*)

Parizianski gave him the sign of the talking finger. Looking face to face, he spoke:

"You come here cranched?"

Parizianski could not hear his own voice, so the words roared like the words on a broken and screeching phone; Martel was startled, but knew that the inquiry was well meant. No one could be better-natured than the burly Pole.

"Vomact called. Top emergency."

"You told him you were cranched?"

"Yes."

"He still made you come?"

"Yes."

"Then all this—it is not for Space? You could not go up-and-out? You are like ordinary men?"

"That's right."

"Then why did he call us?" Some pre-haberman habit made Parizianski wave his arms in inquiry. The hand struck the back of the old man behind them. The slap could be heard throughout the room, but only Martel heard it. Instinctively, he scanned Parizianski and the old scanner, and they scanned him back. Only then did the old man ask why Martel had scanned him. When Martel explained that he was under the wire, the old man moved swiftly away to pass on the news that there was a cranched scanner present at the tie-in.

Even this minor sensation could not keep the attention of most of the scanners from the worry about the top emergency. One young man, who had scanned his first transit just the year before, dramatically interposed himself between Parizianski and Martel. He dramatically flashed his tablet at them:

Is Vmct mad?

The older men shook their heads. Martel, remembering that it had not been too long that the young man had been haberman, mitigated the dead solemnity of the denial with a friendly smile. He spoke in a normal voice, saying:

"Vomact is the senior of scanners. I am sure that he could not go mad. Would he not see it on his boxes first?"

Martel had to repeat the question, speaking slowly and mouthing his words before the young scanner could understand the comment. The young man tried to make his face smile, and twisted it into a comic mask. But he took up his tablet and scribbled:

Yr rght.

Chang broke away from his friend and came over, his half-Chinese face gleaming in the warm evening. (It's strange, thought Martel, that more Chinese don't become scanners. Or not so strange perhaps, if you think that they never fill their quota of habermans. Chinese love good living too much. The ones who do scan are all good ones.) Chang saw that Martel was cranched, and spoke with voice:

"You break precedents. Luci must be angry to lose you?"

"She took it well. Chang, that's strange."

"What?"

"I'm cranched, and I can hear. Your voice sounds all right. How did you learn to talk like—like an ordinary person?"

"I practiced with soundtracks. Funny you noticed it. I think I am the only scanner in or between the Earths who can pass for an ordinary man. Mirrors and soundtracks. I found out how to act."

"But you don't . . . ?"

"No. I don't feel, or taste, or hear, or smell things, any more than you do. Talking doesn't do me much good. But I notice that it cheers up the people around me."

"It would make a difference in the life of Luci."

Chang nodded sagely. "My father insisted on it. He said, 'You may be proud of being a scanner. I am sorry you are not a man. Conceal your defects.' So I tried. I wanted to tell the old boy about the up-and-out, and what we did there, but it did not matter. He said, 'Airplanes were good enough for Confucius, and they are for me too.' The old humbug! He tries so hard to be a Chinese when he can't even read Old Chinese. But he's got wonderful good sense, and for somebody going on two hundred he certainly gets around."

Martel smiled at the thought: "In his airplane?"

Chang smiled back. This discipline of his facial muscles was amazing; a bystander would not think that Chang was a haberman, controlling his eyes, cheeks, and lips by cold intellectual control. The expression had the spontaneity of life. Martel felt a flash of envy for Chang when he looked at the dead cold faces of Parizianski and the others. He knew that he himself looked fine: but why shouldn't he? He was cranched. Turning to Parizianski he said,

"Did you see what Chang said about his father? The old boy uses an airplane."

Parizianski made motions with his mouth, but the sounds meant nothing. He took up his tablet and showed it to Martel and Chang.

Bzz bzz. Ha ha. Gd ol' boy.

At that moment, Martel heard steps out in the corridor. He could not help looking toward the door. Other eyes followed the direction of his glance.

Vomact came in.

The group shuffled to attention in four parallel lines. They scanned one another. Numerous hands reached across to adjust the electrochemical controls on chestboxes which had begun to load up. One scanner held out a broken finger which his counter-scanner had discovered, and submitted it for treatment and splinting.

Vomact had taken out his staff of office. The cube at the top flashed red light through the room, the lines re-formed, and all scanners gave the sign meaning, *Present and ready*!

Vomact countered with the stance signifying, *I am the senior and take command.*

Talking fingers rose in the counter-gesture, *We concur and commit ourselves.*

Vomact raised his right arm, dropped the wrist as though it were broken, in a queer searching gesture, meaning: *Any men around? Any habermans not tied? All clear for the scanners?*

Alone of all those present, the cranched Martel heard the queer rustle of feet as they all turned completely around without leaving position, looking sharply at one another and flashing their beltlights into the dark corners of the great room. When again they faced Vomact, he made a further sign:

All clear. Follow my words.

Martel noticed that he alone relaxed. The others could not know the meaning of relaxation with the minds blocked off up there in their skulls, connected only with the eyes, and the rest of the body connected with the mind only by controlling non-sensory nerves and the instrument boxes on their chests. Martel realized that, cranched as he was, he had expected to hear Vomact's voice: the senior had been talking for some time. No sound escaped his lips. (Vomact never bothered with sound.)

"...and when the first men to go up-and-out went to the moon, what did they find?"

"Nothing," responded the silent chorus of lips.

"Therefore they went farther, to Mars and to Venus. The ships went out year by year, but they did not come back until the Year One of Space. Then did a ship come back with the first effect. Scanners, I ask you, what is the first effect?"

"No one knows. No one knows."

"No one will ever know. Too many are the variables. By what do we know the first effect?"

"By the great pain of space," came the chorus.

"And by what further sign?"

"By the need, oh the need for death."

Vomact again: "And who stopped the need for death?"

"Henry Haberman conquered the first effect, in the Year Eighty-three of Space."

"And, Scanners, I ask you, what did he do?"

"He made the habermans."

"How, O Scanners, are habermans made?"

"They are made with the cuts. The brain is cut from the heart, the lungs. The brain is cut from the ears, the nose. The brain is cut from the mouth, the belly. The brain is cut from desire, and pain. The brain is cut from the world. Save for the eyes. Save for the control of the living flesh."

"And how, O Scanners, is flesh controlled?"

"By the boxes set in the flesh, the controls set in the chest, the signs made to rule the living body, the signs by which the body lives."

"How does a haberman live and live?"

"The haberman lives by control of the boxes."

"Whence come the habermans?"

Martel felt in the coming response a great roar of broken voices echoing through the room as the scanners, habermans themselves, put sound behind their mouthings:

"Habermans are the scum of mankind. Habermans are the weak, the cruel, the credulous, and the unfit. Habermans are the sentenced-to-more-than-death. Habermans live in the mind alone. They are killed for space but they live for space. They master the ships that connect the Earths. They live in the great pain while ordinary men sleep in the cold, cold sleep of the transit."

"Brothers and Scanners, I ask you now: are we habermans or are we not?"

"We are habermans in the flesh. We are cut apart, brain and flesh. We are ready to go to the up-and-out. All of us have gone through the haberman device."

"We are habermans then?" Vomact's eyes flashed and glittered as he asked the ritual question.

Again the chorused answer was accompanied by a roar of voices heard only by Martel: "Habermans we are, and more, and more. We are the chosen who are habermans by our own free will. We are the agents of the Instrumentality of Mankind."

"What must the others say to us?"

"They must say to us, 'You are the bravest of the brave, the most skillful of the skilled. All mankind owes most honor to the scanner, who unites the Earths of mankind. Scanners are the protectors of the habermans. They are the judges in the up-and-out. They make men live in the place where men need desperately to die. They are the most honored of mankind, and even the chiefs of the Instrumentality are delighted to pay them homage!' "

Vomact stood more erect: "What is the secret duty of the scanner?"

"To keep secret our law, and to destroy the acquirers thereof."

"How to destroy?"

"Twice to the *Overload*, back and *Dead*."

"If habermans die, what the duty then?"

The scanners all compressed their lips for answer. (Silence was the code.) Martel, who—long familiar with the code—was a little bored with the proceedings, noticed that Chang was breathing too heavily; he reached over and adjusted Chang's lung-control and received the thanks of Chang's eyes. Vomact observed the interruption and glared at them both. Martel relaxed, trying to imitate the dead cold stillness of the others. It was so hard to do, when you were cranched.

"If others die, what the duty then?" asked Vomact.

"Scanners together inform the Instrumentality. Scanners

together accept the punishment. Scanners together settle the case."

"And if the punishment be severe?"

"Then no ships go."

"And if scanners be not honored?"

"Then no ships go."

"And if a scanner goes unpaid?"

"Then no ships go."

"And if the Others and the Instrumentality are not in all ways at all times mindful of their proper obligation to the scanners?"

"Then no ships go."

"And what, O Scanners, if no ships go?"

"The Earths fall apart. The Wild comes back in. The Old Machines and the Beasts return."

"What is the first known duty of a scanner?"

"Not to sleep in the up-and-out."

"What is the second duty of a scanner?"

"To keep forgotten the name of fear."

"What is the third duty of a scanner?"

"To use the wire of Eustace Cranch only with care, only with moderation." Several pair of eyes looked quickly at Martel before the mouthed chorus went on. "To cranch only at home, only among friends, only for the purpose of remembering, of relaxing, or of begetting."

"What is the word of the scanner?"

"Faithful though surrounded by death."

"What is the motto of the scanner?"

"Awake though surrounded by silence."

"What is the work of the scanner?"

"Labor even in the heights of the up-and-out, loyalty even in the depths of the Earths."

"How do you know a scanner?"

"We know ourselves. We are dead though we live. And we talk with the tablet and the nail."

"What is this code?"

"This code is the friendly ancient wisdom of scanners, briefly put that we may be mindful and cheered by our loyalty to one another."

At this point the formula should have run: "We complete the code. Is there work or word for the scanners?" But Vomact said, and he repeated:

"Top emergency. Top emergency."

They gave him the sign, *Present and ready!*

He said, with every eye straining to follow his lips:

"Some of you know the work of Adam Stone?"

Martel saw lips move, saying: "The Red Asteroid. The Other who lives at the edge of Space."

"Adam Stone has gone to the Instrumentality, claiming success for his work. He says that he has found how to screen out the pain of space. He says that the up-and-out can be made safe for ordinary men to work in, to stay awake in. He says that there need be no more scanners."

Beltlights flashed on all over the room as scanners sought the right to speak. Vomact nodded to one of the older men. "Scanner Smith will speak."

Smith stepped slowly up into the light, watching his own feet. He turned so that they could see his face. He spoke: "I say that this is a lie. I say that Stone is a liar. I say that the Instrumentality must not be deceived."

He paused. Then, in answer to some question from the audience which most of the others did not see, he said:

"I invoke the secret duty of the scanners."

Smith raised his right hand for emergency attention:

"I say that Stone must die."

Martel, still cranched, shuddered as he heard the boos, groans, shouts, squeaks, grunts and moans which came from the scanners who forgot noise in their excitement and strove to make their dead bodies talk to one another's deaf ears. Beltlights flashed wildly all over the room. There was a rush for the rostrum and scanners milled around at the top, vying for attention until Parizianski—by sheer bulk—shoved the others aside and down, and turned to mouth at the group.

"Brother Scanners, I want your eyes."

The people on the floor kept moving, with their numb bodies jostling one another. Finally Vomact stepped up in front of Parizianski, faced the others, and said:

"Scanners, be scanners! Give him your eyes."

Parizianski was not good at public speaking. His lips moved too fast. He waved his hands, which took the eyes of the others away from his lips. Nevertheless, Martel was able to follow most of the message:

". . . can't do this. Stone may have succeeded. If he has succeeded, it means the end of the scanners. It means the end of the habermans, too. None of us will have to fight in the up-and-out. We won't have anybody else going under the wire for a few hours or days of being human. Everybody will be Other. Nobody will have to cranch, never again. Men can be men. The habermans can be killed decently and properly, the way men were killed in the old days, without anybody keeping them alive. They won't have to work in the up-and-out! There will be no more great pain—think of it! No . . . more . . . great . . . pain! How do we know that Stone is a liar—" Lights began flashing directly into his eyes. (The rudest insult of scanner to scanner was this.)

Vomact again exercised authority. He stepped in front of Parizianski and said something which the others could not see. Parizianski stepped down from the rostrum. Vomact again spoke:

"I think that some of the scanners disagree with our brother Parizianski. I say that the use of the rostrum be suspended till we have had a chance for private discussion. In fifteen minutes I will call the meeting back to order."

Martel looked around for Vomact when the senior had rejoined the group on the floor. Finding the senior, Martel wrote swift script on his tablet, waiting for a chance to thrust the tablet before the senior's eyes. He had written:

Am crnchd. Rspctfly requst prmissn lv now, stnd by fr orders.

Being cranched did strange things to Martel. Most meetings that he attended seemed formal, hearteningly ceremonial, lighting up the dark inward eternities of habermanhood. When he was not cranched, he noticed his body no more than a marble bust notices its marble pedestal. He had stood with them before. He had stood with them effortless hours, while the long-winded ritual broke through the terrible loneliness behind his eyes, and made him feel that the scanners, though a confraternity of the damned, were none the less forever honored by the professional requirements of their mutilation.

This time, it was different. Coming cranched, and in full possession of smell-sound-taste-feeling, he reacted more or less as a normal man would. He saw his friends and colleagues as a lot of cruelly driven ghosts, posturing out the meaningless ritual of their indefeasible damnation. What difference did anything make, once you were a haberman? Why all this talk about habermans and scanners? Habermans were criminals or heretics, and scanners were gentlemen-volunteers, but they were all in the same fix—except that scanners were deemed worthy of the short-time return of the cranching wire, while habermans were simply disconnected while the ships lay in port and were left suspended until they should be awakened, in some hour of emergency or trouble, to work out another spell of their damnation. It was a rare haberman that you saw on the street—someone of special merit or bravery, allowed to look at mankind from the terrible prison of his own mechanified body. And yet, what scanner ever pitied a haberman? What scanner ever honored a haberman except perfunctorily in the line of duty? What had the scanners as a guild and a class ever done for the habermans, except to murder them with a twist of the wrist whenever a haberman, too long beside a scanner, picked up the tricks of the scanning trade and learned how to live at his own will, not the will the scanners imposed? What could the Others, the ordinary men, know of what went on inside the ships? The Others slept in their cylinders, mercifully unconscious until they woke up on whatever other Earth they had consigned themselves to. What could the Others know of the men who had to stay alive within the ship?

What could any Other know of the up-and-out? What Other could look at the biting acid beauty of the stars in open space? What could they tell of the great pain, which started quietly in the marrow, like an ache, and proceeded by the fatigue and nausea of each separate nerve cell, brain cell, touchpoint in the body, until life itself became a terrible aching hunger for silence and for death?

He was a scanner. All right, he *was* a scanner. He had been a scanner from the moment when, wholly normal, he had stood in the sunlight before a subchief of the Instrumentality, and had sworn:

"I pledge my honor and my life to mankind. I sacrificed myself willingly for the welfare of mankind. In accepting the perilous austere honor, I yield all my rights without exception to the honorable chiefs of the Instrumentality and to the honored Confraternity of Scanners."

He had pledged.

He had gone into the haberman device.

He remembered his hell. He had not had such a bad one, even though it had seemed to last a hundred-million years, all of them without sleep. He had learned to feel with his eyes. He had learned to see despite the heavy eyeplates set back of his eyeballs to insulate his eyes from the rest of him. He had learned to watch his skin. He still remembered the time he had noticed dampness on his shirt, and had pulled out his scanning mirror only to discover that he had worn a hole in his side by leaning against a vibrating machine. (A thing like that could not happen to him now; he was too adept at reading his own instruments.) He remembered the way that he had gone up-and-out, and the way that the great pain beat into him, despite the fact that his touch, smell, feeling, and hearing were gone for all ordinary purposes. He remembered killing habermans, and keeping others alive, and standing for months beside the honorable scanner-pilot while neither of them slept. He remembered going ashore on Earth Four, and remembered that he had not enjoyed it, and had realized on that day that there was no reward.

Martel stood among the other scanners. He hated their awkwardness when they moved, their immobility when they stood still. He hated the queer assortment of smells which their bodies yielded unnoticed. He hated the grunts and groans and squawks which they emitted from their deafness. He hated them, and himself.

How could Luci stand him? He had kept his chestbox reading *Danger* for weeks while he courted her, carrying the cranch wire about with him most illegally, and going direct from one cranch to the other without worrying about the fact his indicators all crept up to the edge of *Overload*. He had wooed her without thinking of what would happen if she did say, "Yes." She had.

"And they lived happily ever after." In old books they did, but how could they, in life? He had had eighteen days under the wire in the whole of the past year! Yet she had loved him. She still loved him. He knew it. She fretted about him through the long months that he was in the up-and-out. She tried to make home mean something to him even when he was haberman, make food pretty when it could not be tasted, make herself lovable when she could not be kissed— or might as well not, since a haberman body meant no more than furniture. Luci was patient.

And now, Adam Stone! (He let his tablet fade: how could he leave, now?)

God bless Adam Stone?

Martel could not help feeling a little sorry for himself. No longer would the high keen call of duty carry him through two hundred or so years of the Others' time, two million private eternities of his own. He could slouch and relax. He could forget high space, and let the up-and-out be tended by Others. He could cranch as much as he dared. He could be almost normal—almost—for one year or five years or no years. But at least he could stay with Luci. He could go with her into the Wild, where there were Beasts and Old Machines still roving the dark places. Perhaps he would die in the excitement of the hunt, throwing spears at an ancient manshonyagger as it leapt from its lair, or tossing hot spheres at the tribesmen of the Unforgiven who still roamed the Wild. There was still life to live, still a good normal death to die, not the moving of a needle out in the silence and agony of space!

He had been walking about restlessly. His ears were at-tuned to the sounds of normal speech, so that he did not feel like watching the mouthings of his brethren. Now they seemed to have come to a decision. Vomact was moving to the rostrum. Martel looked about for Chang, and went to stand beside him. Chang whispered.

"You're as restless as water in mid-air! What's the mat-ter? Decranching?"

They both scanned Martel, but the instruments held steady and showed no sign of the cranch giving out.

The great light flared in its call to attention. Again they formed ranks. Vomact thrust his lean old face into the glare, and spoke:

"Scanners and Brothers, I call for a vote." He held himself in the stance which meant: *I am the senior and take command.*

A beltlight flashed in protest.

It was old Henderson. He moved to the rostrum, spoke to Vomact, and—with Vomact's nod of approval—turned full-face to repeat his question:

"Who speaks for the scanners out in space?"

No beltlight or hand answered.

Henderson and Vomact, face to face, conferred for a few moments. Then Henderson faced them again:

"I yield to the senior in command. But I do not yield to a meeting of the Confraternity. There are sixty-eight scanners, and only forty-seven present, of whom one is cranched and U.D. I have therefore proposed that the senior in command assume authority only over an emergency committee of the Confraternity, not over a meeting. Is that agreed and understood by the honorable scanners?"

Hands rose in assent.

Chang murmured in Martel's ear, "Lot of difference that makes! Who can tell the difference between a meeting and a committee?" Martel agreed with the words, but was even more impressed with the way that Chang, while haberman, could control his own voice.

Vomact resumed chairmanship: "We now vote on the question of Adam Stone.

"First, we can assume that he has not succeeded, and that his claims are lies. We know that from our practical experience as scanners. The pain of space is only part of scanning"

(*But the essential part, the basis of it all*, thought Martel) "and we can rest assured that Stone cannot solve the problem of space discipline."

"That tripe again," whispered Chang, unheard save by Martel.

"The space discipline of our confraternity has kept high space clean of war and dispute. Sixty-eight disciplined men control all high space. We are removed by our oath and our haberman status from all Earthly passions.

"Therefore, if Adam Stone has conquered the pain of space, so that Others can wreck our confraternity and bring to space the trouble and ruin which afflicts Earths, I say that Adam Stone is wrong. If Adam Stone succeeds, scanners live in vain!

"Secondly, if Adam Stone has not conquered the pain of space, he will cause great trouble in all the Earths. The Instrumentality and the subchiefs may not give us as many habermans as we need to operate the ships of mankind. There will be wild stories, and fewer recruits, and, worst of all, the discipline of the Confraternity may relax if this kind of nonsensical heresy is spread around.

"Therefore, if Adam Stone has succeeded, he threatens the ruin of the Confraternity and should die.

"I move the death of Adam Stone."

And Vomact made the sign, *The honorable scanners are pleased to vote.*

Martel grabbed wildly for his beltlight. Chang, guessing ahead, had his light out and ready; its bright beam, voting *No*, shone straight up at the ceiling. Martel got his light out and threw its beam upward in dissent. Then he looked around. Out of the forty-seven present, he could see only five or six glittering.

Two more lights went on. Vomact stood as erect as a frozen corpse. Vomact's eyes flashed as he stared back and forth over the group, looking for lights. Several more went on. Finally Vomact took the closing stance:

May it please the scanners to count the vote.

Three of the older men went up on the rostrum with Vomact. They looked over the room. (Martel thought: *These damned ghosts are voting on the life of a real man, a live man! They have no right to do it. I'll tell the Instrumentality!* But he knew that he would not. He thought of Luci and what she might gain by the triumph of Adam Stone: the heart-breaking folly of the vote was then almost too much for Martel to bear.)

All three of the tellers held up their hands in unanimous agreement on the sign of the number: *Fifteen against.*

Vomact dismissed them with a bow of courtesy. He turned and again took the stance: *I am the senior and take command.*

Marveling at his own daring, Martel flashed his beltlight on. He knew that any one of the bystanders might reach over and twist his heartbox to *Overload* for such an act. He felt Chang's hand reaching to catch him by the aircoat. But he eluded Chang's grasp and ran, faster than a scanner should, to the platform. As he ran, he wondered what appeal to make. It was no use talking common sense. Not now. It had to be law.

He jumped up on the rostrum beside Vomact, and took the stance: *Scanners, an Illegality!*

He violated good custom while speaking, still in the stance: "A committee has no right to vote death by a majority vote. It takes two-thirds of a full meeting."

He felt Vomact's body lunge behind him, felt himself falling from the rostrum, hitting the floor, hurting his knees and his touch-aware hands. He was helped to his feet. He was scanned. Some scanner he scarcely knew took his instruments and toned him down.

Immediately Martel felt more calm, more detached, and hated himself for feeling so.

He looked up at the rostrum. Vomact maintained the stance signifying: *Order!*

The scanners adjusted their ranks. The two scanners next to Martel took his arms. He shouted at them, but they looked away, and cut themselves off from communication altogether.

Vomact spoke again when he saw the room was quiet: "A scanner came here cranched. Honorable Scanners, I apologize for this. It is not the fault of our great and worthy scanner and friend, Martel. He came here under orders. I told him not to de-cranch. I hoped to spare him an unnecessary haberman. We all know how happily Martel is married, and we wish his brave experiment well. I like Martel. I respect his judgment. I wanted him here. I knew you wanted him here. But he is cranched. He is in no mood to share in the lofty business of the scanners. I therefore propose a solution which will meet all the requirements of fairness. I propose that we rule Scanner Martel out of order for his violation of rules. This violation would be inexcusable if Martel were not cranched.

"But at the same time, in all fairness to Martel, I further propose that we deal with the points raised so improperly by our worthy but disqualified brother."

Vomact gave the sign, *The honorable scanners are pleased to vote.* Martel tried to reach his own beltlight; the dead strong hands held him tightly and he struggled in vain. One lone light shone high: Chang's, no doubt.

Vomact thrust his face into the light again: "Having the approval of our worthy scanners and present company for the general proposal, I now move that this committee declare itself to have the full authority of a meeting, and that this committee further make me responsible for all misdeeds

which this committee may enact, to be held answerable before the next full meeting, but not before any other authority
beyond the closed and secret ranks of scanners."

Flamboyantly this time, his triumph evident, Vomact as-
sumed the *vote* stance.

Only a few lights shone: far less, patently, than a mi-
nority of one-fourth.

Vomact spoke again. The light shone on his high calm
forehead, on his dead relaxed cheekbones. His lean cheeks
and chin were halfshadowed, save where the lower light
picked up and spotlighted his mouth, cruel even in repose.
(Vomact was said to be a descendant of some ancient lady
who had traversed, in an illegitimate and inexplicable fashion, some hundreds of years of time in a single night. Her
name, the Lady Vomact, had passed into legend; but her
blood and her archaic lust for mastery lived on in the mute
masterful body of her descendant. Martel could believe the
old tales as he stared at the rostrum, wondering what
untraceable mutation had left the Vomact kin as predators
among mankind.) Calling loudly with the movement of his
lips, but still without sound, Vomact appealed:

"The honorable committee is now pleased to reaffirm the
sentence of death issued against the heretic and enemy,
Adam Stone." Again the *vote* stance.

Again Chang's light shone lonely in its isolated protest.

Vomact then made his final move:

"I call for the designation of the senior scanner present
as the manager of the sentence. I call for authorization to
him to appoint executioners, one or many, who shall make
evident the will and majesty of scanners. I ask that I be accountable for the deed, and not for the means. The deed is a
noble deed, for the protection of mankind and for the honor
of the scanners; but of the means it must be said that they
are to be the best at hand, and no more. Who knows the true

way to kill an Other, here on a crowded and watchful Earth? This is no mere matter of discharging a cylindered sleeper, no mere question of upgrading the needle of a haberman. When people die down here, it is not like the up-and-out. They die reluctantly. Killing within the Earth is not our usual business, O Brothers and Scanners, as you know well. You must choose me to choose my agent as I see fit. Otherwise the common knowledge will become the common betrayal whereas if I alone know the responsibility, I alone could betray us, and you will not have far to look in case the Instrumentality comes searching." (*What about the killer you choose?* thought Martel. *He too will know unless—unless you silence him forever.*)

Vomact went into the stance: *The honorable scanners are pleased to vote.*

One light of protest shone; Chang's, again.

Martel imagined that he could see a cruel joyful smile on Vomact's dead face—the smile of a man who knew himself righteous and who found his righteousness upheld and affirmed by militant authority.

Martel tried one last time to come free.

The dead hands held. They were locked like vises until their owners' eyes unlocked them: how else could they hold the piloting month by month?

Martel then shouted: "Honorable Scanners, this is judicial murder."

No ear heard him. He was cranched, and alone.

Nonetheless, he shouted again: "You endanger the Confraternity."

Nothing happened.

The echo of his voice sounded from one end of the room to the other. No head turned. No eyes met his.

Martel realized that as they paired for talk, the eyes of the scanners avoided him. He saw that no one desired to watch his speech. He knew that behind the cold faces of his friends there lay compassion or amusement. He knew that they knew him to be cranched—absurd, normal, manlike, temporarily no scanner. But he knew that in this matter the wisdom of scanners was nothing. He knew that only a cranched scanner could feel with his very blood the outrage and anger which deliberate murder would provoke among the Others. He knew that the Confraternity endangered itself, and knew that the most ancient prerogative of law was the monopoly of death. Even the ancient nations, in the times of the Wars, before the Beasts, before men went into the up-and-out—even the ancients had known this. How did they say it? *Only the state shall kill.* The states were gone but the Instrumentality remained, and the Instrumentality could not pardon things which occurred within the Earths but beyond its authority. Death in space was the business, the right of the scanners: how could the Instrumentality enforce its laws in a place where all men who wakened, wakened only to die in the great pain? Wisely did the Instrumentality leave space to the scanners, wisely had the Confraternity not meddled inside the Earths. And now the Confraternity itself was going to step forth as an outlaw band, as a gang of rogues as stupid and reckless as the tribes of the Unforgiven!

Martel knew this because he was cranched. Had he been haberman, he would have thought only with his mind, not with his heart and guts and blood. How could the other scanners know?

Vomàct returned for the last time to the rostrum: *The committee has met and its will shall be done.* Verbally he added: "Senior among you, I ask your loyalty and your silence."

At that point, the two scanners let his arms go. Martel rubbed his numb hands, shaking his fingers to get the circulation back into the cold fingertips. With real freedom, he began to think of what he might still do. He scanned himself: the cranching held. He might have a day. Well, he could go on even if haberman, but it would be inconvenient, having to talk with finger and tablet. He looked about for Chang. He saw his friend standing patient and immobile in a quiet corner. Martel moved slowly, so as not to attract any more attention to himself than could be helped. He faced Chang, moved until his face was in the light, and then articulated:

"What are we going to do? You're not going to let them kill Adam Stone, are you? Don't you realize what Stone's work will mean to us, if it succeeds? No more scanners. No more habermans. No more pain in the up-and-out. I tell you, if the others were all cranched, as I am, they would see it in a human way, not with the narrow crazy logic which they used in the meeting. We've got to stop them. How can we do it? What are we going to do? What does Parizianski think? Who has been chosen?"

"Which question do you want me to answer?"

Martel laughed. (It felt good to laugh, even then; it felt like being a man.) "Will you help me?"

Chang's eyes flashed across Martel's face as Chang answered: "No. No. No."

"You won't help?"

"No."

"Why not, Chang? Why not?"

"I am a scanner. The vote has been taken. You would do the same if you were not in this unusual condition."

"I'm not in an unusual condition. I'm cranched. That merely means that I see things the way that the Others would. I see the stupidity. The recklessness. The selfishness. It is murder."

"What is murder? Have you not killed? You are not one of the Others. You are a scanner. You will be sorry for what you are about to do, if you do not watch out."

"But why did you vote against Vomact then? Didn't you too see what Adam Stone means to all of us? Scanners will live in vain. Thank God for that! Can't you see it?"

"No."

"But you talk to me, Chang. You are my friend?"

"I talk to you. I am your friend. Why not?"

"But what are you going to do?"

"Nothing, Martel. Nothing."

"Will you help me?"

"No."

"Not even to save Stone?"

"No."

"Then I will go to Parizianski for help."

"It will do you no good."

"Why not? He's more human than you, right now."

"He will not help you, because he has the job. Vomact designated him to kill Adam Stone."

Martel stopped speaking in mid-movement. He suddenly took the stance: *I thank you, Brother, and I depart.*

At the window he turned and faced the room. He saw that Vomact's eyes were upon him. He gave the stance, *I thank you, Brother, and I depart,* and added the flourish of respect which is shown when seniors are present. Vomact caught the sign, and Martel could see the cruel lips move. He thought he saw the words ". . . take good care of yourself . . ." but did not wait to inquire. He stepped backward and dropped out the window.

Once below the window and out of sight, he adjusted his aircoat to a maximum speed. He swam lazily in the air, scanning himself thoroughly, and adjusting his adrenal intake down. He then made the movement of release, and felt the cold air rush past his face like running water.

Adam Stone had to be at Chief Downport.

Adam Stone had to be there.

Wouldn't Adam Stone be surprised in the night? Surprised to meet the strangest of beings, the first renegade among scanners. (Martel suddenly appreciated that it was of himself he was thinking. Martel the Traitor to Scanners! That sounded strange and bad. But what of Martel, the Loyal to Mankind? Was that not compensation? And if he won, he won Luci. If he lost, he lost nothing—an unconsidered and expendable haberman. It happened to be himself. But in contrast to the immense reward, to mankind, to the Confraternity, to Luci, what did that matter?)

Martel thought to himself: "Adam Stone will have two visitors tonight. Two scanners, who are the friends of one another." He hoped that Parizianski was still his friend.

"And the world," he added, "depends on which of us gets there first."

Multifaceted in their brightness, the lights of Chief Downport began to shine through the mist ahead. Martel could see the outer towers of the city and glimpsed the phosphorescent periphery which kept back the Wild, whether Beasts, Machines, or the Unforgiven.

Once more Martel invoked the lords of his chance: "Help me to pass for an Other!"

Within the Downport, Martel had less trouble than he thought. He draped his aircoat over his shoulder so that it concealed the instruments. He took up his scanning mirror, and made up his face from the inside, by adding tone and animation to his blood and nerves until the muscles of his face glowed and the skin gave out a healthy sweat. That way he looked like an ordinary man who had just completed a long night flight.

After straightening out his clothing, and hiding his tablet within his jacket, he faced the problem of what to do about the talking finger. If he kept the nail, it would show him to be a scanner. He would be respected, but he would be identified. He might be stopped by the guards whom the Instrumentality had undoubtedly set around the person of Adam Stone. If he broke the nail—But he couldn't! No scanner in the history of the Confraternity had ever willingly broken his nail. That would be resignation, and there was no such thing. The only way *out*, was in the up-and-out! Martel put his finger to his mouth and bit off the nail. He looked at the now-queer finger, and sighed to himself.

He stepped toward the city gate, slipping his hand into his jacket and running up his muscular strength to four times normal. He started to scan, and then realized that his instruments were masked. *Might as well take all the chances at once*, he thought.

The watcher stopped him with a searching wire. The sphere thumped suddenly against Martel's chest.

"Are you a man?" said the unseen voice. (Martel knew that as a scanner in haberman condition, his own field-charge would have illuminated the sphere.)

"I am a man." Martel knew that the timbre of his voice had been good; he hoped that it would not be taken for that of a manshonyagger or a Beast or an Unforgiven one, who with mimicry sought to enter the cities and ports of mankind.

"Name, number, rank, purpose, function, time departed."

"Martel." He had to remember his old number, not Scanner 34. "Sunward 4234, 782nd Year of Space. Rank, rising subchief." That was no lie, but his substantive rank. "Purpose, personal and lawful within the limits of this city. No function of the Instrumentality. Departed Chief Outport 2019 hours." Everything now depended on whether he was believed, or would be checked against Chief Outport.

The voice was flat and routine: "Time desired within the city."

Martel used the standard phrase: "Your honorable sufferance is requested."

He stood in the cool night air, waiting. Far above him, through a gap in the mist, he could see the poisonous glittering in the sky of scanners. *The stars are my enemies*, he thought: *I have mastered the stars but they hate me. Ho, that sounds ancient! Like a book. Too much cranching.*

The voice returned: "Sunward 4234 dash 782 rising subchief Martel, enter the lawful gates of the city. Welcome. Do you desire food, raiment, money, or companionship?" The voice had no hospitality in it, just business. This was certainly different from entering a city in a scanner's role! Then the petty officers came out, and threw their beltlights on their fretful faces, and mouthed their words with preposterous deference, shouting against the stone deafness of scanner's ears. So that was the way that a subchief was treated: matter of fact, but not bad. Not bad.

Martel replied: "I have that which I need, but beg of the city a favor. My friend Adam Stone is here. I desire to see him, on urgent and personal lawful affairs."

The voice replied: "Did you have an appointment with Adam Stone?"

"No."

"The city will find him. What is his number?"

"I have forgotten it."

"You have forgotten it? Is not Adam Stone a magnate of the Instrumentality? Are you truly his friend?"

"Truly." Martel let a little annoyance creep into his voice. "Watcher, doubt me and call your subchief."

"No doubt implied. Why do you not know the number? This must go into the record," added the voice.

"We were friends in childhood. He has crossed the—" Martel started to say "the up-and-out" and remembered that the phrase was current only among scanners. "He has leapt from Earth to Earth, and has just now returned. I knew him well and I seek him out. I have word of his kith. May the Instrumentality protect us!"

"Heard and believed. Adam Stone will be searched."

At a risk, though a slight one, of having the sphere sound an alarm for *nonhuman*, Martel cut in on his scanner speaker within his jacket. He saw the trembling needle of light await his words and he started to write on it with his blunt finger. *That won't work*, he thought, and had a moment's panic until he found his comb, which had a sharp enough tooth to write. He wrote: "Emergency none. Martel Scanner calling Parizianski Scanner."

The needle quivered and the reply glowed and faded out: "Parizianski Scanner on duty and D.C. Calls taken by Scanner Relay."

Martel cut off his speaker.

Parizianski was somewhere around. Could he have crossed the direct way, right over the city wall, setting off the alert, and invoking official business when the petty officers overtook him in mid-air? Scarcely. That meant that a number of other scanners must have come in with Parizianski, all of them pretending to be in search of a few of the tenuous pleasures which could be enjoyed by a haberman, such as the sight of the newspictures or the viewing of beautiful women in the Pleasure Gallery. Parizianski was around, but he could not have moved privately, because Scanner Central registered him on duty and recorded his movements city by city.

The voice returned. Puzzlement was expressed in it. "Adam Stone is found and awakened. He has asked pardon of the Honorable, and says he knows no Martel. Will you see Adam Stone in the morning? The city will bid you welcome."

Martel ran out of resources. It was hard enough mimicking a man without having to tell lies in the guise of one.

Martel could only repeat: "Tell him I am Martel. The husband of Luci."

"It will be done."

Again the silence, and the hostile stars, and the sense that Parizianski was somewhere near and getting nearer; Martel felt his heart beating faster. He stole a glimpse at his chestbox and set his heart down a point. He felt calmer, even though he had not been able to scan with care.

The voice this time was cheerful, as though an annoyance had been settled: "Adam Stone consents to see you. Enter Chief Downport, and welcome."

The little sphere dropped noiselessly to the ground and the wire whispered away into the darkness. A bright arc of narrow light rose from the ground in front of Martel and swept through the city to one of the higher towers—apparently a hostel, which Martel had never entered. Martel plucked his aircoat to his chest for ballast, stepped heel-and-toe on the beam, and felt himself whistle through the air to an entrance window which sprang up before him as suddenly as a devouring mouth.

A tower guard stood in the doorway. "You are awaited, sir. Do you bear weapons, sir?"

"None," said Martel, grateful that he was relying on his own strength.

The guard led him past the check-screen. Martel noticed the quick flight of a warning across the screen as his instruments registered and identified him as a scanner. But the guard had not noticed it.

The guard stopped at a door. "Adam Stone is armed. He is lawfully armed by authority of the Instrumentality and by the liberty of this city. All those who enter are given warning."

Martel nodded in understanding at the man and went in.

Adam Stone was a short man, stout and benign. His gray

hair rose stiffly from a low forehead. His whole face was red and merry-looking. He looked like a jolly guide from the Pleasure Gallery, not like a man who had been at the edge of the up-and-out, fighting the great pain without haberman protection.

He stared at Martel. His look was puzzled, perhaps a little annoyed, but not hostile.

Martel came to the point. "You do not know me. I lied. My name is Martel, and I mean you no harm. But I lied. I beg the honorable gift of your hospitality. Remain armed. Direct your weapon against me—"

Stone smiled: "I am doing so," and Martel noticed the small wirepoint in Stone's capable, plump hand.

"Good. Keep on guard against me. It will give you confidence in what I shall say. But do, I beg you, give us a screen of privacy. I want no casual lookers. This is a matter of life and death."

"First: whose life and death?" Stone's face remained calm, his voice even.

"Yours, and mine, and the worlds'."

"You are cryptic but I agree." Stone called through the doorway: "Privacy please." There was a sudden hum, and all the little noises of the night quickly vanished from the air of the room.

Said Adam Stone: "Sir, who are you? What brings you here?"

"I am Scanner 34."

"You a scanner? I don't believe it."

For answer, Martel pulled his jacket open, showing his chestbox. Stone looked up at him, amazed. Martel explained:

"I am cranched. Have you never seen it before?"

"*Not with men.* On animals. Amazing! But—what do you want?"

"The truth. Do you fear me?"

"Not with this," said Stone, grasping the wirepoint. "But I shall tell you the truth."

"Is it true that you have conquered the great pain?"

Stone hesitated, seeking words for an answer.

"Quick, can you tell me how you have done it, so that I may believe you?"

"I have loaded the ships with life."

"Life?"

"Life. I don't know what the great pain is, but I did find that in the experiments, when I sent out masses of animals or plants, the life in the center of the mass lived longest. I built ships—small ones, of course—and sent them out with rabbits, with monkeys—"

"Those are Beasts?"

"Yes. With small Beasts. And the Beasts came back unhurt. They came back because the walls of the ships were filled with life. I tried many kinds, and finally found a sort of life which lives in the waters. Oysters. Oyster-beds. The outermost oysters died in the great pain. The inner ones lived. The passengers were unhurt."

"But they were Beasts?"

"Not only Beasts. Myself."

"You!"

"I came through space alone. Through what you call the up-and-out, alone. Awake and sleeping. I am unhurt. If you do not believe me, ask your brother scanners. Come and see my ship in the morning. I will be glad to see you then, along with your brother scanners. I am going to demonstrate before the chiefs of the Instrumentality."

Martel repeated his question: "You came here alone?"

Adam Stone grew testy: "Yes, alone. Go back and check your scanner's register if you do not believe me. You never put me in a bottle to cross Space."

Martel's face was radiant. "I believe you now. It is true. No more scanners. No more habermans. No more cranching."

Stone looked significantly toward the door.

Martel did not take the hint. "I must tell you that—"

"Sir, tell me in the morning. Go enjoy your cranch. Isn't it supposed to be pleasure? Medically I know it well. But not in practice."

"It is pleasure. It's normality—for a while. But listen. The scanners have sworn to destroy you, and your work."

"What!"

"They have met and have voted and sworn. You will make scanners unnecessary, they say. You will bring the ancient wars back to the world, if scanning is lost and the scanners live in vain!"

Adam Stone was nervous but kept his wits about him: "You're a scanner. Are you going to kill me—or try?"

"No, you fool. I have betrayed the Confraternity. Call guards the moment I escape. Keep guards around you. I will try to intercept the killer."

Martel saw a blur in the window. Before Stone could turn, the wirepoint was whipped out of his hand. The blur solidified and took form as Parizianski.

Martel recognized what Parizianski was doing: *High speed.*

Without thinking of his cranch, he thrust his hand to his chest, set himself up to *High speed* too. Waves of fire, like the great pain, but hotter, flooded over him. He fought to keep his face readable as he stepped in front of Parizianski and gave the sign,

Top emergency.

Parizianski spoke, while the normally moving body of Stone stepped away from them as slowly as a drifting cloud: "Get out of my way. I am on a mission."

"I know it. I stop you here and now. Stop. Stop. Stop. Stone is right."

Parizianski's lips were barely readable in the haze of pain which flooded Martel. (He thought: *God, God, God of the ancients! Let me hold on! Let me live under Overload just long enough!*) Parizianski was saying: "Get out of my way. By order of the Confraternity, get out of my way!" And Parizianski gave the sign, *Help I demand in the name of my duty!*

Martel choked for breath in the syruplike air. He tried one last time: "Parizianski, friend, friend, my friend. Stop. Stop." (No scanner had ever murdered scanner before.)

Parizianski made the sign: *You are unfit for duty, and I will take over.*

Martel thought, *For the first time in the world!* as he reached over and twisted Parizianski's brainbox up to *Overload*. Parizianski's eyes glittered in terror and understanding. His body began to drift down toward the floor.

Martel had just strength to reach his own chestbox. As he faded into haberman or death, he knew not which, he felt his fingers turning on the control of speed, turning down. He tried to speak, to say, "Get a scanner, I need help, get a scanner . . ."

But the darkness rose about him, and the numb silence clasped him.

Martel awakened to see the face of Luci near his own.

He opened his eyes wider, and found that he was hearing—hearing the sound of her happy weeping, the sound of her chest as she caught the air back into her throat.

He spoke weakly: "Still cranched? Alive?"

Another face swam into the blur beside Luci's. It was Adam Stone. His deep voice rang across immensities of space before coming to Martel's hearing. Martel tried to read

Stone's lips, but could not make them out. He went back to listening to the voice:

"... not cranched. Do you understand me? Not cranched!"

Martel tried to say: "But I can hear! I can feel!" The others got his sense if not his words.

Adam Stone spoke again:

"You have gone back through the haberman. I put you back first. I didn't know how it would work in practice, but I had the theory all worked out. You don't think the Instrumentality would waste the scanners, do you? You go back to normality. We are letting the habermans die as fast as the ships come in. They don't need to live any more. But we are restoring the scanners. You are the first. Do you understand? You are the first. Take it easy, now."

Adam Stone smiled. Dimly behind Stone, Martel thought that he saw the face of one of the chiefs of the Instrumentality. That face, too, smiled at him, and then both faces disappeared upward and away.

Martel tried to lift his head, to scan himself. He could not. Luci stared at him, calming herself, but with an expression of loving perplexity. She said,

"My darling husband! You're back again, to stay!"

Still, Martel tried to see his box. Finally he swept his hand across his chest with a clumsy motion. There was nothing there. The instruments were gone. He was back to normality but still alive.

In the deep weak peacefulness of his mind, another troubling thought took shape. He tried to write with his finger, the way that Luci wanted him to, but he had neither pointed fingernail nor scanner's tablet. He had to use his voice. He summoned up his strength and whispered:

"Scanners?"

"Yes, darling? What is it?"

"Scanners?"

"Scanners. Oh, yes, darling, they're all right. They had to arrest some of them for going into *High speed* and running away. But the Instrumentality caught them all—all those on the ground—and they're happy now. Do you know, darling," she laughed, "some of them didn't want to be restored to normality. But Stone and the chiefs persuaded them."

"Vomact?"

"He's fine, too. He's staying cranched until he can be restored. Do you know, he has arranged for scanners to take new jobs. You're all to be deputy chiefs for Space. Isn't that nice? But he got himself made chief for Space. You're all going to be pilots, so that your fraternity and guild can go on. And Chang's getting changed right now. You'll see him soon."

Her face turned sad. She looked at him earnestly and said: "I might as well tell you now. You'll worry otherwise. There has been one accident. Only one. When you and your friend called on Adam Stone, your friend was so happy that he forgot to scan, and he let himself die of *Overload*."

"Called on Stone?"

"Yes. Don't you remember? Your friend."

He still looked surprised, so she said:

"Parizianski."

SCANNERS LIVE IN VAIN:
UNDER THE WIRE WITH THE HABERMANS

One essential component of great science fiction is strangeness. The story must take the reader someplace new and show him something he has never seen before. The strangeness may reside in the landscape, as in the Aldiss story "Hothouse" in the pages ahead; it may lie in the situation that generates the plot, as in "Fondly Fahrenheit" or "Four in One"; it may be found in the sociocultural assumptions of the story, as in "The Monsters"; it may lie in the emotional nature of the protagonists, as in "No Woman Born." It may even be a linguistic strangeness: the clinesterton bead-emung scene of "Common Time" exemplifies that. But it must be there.

Cordwainer Smith's "Scanners Live in Vain," one of the classic stories of science fiction, provides that essential degree of strangeness in two ways: by sheer originality of concept, and by a deceptive and eerie simplicity of narrative. It was the first published story of a remarkable man and a remarkable writer, and when it appeared in 1950—in what was little more than an amateur magazine—it set off reverberations that opened the way for an extraordinary career. For me it was a revelation. I read it over and over, astonished by its power. It had for me the fundamental science-fiction quality that I had been searching for ever since I discovered Wells' *Time Machine* and Lovecraft's *Shadow out of Time*, and for which I continue to search to this day, some forty years later: it thrust me into a place that was utterly new to me, and imbued me with a residue of haunting images and impressions and feelings that I knew would never leave me.

Within the close-knit world of science fiction, the story and its mysterious author caused an immediate sensation. "Cordwainer Smith" was plainly a pseudonym, but the identity behind it remained a well-kept secret for a dozen years. Because the story showed such mastery, it seemed unlikely that it was the work of a novice; and so there were those who speculated that it had been done by the versatile Henry Kuttner, or perhaps Theodore Sturgeon, or A. E. van Vogt. But none of those writers owned up to it; and it was only in the 1960s that we learned that the true author of "Scanners Live in Vain" was one Paul M. A. Linebarger, who had been a linguist, a psychiatrist, a professor of Asian politics at Johns Hopkins University, an advisor to U.S. Intelligence in the Far East during World War II and to President Kennedy twenty years later, and a great many other things in a crowded life cruelly shortened to 53 years.

More so than any other science-fiction writer I can think of, Linebarger had had close experience with alien cultures from childhood on, and I think the power of his science fiction sprang primarily from that. His father was an international financier and diplomat, and young Paul attended schools in Hawaii, China, and Germany before he was ten years old. When he was thirteen he returned to China, remaining there through his adolescence. It was that country that seems to have had the most profound influence on him. He grew up fluent in six languages, and he was at home both in Oriental and Occidental cultures. Somehow science fiction caught his fancy along the way, and he began writing stories for his own amusement, drawing on his knowledge of Chinese literary techniques. The earliest of these went unpublished and have been lost; but in 1945, while serving at the Pentagon, he produced "Scanners Live in Vain" and started it on its journey through the science-fiction magazines.

The only magazine of that period that had risen above the slam-bang pulp-magazine tradition of action fiction was John Campbell's *Astounding*; but the very strangeness that makes "Scanners" such an important story must have made it unpalatable to the conservative Campbell. So it bounced around from *Amazing Stories* to *Planet Stories* to *Thrilling Wonder Stories* before finding a home in *Fantasy Book*, a West Coast magazine published by a longtime s-f hobbyist in an edition of a few thousand copies. There I came upon it, for I was so voracious in my quest for science fiction then that I hunted down even such obscurities as *Fantasy Book*. But only a fluke brought Cordwainer Smith to the attention of a wider audience. The writer, editor, and literary agent Frederik Pohl happened to have a story in the same issue of *Fantasy Book* and, leafing through the magazine, he discovered "Scanners," to his great astonishment. A year or so later he included it in *Beyond the End of Time*, an anthology he edited for a major paperback house, and nothing was quite the same again in science fiction. For "Scanners" proved to be the first story in a history of the future spanning thousands of years and coming eventually to fill ten volumes, and "Cordwainer Smith," though, in fact, fundamentally inimitable, came to be one of the most widely imitated science-fiction writers of the fertile period that began in the mid-1960s.

I am unable to think in Chinese and, probably, so are you; and most of us lack Paul Linebarger's intimate acquaintance with the Far East. Therefore we are unable really to attain that quality of non-Westernness that made Cordwainer Smith's fiction seem almost like the work of a visitor from the far future dwelling in our midst. We can aspire after strangeness, and perhaps we can find some of our own to use in our work; but Linebarger's unique tone and method, though easy enough to copy, loses all vitality and power when employed by other hands. Still, we can study what he did, and try to learn from his example.

The title is immediately arresting: "Scanners Live in Vain." What are *scanners?* We don't know, of course. But they live in vain. Why? Most story titles are descriptive in nature: "A Martian Odyssey," "Nightfall," "The Weapon Shops," "The Nine Billion Names of God," "First Contact." But "Scanners Live in Vain" is a *statement.* It is a complete sentence, in the present indicative, *telling* us something. What, though? We have no idea what it means; but we want to find out.

So we begin to read and are plunged instantly into mystery and tension: "Martel was angry. He did not even adjust his blood away from anger." Two sentences, and we have the initial announcement of conflict that every effective storyteller since Homer has known to be the best way of starting a story, followed by an indication—"He did not even adjust his blood away from anger"—that we are entering an unfamiliar frame of reference, a strange science-fiction world. In the paragraphs that follow, Smith builds and reinforces a sense of strangeness by introducing unknown and unexplained terminology: first *scanner*, then *cranch*, then *habermans, up-and-out, under the wire.* These concepts are utterly familiar to his characters, of course, as much so as *policeman* and *telephone* and *newspaper* are to us; and they are familiar to the author, too, probably because he has devised them first while sketching the outline of his story, and has come to know them well during the planning stage. Now he can throw them at us with confidence. *He* sees nothing bewildering about the term *cranching*, and because he is so self-assured, we will stick around to find out what it means. (When a science-fiction writer seems to be making up his terminology as he goes along, blithely tossing in this or that ad-hoc coinage whenever he finds he needs one, readers quickly sense it, and their willingness to accept the invented world as a real one rapidly wavers. The trick is to work it all out ahead of time and internalize it thoroughly, so that the writer appears to be reporting the movements of his characters through a solid and plausible and fully experienced world that happens not to be this one. If it's done right, the reader will quickly come to feel at home there.)

Of course, there are limits to how far this technique can be carried. A story that presents the reader with fifty strange terms on the first page ("It was mid-Sneel, the quonking season. Calmly Blargelon thrikkeled his blorch, and a smile slowly spread across his face as the Git-Snup Effect awakened in him. Across the room the valiblog uncoiled his-her's filmy snabbish and began to vorken") will probably arouse annoyance rather than fascination. But Smith is restrained: though he gives us little background information, he allows us to establish hierarchies among the unknowns (scanners, whoever they are, are superior to habermans, whoever *they* are, and cranching, whatever *that* is, is something done with the aid of a *cranching wire*; the *up-and-out*, though we have never heard of it before, seems clearly to be a term for space) and sets everything forth in spare, simple prose. Here, his early training in Chinese probably served him in good stead. Chinese, after all, is a language in which complex terms are reduced to simple component terms so that they can be dealt with in an ideographic form of writing. Thus we find things like "One Chicken Three Flavors" and "Hot and Sour Soup" on the menus of Chinese restaurants; and *up-and-out* sounds to me like a translation of a perfectly good Chinese metaphor both for space and the process of reaching it.

His knowledge of Chinese, also, may be behind Smith's extreme sparseness and simplicity of style, which is so valuable both in helping the reader absorb all this unexplained material and in creating the mood of strangeness. Adverbs and adjectives are rare in his prose. Sentences are short. Rhythms are insistent and often choppy. (Note the paragraphs near the beginning of the story, from "He saw by her look of stricken assent" through "She turned her back to him again." Nearly every sentence begins with a personal pronoun. There are few subordinate clauses. Most sentences are simple declarative announcements of external events: "She snapped the small plug into the high-burden control. . . . She helped him to sit down. . . . She turned then, full-face toward him. . . .") There are odd but always comprehensible locutions, too, which aid in setting the mood. Smith speaks of "calling" an emergency, of making food "pretty," of faces that "disappeared upward and away." These unexpected turns of phrase rise startlingly out of Smith's unadorned prose to brilliant effect.

Smith also understands how to create drama. The thirteen-paragraph prologue begins with anger and ends with pain, a powerful emotional progression. In that short span Martel has awakened in haberman condition, he has struggled to regain contact with his wife, and he has cranched; that is, he has returned to the world of ordinary mortals. We have been launched into the bizarre world of the scanners and are intensely eager to know more about it, and now the story proper can begin.

We know we are somewhere in the far future. Lamb chops have been forgotten. Mankind is ruled by something called the Instrumentality, never described in detail. (The "iceberg technique," by which nine-tenths of a story's background remains submerged and is not allowed to surface, is an important mood-creating device in science fiction.) Space travel is an established fact; but those who go forth into the up-and-out experience what is known as the "great pain of space," a startling and original concept. (What causes it? Cosmic radiation? Psychic vibrations between the worlds? Smith feels no need to tell us. It is there; this story is about mankind's way of dealing with it.)

When he begins to move into the heart of his story—the gathering of scanners at Central Tie-in, and the decision to kill Adam Stone—Smith makes a brilliant choice of narrative strategy that allows him to portray the Scanner society both from within and without while using only one character's viewpoint. *Vomact makes Martel come to the meeting while he is still cranched.* There's no time for him to return to normal scanner mode; and so he finds himself in the role of a detached observer among his own people. It's a magnificently effective device: Martel is a legitimate member of the group but he looks at his fellow scanners from the outside, as we must. As a result, our identification with Martel is tightened. Scanners, when they are in haberman mode, are rigid, austere, robotic figures, more dead than alive, alien and remote to us. But we perceive Martel as a human being, complex and troubled. What might have been an impossibly cold and uninvolving story is made accessible to us. We care about Martel; and we believe it when he rebels against his fellow scanners and sets out to save Adam Stone.

Gradually, as the main narrative that centers about the scanners' fears of obsolescence unfolds, Smith drops in a few more far-future terms, none of which he tries to explain—manshonyaggers, the Others, the Unforgiven, the Old Machines, the Beasts. Some we can work out from the context, some are left mysterious. There are not so many of them that they overwhelm the narrative, and they are always secondary to the initial set, scanners and habermans and cranching. Smith has introduced that basic set of strange terms in the first few pages, and the story, if it is to satisfy the reader, must be devoted to manipulation and development of the substance behind those initially given terms. Additional ones, as they appear, serve only as embellishments and decorations. A writer who has invented habermans, scanners, and the Great Pain of Space in the first few pages of his story has enough on his hands; it would be a technical mistake to try to throw in yet another major concept midway through.

But Smith's secondary embellishments and decorations have an important purpose. By hinting throughout at other things going on outside the immediate focus of the story—the manshonyaggers, say, or the "times of the Wars" before the Beasts and the up-and-out— Smith gives it breadth and scope with just a few quick strokes. A short story does not have to be a total history of everything that has happened in the writer's imagined future world; but it gains in power if it seems to be a brief episode against a much larger background.

The stark and sometimes exotic rhythms of the prose often allow Smith to get away with things that would appear to be technical errors in the hands of another writer. By adopting a deliberately primitive tone, as if his story were a translation from some other language used in a remote era in another land, he shrewdly forestalls the criticism that might have been appropriate had he used a more "contemporary" realistic mode. For instance, it is irritating when a writer forces one of his characters to tell another something that both of them already know, simply to get the information before the reader. Yet Smith does just that in the scene between Martel and Luci, having Luci tell Martel the scanner, "All Mankind owes most honor to the scanner, who unites the Earths of mankind. Scanners are the protectors of the habermans. They are the judges in the up-and-out. . . ." None of this is news to Martel; and no one writing a piece of realistic fiction could safely indulge in such a speech. Smith justifies it by telling us that she is reciting these things "like a tale told a thousand times to reassure herself." And because his prose, while simple, is actually highly mannered in its stylized simplicity, he manages to bring it off by making the passage seem almost a ritualistic litany. In the scene at Central Tie-in that follows, he does the same thing on a much greater scale, and this time it actually *is* a ritualistic litany, a sort of responsory chanted by Vomact and the scanners. It is tremendously effective: we suspend not only disbelief but our annoyance over this sort of technical flaw in storytelling, and the chanting of the scanners both gives us all manner of useful background information and adds significantly to the haunting tone of the story.

Smith is aware, of course, that having characters tell each other things that they already know is generally regarded as undesirable in fiction. He signals this a couple of pages later by having Martel show irritation at the "long-winded ritual" of the scanners, whom he sees as "a lot of cruelly driven ghosts." And when he needs to convey even more information at that point he simply offers it in straightforward and conventional exposition. ("Habermans were criminals or heretics, and scanners were gentleman-volunteers. . . .") Great hunks of flatfooted exposition can be horrendously boring in a science-fiction story, however necessary the information they contain may be. But at this stage, midway through the story, Smith has already hooked the reader with his cunning and tantalizing display of unexplained material; now he knows he can abandon that sly technique and safely lay out the explanations he still needs to convey. No one will be bored: the plot is in motion and we are all desperately eager to know what is going on. It is the right moment for a welcome bit of straightforward exposition.

The ending of the story is perhaps its one weak point: Martel awakening from unconsciousness to hear Luci and Stone telling him that all remaining strands of the plot have been tidied up while he was out cold. ("Do you know, he has arranged for scanners to take new jobs. You're all to be deputy chiefs for Space. Isn't that nice?") Here, and only here, we realize that we are reading the work of a beginner. A more experienced practitioner would probably have brought the story to its close with some or all of the restructuring of scanner society still undone, and Martel looking forward to the changes yet to come. No matter: it's a small failing in a story otherwise so strong.

The use of such an array of strikingly original narrative strategies to create a unique and unforgettable view of the future is what made some of us think, back in 1950, that we were reading some well-known master of the craft who was hiding behind false whiskers. Even in his first published story Cordwainer Smith was an astonishingly adept storyteller.

But we must remember that he had been writing fiction privately for many years, doubtless learning the tricks of his trade very well indeed during that secret apprenticeship. And we should remember, also, that this man was an authority on Asian politics and on the tactics of revolution, and that about the same time as "Scanners Live in Vain," he was writing *Psychological Warfare* (Infantry Journal Press, 1948), which is still considered a basic text on that subject. He was a man who knew how to hold the interest of an audience because he understood the art of manipulating the intellects and emotions of human beings. Which is, after all, what writing fiction really is.

HOTHOUSE
BRIAN W. ALDISS

My vegetable love should grow
Vaster than empires and more slow.
Andrew Marvell

I

The heat, the light, the humidity—these were constant and had remained constant for ... but nobody knew how long. Nobody cared any more for the big questions that begin "How long ...?" or "Why ...?" It was no longer a place for mind. It was a place for growth, for vegetables. It was like a hothouse.

In the green light, some of the children came out to play. Alert for enemies, they ran along the branch, calling to each other in soft voices. A fast growing berrywhisk moved upwards to one side, its sticky crimson mass of berries gleaming. Clearly it was intent on seeding and would offer the children no harm. They scuttled past it. Beyond the margin of the group strip, some nettlemoss had sprung up during their period of sleep. It stirred as the children approached.

"Kill it," Toy said simply. She was the head child of the group. She was ten. The others obeyed her. Unsheathing the sticks every child carried in imitation of every adult, they scraped at the nettlemoss. They scraped at it and hit it. Excitement grew in them as they beat down the plant, squashing its poisoned tips.

Clat fell forward in her excitement. She was only five, the youngest of the group's children. Her hands fell among the poisonous stuff. She cried aloud and rolled aside. The other children also cried, but did not venture into the nettlemoss to save her.

Struggling out of the way, little Clat cried again. Her fingers clutched at the rough bark—then she was tumbling from the branch.

The children saw her fall onto a great spreading leaf several lengths below, clutch it, and lie there quivering on the quivering green. She looked up pitifully.

"Fetch Lily-yo," Toy told Gren. Gren sped back along the branch to get Lily-yo. A tigerfly swooped out of the air at him, humming its anger deeply. He struck it aside with a hand, not pausing. He was nine, a rare man child, very brave already, and fleet and proud. Swiftly he ran to the Headwoman's hut.

Under the branch, attached to its underside, hung eighteen great homemaker nuts. Hollowed out they were, and cemented into place with the cement distilled from the acetoyle plant. Here lived the eighteen members of the group, one to each homemaker's nut—the Headwoman, her five women, their man, and the eleven surviving children.

Hearing Gren's cry, out came Lily-yo from her nuthut, climbing up a line to stand on the branch beside him.

HOTHOUSE

"Clat falls!" cried Gren.

With her stick, Lily-yo rapped sharply on the bough before running on ahead of the child.

Her signal called out the other six adults, the women Flor, Daphe, Hy, Ivin, and Jury, and the man Haris. They hastened from their nuthuts, weapons ready, poised for attack or flight.

As Lily-yo ran, she whistled on a sharp split note.

Instantly to her from the thick foliage nearby came a dumbler, flying to her shoulder. The dumbler rotated, a fleecy umbrella whose separate spokes controlled its direction. It matched its flight to her movement.

Both children and adults gathered around Lily-yo when she looked down at Clat, still sprawled some way below on her leaf.

"Lie still, Clat! Do not move!" called Lily-yo. "I will come to you." Clat obeyed that voice, though she was in pain and fear.

Lily-yo climbed astride the hooked base of the dumbler, whistling softly to it. Only she of the group had fully mastered the art of commanding dumblers. These dumblers were the half-sentient spores of the whistlethistle. The tips of their feathered spokes carried seeds; the seeds were strangely shaped, so that a light breeze whispering in them made them into ears that listened to every advantage of the wind that would spread their propagation. Humans, after long years of practice, could use these crude ears for their own purposes and instructions, as Lily-yo did now.

The dumbler bore her down to the rescue of the helpless child. Clat lay on her back, watching them come, hoping to herself. She was still looking up when green teeth sprouted through the leaf all about her.

"Jump, Clat!" Lily-yo cried.

The child had time to scramble to her knees. Vegetable

349

predators are not so fast as humans. Then the green teeth snapped shut about her waist.

Under the leaf, a trappersnapper had moved into position, sensing the presence of prey through the single layer of foliage. It was a horny, caselike affair, just a pair of square jaws hinged and with many long teeth. From one corner of it grew a stalk, very muscular and thicker than a human. It looked like a neck. Now it bent, carrying Clat away, down to its true mouth, which lived with the rest of the plant far below on the unseen forest Ground, slobbering in darkness and wetness and decay.

Whistling, Lily-yo directed her dumbler back up to the home bough. Nothing now could be done for Clat. It was the way.

Already the rest of the group was dispersing. To stand in a bunch was to invite trouble from the unnumbered enemies of the forest. Besides, Clat's was not the first death they had witnessed.

Lily-yo's group had once been of seven underwomen and two men. Two women and one man had fallen to the green. Among them, the eight women had borne twenty-two children to the group, four of them being man children. Deaths of children were many, always. Now that Clat was gone, over half the children had fallen to the green. Only two man children were left, Gren and Veggy.

Lily-yo walked back along the branch in the green light. The dumbler drifted from her unheeded, obeying the silent instructions of the forest air, listening for word of a seeding place. Never had there been such an overcrowding of the world. No bare places existed. The dumblers sometimes drifted through the jungles for centuries waiting to alight.

Coming to a point above one of the nuthuts, Lily-yo lowered herself into it by the creeper. This had been Clat's nuthut. The headwoman could hardly enter it, so small was the door. Humans kept their doors as narrow as possible, enlarging them as they grew. It helped to keep out unwanted visitors.

All was tidy in the nuthut. From the interior soft fiber a bed had been cut; there the five-year-old had slept when a feeling for sleep came among the unchanging forest green. On the cot lay Clat's soul. Lily-yo took it and thrust it into her belt.

She climbed out onto the creeper, took her knife, and began to slash at the place where the bark of the tree had been cut away and the nuthut was attached to the living wood. After several slashes the cement gave. Clat's nuthut hinged down, hung for a moment, then fell.

As it disappeared among huge coarse leaves, there was a flurry of foliage. Something was fighting for the privilege of devouring the huge morsel.

Lily-yo climbed back onto the branch. For a moment she paused to breathe deeply. Breathing was more trouble than it had been. She had gone on too many hunts, borne too many children, fought too many fights. With a rare and fleeting knowledge of herself, she glanced down at her bare green breasts. They were less plump than they had been when she first took the man Haris to her; they hung lower. Their shape was less beautiful.

By instinct she knew her youth was over. By instinct she knew it was time to Go Up.

The group stood near the Hollow, awaiting her. She ran to them. The Hollow was like an upturned armpit, formed where the branch joined the trunk. In the Hollow collected their water supply.

Silently, the group was watching a line of termights climb the trunk. One of the termights now and again signaled greetings to the humans. The humans waved back. As far as they had allies at all, the termights were their allies. Only five great families survived here in the allconquering vegetable world; the tigerflies, the treebees, the plantants, and the termights were social insects, mighty and invincible. And the fifth family was man, lowly and easily killed; not organized as the insects were, but not extinct—the last animal species remaining.

Lily-yo came up to the group. She too raised her eyes to follow the moving line of termights until it disappeared into the layers of green. The termights could live on any level of the great forest, in the Tips or down on the Ground. They were the first and last of insects; as long as anything lived, the termights and tigerflies would.

Lowering her eyes, Lily-yo called to the group.

When they looked, she brought out Clat's soul, lifting it above her head to show to them.

"Clat has fallen to the green," she said. "Her soul must go to the Tips, according to the custom. Flor and I will take it at once, so that we can go with the termights. Daphe, Hy, Ivin, Jury, you guard well the man Haris and the children till we return."

The women nodded solemnly. Then they came one by one to touch Clat's soul.

The soul was roughly carved of wood into the shape of a woman. As a child was born, so with rites its male parent carved it a soul, a doll, a totem soul—for in the forest when one fell to the green there was scarely ever a bone surviving to be buried. The soul survived for burial in the Tips.

As they touched the soul, Gren adventurously slipped from the group. He was nearly as old as Toy, as active and as strong. Not only had he power to run. He could climb. He could swim. Ignoring the cry of his friend Veggy, he scampered into the Hollow and dived into the pool.

Below the surface, opening his eyes, he saw a world of

bleak clarity. A few green things like clover leaves grew at his approach, eager to wrap around his legs. Gren avoided them with a flick of his hand as he shot deeper. Then he saw the crocksock—before it saw him.

The crocksock was an aquatic plant, semiparasitic by nature. Living in hollows, it sent down its saw-toothed suckers into the trees' sap. But the upper section of it, rough and tongue-shaped like a sock, could also feed. It unfolded, wrapping around Gren's left arm, its fibers instantly locking to increase the grip.

Gren was ready for it.

With one slash of his knife, he clove the crocksock in two, leaving the lower half to thrash uselessly at him. Before he could rise to the surface, Daphe the skilled huntress was beside him, her face angered, bubbles flashing out silverlike fish from between her teeth. Her knife was ready to protect him.

He grinned at her as he broke surface and climbed out onto the dry bank. Nonchalantly he shook himself as she climbed beside him.

" 'Nobody runs or swims or climbs alone,' " Daphe called to him, quoting one of the laws. "Gren, have you no fear? Your head is an empty burr!"

The other women too showed anger. Yet none of them touched Gren. He was a man child. He was tabu. He had the magic powers of carving souls and bringing babies—or would have when fully grown, which would be soon now.

"I am Gren, the man child!" he boasted to them. His eyes sought Haris's for approval. Haris merely looked away. Now that Gren was so big, Haris did not cheer as once he had, though the boy's deeds were braver than before.

Slightly deflated, Gren jumped about, waving the strip of crocksock still wrapped around his left arm. He called and boasted at the women to show how little he cared for them.

"You are a baby yet," hissed Toy. She was ten, his senior by one year. Gren fell quiet.

Scowling, Lily-yo said, "The children grow too old to manage. When Flor and I have been to the Tips to bury Clat's soul, we shall return and break up the group. Time has come for us to part. Guard yourselves!"

It was a subdued group that watched their leader go. All knew that the group had to split; none cared to think about it. Their time of happiness and safety—so it seemed to all of them—would be finished, perhaps forever. The children would enter a period of lonely hardship, fending for themselves. The adults embarked on old age, trial, and death when they Went Up into the unknown.

2

Lily-yo and Flor climbed the rough bark easily. For them it was like going up a series of more or less symmetrically placed rocks. Now and again they met some kind of vegetable enemy, a thinpin or a pluggyrug, but these were small-fry, easily dispatched into the green gloom below. Their enemies were the termights' enemies, and the moving column had already dealt with the foes in its path. Lily-yo and Flor climbed close to the termights, glad of their company.

They climbed for a long while. Once they rested on an empty branch, capturing two wandering burrs, splitting them, and eating their oily white flesh. On the way up, they had glimpsed one or two groups of humans on different branches; sometimes these groups waved shyly, sometimes not. Now they were too high for humans.

Nearer the Tips, new danger threatened. In the safer middle layers of the forest the humans lived, avoided the perils of the Tips or the Ground.

"Now we move on," Lily-yo told Flor, getting to her feet when they had rested. "Soon we will be at the Tips."

A commotion silenced the two women. They looked up, crouching against the trunk for protection. Above their heads, leaves rustled as death struck.

A leapycreeper flailed the rough bark in a frenzy of greed, attacking the termight column. The leapycreeper's roots and stems were also tongues and lashes. Whipping around the trunk, it thrust its sticky tongues into the termights.

Against this particular plant, flexible and hideous, the insects had little defense. They scattered but kept doggedly climbing up, each perhaps trusting in the blind law of averages to survive.

For the humans, the plant was less of a threat—at least when met on a branch. Encountered on a trunk, it could easily dislodge them and send them helplessly falling to the green.

"We will climb on another trunk," Lily-yo said.

She and Flor ran deftly along the branch, once jumping a bright parasitic bloom around which treebees buzzed, a forerunner of the world of color above them.

A far worse obstacle lay waiting in an innocent-looking hole in the branch. As Flor and Lily-yo approached, a tigerfly zoomed up at them. It was all but as big as they were, a terrible thing that possessed both weapons and intelligence—and malevolence. Now it attacked only through viciousness, its eyes large, its mandibles working, its transparent wings beating. Its head was a mixture of shaggy hair and armor-plating, while behind its slender waist lay the great swivel-plated body, yellow and black, sheathing a lethal sting on its tail.

It dived between the women, aiming to hit them with its wings. They fell flat as it sped past. Angrily, it tumbled against the branch as it turned on them again; its golden-brown sting flicked in and out.

"I'll get it!" Flor said. A tigerfly had killed one of her babes.

Now the creature came in fast and low. Ducking, Flor reached up and seized its shaggy hair, swinging the tigerfly off balance. Quickly she raised her sword. Bringing it down in a mighty sweep, she severed that chitinous and narrow waist.

The tigerfly fell away in two parts. The two women ran on.

The branch, a main one, did not grow thinner. Instead, it ran on for another twenty yards and grew into another trunk. The tree, vastly old, the longest lived organism ever to flourish on this little world, had a myriad of trunks. Very long ago—two thousand million years past—trees had grown in many kinds, depending on soil, climate, and other conditions. As temperatures climbed, they proliferated and came into competition with each other. The banyan, thriving in the heat, using its complex system of selfrooting branches, gradually established ascendancy over the other species. Under pressure, it evolved and adapted. Each banyan spread out farther and farther, sometimes doubling back on itself for safety. Always it grew higher and crept wider, protecting its parent stem as its rivals multiplied, dropping down trunk after trunk, throwing out branch after branch, until at last it learned the trick of growing into its neighbor banyan, forming a thicket against which no other tree could strive. Their complexity became unrivaled, their immortality established.

On this great continent where the humans lived, only one banyan tree grew now. It had become first King of the forest, then it had become the forest itself. It had conquered the deserts and the mountains and the swamps. It filled the continent with its interlaced scaffolding. Only before the wider rivers or at the margins of the sea, where the deadly seaweeds could assail it, did the tree not go.

And at the terminator, where all things stopped and night began, there too the tree did not go.

The women climbed slowly now, alert as the odd tigerfly zoomed in their direction. Splashes of color grew everywhere, attached to the tree, hanging from lines, or drifting free. Lianas and fungi blossomed. Dumblers moved mournfully through the tangle. As they gained height, the air grew fresher and color rioted, azures and crimsons, yellows and mauves, all the beautifully tinted snares of nature.

A dripperlip sent its scarlet dribbles of gum down the trunk. Several thinpins, with vegetable skill, stalked the drops, pounced, and died. Lily-yo and Flor went by on the other side.

Slashweed met them. They slashed back and climbed on.

Many fantastic plant forms there were, some like birds, some like butterflies. Ever and again, whips and hands shot out.

"Look!" Flor whispered. She pointed above their heads.

The tree's bark was cracked almost invisibly. Almost invisibly, a part of it moved. Thrusting her stick out at arm's length, Flor eased herself up until stick and crack were touching. Then she prodded.

A section of the bark gaped wide, revealing a pale, deadly mouth. An oystermaw, superbly camouflaged, had dug itself into the tree. Jabbing swiftly, Flor thrust her stick into the trap. As the jaws closed, she pulled with all her might, Lily-yo steadying her. The oystermaw, taken by surprise, was wrenched from its socket.

Opening its maw in shock, it sailed outward through the air. A rayplane took it without trying.

Lily-yo and Flor climbed on.

The Tips was a strange world of its own, the vegetable kingdom at its most imperial and most exotic.

If the banyan ruled the forest, *was* the forest, then the traversers ruled the Tips. The traversers had formed the typical landscape of the Tips. Theirs were the great webs trailing everywhere, theirs the nests built on the tips of the tree.

When the traversers deserted their nests, other creatures built there, other plants grew, spreading their bright colors to the sky. Debris and droppings knitted these nests into solid platforms. Here grew the burnurn plant, which Lily-yo sought for the soul of Clat.

Pushing and climbing, the two women finally emerged onto one of these platforms. They took shelter from the perils of the sky under a great leaf and rested from their exertions. Even in the shade, even for them, the heat of the Tips was formidable. Above them, paralyzing half the heaven, burned a great sun. It burned without cease, always fixed and still at one point in the sky, and so would burn until that day—now no longer impossibly distant—when it burned itself out.

Here in the Tips, relying on that sun for its strange method of defense, the burnurn ruled among stationary plants. Already its sensitive roots told it that intruders were near. On the leaf above them, Lily-yo and Flor saw a circle of light move. It wandered over the surface, paused, contracted: The leaf smoldered and burst into flames. Focusing one of its urns on them, the plant was fighting them with its terrible weapon—fire!

"Run!" Lily-yo commanded, and they dashed behind the top of a whistlethistle, hiding beneath its thorns, peering out at the burnurn plant.

It was a splendid sight.

High reared the plant, displaying perhaps half a dozen cerise flowers, each flower larger than a human. Other flowers, fertilized, had closed together, forming many-sided urns.

Later stages still could be seen, where the color drained from the urns as seed swelled at the base of them. Finally, when the seed was ripe, the urn—now hollow and immensely strong—turned transparent as glass and became a heat weapon the plant could use even after its seeds were scattered.

Every vegetable and creature shrank from fire—except humans. They alone could deal with the burnurn plant and use it to advantage.

Moving cautiously, Lily-yo stole forth and cut off a big leaf which grew through the platform on which they stood. A pluggyrug launched a spine at her from underneath, but she dodged it. Seizing the leaf, so much bigger than herself, she ran straight for the burnurn, hurling herself among its foliage and shinning to the top of it in an instant, before it could bring its urn-shaped lenses up to focus on her.

"Now!" she cried to Flor.

Flor was already on the move, sprinting forward.

Lily-yo raised the leaf above the burnurn, holding it between the plant and the sun. As if realizing that this ruined its method of defense, the plant drooped in the shade as though sulking. Its flowers and its urns hung down limply.

Her knife out ready, Flor darted forward and cut off one of the great transparent urns. Together the two women dashed back for the cover of the whistlethistle while the burnurn came back to furious life, flailing its urns as they sucked in the sun again.

They reached cover just in time. A vegbird swooped out of the sky at them—and impaled itself on a thorn.

Instantly, a dozen scavengers were fighting for the body. Under cover of the confusion, Lily-yo and Flor attacked the urn they had won. Using both their knives and all their strength, they prized up one side far enough to put Clat's soul inside the urn. The side instantly snapped back into place again, an airtight join. The soul stared woodenly out at them through the transparent facets.

"May you Go Up and reach heaven," Lily-yo said.

It was her business to see the soul stood at least a sporting chance of doing so. With Flor, she carried the urn across to one of the cables spun by a traverser. The top end of the urn, where the seed had been, was enormously sticky. The urn adhered easily to the cable and hung there in the sun.

Next time a traverser climbed up the cable, the urn stood an excellent chance of sticking like a burr to one of its legs. Thus it would be carried away to heaven.

As they finished the work, a shadow fell over them. A mile-long body drifted down toward them. A traverser, a gross vegetable-equivalent of a spider, was descending to the Tips.

Hurriedly, the women burrowed their way through the platform. The last rites for Clat had been carried out: it was time to return to the group.

Before they climbed down again to the green world of middle levels, Lily-yo looked back.

The traverser was descending slowly, a great bladder with legs and jaws, fibery hair covering most of its bulk. To her it was like a god, with the powers of a god. It came down a cable, floated nimbly down the strand trailing up into the sky.

As far as could be seen, cables slanted up from the jungle, pointing like slender drooping fingers to heaven. Where the sun caught them, they glittered. They all trailed up in the same direction, toward a floating silver half-globe, remote and cool, but clearly visible even in the glare of eternal sunshine.

Unmoving, steady, the half-moon remained always in the same sector of the sky.

Through the eons, the pull of this moon had gradually

slowed the axial revolution of its parent planet to a standstill, until day and night slowed, and became fixed forever, day always on one side of the planet, night on the other. At the same time, a reciprocal braking effect had checked the moon's apparent flight. Drifting farther from Earth, the moon had shed its role as Earth's satellite and rode along in Earth's orbit, an independent planet in its own right. Now the two bodies, for what was left of the afternoon of eternity, faced each other in the same relative position. They were locked face to face, and so would be, until the sands of time ceased to run, or the sun ceased to shine.

And the multitudinous strands of cable floated across the gap, uniting the worlds. Back and forth the traversers could shuttle at will, vegetable astronauts huge and insensible, with Earth and Luna both enmeshed in their indifferent net.

With surprising suitability, the old age of the Earth was snared about with cobwebs.

3

The journey back to the group was fairly uneventful. Lily-yo and Flor traveled at an easy pace, sliding down again into the middle levels of the tree. Lily-yo did not press forward as hard as usual, for she was reluctant to face the breakup of the group.

She could not express her few thoughts easily.

"Soon we must Go Up like Clat's soul," she said to Flor, as they climbed down.

"It is the way," Flor answered, and Lily-yo knew she would get no deeper word on the matter than that. Nor could she frame deeper words herself; human understandings trickled shallow these days.

The group greeted them soberly when they returned.

Being weary, Lily-yo offered them a brief salutation and retired to her nuthut. Jury and Ivin soon brought her food,
setting not so much as a finger inside her home, that being
tabu. When she had eaten and slept, she climbed again onto
the home strip of branch and summoned the others.

"Hurry!" she called, staring fixedly at Haris, who was not
hurrying. Why should a difficult thing be so precious—or a
precious thing so difficult?

At that moment, while her attention was diverted, a long
green tongue licked out from behind the tree trunk. Uncur-
ling, it hovered daintily for a second. It took Lily-yo around
the waist, pinning her arms to her side, lifting her off the
branch. Furiously she kicked and cried.

Haris pulled a knife from his belt, leaped forward with
eyes slitted, and hurled the blade. Singing, it pierced the
tongue and pinned it to the rough trunk of the tree.

Haris did not pause after throwing. As he ran toward the
pinioned tongue, Daphe and Jury ran behind him, while Flor
scuttled the children to safety. In its agony, the tongue eased
its grip on Lily-yo.

Now a terrific thrashing had set in on the other side of
the tree trunk: the forest seemed full of its vibrations. Lily-
yo whistled up two dumblers, fought her way out of the
green coils around her, and was now safely back on the
branch. The tongue, writhing in pain, flicked about mean-
inglessly. Weapons out, the four humans moved forward to
deal with it.

The tree itself shook with the wrath of the trapped creature. Edging cautiously around the trunk, they saw it. Its
great vegetable mouth distorted, a wiltmilt stared back at
them with the hideous palmate pupil of its single eye. Furiously it hammered itself against the tree, foaming and
mouthing. Though they had faced wiltmilts before, yet the
humans trembled.

The wiltmilt was many times the girth of the tree trunk at its present extension. If necessary, it could have extended itself up almost to the Tips, stretching and becoming thinner as it did so. Like an obscene jack-in-the-box, it sprang up from the Ground in search of food, armless, brainless, gouging its slow way over the forest floor on wide and rooty legs.

"Pin it!" Lily-yo cried.

Concealed all along the branch were sharp stakes kept for such emergencies. With these they stabbed the writhing tongue that cracked like a whip about their heads. At last they had a good length of it secured, staked down to the tree. Though the wiltmilt writhed, it would never get free now.

"Now we must leave and Go Up," Lily-yo said.

No human could ever kill a wiltmilt. But already its struggles were attracting predators, the thinpins—those mindless sharks of the middle levels—rayplanes, trappersnappers, gargoyles, and smaller vegetable vermin. They would tear the wiltmilt to living pieces and continue until nothing of it remained—and if they happened on a human at the same time . . . well, it was the way.

Lily-yo was angry. She had brought on this trouble. She had not been alert. Alert, she would never have allowed the wiltmilt to catch her. Her mind had been tied with thought of her own bad leadership. For she had caused two dangerous trips to be made to the Tips where one would have done. If she had taken all the group with her when Clat's soul was disposed of, she would have saved this second ascent. What ailed her brain that she had not seen this beforehand?

She clapped her hands. Standing for shelter under a giant leaf, she made the group come about her. Sixteen pairs of eyes stared trustingly at her. She grew angry to see how they trusted her.

"We adults grow old," she told them. "We grow stupid. I grow stupid. I am not fit to lead you anymore. The time is come for the adults to Go Up and return to the gods who made us. Then the children will be on their own. They will be the group. Toy will lead the group. By the time you are sure of your group, Gren and soon Veggy will be old enough to give you children. Take care of the man children. Let them not fall to the green, or the group dies. Better to die yourself than let the group die."

Lily-yo had never made, the others had never heard, so long a speech. Some of them did not understand it all. What of this talk about falling to the green? One did or one did not: it needed no talk. Whatever happened was the way, and talk could not touch it.

May, a girl child, said cheekily, "On our own we can enjoy many things."

Reaching out, Flor clapped her on an ear.

"First you make the hard climb to the Tips," she said.

"Yes, move," Lily-yo said. She gave the order for climbing, who should lead, who follow.

About them the forest throbbed, green creatures sped and snapped as the wiltmilt was devoured.

"The climb is hard. Begin quickly," Lily-yo said, looking restlessly about her.

"Why climb?" Gren asked rebelliously. "With dumblers we can fly easily to the Tips and suffer no pain."

It was too complicated to explain to him that a human drifting in the air was far more vulnerable than a human shielded by a trunk, with the good rough bark nodules to squeeze between in case of attack.

"While I lead, you climb," Lily-yo said. She could not hit Gren; he was a tabu man child.

They collected their souls from their nuthuts. There was no pomp about saying good-bye to their old home. Their souls went in their belts, their swords—the sharpest, hardest thorns available—went in their hands. They ran along the branch after Lily-yo, away from the disintegrating wiltmilt, away from their past.

Slowed by the younger children, the journey up to the Tips was long. Although the humans fought off the usual hazards, the tiredness growing in small limbs could not be fought. Halfway to the Tips, they found a side branch to rest on, for there grew a fuzzypuzzle, and they sheltered in it.

The fuzzypuzzle was a beautiful, disorganized fungus. Although it looked like nettlemoss on a larger scale, it did not harm humans, drawing in its poisoned pistils as if with disgust when they came to it. Ambling in the eternal branches of the tree, fuzzypuzzles desired only vegetable food. So the group climbed into the middle of it and slept. Guarded among the waving viridian and yellow stalks, they were safe from nearly all forms of attack.

Flor and Lily-yo slept most deeply of the adults. They were tired by their previous journey. Haris the man was the first to awake knowing something was wrong. As he roused, he woke up Jury by poking her with his stick. He was lazy; besides, it was his duty to keep out of danger. Jury sat up. She gave a shrill cry of alarm and jumped up at once to defend the children.

Four winged things had invaded the fuzzypuzzle. They had seized Veggy, the man child, and Bain, one of the younger girl children, gagging and tying them before the pair could wake properly.

At Jury's cry, the winged ones looked round.

They were flymen!

In some respects they resembled humans. That is to say, they had one head, two long and powerful arms, stubby legs, and strong fingers on hands and feet. But instead of smooth green skin, they were covered in a glittering horny substance, here black, here pink. And large scaly wings resembling those of a vegbird grew from their wrists to their ankles. Their faces were sharp and clever. Their eyes glittered.

When they saw the humans waking, the flymen grabbed up the two captive children. Bursting through the fuzzypuzzle, which did not harm them, they ran toward the edge of the branch to jump off.

Flymen were crafty enemies, seldom seen but much dreaded by the group. They worked by stealth. Though they did not kill unless forced to, they stole children. Catching them was hard. Flymen did not fly properly, but the crash glides they fell into carried them swiftly away through the forest, safe from human reprisal.

Jury flung herself forward with all her might, Ivin behind her. She caught an ankle, seized part of the leathery tendon of wing where it joined the foot, and clung on. One of the flymen holding Veggy staggered with her weight, turning as he did so to free himself. His companion, taking the full weight of the boy child, paused, dragging out a knife to defend himself.

Ivin flung herself at him with savagery. She had mothered Veggy: he should not be taken away. The flyman's blade came to meet her. She threw herself on it. It ripped her stomach till the brown entrails showed, and she toppled from the branch with no cry. There was a commotion in the foliage below as trappersnappers fought for her.

Deciding he had done enough, the flyman dropped the bound Veggy and left his friend still struggling with Jury. He spread his wings, taking off heavily after the two who had borne Bain away between them into the green thicket.

All the group were awake now. Lily-yo silently untied Veggy, who did not cry, for he was a man child. Meanwhile, Haris knelt by Jury and her winged opponent, who fought without words to get away. Quickly, Haris brought out a knife.

"Don't kill me. I will go!" cried the flyman. His voice was harsh, his words hardly understandable. The mere strangeness of him filled Haris with savagery, so that his lips curled back and his tongue came thickly between his bared teeth.

He thrust his knife deep between the flyman's ribs, four times over, till the blood poured over his clenched fist.

Jury stood up gasping and leaned against Ivin. "I grow old," she said. "Once it was no trouble to kill a flyman."

She looked at the man Haris with gratitude. He had more than one use.

With one foot she pushed the limp body over the edge of the branch. It rolled messily, then dropped. Its old wizened wings tucked uselessly about its head, the flyman fell to the green.

4

They lay among the sharp leaves of two whistlethistle plants, dazed by the bright sun but alert for new dangers. Their climb had been completed. Now the nine children saw the Tips for the first time—and were struck mute by it.

Once more Lily-yo and Flor lay siege to a burnurn, with Daphe helping them. As the plant slumped defenselessly in the shadow of their upheld leaves, Daphe severed six of the great transparent pods that were to be their coffins. Hy helped her carry them to safety, after which Lily-yo and Flor dropped their leaves and ran for the shelter of the whistle-thistles.

A cloud of paperwings drifted by, their colors startling to eyes generally submerged in green: sky-blues and yellows and bronzes and a viridian that flashed like water.

One of the paperwings alighted fluttering on a tuft of emerald foliage near the watchers. The foliage was a dripperlip. Almost at once the paperwing turned gray as its small nourishment content was sucked out. It disintegrated like ash.

Rising cautiously, Lily-Yo led the group over to the nearest cable of traverser web. Each adult carried her own urn.

The traversers, largest of all creatures, vegetable or otherwise, could never go into the forest. They spurted out their line among the upper branches, securing it with side strands.

Finding a suitable cable with no traverser in sight, Lily-yo turned, signaling for the urns to be put down. She spoke to Toy, Gren, and the seven other children.

"Now help us climb with our souls into our burnurns. See us tight in. Then carry us to the cable and stick us to it. Then good-bye. We Go Up. You are the group now."

Toy momentarily hesitated. She was a slender girl, her breasts like pear-fruit.

"Do not go, Lily-yo," she said. "We still need you."

"It is the way," Lily-yo said firmly.

Prizing open one of the facets of her urn, she slid into her coffin. Helped by the children, the other adults did the same. From habit, Lily-yo glanced to see that Haris was safe.

They were all in now, and helpless. Inside the urns it was surprisingly cool.

The children carried the coffins between them, glancing nervously up at the sky meanwhile. They were afraid. They felt helpless. Only the bold man child Gren looked as if he were enjoying their new sense of independence. He more than Toy directed the others in the placing of the urns upon the traverser's cable.

Lily-yo smelled a curious smell in the urn. As it soaked through her lungs, her senses became detached. Outside, the scene which had been clear, clouded and shrank. She saw she hung suspended on a traverser cable above the treetops, with Flor, Haris, Daphe, Hy and Jury in other urns nearby, hanging helplessly. She saw the children, the new group, run to shelter. Without looking back, they dived into the muddle of foliage on the platform and disappeared.

The traverser hung ten and a half miles above the Tips, safe from its enemies. All about it, space was indigo, and the invisible rays of space bathed it and nourished it. Yet the traverser was still dependent on Earth for some food. After many hours of vegetative dreaming, it swung itself over and climbed down a cable.

Other traversers hung motionless nearby. Occasionally one would blow a globe of oxygen or hitch a leg to try and dislodge a troublesome parasite. Theirs was a leisureliness never attained before. Time was not for them; the sun was theirs, and would ever be until it became unstable, turned nova, and burned both them and itself out.

The traverser fell fast, its feet twinkling, hardly touching the cable, fell straight to the forest, plunging toward the leafy cathedrals of the forest. Here in the air lived its enemies, enemies many times smaller, many times more vicious, many times more clever. Traversers were prey to one of the last families of insect, the tigerflies.

Only tigerflies could kill traversers—kill in their own insidious, invincible way.

Over the long slow eons as the sun's radiation increased, vegetation had evolved to undisputed supremacy. The wasps had developed too, keeping pace with the new developments. They grew in numbers and size as the animal kingdom fell into eclipse and dwindled into the rising tide of green. In time they became the chief enemies of the spiderlike traversers. Attacking in packs, they could paralyze the primitive nerve centers, leaving the traversers to stagger to their own destruction. The tigerflies also laid their eggs in tunnels bored into the stuff of their enemies' bodies; when the eggs hatched, the larvae fed happily on living flesh.

This threat it was, more than anything, that had driven the traversers farther and farther into space many millennia past. In this seemingly inhospitable region, they reached their full and monstrous flowering.

Hard radiation became a necessity for them. Nature's first astronauts, they changed the face of the firmament. Long after man had rolled up his affairs and retired to the trees whence he came, the traversers reconquered that vacant pathway he had lost. Long after intelligence had died from its peak of dominance, the traversers linked indissolubly the green globe and the white—with that antique symbol of neglect, a spider's web.

The traverser scrambled down among the upper leaves, erecting the hairs on its back, where patchy green and black afforded it natural camouflage. On its way down it had collected several creatures caught fluttering in its cables. It sucked them peacefully. When the soupy noises stopped, it vegetated.

Buzzing roused it from its doze. Yellow and black stripes zoomed before its crude eyes. A pair of tigerflies had found it.

With great alacrity, the traverser moved. Its massive bulk, contracted in the atmosphere, had an overall length of over a mile, yet it moved lightly as pollen, scuttling up a cable back to the safety of vacuum.

As it retreated, its legs brushing the web, it picked up various spores, burrs, and tiny creatures that adhered there. It also picked up six burnurns, each containing an insensible human, which swung unregarded from its shin.

Several miles up, the traverser paused. Recovering from its fright, it ejected a globe of oxygen, attaching it gently to a cable. It paused. Its palps trembled. Then it headed out toward deep space, expanding all the time as pressure dropped.

Its speed increased. Folding its legs, the traverser began to eject fresh web from the spinnerets under its abdomen. So it propelled itself, a vast vegetable almost without feeling, rotating slowly to stabilize its temperature.

Hard radiations bathed it. The traverser basked in them. It was in its element.

Daphe roused. She opened her eyes, gazing without intelligence. What she saw had no meaning. She only knew she had Gone Up. This was a new existence and she did not expect it to have meaning.

Part of the view from her urn was eclipsed by stiff yellowy wisps that might have been hair or straw. Everything else was uncertain, being washed either in blinding light or deep shadow. Light and shadow revolved.

Gradually Daphe identified other objects. Most notable was a splendid green half-ball mottled with white and blue. Was it a fruit? To it trailed cables, glinting here and there, many cables, silver or gold in the crazy light. Two traversers she recognized at some distance, traveling fast, looking mummified. Bright points of light sparkled painfully. All was confusion.

This was where gods lived.

Daphe had no feeling. A curious numbness kept her without motion or the wish to move. The smell in the urn was strange. Also the air seemed thick. Everything was like an evil dream. Daphe opened her mouth, her jaw sticky and slow to respond. She screamed. No sound came. Pain filled her. Her sides in particular ached.

Even when her eyes closed again, her mouth hung open.

* * *

Like a great shaggy balloon, the traverser floated down to the moon.

It could hardly be said to think, being a mechanism or little more. Yet somewhere in it the notion stirred that its pleasant journey was too brief, that there might be other directions in which to sail. After all, the hated tigerflies were almost as many now, and as troublesome, on the moon as on the earth. Perhaps somewhere there might be a peaceful place, another of these half-round places with green stuff, in the middle of warm delicious rays. . . .

Perhaps sometime it might be worth sailing off on a full belly and a new course. . . .

Many traversers hung above the moon. Their nets straggled untidily everywhere. This was their happy base, better liked than the earth, where the air was thick and their limbs were clumsy. This was the place they had discovered first—except for some puny creatures who had been long gone before they arrived. They were the last lords of creation. Largest and lordliest, they enjoyed their long lazy afternoon's supremacy.

The traverser slowed, spinning out no more cable. In leisurely fashion, it picked its way through a web and drifted down to the pallid vegetation of the moon. . . .

Here were conditions very unlike those on the heavy planet. The many-trunked banyans had never gained supremacy here; in the thin air and low gravity they outgrew their strength and collapsed. In their place, monstrous celeries and parsleys grew, and it was into a bed of these that the traverser settled. Hissing from its exertions, it blew off a great cloud of oxygen and relaxed.

As it settled down into the foliage, its great sack of body rubbed against the stems. Its legs too scraped into the mass of leaves. From legs and body a shower of light debris was dislodged—burrs, seeds, grit, nuts, and leaves caught up in its sticky fibers back on distant earth. Among this detritus were six seed casings from a burnurn plant. They rolled over the ground and came to a standstill.

Haris the man was the first to awaken. Groaning with an unexpected pain in his sides, he tried to sit up. Pressure on his forehead reminded him of where he was. Doubling up knees and arms, he pushed against the lid of his coffin.

Momentarily, it resisted him. Then the whole urn crumbled into pieces, sending Haris sprawling. The rigors of total vacuum had destroyed its cohesive powers.

Unable to pick himself up, Haris lay where he was. His head throbbed, his lungs were full of an unpleasant odor. Eagerly he gasped in fresh air. At first it seemed thin and chill, yet he sucked it in with gratitude.

After a while, he was well enough to look about him.

Long yellow tendrils were stretching out of a nearby thicket, working their way gingerly toward him. Alarmed, he looked about for a woman to protect him. None was there. Stiffly, his arms so stiff, he pulled his knife from his belt, rolled over on one side, and lopped the tendrils off as they reached him. This was an easy enemy!

Haris cried. He screamed. He jumped unsteadily to his feet, yelling in disgust at himself. Suddenly he had noticed he was covered in scabs. Worse, as his clothes fell in shreds from him, he saw that a mass of leathery flesh grew from his arms, his ribs, his legs. When he lifted his arms, the mass stretched out almost like wings. He was spoiled, his handsome body ruined.

A sound made him turn, and for the first time he remembered his fellows. Lily-yo was struggling from the remains of her burnurn. She raised a hand in greeting.

To his horror, Haris saw that she bore disfigurements like his own. In truth, at first he scarcely recognized her. She resembled nothing so much as one of the hated flymen. He flung himself to the ground and wept as his heart expanded in fear and loathing.

Lily-yo was not born to weep. Disregarding her own painful deformities, breathing laboriously, she cast about, seeking the other four coffins.

Flor's was the first she found, half buried though it was. A blow with a stone shattered it, Lily-yo lifted up her friend, as hideously transformed as she, and in a short while Flor roused. Inhaling the strange air raucously, she too sat up. Lily-yo left her to seek the others. Even in her dazed state, she thanked her aching limbs for feeling so light.

Daphe was dead. She lay stiff and purple in her urn. Though Lily-yo shattered it and called aloud, Daphe did not stir. Her swollen tongue stayed dreadfully protruding from her mouth. Daphe was dead, Daphe who had lived, Daphe who had been the sweet singer.

Hy also was dead, a poor shriveled thing lying in a coffin that had cracked on its arduous journey between the two worlds. When that coffin shattered under Lily-yo's blow, Hy fell away to powder. Hy was dead. Hy who had been born a man child. He always so fleet of foot.

Jury's urn was the last. She stirred as the headwoman reached her. A minute later, she was sitting up, eyeing her deformities with a stoical distaste, breathing the sharp air. Jury lived.

Haris staggered over to the women. In his hand he carried his soul.

"Four of us!" he exclaimed. "Have we been received by the gods or no?"

"We feel pain—so we live," Lily-yo said. "Daphe and Hy have fallen to the green."

Bitterly, Haris flung down his soul and trampled it under-foot.

"Look at us! Better be dead!" he said.

"Before we decide that, we will eat," said Lily-yo.

Painfully, they retreated into the thicket, alerting themselves once more to the idea of danger. Flor, Lily-yo, Jury, Haris, each supported the other. The idea of tabu had somehow been forgotten.

5

"No proper trees grow here," Flor protested, as they pushed among giant celeries whose crests waved high above their heads.

"Take care!" Lily-yo said. She pulled Flor back. Something rattled and snapped like a chained dog, missing Flor's leg by inches.

A trappersnapper, having missed its prey, was slowly reopening its jaws, baring its green teeth. This one was only a shadow of the terrible trappersnappers spawned on the jungle floors of earth. Its jaws were weaker, its movements far more circumscribed. Without the shelter of the giant banyans, the trappersnappers were disinherited.

Something of the same feeling overcame the humans. They and their ancestors for countless generations had lived in the high trees. Safety was arboreal. Here there were only celery and parsley trees, offering neither the rock-steadiness nor the unlimited boughs of the giant banyan.

So they journeyed, nervous, lost, in pain, knowing neither where they were nor why they were.

They were attacked by leapycreepers and sawthorns, and beat them down. They skirted a thicket of nettlemoss taller and wider than any to be met with on earth. Conditions that worked against one group of vegetation favored others. They climbed a slope and came on a pool fed by a stream. Over the pool hung berries and fruits, sweet to taste, good to eat.

"This is not so bad," Haris said. "Perhaps we can still live."

Lily-yo smiled at him. He was the most trouble, the most lazy; yet she was glad he was still here. When they bathed in the pool, she looked at him again. For all the strange scales that covered him, and the two broad sweeps of flesh that hung by his side, he was still good to look on just because he was Haris. She hoped she was also comely. With a burr she raked her hair back; only a little of it fell out.

When they had bathed, they ate. Haris worked then, collecting fresh knives from the bramblebushes. They were not as tough as the ones on earth, but they would have to do. Then they rested in the sun.

The pattern of their lives was completely broken. More by instinct than intelligence they had lived. Without the group, without the tree, without the earth, no pattern guided them. What was the way or what was not became unclear. So they lay where they were and rested.

As she lay there, Lily-yo looked about her. All was strange, so that her heart beat faintly.

Though the sun shone bright as ever, the sky was as deep blue as a vandalberry. And the half-globe in the sky was monstrous, all streaked with green and blue and white, so that Lily-yo could not know it for somewhere she had lived. Phantom silver lines pointed to it, while nearer at hand the tracery of traverser webs glittered, veining the whole sky. Traversers moved over it like clouds, their great bodies slack.

All this was their empire, their creation. On their first journeys here, many millennia ago, they had literally laid the seeds of this world. To begin with, they had withered and died by the thousand on the inhospitable ash. But even the dead had brought their little legacies of oxygen, soil, spores, and seed, some of which later sprouted on the fruitful corpses. Under the weight of dozing centuries, they gained a sort of foothold.

They grew. Stunted and ailing in the beginning, they grew. With vegetal tenacity, they grew. They exhaled. They spread. They thrived. Slowly the broken wastes of the moon's lit face turned green. In the craters creepers grew. Up the ravaged slopes the parsleys crawled. As the atmosphere deepened, so the magic of life intensified, its rhythm strengthened, its tempo increased. More thoroughly than another dominant species had once managed to do, the traversers colonized the moon.

Lily-yo could know or care little about any of this. She turned her face from the sky.

Flor had crawled over to Haris the man. She lay against him in the circle of his arms, half under the shelter of his new skin, and she stroked his hair.

Furious, Lily-yo jumped up, kicked Flor on the shin, and then flung herself upon her, using teeth and nails to pull her away. Jury ran to join in.

"This is not time for mating!" Lily-yo cried.

"Let me *go!*" cried Flor.

Haris in his startlement jumped up. He stretched his arms, waved them, and rose effortlessly into the air.

"Look!" he shouted in alarmed delight.

Over their heads he circled once, perilously. Then he lost his balance and came sprawling head first, mouth open in fright. Head first he pitched into the pool.

Three anxious, awe-struck, love-struck female humans dived after him in unison.

While they were drying themselves, they heard noises in the forest. At once they became alert, their old selves. They drew their new swords and looked to the thicket.

The wiltmilt when it appeared was not like its Earthly

brothers. No longer upright like a jack-in-the-box, it groped its way along like a caterpillar.

The humans saw its distorted eye break from the celeries. Then they turned and fled.

Even when the danger was left behind, they moved rapidly, not knowing what they sought. Once they slept, ate, and then again pressed on through the unending growth, the undying daylight, until they came to where the jungle gaped.

Ahead of them, everything seemed to cease and then go on again.

Cautiously they approached. The ground underfoot had been badly uneven. Now it broke altogether into a wide crevasse. Beyond the crevasse the vegetation grew again—but how did humans pass the gulf? The four of them stood anxiously where the ferns ended, looking across at the far side.

Haris the man screwed his face in pain to show he had a troublesome idea in his head.

"What I did before—going up in the air," he began awkwardly. "If we do it again now, all of us, we go in the air across to the other side."

"No!" Lily-yo said. "When you go up you come down hard. You will fall to the green!"

"I will do better than before."

"No!" repeated Lily-yo. "You are not to go."

"Let him go," Flor said.

The two women turned to glare at each other. Taking his chance, Haris raised his arms, waved them, rose slightly from the ground, and began to use his legs too. He moved forward over the crevasse before his nerve broke.

As he fluttered down, Flor and Lily-yo, moved by instinct, dived into the gulf after him. Spreading their arms, they glided about him, shouting. Jury remained behind, crying in baffled anger down to them.

Regaining a little control, Haris landed heavily on an

outcropping ledge. The two women alighted chattering and scolding beside him. They looked up. Two lips fringed with green fern sucked a narrow purple segment of sky. Jury could not be seen, though her cries still echoed down to them.

Behind the ledge on which they stood, a tunnel ran into the cliff. All the rock face was peppered with similar holes, so that it resembled a sponge. From the hole behind the ledge ran three flymen, two male and one female. They rushed out with ropes and spears.

Flor and Lily-yo were bending over Haris. Before they had time to recover, they were knocked sprawling and tied with the ropes. Helpless, Lily-yo saw other flymen launch themselves from other holes and come gliding in to help secure them. Their flight seemed more sure, more graceful, than it had on earth. Perhaps the way humans were lighter here had something to do with it.

"Bring them in!" the flymen cried to each other. Their sharp, clever faces jostled around eagerly as they hoisted up their captives and bore them into the tunnel.

In their alarm, Lily-yo, Flor, and Haris forgot about Jury, still crouching on the lip of the crevasse. They never saw her again. A pack of thinpins got her.

The tunnel sloped gently down. Finally it curved and led into another which ran level and true. This in its turn led into an immense cavern with regular sides and a regular roof. Gray daylight flooded in at one end, for the cavern stood at the bottom of the crevasse.

To the middle of this cavern the three captives were brought. Their knives were taken from them and they were released. As they huddled together uneasily, one of the flymen stood forward and spoke.

"We will not harm you unless we must," he said. "You come by traverser from the Heavy World. You are new here. When you learn our ways, you will join us."

"I am Lily-yo," Lily-yo proudly said. "Let me go. We three are humans. You are flymen."

"Yes, you are humans, we are flymen. Also we are humans, you are flymen. Now you know nothing. Soon you will know, when you have seen the Captives. They will tell you many things."

"I am Lily-yo. I know many things."

"The Captives will tell you many more things."

"If there were many more things, then I would know them."

"I am Band Appa Bondi and I say come to see the Captives. Your talk is stupid Heavy World talk, Lily-yo."

Several flymen began to look aggressive, so that Haris nudged Lily-yo and muttered, "Let us do what he asks."

Grumpily, Lily-yo let herself and her two companions be led to another chamber. This one was partially ruined, and it stank. At the far end of it, a fall of cindery rock marked where the roof had fallen in, while a shaft of the unremitting sunlight burned on the floor, sending up a curtain of golden light about itself. Near this light were the Captives.

"Do not fear to see them. They will not harm you." Band Appa Bondi said, going forward.

The encouragement was needed, for the Captives were not prepossessing.

Eight of them there were, eight Captives, kept in eight great burnurns big enough to serve them as narrow cells. The cells stood grouped in a semicircle. Band Appa Bondi led Lily-yo, Flor, and Haris into the middle of this semicircle, where they could survey and be surveyed.

The Captives were painful to look on. All had some kind of deformity. One had no legs. One had no flesh on his lower jaw. One had four gnarled dwarf arms. One had short wings of flesh connecting earlobes and thumbs, so that he lived perpetually with hands half raised to his face. One had boneless arms trailing at his side and one boneless leg. One had monstrous wings which trailed about him like carpet. One was hiding his ill-shaped form away behind a screen of his own excrement, smearing it onto the transparent walls of his cell. And one had a second head, a small, wizened thing growing from the first that fixed Lily-yo with a malevolent eye. This last Captive, who seemed to lead the others, spoke now, using the mouth of his main head.

"I am the Chief Captive. I greet you. You are of the Heavy World. We are of the True World. Now you join us because you are of us. Though your wings and your scars are new, you may join us."

"I am Lily-yo. We three are humans. You are only fly-men. We will not join you."

The Captives grunted in boredom. The Chief Captive spoke again.

"Always this talk from you of the Heavy World! You *have* joined us! You are flymen, we are human. You know little, we know much."

"But we—"

"Stop your stupid talk, woman!"

"We are—"

"Be silent, woman, and listen," Band Appa Bondi said.

"We know much," repeated the Chief Captive. "Some things we will tell you. All who make the journey from the Heavy World become changed. Some die. Most live and grow wings. Between the worlds are many strong rays, not seen or felt, which change our bodies. When you come here, when you come to the True World, you become a true human. The grub of the tigerfly is not a tigerfly until it changes. So humans change."

"I cannot know what he says," Harris said stubbornly, throwing himself down. But Lily-yo and Flor were listening.

"To this True World, as you call it, we come to die," Lily-yo said, doubtingly.

The Captive with the fleshless jaw said, "The grub of the tigerfly thinks it dies when it changes into a tigerfly."

"You are still young," said the Chief Captive. "You begin newly here. Where are your souls?"

Lily-yo and Flor looked at each other. In their flight from the wiltmilt they had heedlessly thrown down their souls. Haris had trampled on his. It was unthinkable!

"You see. You needed them no more. You are still young. You may be able to have babies. Some of those babies may be born with wings."

The Captive with the boneless arms added, "Some may be born wrong, as we are. Some may be born right."

"You are too foul to live!" Haris growled. "Why are you not killed?"

"Because we know all things," the Chief Captive said. Suddenly his second head roused itself and declared, "To be a good shape is not all in life. To know is also good. Because we cannot move well we can—*think*. This tribe of the True World is good and knows these things. So it lets us rule it."

Flor and Lily-yo muttered together.

"Do you say that you poor Captives *rule* the True World?" Lily-yo asked at last.

"We do."

"Then why are you Captives?"

The flyman with earlobes and thumbs connected, making his perpetual little gesture of protest, spoke for the first time.

"To rule is to serve, woman. Those who bear power are slaves to it. Only an outcast is free. Because we are Captives, we have the time to talk and think and plan and know. Those who know command the lives of others."

"No hurt will come to you, Lily-yo," Band Appa Bondi

added. "You will live among us and enjoy your life free from harm."

"No!" the Chief Captive said with both mouths. "Before she can enjoy, Lily-yo and her companion Flor—this other man creature is plainly useless—must help our great plan."

"The invasion?" Bondi asked.

"What else? Flor and Lily-yo, you arrive here at a good time. Memories of the Heavy World and its savage life are still fresh in you. We need such memories. So we ask you to go back there on a great plan we have."

"Go back?" gasped Flor.

"Yes. We plan to attack the Heavy World. You must help to lead our force."

6

The long afternoon of eternity wore on, that long golden road of an afternoon that would somewhere lead to an everlasting night. Motion there was, but motion without event—except for those negligible events that seemed so large to the creatures participating in them.

For Lily-yo, Flor, and Haris there were many events. Chief of these was that they learned to fly properly.

The pains associated with their wings soon died away as the wonderful new flesh and tendons strengthened. To sail up in the light gravity became an increasing delight—the ugly flopping movements of flymen on the Heavy World had no place here.

They learned to fly in packs, and then to hunt in packs. In time they were trained to carry out the Captives' plan.

The series of accidents that had first delivered humans to this world in burnurns had been a fortunate one, growing more fortunate as millennia tolled away. For gradually the humans adapted better to the True World. Their survival factor became greater, their power surer. And all this as on the Heavy World conditions grew more and more adverse to anything but the giant vegetables.

Lily-yo at least was quick to see how much easier life was in these new conditions. She sat with Flor and a dozen others eating pulped pluggyrug, before they did the Captives' bidding and left for the Heavy World.

It was hard to express all she felt.

"Here we are safe," she said, indicating the whole green land that sweltered under the silver network of webs.

"Except from the tigerflies," Flor agreed.

They rested on a bare peak, where the air was thin and even the giant creepers had not climbed. The turbulent green stretched away below them, almost as if they were on Earth— although here it was continually checked by the circular formations of rock.

"This world is smaller," Lily-yo said, trying again to make Flor know what was in her head. "Here we are bigger. We do not need to fight so much."

"Soon we must fight."

"Then we can come back here again. This is a good place, with nothing so savage and with not so many enemies. Here the groups could live without so much fear. Veggy and Toy and May and Gren and the other little ones would like it here."

"They would miss the trees."

"We shall soon miss the trees no longer. We have wings instead."

This idle talk took place beneath the unmoving shadow of a rock. Overhead, silver blobs against a purple sky, the traversers went, walking their networks, descending only occasionally to the celeries far below. As Lily-yo fell to watching these creatures, she thought in her mind of the grand plan the Captives had hatched. She flicked it over in a series of vivid pictures.

Yes, the Captives knew. They could see ahead as she could not. She and those about her had lived like plants, doing what came. The Captives were not plants. From their cells they saw more than those outside.

This, the Captives saw: that the few humans who reached the True World bore few children, because they were old, or because the rays that made their wings grow made their seed die; that it was good here, and would be better still with more humans; that one way to get more humans here was to bring babies and children from the Heavy World.

For countless time, this had been done. Brave flymen had traveled back to that other world and stolen children. The flymen who had once attacked Lily-yo's group on their climb to the Tips had been on that mission. They had taken Bain to bring her to the True World in burnurns—and had not been heard of since.

Many perils and mischances lay in that long double journey. Of those who set out, few returned.

Now the Captives had thought of a better and more daring scheme.

"Here comes a traverser," Band Appa Bondi said. "Let us be ready to move."

He walked before the pack of twelve flyers who had been chosen for this new attempt. He was the leader. Lily-yo, Flor, and Haris were in support of him, together with eight others, three male, five female. Only one of them, Band Appa Bondi himself, had been carried to the True World as a boy.

Slowly the pack stood up, stretching their wings. The moment for their great adventure was here. Yet they felt little fear; they could not look ahead as the Captives did, except perhaps for Band Appa Bondi and Lily-yo. She strengthened her will by saying, "It is the way." Then they all spread their arms wide and soared off to meet the traverser.

The traverser had eaten.

It had caught one of its most tasty enemies, a tigerfly, in a web, and had sucked it till only a shell was left. Now it sank down into a bed of celeries, crushing them under its great bulk. Gently, it began to bud. Afterward, it would head out for the great black gulfs, where heat and radiance called it. It had been born on this world. Being young, it had never yet made that dreaded, desired journey.

Its buds burst up from its back, hung over, popped, fell to the ground, and scurried away to bury themselves in the pulp and dirt where they might begin their ten thousand years' growth in peace.

Young though it was, the traverser was sick. It did not know this. The enemy tigerfly had been at it, but it did not know this. Its vast bulk held little sensation.

The twelve humans glided down and landed on its back, low down on the abdomen in a position hidden from the creature's cluster of eyes. They sank among the tough shoulder-high fibers that served the traverser as hair, and looked about them. A rayplane swooped overhead and disappeared. A trio of tumbleweeds skittered into the fibers and were seen no more. All was as quiet as if they lay on a small deserted hill.

At length they spread out and moved along in line, heads down, eyes searching, Band Appa Bondi at one end, Lily-yo at the other. The great body was streaked and pitted and scarred, so that progress down the slope was not easy. The fiber grew in patterns of different shades, green, yellow, black, breaking up the traverser's bulk when seen from the air, serving it as natural camouflage. In many places, tough parasitic plants had rooted themselves, drawing their nourishment entirely from their host; most of them would die when the traverser launched itself out between worlds.

The humans worked hard. Once they were thrown flat when the traverser changed position. As the slope down which they moved grew steeper, so progress became more slow.

"Here!" cried Y Coyin, one of the women.

At last they had found what they sought, what the Captives sent them to seek.

Clustering around Y Coyin with their knives out, the pack looked down.

Here the fibers had been neatly champed away in swathes, leaving a bare patch as far across as a human was long. In this patch was a round scab. Lily-yo felt it. It was immensely hard.

Lo Jint put his ear to it. Silence.

They looked at each other.

No signal was needed, none given.

Together they knelt, prizing with their knives around the scab. Once the traverser moved, and they threw themselves flat. A bud rose nearby popped, rolled down the slope and fell to the distant ground. A thinpin devoured it as it ran. The humans continued prizing.

The scab moved. They lifted it off. A dark and sticky tunnel was revealed to them.

"I go first," Band Appa Bondi said.

He lowered himself into the hole. The others followed. Dark sky showed roundly above them until the twelfth human was in the tunnel. Then the scab was drawn back into place. A soft slobber of sound came from it as it began to heal back into position again.

They crouched where they were for a long time. They crouched, their knives ready, their wings folded around them, their human hearts beating strongly.

In more than one sense they were in enemy territory. At the best of times, traversers were only allies by accident; they ate humans as readily as they devoured anything else. But this burrow was the work of that yellow and black destroyer, the tigerfly. One of the last true insects to survive, the tough and resourceful tigerflies had instinctively made the most invincible of all living things its prey.

The female tigerfly alights and bores her tunnel into the traverser. Working her way down, she at last stops and prepares a natal chamber, hollowing it from the living traverser, paralyzing the matter with her needletail to prevent its healing again. There she lays her store of eggs before climbing back to daylight. When the eggs hatch, the larvae have fresh and living stuff to nourish them.

After a while, Band Appa Bondi gave a sign and the pack moved forward, climbing awkwardly down the tunnel. A faint luminescence guided their eyes. The air lay heavy and green in their chests. They moved very slowly, very quietly, for they heard movement ahead.

Suddenly the movement was on them.

"Look out!" Band Appa Bondi cried.

From the terrible dark, something launched itself at them.

Before they realized it, the tunnel had curved and widened into the natal chamber. The tigerfly's eggs had hatched. Two hundred larvae with jaws as wide as a man's reach turned on the intruders, snapping in fury and fear.

Even as Band Appa Bondi sliced his first attacker, another had his head off. He fell, and his companions launched themselves over him. Pressing forward, they dodged those clicking jaws.

Behind their hard heads, the larvae were soft and plump. One slash of a sword and they burst, their entrails flowing out. They fought, but knew not how to fight. Savagely the humans stabbed, ducked, and stabbed. No other human died. With backs to the wall they cut and thrust, breaking jaws, ripping flimsy stomachs. They killed unceasingly with neither hate nor mercy until they stood knee deep in slush. The larvae snapped and writhed and died. Uttering a grunt of satisfaction, Haris slew the last of them.

Wearily then, eleven humans crawled back to the tunnel, there to wait until the mess drained away—and then to wait a longer while.

The traverser stirred in its bed of celeries. Vague impulses drifted through its being. Things it had done. Things it had to do. The things it had done had been done, the things it had to do were still to do. Blowing off oxygen, it heaved itself up.

Slowly at first, it swung up a cable, climbing to the network where the air thinned. Always, always before in the eternal afternoon it had stopped here. This time there seemed no reason for stopping. Air was nothing, heat was all, the heat that blistered and prodded and chafed and coaxed increasingly with height. . . .

It blew a jet of cable from a spinneret. Gaining speed, gaining intention, it rocketed its mighty vegetable self out and away from the place where the tigerflies flew. Ahead of it floated a semicircle of light, white and blue and green; it was a useful thing to look at to avoid getting lost.

For this was a lonely place for a young traverser, a terrible-wonderful bright-dark place, so full of nothing. Turn as you speed and you fry well on all sides . . . nothing to trouble you. . . .

. . . Except that deep in your core a little pack of humans use you as an ark for their own purposes. You carry them back to a world that once—so staggeringly long ago—

belonged to their kind; you carry them back so that they may eventually—who knows?—fill another world with their own kind.

For remember, there is always plenty of time.

HOTHOUSE: THE FUZZYPUZZLE ODYSSEY

The strangely transformed future, once again. But "Scanners Live in Vain" takes place, it would seem, only some five or six hundred years from now, a thousand at most: lamb chops may be forgotten, but people still live in cities and use telephones. The world that the formidably gifted British writer Brian Aldiss conjures up for us in "Hothouse" lies enormously farther down the line—millions of years ahead—and the transformation is nearly total. Huge vegetable spiders travel on cables between Earth and the moon, forests consist of a single enormous tree, humans wander like lost children through a terrifying toothy jungle, carrying their souls under their arms.

It is a kind of science fiction that has always held a special excitement for me: visionary fantasy, really, offering wild and vivid leaps of the imagination. It does not spring from close analysis of contemporary trends—as do, for example, such stories as Robert A. Heinlein's "The Roads Must Roll" or Arthur C. Clarke's *The Fountains of Paradise*—so much as it does from the free play of the unchained subconscious: a literature of dreams. The writer, peering into inconceivable depths of time, can hardly venture to say, "This is how it will be." He can say only, "This is my dream of the eons to come." What he offers are visions, not blueprints.

Some of my favorite science-fiction stories belong to this mode: S. Fowler Wright's *The World Below*, Olaf Stapledon's *Last and First Men*, Jack Vance's *The Dying Earth*. I attempted it myself in 1969 in *Son of Man*. I find in such stories the eerie clarity and power of sustained hallucinations. I find that in stories of the near future too: Heinlein's sliding roadways and Clarke's elevator into space are embedded deep in my memory, not far from the place where Vance's wizards and Wright's frog-mouthed horrors dwell. Any well-done stories of the future, even if they are set only thirty or forty years ahead—Orwell's *1984*, say—hold this almost hallucinatory intensity for me. But the story of the remote future, freed as it is from most of the constraints of realism, exerts a special kind of force.

One of the best of its kind is the Aldiss novel variously published as *The Long Afternoon of Earth* and *Hothouse*. Cast in the form of an odyssey—although Gren's long journey, unlike that of Odysseus, has no clear goal in mind, so that perhaps it might better be called a picaresque novel, endlessly stringing its story on the line of the hero's adventures—it carries us through a world that has undergone an astonishing metamorphosis, which is depicted in meticulous detail. Creating that vision of metamorphosis is the author's entire purpose, and it is magnificently realized. Heinlein, in a story like "The Roads Must Roll," was attempting to imagine with utterly plausible conviction the transportation system of the late twentieth century, down to the last rotor bearing and field coil, as he foresaw it in 1940. That our highways today don't look like the ones Heinlein imagined is beside the point: the story is a perfect self-contained prophecy based on the most careful possible analysis of the available data, and its power rises from the clarity with which Heinlein limns his near-future vision. The power of Aldiss' novel grows from the clarity of its vision, too; but where Heinlein was seriously trying to invent a possible future, Aldiss nowhere asks us to believe that his fuzzypuzzles and flymen and dripperlips will someday come to inhabit the Earth. Both writers are sharing their dreams with us, but their intent is different, even if the ultimate result, which is the enhancement of our interior visionary furnishings, is the same.

Since *Hothouse* is a book-length work, you may have been wondering why I have included an extract from it in what is otherwise a collection of short fiction. Since one of the many purposes of this book is to offer my thoughts on the art and craft of writing the science-fiction short story, a piece of a novel may seem out of place here, even if it does fit the *Worlds of Wonder* rubric. But in fact Aldiss first brought *Hothouse* to the reading public as five short stories, which *The Magazine of Fantasy & Science Fiction* published between February and December of 1961; and the following year the series received the Hugo Award of the World Science Fiction Convention, not as a novel but as the collective winner in the Best Short Fiction category. "Hothouse," the story reprinted here, was the first of the group of five, which were combined into book form in the United States in 1962, somewhat abridged, under the title of *The Long Afternoon of Earth*, and at last published complete in 1976 under Aldiss' original title of *Hothouse*.

"Hothouse" is here, therefore, not only for its intrinsic beauty and excitement as a segment of Aldiss' great visionary achievement, but because it demonstrates a significant aspect of the writer's craft: how to construct a work that is at the same time the opening section of a novel and a satisfying short story, complete in itself.

In its form "Hothouse" differs considerably from the other stories collected here, most of which follow the efforts of one protagonist to deal with a single problem, and fit readily into the Kenneth Burke "purpose, passion, perception" framework that is my own basic structural device. In that sense "Hothouse" is not a complete story: it lacks the fulfilled dissonance/opposition/resolution sequence of the Burke formula, and there is no readily apparent central character (though the novel as a whole has one, Gren, who on a larger scale certainly does undergo the Burkean passion). But "Hothouse," though only a slice of the whole, is so vivid that it works independently, all the same. We may be able to see that Gren is to be the protagonist of the novel, and therefore the journey of Lily-yo and the other elders to the Moon is merely a long digression; yet a unity of vision holds the story together even though the unities of plot are not visible. It is a small peep into the huge future, just as "Scanners" is in a very different way. Not all stories need fully rounded denouements.

Sometimes the promise of a fulfillment will serve in place of the real thing—as it does here.

Certainly the story opens swiftly and crisply. There is a one-paragraph prologue. Then comes jeopardy and response, and a death. There is no introspection and at first no explanation: the events unroll, statement by statement; Aldiss merely shows us what is happening, with scarcely any editorial comment. The effect is cinematic. (It doesn't stay that way, or we'd be hopelessly bewildered. But in the earliest pages he gives us only the smallest cues: the prologue, and then, pages later, that Lily-yo is weary and awaiting her time to Go Up. Everything else is implicit in the action, as it would be in a movie.)

The pace is extraordinary. Aldiss dazzles us with unflagging inventiveness: swiftly we encounter berrywhisks, nuthuts, nettlemoss, dumblers, whistlethistles, trappersnappers. The unrelenting flow of strangeness quickly sets the scene for us—a steaming jungle where fantastic perils lurk on all sides and life is short. The names of the creatures are artfully chosen to minimize the need for explanation: without Cordwainer Smith's help we would have no idea what "haberman" or "cranch" meant, but we can make some sort of sense out of Aldiss' vegetable bestiary from the names alone, even though he does give us just enough description—the nettlemoss has poisoned tips, the berrywhisk is a sticky crimson mask, the dumbler is a fleecy umbrella with feathered spokes—to provide us with rich visual data. A flash of color here, a bit of texture there, the sounds of slobbering in the darkness below: Aldiss works on all our senses in turn, a series of brief but telling strokes. His technical control is so tight that he carries us into the heart of his story within moments, a breathless headlong tumble into a bizarre world the likes of which we have never seen or even imagined before. Only after that has been achieved does he slow down long enough to confide bits of background detail directly to us. When the tribe approaches the Tips, he allows himself a little essay on the evolution of the banyan tree—using our name for it, not the tribe's. When the fuzzypuzzle appears, he tells us that it is "a beautiful disorganized fungus." Now that we are snared, he can take the risk of outright Aldiss-to-reader exposition, and he will make more and more use of it as the story (and the book) goes along. But it is the cinematic method of the fast-paced early scenes that creates this work's astonishing initial impact.

Though one cannot find a conventional one-protagonist short-story plot, plot on a larger scale is present and is signalled, as it almost always is, in the earliest passages. The first two sentences after the brief prologue announce the theme of the entire work: "In the green light, some of the children came out to play. Alert for enemies, they ran along the branch, calling to each other in soft voices." Everything is there, tightly encapsulated. *In the green light* lets us know that we are entering an unfamiliar world. *Some of the children* immediately focuses on the protagonists, babes in the woods. *Came out to play* declares the fundamental nature of the world: there is no work to be done in our twentieth-century sense, only the free play of children in the jungle. *Alert for enemies*—yes, they are everywhere. *They ran along the branch*. This book will be about people in motion. *Calling to each other in soft voices*. Seeking to communicate, often against extreme odds. There it is. A beautiful but harsh and dangerous world; a band of innocents in a state of nature. The challenge is survival and the overriding purpose is to maintain the integrity of the tribe and of the human race.

Nearly everything that follows in "Hothouse" can be related to the thematic matter of those two sentences; and when we come to the story's final paragraph, we find that Aldiss has provided a passage that, while taking into account the events we have just been shown, is also a recapitulation of the opening:

Except that deep in your core a little pack of humans use
you as an ark for their own purposes. You carry them back
to a world that once—so staggeringly long ago—belonged
to their kind; you carry them back so that they may

eventually—who knows?—fill another world with their own kind.

So the odyssey will continue, through strangeness after strangeness. Survival of the race, if not of the individual, remains the issue.

In the very last sentence of "Hothouse" Aldiss supplies a second recapitulation—not to the first scene, but to the prologue itself. "For remember, there is always plenty of time," he concludes, deftly taking us back to the statement of vast and unknowable spans of elapsed time that we find in the story's opening sentence, and at the same time aiming us onward to the next story in the sequence, which would be published two months afterward. (This sentence appeared only in the magazine version of "Hothouse." It was deleted in the book version, where it was not needed, since the reader needed only to turn the page to continue.)

An ending of this sort is what I mean when I say that the promise of a fulfillment can sometimes be used in lieu of a real denouement. In such a journey story as this one, there can be no cessation short of death: the point of it is that the characters are doomed to keep moving all the time. Therefore, a closing passage that propels the story into a new set of episodes carries with it the sense, for the moment, of an ending: this phase is closing, another is beginning, and we know that the road goes ever onward. We may realize that what we have just read is not truly complete, but, partial though it may be, it nevertheless has carried us from this place to that place, has given us rewarding vicarious experience along the way, and has set us down with the satisfying feeling that we have not traveled in vain.

Though Aldiss is not greatly concerned with the depiction of character in this segment of what will ultimately be a novel, it is necessary for him to bring on stage his protagonist-to-be, Gren, and establish him for later use. He does this with the same splendid craftsmanship with which he has so swiftly sketched in the jungle world. We see Gren, nine years old, "very brave already, and fleet and proud," knocking a tigerfly aside as he runs, without pausing in the errand he is carrying out. Then he vanishes from our view; the focus shifts to Lily-yo. When Gren reappears a few pages later, we meet him in jeopardy once again: this time a crocksock grabs his left arm. But "Gren was ready for it. With one slash of his knife, he clove the crocksock in two." When he climbs out of the crocksock's pool he grins "nonchalantly." Daphe calls out, "Gren, have you no fear? Your head is an empty burr!" He jumps about boastfully, winning mingled scorn and respect from his comrades. In just a few lines, then, we see Gren: strong, brave, competent, a little absurd in a virile way. As it happens, Aldiss will have no particular use for him in this segment of the novel. But Gren is there, beautifully established, for whenever he will be needed; and readers of the short story have had a lovely little vignette of burgeoning manhood to divert them.

As the shift from Gren to Lily-yo (and later, for a time, to Haris) indicates, Aldiss' use of viewpoint in this story is flexible and supple. Often it is omniscient: Brian Aldiss telling us about banyans, or fuzzy-puzzles, or the changes in the intensity of the sun's radiation. Then he will dart briefly into the sensibility of one of the characters, but rarely very far. We get a glimpse of what Lily-yo is feeling, or Haris, or even a very minor character like Jury. ("A minute later, she was sitting up, eyeing her deformities with a stoical distaste, breathing the sharp air.") These rapid shifts of viewpoint help create the story's fluid pace. In a way, they amount to a structural analog of the jungle's own shimmering swiftness of growth and change. Everything moves, and the camera's eye moves with it; now it is within this member of the tribe, now that one.

"Hothouse" is a stunning vision, as voluptuous a tale of the strange future as Cordwainer Smith's is claustrophobic and austere. Each in its own way is unique and unforgettable. By strikingly different methods these two stories create reality out of unreality, and plant themselves inextricably in the imaginations of their readers.

THE NEW PRIME
JACK VANCE

Music, carnival lights, the slide of feet on waxed oak, perfume, muffled talk and laughter.

Arthur Caversham of twentieth-century Boston felt air along his skin, and discovered himself to be stark naked.

It was at Janice Paget's coming-out party: three hundred guests in formal evening-wear surrounded him.

For a moment he felt no emotion beyond vague bewilderment. His presence seemed the outcome of logical events, but his memory was fogged and he could find no definite anchor of certainty.

He stood a little apart from the rest of the stag line, facing the red and gold calliope where the orchestra sat. The buffet, the punch bowl, the champagne wagons, tended by clowns, were to his right; to the left, through the open flap of the circus tent, lay the garden, now lit by strings of colored lights, red, green, yellow, blue, and he caught a glimpse of a merry-go-round across the lawn.

Why was he here? He had no recollection, no sense of purpose.... The night was warm; the other young men in

397

the full-dress suits must feel rather sticky, he thought. . . . An idea tugged at a corner of his mind. There was a significant aspect of the affair that he was overlooking.

He noticed that the young men nearby had moved away from him. He heard chortles of amusement, astonished exclamations. A girl dancing past saw him over the arm of her escort; she gave a startled squeak, jerked her eyes away, giggling and blushing.

Something was wrong. These young men and women were startled and amazed by his naked skin to the point of embarrassment. The gnaw of urgency came closer to the surface. He must do something. Taboos felt with such intensity might not be violated without unpleasant consequences; such was his understanding. He was lacking garments; these he must obtain.

He looked about him, inspecting the young men who watched him with ribald delight, disgust, or curiosity. To one of these latter he addressed himself.

"Where can I get some clothing?"

The young man shrugged. "Where did you leave yours?"

Two heavyset men in dark blue uniforms entered the tent; Arthur Caversham saw them from the corner of his eye, and his mind worked with desperate intensity.

This young man seemed typical of those around him. What sort of appeal would have meaning for him? Like any other human being, he could be moved to action if the right chord were struck. By what method could he be moved?

Sympathy?

Threats?

The prospect of advantage or profit?

Caversham rejected all of these. By violating the taboo he had forfeited his claim to sympathy. A threat would excite derision, and he had no profit or advantage to offer. The stimulus must be more devious. . . . He reflected that young men customarily banded together in secret societies. In the thousand cultures he had studied this was almost infallibly true. Longhouses, drug-cults, tongs, instruments of sexual initiation—whatever the name, the external aspects were near-identical: painful initiation, secret signs and passwords, uniformity of group conduct, obligation to service. If this young man were a member of such an association, he might react to an appeal to this group-spirit.

Arthur Caversham said, "I've been put in this taboo situation by the brotherhood; in the name of the brotherhood, find me some suitable garments."

The young man stared, taken aback. "Brotherhood? . . . You mean fraternity?" Enlightenment spread over his face. "Is this some kind of hell-week stunt?" He laughed. "If it is, they sure go all the way."

"Yes," said Arthur Caversham. "My fraternity."

The young man said, "This way, then—and hurry, here comes the law. We'll take off under the tent. I'll lend you my topcoat till you make it back to your house."

The two uniformed men, pushing quietly through the dancers, were almost upon them. The young man lifted the flap of the tent, Arthur Caversham ducked under, his friend followed. Together they ran through the many-colored shadows to a little booth painted with gay red and white stripes that was near the entrance to the tent.

"You stay back, out of sight," said the young man. "I'll check out my coat."

"Fine," said Arthur Caversham.

The young man hesitated. "What's your house? Where do you go to school?"

Arthur Caversham desperately searched his mind for an answer. A single fact reached the surface.

"I'm from Boston."

"Boston U? Or MIT? Or Harvard?"

"Harvard."

"Ah." The young man nodded. "I'm Washington and Lee myself. What's your house?"

"I'm not supposed to say."

"Oh," said the young man, puzzled but satisfied. "Well—just a minute. . . ."

Bearwald the Halforn halted, numb with despair and exhaustion. The remnants of his platoon sank to the ground around him, and they stared back to where the rim of the night flickered and glowed with fire. Many villages, many wood-gabled farmhouses had been given the torch, and the Brands from Mount Medallion reveled in human blood.

The pulse of a distant drum touched Bearwald's skin, a deep *thrumm-thrumm-thrumm*, almost inaudible. Much closer he heard a hoarse human cry of fright, then exultant killing-calls, not human. The Brands were tall, black, man-shaped but not men. They had eyes like lamps of red glass, bright white teeth, and tonight they seemed bent on slaughtering all the men of the world.

"Down," hissed Kanaw, his right arm-guard, and Bearwald crouched. Across the flaring sky marched a column of tall Brand warriors, rocking jauntily, without fear.

Bearwald said suddenly, "Men—we are thirteen. Fighting arm to arm with these monsters we are helpless. Tonight their total force is down from the mountain; the hive must be near deserted. What can we lose if we undertake to burn the home-hive of the Brands? Only our lives, and what are these now?"

Kanaw said, "Our lives are nothing; let us be off at once."

"May our vengeance be great," said Broctan the left arm-guard. "May the home-hive of the Brands be white ashes this coming morn. . . ."

Mount Medallion loomed overhead; the oval hive lay in

Pangborn Valley. At the mouth of the valley, Bearwald divided the platoon into two halves, and placed Kanaw in the van of the second. "We move silently twenty yards apart; thus if either party rouses a Brand, the other may attack from the rear and so kill the monster before the vale is roused. Do all understand?"

"We understand."

"Forward then, to the hive."

The valley reeked with an odor like sour leather. From the direction of the hive came a muffled clanging. The ground was soft, covered with runner moss; careful feet made no sound. Crouching low, Bearwald could see the shapes of his men against the sky—here indigo with a violet rim. The angry glare of burning Echevasa lay down the slope to the south.

A sound. Bearwald hissed, and the columns froze. They waited. *Thud-thud-thud-thud* came the steps—then a hoarse cry of rage and alarm.

"Kill, kill the beast!" yelled Bearwald.

The Brand swung his club like a scythe, lifting one man, carrying the body around with the after-swing. Bearwald leapt close, struck with his blade, slicing as he hewed; he felt the tendons part, smelled the hot gush of Brand blood.

The clanging had stopped now, and Brand cries carried across the night.

"Forward," panted Bearwald. "Out with your tinder, strike fire to the hive. Burn, burn, burn. . . ."

Abandoning stealth he ran forward; ahead loomed the dark dome. Immature Brands came surging forth, squeaking and squalling, and with them came the genetrices—twenty-foot monsters crawling on hands and feet, grunting and snapping as they moved.

"Kill!" yelled Bearwald the Halforn. "Kill! Fire, fire, fire!"

He dashed to the hive, crouched, struck spark to tinder,

puffed. The rag, soaked with saltpeter, flared; Bearwald fed it straw, thrust it against the hive. The reed-pulp and withe crackled.

He leapt up as a horde of young Brands darted at him. His blade rose and fell; they were cleft, no match for his frenzy. Creeping close came the great Brand genetrices, three of them, swollen of abdomen, exuding an odor vile to his nostrils.

"Out with the fire!" yelled the first. "Fire, out. The Great Mother is tombed within; she lies too fecund to move. . . . Fire, woe, destruction!" And they wailed, "Where are the mighty? Where are our warriors?"

Thrumm-thrumm-thrumm came the sound of skindrums. Up the valley rolled the echo of hoarse Brand voices.

Bearwald stood with his back to the blaze. He darted forward, severed the head of a creeping genetrix, jumped back. . . . Where were his men? "Kanaw!" he called. "Laida! Theyat! Gyorg! Broctan!"

He craned his neck, saw the flicker of fires. "Men! Kill the creeping mothers!" And leaping forward once more, he hacked and hewed, and another genetrix sighed and groaned and rolled flat.

The Brand voices changed to alarm; the triumphant drumming halted; the thud of footsteps came loud.

At Bearwald's back the hive burnt with a pleasant heat. Within came a shrill keening, a cry of vast pain.

In the leaping blaze he saw the charging Brand warriors. Their eyes glared like embers, their teeth shone like white sparks. They came forward, swinging their clubs, and Bearwald gripped his sword, too proud to flee.

After grounding his air sled Ceistan sat a few minutes inspecting the dead city Therlatch: a wall of earthen brick a hundred feet high, a dusty portal, and a few crumbled roofs lifting above the battlements. Behind the city the desert spread across the near, middle, and far distance to the hazy shapes of the Allune Mountains at the horizon, pink in the light of the twin suns Mig and Pag.

Scouting from above he had seen no sign of life, nor had he expected any, after a thousand years of abandonment. Perhaps a few sand-crawlers wallowed in the heat of the ancient bazaar. Otherwise the streets would feel his presence with great surprise.

Jumping from the air sled, Ceistan advanced toward the portal. He passed under, stood looking right and left with interest. In the parched air the brick buildings stood almost eternal. The wind smoothed and rounded all harsh angles; the glass had been cracked by the heat of day and chill of night; heaps of sand clogged the passageways.

Three streets led away from the portal and Ceistan could find nothing to choose between them. Each was dusty, narrow, and each twisted out of his line of vision after a hundred yards.

Ceistan rubbed his chin thoughtfully. Somewhere in the city lay a brass bound coffer, containing the Crown and Shield Parchment. This, according to tradition, set a precedent for the fiefholder's immunity from energy-tax. Glay, who was Ceistan's liege-lord, having cited the parchment as justification for his delinquency, had been challenged to show validity. Now he lay in prison on charge of rebellion, and in the morning he would be nailed to the bottom of an air sled and sent drifting into the west, unless Ceistan returned with the parchment.

After a thousand years, there was small cause for optimism, thought Ceistan. However, the lord Glay was a fair man and he would leave no stone unturned. . . . If it existed, the chest presumably would lie in state, in the town's Legalic, or the Mosque, or in the Hall of Relics, or possibly in the

Sumptuar. He would search all of these, allowing two hours per building; the eight hours so used would see the end to the pink daylight.

At random he entered the street in the center and shortly came to a plaza at whose far end rose the Legalic, the Hall of Records and Decisions. At the façade Ceistan paused, for the interior was dim and gloomy. No sound came from the dusty void save the sigh and whisper of the dry wind. He entered.

The great hall was empty. The walls were illuminated with frescoes of red and blue, as bright as if painted yesterday. There were six to each wall, the top half displaying a criminal act and the bottom half the penalty.

Ceistan passed through the hall, into the chambers behind. He found but dust and the smell of dust. Into the crypts he ventured, and these were lit by embrasures. There was much litter and rubble, but no brass coffer.

Up and out into the clean air he went, and strode across the plaza to the Mosque, where he entered under the massive architrave.

The Nunciator's Confirmatory lay wide and bare and clean, for the tessellated floor was swept by a powerful draft. A thousand apertures opened from the low ceiling, each communicating with a cell overhead; thus arranged so that the devout might seek counsel with the Nunciator as he passed below without disturbing their attitudes of supplication. In the center of the pavilion a disk of glass roofed a recess. Below was a coffer and in the coffer rested a brassbound chest. Ceistan sprang down the steps in high hopes.

But the chest contained jewels—the tiara of the Old Queen, the chest vellopes of the Gonwand Corps, the great ball, half emerald, half ruby, which in the ancient ages was rolled across the plaza to signify the passage of the old year.

Ceistan tumbled them all back in the coffer. Relics on

this planet of dead cities had no value, and synthetic gems were infinitely superior in luminosity and water.

Leaving the Mosque, he studied the height of the suns. The zenith was past, the moving balls of pink fire leaned to the west. He hesitated, frowning and blinking at the hot earthen walls, considering that not impossibly both coffer and parchment were fable, like so many others regarding dead Therlatch.

A gust of wind swirled across the plaza and Ceistan choked on a dry throat. He spat, and an acrid taste bit his tongue. An old fountain opened in the wall nearby; he examined it wistfully, but water was not even a memory along these dead streets.

Once again he cleared his throat, spat, turned across the city toward the Hall of Relics.

He entered the great nave, past square pillars built of earthen brick. Pink shafts of light struck down from the cracks and gaps in the roof, and he was like a midge in the vast space. To all sides were niches cased in glass, and each held an object of ancient reverence: the armor in which Plange the Forewarned led the Blue Flags; the coronet of the First Serpent; an array of antique Padang skulls; Princess Thermosteraliam's bridal gown of woven cobweb palladium, as fresh as the day she wore it; the original Tablets of Legality; the great conch throne of an early dynasty; a dozen other objects. But the coffer was not among them.

Ceistan sought for entrance to a possible crypt, but except where the currents of dusty air had channeled grooves in the porphyry, the floor was smooth.

Out once more into the dead streets, and now the suns had passed behind the crumbled roofs, leaving the streets in magenta shadow.

With leaden feet, burning throat, and a sense of defeat, Ceistan turned to the Sumptuar, on the citadel. Up the wide steps, under the verdigris-fronted portico into a lobby painted with vivid frescoes. These depicted the maidens of ancient Therlatch at work, at play, amid sorrow and joy: slim creatures with short, black hair and glowing ivory skin, as graceful as water vanes, as round and delectable as chermoyan plums. Ceistan passed through the lobby with many side-glances, reflecting that these ancient creatures of delight were now the dust he trod under his feet.

He walked down a corridor which made a circuit of the building, and from which the chambers and apartments of the Sumptuar might be entered. The wisps of a wonderful rug crunched under his feet, and the walls displayed moldy tatters, once tapestries of the finest weave. At the entrance to each chamber a fresco pictured the Sumptuar maiden and the sign she served; at each of these chambers Ceistan paused, made a quick investigation, and so passed on to the next. The beams slanting in through the cracks served him as a gauge of time, and they flattened ever more toward the horizontal.

Chamber after chamber after chamber. There were chests in some, altars in others, cases of manifestos, triptychs, and fonts in others. But never the chest he sought.

And ahead was the lobby where he had entered the building. Three more chambers were to be searched, then the light would be gone.

He came to the first of these, and this was hung with a new curtain. Pushing it aside, he found himself looking into an outside court, full in the long light of the twin suns. A fountain of water trickled down across steps of apple-green jade into a garden as soft and fresh and green as any in the north. And rising in alarm from a couch was a maiden, as vivid and delightful as any in the frescoes. She had short, dark hair, a face as pure and delicate as the great white frangipani she wore over her ear.

For an instant Ceistan and the maiden stared eye to eye; then her alarm faded and she smiled shyly.

"Who are you?" Ceistan asked in wonder. "Are you a ghost or do you live here in the dust?"

"I am real," she said. "My home is to the south, at the Palram Oasis, and this is the period of solitude to which all maidens of the race submit when aspiring for Upper Instruction. . . . So without fear may you come beside me, and rest, and drink of fruit wine and be my companion through the lonely night, for this is my last week of solitude and I am weary of my aloneness."

Ceistan took a step forward, then hesitated. "I must fulfill my mission. I seek the brass coffer containing the Crown and Shield Parchment. Do you know of this?"

She shook her head. "It is nowhere in the Sumptuar." She rose to her feet, stretching her ivory arms as a kitten stretches. "Abandon your search, and come let me refresh you."

Ceistan looked at her, looked up at the fading light, looked down the corridor to the two doors yet remaining. "First I must complete my search; I owe duty to my lord Glay, who will be nailed under an air sled and sped west unless I bring him aid."

The maiden said with a pout, "Go then to your dusty chamber; and go with a dry throat. You will find nothing, and if you persist so stubbornly, I will be gone when you return."

"So let it be," said Ceistan.

He turned away, marched down the corridor. The first chamber was bare and dry as a bone. In the second and last, a man's skeleton lay tumbled in a corner; this Ceistan saw in the last rosy light of the twin suns.

There was no brass coffer, no parchment. So Glay must die, and Ceistan's heart hung heavy.

He returned to the chamber where he had found the maiden, but she had departed. The fountain had been stopped, and moisture only filmed the stones.

Ceistan called, "Maiden, where are you? Return; my obligation is at an end. . . ."

There was no response.

Ceistan shrugged, turned to the lobby and so outdoors, to grope his way through the deserted twilight street to the portal and his air sled.

Dobnor Daksat became aware that the big man in the embroidered black cloak was speaking to him.

Orienting himself to his surroundings, which were at once familiar and strange, he also became aware that the man's voice was condescending, supercilious.

"You are competing in a highly advanced classification," he said. "I marvel at your . . . ah, confidence." And he eyed Daksat with a gleaming and speculative eye.

Daksat looked down at the floor, frowned at the sight of his clothes. He wore a long cloak of black-purple velvet, swinging like a bell around his ankles. His trousers were of scarlet corduroy, tight at the waist, thigh, and calf, with a loose puff of green cloth between calf and ankle. The clothes were his own, obviously: they looked wrong and right at once, as did the carved gold knuckle-guards he wore on his hands.

The big man in the dark cloak continued speaking, looking at a point over Daksat's head, as if Daksat were nonexistent.

"Clauktaba has won Imagist honors over the years. Bel-Washab was the Korsi Victor last month; Tol Morabait is an acknowledged master of the technique. And then there is Ghisel Ghang of West Ind, who knows no peer in the creation of fire-stars, and Pulakt Havjorska, the Champion of the

Island Realm. So it becomes a matter of skepticism whether you, new, inexperienced, without a fund of images, can do more than embarrass us all with your mental poverty."

Daksat's brain was yet wrestling with his bewilderment, and he could feel no strong resentment at the big man's evident contempt. He said, "Just what is all this? I'm not sure that I understand my position."

The man in the black cloak inspected him quizzically. "So, now you commence to experience trepidation? Justly, I assure you." He sighed, waved his hands. "Well, well—young men will be impetuous, and perhaps you have formed images you considered not discreditable. In any event, the public eye will ignore you for the glories of Clauktaba's geometrics and Ghisel Ghang's star-bursts. Indeed, I counsel you, keep your images small, drab, and confined; you will so avoid the faults of bombast and discord.... Now, it is time to go to your Imagicon. This way, then. Remember, grays, browns, lavenders, perhaps a few tones of ocher and rust; then the spectators will understand that you compete for the schooling alone, and do not actively challenge the masters. This way then...."

He opened a door and led Dobnor Daksat up a stair and so out into the night.

They stood in a great stadium, facing six great screens forty feet high. Behind them in the dark sat tier upon tier of spectators—thousands and thousands, and their sounds came as a soft crush. Daksat turned to see them, but all their faces and their individualities had melted into the entity as a whole.

"Here," said the big man, "this is your apparatus. Seat yourself and I will adjust the ceretemps."

Daksat suffered himself to be placed in a heavy chair, so soft and deep that he felt himself to be floating.

Adjustments were made at his head and neck and the bridge of his nose. He felt a sharp prick, a pressure, a throb, and then a soothing warmth. From the distance, a voice called out over the crowd:

"Two minutes to gray mist! Two minutes to gray mist! Attend, Imagists, two minutes to gray mist!"

The big man stooped over him. "Can you see well?"

Daksat raised himself a trifle. "Yes . . . all is clear."

"Very well. At 'gray mist,' this little filament will glow. When it dies, then it is your screen, and you must imagine your best."

The far voice said, "One minute to gray mist! The order is Pulakt Havjorska, Tol Morabait, Ghisel Ghang, Dobnor Daksat, Clauktaba, and Bel-Washab. There are no handicaps; all colors and shapes are permitted. Relax then, ready your lobes, and now—gray mist!"

The light glowed on the panel of Daksat's chair, and he saw five of the six screens light to a pleasant pearl-gray, swirling a trifle as if agitated, excited. Only the screen before him remained dull. The big man, who stood behind him, reached down, prodded. "Gray mist, Daksat; are you deaf and blind?"

Daksat thought gray mist, and instantly his screen sprang to life, displaying a cloud of silver-gray, clean and clear.

"Humph," he heard the big man snort. "Somewhat dull and without interest—but I suppose good enough. . . . See how Cluktaba's rings with hints of passion already, quivers with emotion."

And Daksat, noting the screen to his right, saw this to be true. The gray, without actually displaying color, flowed and filmed as if suppressing a vast flood of light.

Now, to the far left, on Pulakt Havjorska's screen, color glowed. It was a gambit image, modest and restrained—a green jewel dripping a rain of blue and silver drops which struck a black ground and disappeared in little orange explosions.

Then Tol Morabait's screen glowed: a black and white checkerboard with certain of the squares flashing suddenly green, red, blue, and yellow—warm, searching colors, pure as shafts from a rainbow. The image disappeared in a flush mingled of rose and blue.

Ghisel Ghang wrought a circle of yellow which quivered, brought forth a green halo, which in turn bulged giving rise to a larger band of brilliant black and white. In the center formed a complex kaleidoscopic pattern. The pattern suddenly vanished in a brilliant flash of light; on the screen for an instant or two appeared the identical pattern in a complete new suit of colors. A ripple of sound from the spectators greeted this *tour de force*.

The light on Daksat's panel died. Behind him he felt a prod. "Now."

Daksat eyed the screen and his mind was blank of ideas. He ground his teeth. Anything. Anything. A picture . . . he imagined a view across the meadowlands beside the River Melramy.

"Hm," said the big man behind him. "Pleasant. A pleasant fantasy, and rather original."

Puzzled, Daksat examined the picture on the screen. So far as he could distinguish, it was an uninspired reproduction of a scene he knew well. Fantasy? Was that what was expected? Very well, he'd produce fantasy. He imagined the meadows glowing, molten, white-hot. The vegetation, the old cairns slumped into a viscous seethe. The surface smoothed, became a mirror which reflected the Copper Crags.

Behind him the big man grunted. "A little heavy-handed, that last, and thereby you destroyed the charming effect of those unearthly colors and shapes. . . ."

Daksat slumped back in his chair, frowning, eager for his turn to come again.

Meanwhile Clauktaba created a dainty white blossom with purple stamens on a green stalk. The petals wilted, the stamens discharged a cloud of swirling yellow pollen.

Then Bel-Washab, at the end of the line, painted his screen a luminous underwater green. It rippled, bulged, and a black irregular blot marred the surface. From the center of the blot seeped a trickle of hot gold that quickly meshed and veined the black blot.

Such was the first passage.

There was a pause of several seconds. "Now," breathed the voice behind Daksat, "now the competition begins."

On Pulakt Havjorska's screen appeared an angry sea of color: waves of red, green, blue, an ugly mottling. Dramatically, a yellow shape appeared at the lower right, vanquished the chaos. It spread over the screen, the center went lime-green. A black shape appeared split, bowed softly and easily to both sides. Then turning, the two shapes wandered into the background, twisting, bending with supple grace. Far down a perspective they merged, darted forward like a lance, spread out into a series of lances, formed a slanting pattern of slim black bars.

"Superb!" hissed the big man. "The timing, so just, so exact!"

Tol Morabait replied with a fuscous brown field threaded with crimson lines and blots. Vertical green hatching formed at the left, strode across the screen to the right. The brown field pressed forward, bulged through the green bars, pressed hard, broke, and segments flitted forward to leave the screen. On the black background behind the green hatching, which now faded, lay a human brain, pink, pulsing. The brain sprouted six insectlike legs, scuttled crabwise back into the distance.

Ghisel Ghang brought forth one of his fire-bursts—a small pellet of bright blue exploding in all directions, the tips working and writhing through wonderful patterns in the five colors, blue, violet, white, purple, and light green.

Dobnor Daksat, rigid as a bar, sat with hands clenched and teeth grinding into teeth. Now! Was not his brain as excellent as those of the far lands? Now!

On the screen appeared a tree, conventionalized in greens and blues, and each leaf was a tongue of fire. From these fires wisps of smoke arose on high to form a cloud which worked and swirled, then emptied a cone of rain about the tree. The flames vanished and in their places appeared star-shaped white flowers. From the cloud came a bolt of lightning, shattering the tree to agonized fragments of glass. Another bolt into the brittle heap and the screen exploded in a great gout of white, orange, and black.

The voice of the big man said doubtfully, "On the whole, well done, but mind my warning, and create more modest images, since—"

"Silence!" said Dobnor Daksat in a harsh voice.

So the competition went, round after round of spectacles, some sweet as caramel honey, others as violent as the storms that circle the poles. Color strove with color, patterns evolved and changed, sometimes in glorious cadence, sometimes in the bitter discord necessary to the strength of the image.

And Daksat built dream after dream, while his tension vanished, and he forgot all save the racing pictures in his mind and on the screen, and his images became as complex and subtle as those of the masters.

"One more passage," said the big man behind Daksat, and now the imagists brought forth the master-dreams: Pulakt Havjorska, the growth and decay of a beautiful city; Tol Morabait, a quiet composition of green and white interrupted by a marching army of insects who left a dirty wake, and who were joined in battle by men in painted leather armor and tall hats, armed with short swords and flails. The insects were destroyed and chased off the screen; the dead warriors became bones and faded to twinkling blue dust. Ghisel Ghang created three fire-bursts simultaneously, each different, a gorgeous display.

Daksat imagined a smooth pebble, magnified it to a block of marble, chipped it away to create the head of a beautiful maiden. For a moment she stared forth and varying emotions crossed her face—joy at her sudden existence, pensive thought, and at last fright. Her eyes turned milky opaque blue, the face changed to a laughing sardonic mask, black-cheeked with a fleering mouth. The head tilted, the mouth spat into the air. The head flattened into a black background, the drops of spittle shone like fire, became stars, constellations, and one of these expanded, became a planet with configurations dear to Daksat's heart. The planet hurtled off into darkness, the constellations faded. Dobnor Daksat relaxed. His last image. He sighed, exhausted.

The big man in the black cloak removed the harness in brittle silence. At last he asked, "The planet you imagined in that last screening, was that a creation or a remembrance of actuality? It was none of our system here, and it rang with the clarity of truth."

Dobnor Daksat stared at him, puzzled, and the words faltered in his throat. "But it is—home! This world! Was it not this world?"

The big man looked at him strangely, shrugged, turned away. "In a moment now the winner of the contest will be made known and the jeweled brevet awarded."

The day was gusty and overcast, the galley was low and black, manned by the oarsmen of Belaclaw. Ergan stood on the poop, staring across the two miles of bitter sea to the coast of Racland, where he knew the sharp-faced Racs stood watching from the headlands.

A gout of water erupted a few hundred yards astern.

Ergan spoke to the helmsman. "Their guns have better range than we bargained for. Better stand offshore another mile and we'll take our chances with the current."

Even as he spoke, there came a great whistle and he glimpsed a black pointed projectile slanting down at him. It struck the waist of the galley, exploded. Timber, bodies, metal flew everywhere, and the galley laid its broken back into the water, doubled up and sank.

Ergan, jumping clear, discarded his sword, casque, and greaves almost as he hit the chill gray water. Gasping from the shock, he swam in circles, bobbing up and down in the chop; then, finding a length of timber, he clung to it for support.

From the shores of Racland a longboat put forth and approached, bow churning white foam as it rose and fell across the waves. Ergan turned loose the timber and swam as rapidly as possible from the wreck. Better drowning than capture; there would be more mercy from the famine-fish that swarmed the waters than from the pitiless Racs.

So he swam, but the current took him to the shore, and at last, struggling feebly, he was cast upon a pebbly beach.

Here he was discovered by a gang of Rac youths and marched to a nearby command post. He was tied and flung into a cart and so conveyed to the city Korsapan.

In a gray room he was seated facing an intelligence officer of the Rac secret police, a man with the gray skin of a toad, a moist gray mouth, eager, searching eyes.

"You are Ergan," said the officer. "Emissary to the Bargee of Salomdek. What was your mission?"

Ergan stared back eye to eye, hoping that a happy and convincing response would find his lips. None came, and the truth would incite an immediate invasion of both Belaclaw and Salomdek by the tall, thin-headed Rac soldiers, who wore black uniforms and black boots.

Ergan said nothing. The officer leaned forward. "I ask you once more; then you will be taken to the room below." He said "room below" as if the words were capitalized, and he said it with soft relish.

Ergan, in a cold sweat, for he knew of the Rac torturers, said, "I am not Ergan; my name is Ervard; I am an honest trader in pearls."

"This is untrue," said the Rac. "Your aide was captured, and under the compression pump he blurted up your name with his lungs."

"I am Ervard," said Ergan, his bowels quaking.

The Rac signaled. "Take him to the Room Below."

A man's body, which has developed nerves as outposts against danger, seems especially intended for pain, and co-operates wonderfully with the craft of the torturer. These characteristics of the body had been studied by the Rac specialists, and other capabilities of the human nervous system had been blundered upon by accident. It had been found that certain programs of pressure, heat, strain, friction, torque, surge, jerk, sonic and visual shock, vermin, stench, and vileness created cumulative effects, whereas a single method, used to excess, lost its stimulation thereby.

All this lore and cleverness was lavished upon Ergan's citadel of nerves, and they inflicted upon him the entire gamut of pain: the sharp twinges, the dull, lasting joint-aches which groaned by night, the fiery flashes, the assaults of filth and lechery, together with shocks of occasional tenderness when he would be allowed to glimpse the world he had left.

Then back to the Room Below.

But always: "I am Ervard the trader." And always he tried

to goad his mind over the tissue barrier to death, but always the mind hesitated at the last toppling step, and Ergan lived.

The Racs tortured by routine, so that the expectation, the approach of the hour, brought as much torment as the act itself. And then the heavy, unhurried steps outside the cell, the feeble thrashing around to evade, the harsh laughs when they cornered him and carried him forth, and the harsh laughs when three hours later they threw him sobbing and whimpering back to the pile of straw that was his bed.

"I am Ervard," he said, and trained his mind to believe that this was the truth, so that never would they catch him unaware. "I am Ervard! I am Ervard, I trade in pearls!"

He tried to strangle himself on straw, but a slave watched always, and this was not permitted.

He attempted to die by self-suffocation, and would have been glad to succeed, but always as he sank into blessed numbness, so did his mind relax and his motor nerves take up the mindless business of breathing once more.

He ate nothing, but this meant little to the Racs, as they injected him full of tonics, sustaining drugs, and stimulants, so that he might always be keyed to the height of his awareness.

"I am Ervard," said Ergan, and the Racs gritted their teeth angrily. The case was now a challenge; he defied their ingenuity, and they puzzled long and carefully upon refinements and delicacies, new shapes to the iron tools, new types of jerk ropes, new directions for the strains and pressures. Even when it was no longer important whether he was Ergan or Ervard, since war now raged, he was kept and maintained as a problem, an ideal case; so he was guarded and cosseted with even more than usual care, and the Rac torturers mulled over their techniques, making changes here, improvements there.

Then one day the Belaclaw galleys landed and the feather-crested soldiers fought past the walls of Korsapan.

The Racs surveyed Ergan with regret. "Now we must go, and still you will not submit to us."

"I am Ervard," croaked that which lay on the table. "Ervard the trader."

A splintering crash sounded overhead.

"We must go," said the Racs. "Your people have stormed the city. If you tell the truth, you may live. If you lie, we kill you. So there is your choice. Your life for the truth."

"The truth?" muttered Ergan. "It is a trick—" And then he caught the victory chant of the Belaclaw soldiery. "The truth? Why not? . . . Very well." And he said, "I am Ervard," for now he believed this to be the truth.

Galactic Prime was a lean man with reddish-brown hair, sparse across a fine arch of skull. His face, undistinguished otherwise, was given power by great dark eyes flickering with a light like fire behind smoke. Physically, he had passed the peak of his youth; his arms and legs were thin and loose jointed; his head inclined forward as if weighted by the intricate machinery of his brain.

Arising from the couch, smiling faintly, he looked across the arcade to the eleven Elders. They sat at a table of polished wood, backs to a wall festooned with vines. They were grave men, slow in their motions, and their faces were lined with wisdom and insight. By the ordained system, Prime was the executive of the universe, the Elders the deliberative body, invested with certain restrictive powers.

"Well?"

The Chief Elder without haste raised his eyes from the computer. "You are the first to arise from the couch."

Prime turned a glance up the arcade, still smiling faintly. The others lay variously: some with arms clenched, rigid as bars; others huddled in fetal postures. One had slumped from the couch half to the floor; his eyes were open, staring at remoteness.

Prime returned his gaze to the Chief Elder, who watched him with detached curiosity. "Has the optimum been established?"

The Chief Elder consulted the computer. "Twenty-six thirty-seven is the optimum score."

Prime waited, but the Chief Elder said no more. Prime stepped to the alabaster balustrade beyond the couches. He leaned forward, looked out across the vista—miles and miles of sunny haze, with a twinkling sea in the distance. A breeze blew past his face, ruffling the scant russet strands of his hair. He took a deep breath, flexed his fingers and hands, for the memory of the Rac torturers was still heavy on his mind. After a moment he swung around, leaned back, resting his elbows upon the balustrade. He glanced once more down the line of couches; there were still no signs of vitality from the candidates.

"Twenty-six thirty-seven," he muttered. "I venture to estimate my own score at twenty-five ninety. In the last episode I recall an incomplete retention of personality."

"Twenty-five seventy-four," said the Chief Elder. "The computer judged Bearwald the Halforn's final defiance of the Brand warriors unprofitable."

Prime considered. "The point is well made. Obstinacy serves no purpose unless it advances a predetermined end. It is a flaw I must seek to temper." He looked along the line of Elders, from face to face. "You make no enunciations, you are curiously mute."

He waited; the Chief Elder made no response.

"May I inquire the high score?"

"Twenty-five seventy-four."

Prime nodded. "Mine."

"Yours is the high score," said the Chief Elder.

Prime's smile disappeared: a puzzled line appeared across his brow. "In spite of this, you are still reluctant to confirm my second span of authority; there are still doubts among you."

"Doubts and misgivings," replied the Chief Elder.

Prime's mouth pulled in at the corners, although his brows were still raised in polite inquiry. "Your attitude puzzles me. My record is one of selfless service. My intelligence is phenomenal, and in this final test, which I designed to dispel your last doubts, I attained the highest score. I have proved my social intuition and flexibility, my leadership, devotion to duty, imagination, and resolution. In every commensurable aspect, I fulfill best the qualifications for the office I hold."

The Chief Elder looked up and down the line of his fellows. There were none who wished to speak. The Chief Elder squared himself in his chair, sat back.

"Our attitude is difficult to represent. Everything is as you say. Your intelligence is beyond dispute, your character is exemplary, you have served your term with honor and devotion. You have earned our respect, admiration, and gratitude. We realize also that you seek this second term from praiseworthy motives: you regard yourself as the man best able to coordinate the complex business of the galaxy."

Prime nodded grimly. "But you think otherwise."

"Our position is perhaps not quite so blunt."

"Precisely what is your position?" Prime gestured along the couches. "Look at these men. They are the finest of the galaxy. One man is dead. That one stirring on the third couch has lost his mind; he is a lunatic. The others are sorely shaken. And never forget that this test has been expressly designed to measure the qualities essential to the Galactic Prime."

"This test has been of great interest to us," said the Chief Elder mildly. "It has considerably affected our thinking."

Prime hesitated, plumbing the unspoken overtones of the words. He came forward, seated himself across from the line of Elders. With a narrow glance he searched the faces of the eleven men, tapped once, twice, three times with his fingertips on the polished wood, leaned back in the chair.

"As I have pointed out, the test has gauged each candidate for the exact qualities essential to the optimum conduct of office, in this fashion: Earth of the twentieth century is a planet of intricate conventions; on Earth the candidate, as Arthur Caversham, is required to use his social intuition—a quality highly important in this galaxy of two billion suns. On Belotsi, Bearwald the Halforn is tested for courage and the ability to conduct positive action. At the dead city Therlatch on Praesepe Three, the candidate, as Ceistan, is rated for devotion to duty, and as Dobnor Daksat at the Imagicon on Staff, his creative conceptions are rated against the most fertile imaginations alive. Finally as Ergan, on Chankozar, his will, persistence, and ultimate fiber are explored to their extreme limits.

"Each candidate is placed in the identical set of circumstances by a trick of temporal, dimensional, and cerebroneural meshing, which is rather complicated for the present discussion. Sufficient that each candidate is objectively rated by his achievements, and that the results are commensurable."

He paused, looked shrewdly along the line of grave faces. "I must emphasize that although I myself designed and arranged the test, I thereby gained no advantage. The mnemonic synapses are entirely disengaged from incident to incident, and only the candidate's basic personality acts. All were tested under precisely the same conditions. In my opinion the scores registered by the computer indicate an objective and reliable index of the candidate's ability for the highly responsible office of Galactic Executive."

The Chief Elder said, "The scores are indeed significant."

"Then—you approve my candidacy?"

The Chief Elder smiled. "Not so fast. Admittedly you are intelligent, admittedly you have accomplished much during your term as Prime. But much remains to be done."

"Do you suggest that another man would have achieved more?"

The Chief Elder shrugged. "I have no conceivable way of knowing. I point out your achievements, such as the Glenart civilization, the Dawn Time on Masilis, the reign of King Karal on Aevir, the suppression of the Arkid Revolt. There are many such examples. But there are also shortcomings: the totalitarian governments on Earth, the savagery on Belotsi and Chankozar, so pointedly emphasized in your test. Then there is the decadence of the planets in the Eleven Hundred Ninth Cluster, the rise of the priest-kings on Fiir, and much else."

Prime clenched his mouth and the fires behind his eyes burnt more brightly.

The Chief Elder continued. "One of the most remarkable phenomena of the galaxy is the tendency of humanity to absorb and manifest the personality of the Prime. There seems to be a tremendous resonance which vibrates from the brain of the Prime through the minds of man from Center to the outer fringes. It is a matter which should be studied, analyzed, and subjected to control. The effect is as if every thought of the Prime is magnified a billion-fold, as if every mood sets the tone for a thousand civilizations, every facet of his personality reflects in the ethics of a thousand cultures."

Prime said tonelessly, "I have remarked this phenomenon and have thought much on it. Prime's commands are promulgated in such a way as to exert subtle rather than overt influence; perhaps here is the background of the matter. In any event, the fact of this influence is even more reason to select for the office a man of demonstrated virtue."

"Well put," said the Chief Elder. "Your character is indeed beyond reproach. However, we of the Elders are concerned by the rising tide of authoritarianism among the planets of the galaxy. We suspect that this principle of resonance is at work. You are a man of intense and indomitable will, and we feel that your influence has unwittingly prompted an irruption of autarchies."

Prime was silent a moment. He looked down the line of couches where the other candidates were recovering awareness. They were men of various races: a pale Northkin of Palast, a stocky red Hawolo, a gray-haired gray-eyed Islander from the Sea Planet—each the outstanding man of the planet of his birth. Those who had returned to consciousness sat quietly, collecting their wits, or lay back on the couch, trying to expunge the test from their minds. There had been a toll taken: one lay dead, another bereft of his wits crouched whimpering beside his couch.

The Chief Elder said, "The objectionable aspects of your character are perhaps best exemplified by the test itself."

Prime opened his mouth; the Chief Elder held up his hand. "Let me speak; I will try to deal fairly with you. When I am done, you may say your say.

"I repeat that your basic direction is displayed by the details of the test that you devised. The qualities you measured were those which you considered the most important: that is, those ideals by which you guide your own life. This arrangement I am sure was completely unconscious, and hence completely revealing. You conceive the essential characteristics of the Prime to be social intuition, aggressiveness, loyalty, imagination, and dogged persistence. As a man of strong character you seek to exemplify these ideals in your own conduct; therefore it is not at all surprising that in this test, designed by you, with a scoring system calibrated by you, your score should be highest.

"Let me clarify the idea by an analogy. If the Eagle were conducting a test to determine the King of Beasts, he would rate all the candidates on their ability to fly; necessarily he would win. In this fashion the Mole would consider ability to dig important; by his system of testing *he* would inevitably emerge King of Beasts."

Prime laughed sharply, ran a hand through his sparse red-brown locks. "I am neither Eagle nor Mole."

The Chief Elder shook his head. "No. You are zealous, dutiful, imaginative, indefatigable—so you have demonstrated, as much by specifying tests for these characteristics as by scoring high in these same tests. But conversely, by the very absence of other tests you demonstrate deficiencies in your character."

"And these are?"

"Sympathy. Compassion. Kindness." The Chief Elder settled back in his chair. "Strange. Your predecessor two times removed was rich in these qualities. During his term, the great humanitarian systems based on the idea of human brotherhood sprang up across the universe. Another example of resonance—but I digress."

Prime said with a sardonic twitch of his mouth, "May I ask this: have you selected the next Galactic Prime?"

The Chief Elder nodded. "A definite choice has been made."

"What was his score in the test?"

"By your scoring system—seventeen eighty. He did poorly as Arthur Caversham; he tried to explain the advantages of nudity to the policeman. He lacked the ability to concoct an instant subterfuge; he has little of your quick craft. As Arthur Caversham he found himself naked. He is sincere and straightforward, hence tried to expound the positive motivations for his state, rather than discover the means to evade the penalties."

"Tell me more about this man," said Prime shortly.

"As Bearwald the Halforn, he led his band to the hive of the Brands on Mount Medallion, but instead of burning the hive, he called forth to the queen, begging her to end the useless slaughter. She reached out from the doorway, drew him within and killed him. He failed—but the computer still rated him highly on his forthright approach.

"At Therlatch, his conduct was as irreproachable as yours, and at the Imagicon his performance was adequate. Yours approached the brilliance of the Master Imagists, which is high achievement indeed.

"The Rac tortures are the most trying element of the test. You knew well you could resist limitless pain; therefore you ordained that all other candidates must likewise possess this attribute. The new Prime is sadly deficient here. He is sensitive, and the idea of one man intentionally inflicting pain upon another sickens him. I may add that none of the candidates achieved a perfect count in the last episode. Two others equaled your score—"

Prime evinced interest. "Which are they?"

The Chief Elder pointed them out—a tall hard-muscled man with rock-hewn face standing by the alabaster balustrade gazing moodily out across the sunny distance, and a man of middle age who sat with his legs folded under him, watching a point three feet before him with an expression of imperturbable placidity.

"One is utterly obstinate and hard," said the Chief Elder. "He refused to say a single word. The other assumes an outer objectivity when unpleasantness overtakes him. Others among the candidates fared not so well; therapy will be necessary in almost all cases."

Their eyes went to the witless creature with vacant eyes who padded up and down the aisle, humming and muttering quietly to himself.

"The tests were by no means valueless," said the Chief Elder. "We learned a great deal. By your system of scoring, the competition rated you most high. By other standards which we Elders postulated, your place was lower."

With a tight mouth, Prime inquired, "Who is this paragon of altruism, kindliness, sympathy, and generosity?"

The lunatic wandered close, fell on his hands and knees, crawled whimpering to the wall. He pressed his face to the cool stone, stared blankly up at Prime. His mouth hung loose, his chin was wet, his eyes rolled apparently free of each other.

The Chief Elder smiled in great compassion; he stroked the mad creature's head. "This is he. Here is the man we select."

The old Galactic Prime sat silent, mouth compressed, eyes burning like far volcanoes.

At his feet the new Prime, Lord of Two Billion Suns, found a dead leaf, put it into his mouth and began to chew.

THE NEW PRIME:
SIX PLOTS FOR THE PRICE OF ONE

It ought to be apparent by now that the essence of science fiction for me is *wonder*. I don't mean to minimize the importance of such things as a clever plot, a graceful style, insight into character, an intellectually stimulating idea, a swift narrative pace. All of those are basic requirements of good fiction, whether science fiction or not. But they are available in other kinds of fiction. I can go to John Updike for style, to Faulkner for character, to Dostoievski for plot, to Thomas Mann for ideas, to Graham Greene for pace—or, for that matter, to any of those writers for all of those qualities. But not one of them can deliver those moments of visionary power that science fiction has brought me since those long-ago days when I first wandered goggle-eyed through the pages of Wells' *The Time Machine* and Lovecraft's *The Shadow out of Time*.

Of contemporary science fiction writers, none, I think, has been more consistently "wonder-ful" for me than Jack Vance. His specialty, which has been the hallmark of his work in a brilliant career stretching across more than forty years, is exotica: vivid portrayals of bizarre cultures or astonishing landscapes. His characters tend toward the eccentric, his style is formal and elegant and baroquely sensuous, and his inventiveness is probably unparalleled in our field. Through such works as *To Live Forever, Big Planet, Emphyrio*, and the *Durdane* trilogy he has shaped and enriched my imagination like no other writer.

I first discovered my affinity for Vance's work in 1950, when his "New Bodies for Old," a lively and flamboyant adventure, appeared in the revitalized and suddenly top-grade pulp magazine *Thrilling Wonder Stories*. (The same issue included fiction by Henry Kuttner, Arthur C. Clarke, and L. Ron Hubbard, and the letter column in the back held contributions by such eager young fans as Marion Zimmer Bradley, A. J. Budrys, and a kid from Brooklyn who signed himself "Bob" Silverberg.) What caught my attention in the Vance story were passages like this:

"Every man amuses himself as best he knows how. My current interest is building the Empyrean Tower." His voice took on a deep exalted ring. "It shall rise three miles into the air! There is a banquet hall with a floor of alternate silver and copper strips, a quarter mile wide, a quarter mile high, ringed with eight glass balconies. There will be garden terraces like nothing else on earth, with fountains, water-falls, running brooks. One floor will be a fairyland out of the ancient days, peopled with beautiful nymphs.

"Others will display the earth at stages in its history. There will be museums, conservatories of various musical styles, studios, workshops, laboratories for every known type of research, sections given to retail shops. There will be beautiful chambers and balconies designed for nothing except to be wandered through, sections devoted to the—let us say, worship of Astarte. There will be halls full of toys, a hundred restaurants staffed by gourmets, a thousand taverns serving liquid dreams. . . ."

Vision, gorgeous excess, playfulness, even some bombast, all set against a background of skulduggery and intrigue: I loved it. Vance had already published a dozen stories, all of which I had read in the previous two or three years, but this was the first to make a real impression. I began to watch for his work. And toward the end of the year came an extraordinary treat. The first issue of *Worlds Beyond*, an attractive and greatly appealing magazine edited by Damon Knight, offered a moody, mysterious Vance piece called "The Loom of Darkness" that turned out to be an extract from a new Vance novel, *The Dying Earth*, from the same publisher as the magazine. This is how the back cover advertisement for the novel began:

Time had worn out the sun, and earth was spinning quickly toward eternal darkness. In the forests strange animals hid behind twisted trees, plotting death; in the cities men made constant revel and sought sorcery to cheat the dying world.

In this dark and frenzied atmosphere Jack Vance has set his finest novel, *The Dying Earth*, a story of love and death and magic and the rediscovery of science. Through this time, fabulously far from now, wander men and women and artificial creatures from the vats. . . .

I knew at once it would be my kind of stuff. I set out immediately to buy a copy. What I didn't know was that both the magazine and the companion line of paperbacks had been killed almost at the moment of their birth by a hasty decision of the publisher, and *The Dying Earth* had received only random and spotty distribution. I think I looked everywhere in New York for a copy, seeking it lucklessly after school on dark wintry afternoons in odd corners of the city. With the greatest clarity, I recall my delight that Christmas when a friend who had actually found one gave me his copy after he had read it. Miracle of miracles, the book came close to living up to my hopes for it: a small masterpiece, unforgettable in its portrait of a mysterious distant future. Though it has been reprinted many times, I still have my much-sought copy of the scruffy-looking original edition, which is inordinately prized by collectors today.

Worlds Beyond, that beautiful but doomed little magazine, lasted for two more issues, which were released only because they were too far along in the production process to abandon. Its contents page was brightened by such names as Franz Kafka, Rudyard Kipling, and E. B. White, along with outstanding work by the s-f regulars of the day, C. M. Kornbluth, William Tenn, Fredric Brown. Vance reappeared in the final issue with a story called "Brain of the Galaxy," which held for me the same wonder and power as his other work that year—indeed, seemed to surpass it in the intensity of its visions. That is the story I have reprinted here—under what seems to have been Vance's preferred title for it, "The New Prime."

What is so astonishing about this story is its profligacy. In something like eight thousand words Vance devises—and almost immediately tosses away—enough science-fiction concepts to see any other writer through an entire novel. The tactic is deliberate: the whole point of Vance's story is to carry us quickly through a series of quick unrelated scenes, which actually are related in a way not immediately apparent. Each must have its own sharply distinct background, and so we are shown tantalizing glimpses: the torturers of Racland, the dead city of Therlatch, the ferocious Brands of Mount

Medallion, and the rest. At least one of these—the Imagicon at which Dobnor Daksat competes with such notable skill—is a major invention, which calls forth from Vance some of his most powerful writing. (It is, probably not by coincidence, the longest of the five test sequences.) Even in this masterly dream-shaping sequence, though, Vance is content to demonstrate his own skill and move quickly onward; the Imagicon and those who take part in its competition are merely incidental to the real story, not a central element at all.

"The New Prime" differs in structure from the other stories represented here. Instead of following the problems of a single protagonist or group of protagonists facing one problem or progression of problems, it is built of seemingly unrelated threads that only gradually unite. This is a storytelling tactic that can be highly effective in the right hands, though the usual result when it is employed by beginners is diffuse and irritating. The writer must be prepared to surrender the effect of involving the reader emotionally in the story, since the constantly shifting focus destroys reader identification with the protagonists again and again. On the other hand, this structural device can build considerable suspense, provided each section is compelling of itself: the reader, though baffled, keeps on going, wondering where the writer is taking him. If the writing is confident enough, the reader never loses hope that the story will get somewhere if only he is patient long enough. Inducing patience in the reader is simply another way of saying that suspense has been created. A reader who becomes impatient with a story will simply toss it aside. (Though it should be noted that in storytelling there is impatience and impatience. The good impatience is the sort that makes the reader turn the pages as fast as he can read, because he is so eager to know what happens next. The bad impatience is the kind that evokes restlessness, boredom, and the discarding of the story unfinished.)

Though the story seems at first glance to have no coherence at all, Vance's ingenuity and his skill at plotting hold us here. He achieves this by a dazzling technical maneuver: each of the five ostensibly unrelated episodes is actually a miniature story, complete in itself, with beginning, middle, and end. Arthur Caversham, dumped down naked at the formal gathering in a classic use of the nightmare fantasy as narrative hook, finds a way to deal with his embarrassing predicament. Bearwald the Halforn, facing an army of implacable monsters with only a dozen comrades, battles nobly and goes down to glorious defeat. Ceistan, seeking the vital Crown and Shield Parchment his master needs, strives loyally and fails interestingly. (Note in this sequence the typically Vancean names of the buildings: the Legalic, the Sumptuar, the Nunciator's Confirmatory.) Dobnor Daksat's Imagicon contest has color, conflict, and a fascinatingly ambiguous resolution. And the torment of Ergan at the hands of the Racs leads to a beautifully wry moment of insight. Each of these sequences, spun out to five thousand words, would have made a fine short story in its own right, which is why they hold our attention even though as we proceed through them we have no idea why Vance is offering them to us in such swift succession.

The main story—the choosing of the New Prime—is audaciously withheld until the final scene of the whole work. Not a clue do we have until then that there is any larger structure; no prologue, no interpolated italicized linkages between sections. At last we are allowed to see: all these little stories are phases in a galactic election process. Retroactively, the structure of the story arises and the unrelated stories acquire a relationship. And now the outer story, so belatedly set in motion, can drive onward to its ironic conclusion. It is a remarkable stunt, an enviable tour de force, six stories for the price of one. "The New Prime" demonstrates Jack Vance's cool willingness to take risks with his audience, his distinctive prose manner, and above all the fertility of his imagination.

Vance is not a writer whose manner can safely be imitated: his idiosyncratic style and sardonic, mordant view of the world make him so much his own man that another writer trying to use Vance's voice will seem pitifully derivative. But his generosity of invention is something we can all try to emulate. His stories of distant worlds and remote times surge and throb with the vitality of his strange, wonderful visions, and remain to haunt the souls of his readers forever after.

COLONY
PHILIP K. DICK

M ajor Lawrence Hall bent over the binocular microscope, correcting the fine adjustment.

"Interesting," he murmured.

"Isn't it? Three weeks on this planet and we've yet to
find a harmful life-form." Lieutenant Friendly sat down on
the edge of the lab table, avoiding the culture bowls. "What
kind of place is this? No disease germs, no lice, no flies, no
rats, no—"

"No whisky or red light districts." Hall straightened up.
"Quite a place. I was sure this brew would show something
along the lines of Terra's *Eberthella typhi*. Or the Martian
sand rot corkscrew."

"But the whole planet's harmless. You know, I'm wondering whether this is the Garden of Eden our ancestors fell
out of."

"Were pushed out of."

Hall wandered over to the window of the lab and contemplated the scene beyond. He had to admit it was an attractive sight. Rolling forests and hills, green slopes alive
with flowers and endless vines; waterfalls and hanging moss;

fruit trees, acres of flowers, lakes. Every effort had been made to preserve intact the surface of Planet Blue—as it had been designated by the original scout ship, six months earlier.

Hall sighed. "Quite a place. I wouldn't mind coming back here again some time."

"Makes Terra seem a little bare." Friendly took out his cigarettes; then put them away again. "You know, the place has a funny effect on me. I don't smoke any more. Guess that's because of the way it looks. It's so—so damn pure. Unsullied. I can't smoke or throw papers around. I can't bring myself to be a picnicker."

"The picnickers'll be along soon enough." Hall said. He went back to the microscope. "I'll try a few more cultures. Maybe I'll find a lethal germ yet."

"Keep trying." Lieutenant Friendly hopped off the table. "I'll see you later and find out if you've had any luck. There's a big conference going on in Room One. They're almost ready to give the go-ahead to the E.A. for the first load of colonists to be sent out."

"Picnickers!"

Friendly grinned. "Afraid so."

The door closed after him. His bootsteps echoed down the corridor. Hall was alone in the lab.

He sat for a time in thought. Presently he bent down and removed the slide from the stage of the microscope, selected a new one and held it up to the light to read the marking. The lab was warm and quiet. Sunlight streamed through the windows and across the floor. The trees outside moved a little in the wind. He began to feel sleepy.

"Yes, the picnickers," he grumbled. He adjusted the new slide into position. "And all of them ready to come in and cut down the trees, tear up the flowers, spit in the lakes, burn up the grass. With not even the common cold virus around to—"

He stopped, his voice choked off—

Choked off, because the two eyepieces of the microscope had twisted suddenly around his windpipe and were trying to strangle him. Hall tore at them, but they dug relentlessly into his throat, steel prongs closing like the claws of a trap.

Throwing the microscope on to the floor, he leaped up. The microscope crawled quickly towards him, hooking around his leg. He kicked it loose with his other foot, and drew his blast pistol.

The microscope scuttled away, rolling on its coarse adjustments. Hall fired. It disappeared in a cloud of metallic particles.

"Good God!" Hall sat down weakly, mopping his face. "What the—?" He massaged his throat. "What the hell!"

The council room was packed solid. Every officer of the Planet Blue unit was there. Commander Stella Morrison tapped on the big control map with the end of a slim plastic pointer.

"This long flat area is ideal for the actual city. It's close to water, and weather conditions vary sufficiently to give the settlers something to talk about. There are large deposits of various minerals. The colonists can set up their own factories. They won't have to do any importing. Over here is the biggest forest on the planet. If they have any sense, they'll leave it. But if they want to make newspapers out of it, that's not our concern."

She looked around the room at the silent men.

"Let's be realistic. Some of you have been thinking we shouldn't send the okay to the Emigration Authority, but keep the planet our own selves, to come back to. I'd like that as much as any of the rest of you, but we'd just get into a lot of trouble. It's not *our* planet. We're here to do a certain job. When the job is done, we move along. And it is almost done. So let's forget it. The only thing left to do is flash the go-ahead signal and then begin packing our things."

"Has the lab report come in on bacteria?" Vice-Commander Wood asked.

"We're taking special care to look out for them, of course. But the last I heard nothing had been found. I think we can go ahead and contact the E.A. Have them send a ship to take us off and bring in the first load of settlers. There's no reason why—" she stopped.

A murmur was swelling through the room. Heads turned towards the door.

Commander Morrison frowned. "Major Hall, may I remind you that when the council is in session no one is permitted to interrupt!"

Hall swayed back and forth, supporting himself by holding on to the door knob. He gazed vacantly around the council room. Finally his glassy eyes picked out Lieutenant Friendly, sitting half-way across the room.

"Come here," he said hoarsely.

"Me?" Friendly sank further down in his chair.

"Major, what is the meaning of this?" Vice-Commander Wood cut in angrily. "Are you drunk or are—?" He saw the blast gun in Hall's hand. "Is something wrong, Major?"

Alarmed, Lieutenant Friendly got up and grabbed Hall's shoulder. "What is it? What's the matter?"

"Come to the lab."

"Did you find something?" The Lieutenant studied his friend's rigid face. "What is it?"

"Come on." Hall started down the corridor. Friendly following. Hall pushed the laboratory door open, stepped inside slowly.

"What is it?" Friendly repeated.

"My microscope."

"Your microscope? What about it?" Friendly squeezed past him into the lab. "I don't see it."

"It's gone."

"Gone? Gone where?"

"I blasted it."

"You blasted it?" Friendly looked at the other man. "I don't get it. Why?"

Hall's mouth opened and closed, but no sound came out.

"Are you all right?" Friendly asked in concern. Then he bent down and lifted a black plastic box from a shelf under the table. "Say, is this a gag?"

He removed Hall's microscope from the box. "What do you mean, you blasted it? Here it is, in its regular place. Now, tell me what's going on? You saw something on a slide? Some kind of bacteria? Lethal? Toxic?"

Hall approached the microscope slowly. It was his, all right. There was the nick just above the fine adjustment. And one of the stage clips was slightly bent. He touched it with his finger.

Five minutes ago this microscope had tried to kill him. And he knew he had blasted it out of existence.

"You sure you don't need a psych test?" Friendly asked anxiously. "You look like post-trauma to me, or worse."

"Maybe you're right," Hall muttered.

The robot psyche tester whirred, integrating and gestalting. At last its colour code lights changed from red to green.

"Well?" Hall demanded.

"Severe disturbance. Instability ratio up above ten."

"That's over danger?"

"Yes. Eight is danger. Ten is unusual, especially for a person of your index. You usually show about a four."

Hall nodded wearily. "I know."

"If you could give me more data—"

Hall set his jaw. "I can't tell you any more."

"It's illegal to hold back information during a psyche test," the machine said peevishly. "If you do that you deliberately distort my findings."

Hall rose. "I can't tell you any more. But you do record a high degree of unbalance for me?"

"There's a high degree of psychic disorganization. But what it means, or why it exists, I can't say."

"Thanks." Hall clicked the tester off. He went back to his own quarters. His head whirled. Was he out of his mind? But he had fired his blast gun at *something*. Afterwards, he had tested the atmosphere in the lab, and there were metallic particles in suspension, especially near the place he had fired his blast gun at the microscope.

But how could a thing like that be? A microscope coming to life, trying to kill him!

Anyhow, Friendly had pulled it out of its box, whole and sound. But how had it got back in the box?

He stripped off his uniform and entered the shower. While he ran warm water over his body he meditated. The robot psyche tester had showed his mind was severely disturbed, but that could have been the result, rather than the cause, of the experience. He had started to tell Friendly about it but he had stopped. How could he expect anyone to believe a story like that?

He shut off the water and reached out for one of the towels on the rack.

The towel wrapped around his wrist, yanking him against the wall. Rough cloth pressed over his mouth and nose. He fought wildly, pulling away. All at once the towel let go. He fell, sliding to the floor, his head striking the wall. Stars shot around him; then violent pain.

Sitting in a pool of warm water, Hall looked up at the towel rack. The towel was motionless now, like the others with it. Three towels in a row, all exactly alike, all unmoving. Had he dreamed it?

He got shakily to his feet, rubbing his head. Carefully avoiding the towel rack, he edged out of the shower and into his room. He pulled a new towel from the dispenser in a gingerly manner. It seemed normal. He dried himself and began to put his clothes on.

His belt got him around the waist and tried to crush him. It was strong—it had reinforced metal links to hold his leggings and his gun. He and the belt rolled silently on the floor, struggling for control. The belt was like a furious metal snake, whipping and lashing at him. At last he managed to get his hand around his blaster.

At once the belt let go. He blasted it out of existence and then threw himself down in a chair, gasping for breath.

The arms of the chair closed around him. But this time the blaster was ready. He had to fire six times before the chair fell limp and he was able to get up again.

He stood half-dressed in the middle of the room, his chest rising and falling.

"It isn't possible," he whispered. "I must be out of my mind."

Finally he got his leggings and boots on. He went outside into the empty corridor. Entering the lift, he ascended to the top floor.

Commander Morrison looked up from her desk as Hall stepped through the robot clearing screen. It pinged.

"You're armed," the Commander said accusingly.

Hall looked down at the blaster in his hand. He put it down on the desk. "Sorry."

"What do you want? What's the matter with you? I have a report from the testing machine. It says you've hit a ratio of ten within the last twenty-four-hour period." She studied him intently. "We've known each other for a long time, Lawrence. What's happening to you?"

Hall took a deep breath. "Stella, earlier today, my microscope tried to strangle me."

Her blue eyes widened. "What!"

"Then, when I was getting out of the shower, a bath towel tried to smother me. I got by it, but while I was dressing, my belt—" he stopped. The Commander had got to her feet.

"Guards!" she called.

"Wait, Stella." Hall moved towards her. "Listen to me. This is serious. There's something wrong. Four times things have tried to kill me. Ordinary objects suddenly turned lethal. Maybe it's what we've been looking for. Maybe this is—"

"Your microscope tried to kill you?"

"It came alive. Its stems got me around the windpipe."

There was a long silence. "Did anyone see this happen besides you?"

"No."

"What did you do?"

"I blasted it."

"Are there any remains?"

"No," Hall admitted reluctantly. "As a matter of fact, the microscope seems to be all right, again. The way it was before. Back in its box."

"I see." The Commander nodded to the two guards who had answered her call. "Take Major Hall down to Captain Taylor and have him confined until he can be sent back to Terra for examination."

She watched calmly as the two guards took hold of Hall's arms with magnetic grapples.

"Sorry, Major," she said. "Unless you can prove any of your story, we've got to assume it's a psychotic projection on your part. And the planet isn't well enough policed for us to allow a psychotic to run around loose. You could do a lot of damage."

The guards moved him towards the door. Hall went un-protestingly. His head rang, rang and echoed. Maybe she was right. Maybe he was out of his mind.

They came to Captain Taylor's offices. One of the guards rang the buzzer.

"Who is it?" the robot door demanded shrilly.

"Commander Morrison orders this man put under the Captain's care."

There was a hesitant pause, then: "The Captain is busy."

"This is an emergency."

The robot's relays clicked while it made up its mind. "The Commander sent you?"

"Yes. Open up."

"You may enter," the robot conceded finally. It drew its locks back, releasing the door.

The guard pushed the door open. And stopped.

On the floor lay Captain Taylor, his face blue, his eyes gaping. Only his head and his feet were visible. A red and white scatter rug was wrapped around him, squeezing, strain-ing tighter and tighter.

Hall dropped to the floor and pulled at the rug. "Hurry!" he barked. "Grab it!"

The three of them pulled together. The rug resisted.

"Help," Taylor cried weakly.

"We're trying!" They tugged frantically. At last the rug came away in their hands. It flopped off rapidly towards the open door. One of the guards blasted it.

Hall ran to the vidscreen and shakily dialled the Com-mander's emergency number.

Her face appeared on the screen.

"See!" he gasped.

She stared past him to Taylor lying on the floor, the two guards kneeling beside him, their blasters still out.

"What—what happened?"

"A rug attacked him." Hall grinned without amusement. "Now who's crazy?"

"We'll send a guard unit down." She blinked. "Right away. But how—"

"Tell them to have their blasters ready. And better make that a general alarm to *everyone*."

Hall placed four items on Commander Morrison's desk: a microscope, a towel, a metal belt, and a small red and white rug.

She edged away nervously. "Major, are you sure—?"

"They're all right, *now*. That's the strangest part. This towel. A few hours ago it tried to kill me. I got away by blasting it to particles. But here it is, back again. The way it always was. Harmless."

Captain Taylor fingered the red and white rug warily. "That's my rug. I brought it from Terra. My wife gave it to me. I—I trusted it completely."

They all looked at each other.

"We blasted the rug, too," Hall pointed out.

There was silence.

"Then what was it that attacked me?" Captain Taylor asked. "If it wasn't this rug?"

"It looked like this rug," Hall said slowly. "And what attacked me looked like this towel."

Commander Morrison held the towel up to the light. "It's just an ordinary towel! It couldn't have attacked you."

"Of course not," Hall agreed. "We've put these objects through all the tests we can think of. They're just what they're supposed to be, all elements unchanged. Perfectly stable non-organic objects. It's impossible that *any* of these could have come to life and attacked us."

"But something did," Taylor said. "Something attacked me. And if it wasn't this rug, what was it?"

Lieutenant Dodds felt around on the dresser for his gloves. He was in a hurry. The whole unit had been called to emergency assembly.

"Where did I—?" he murmured. "What the hell!"

For on the bed were *two* pairs of identical gloves, side by side.

Dodds frowned, scratching his head. How could it be? He owned only one pair. The others must be somebody else's. Bob Wesley had been in the night before, playing cards. Maybe he had left them.

The vidscreen flashed again. "All personnel, report at once. All personnel, report at once. Emergency assembly of all personnel."

"All right!" Dodds said impatiently. He grabbed up one of the pairs of gloves, sliding them on to his hands.

As soon as they were in place, the gloves carried his hands down to his waist. They clamped his fingers over the butt of his gun, lifting it from his holster.

"I'll be damned," Dodds said. The gloves brought the blast gun up, pointing it at his chest.

The fingers squeezed. There was a roar. Half of Dodds' chest dissolved. What was left of him fell slowly to the floor, the mouth still open in amazement.

Corporal Tenner hurried across the ground towards the main building, as soon as he heard the wail of the emergency alarm.

At the entrance to the building he stopped to take off his metal-cleated boots. Then he frowned. By the door were two safety mats instead of one.

Well, it didn't matter. They were both the same. He

stepped on to one of the mats and waited. The surface of the mat sent a flow of high-frequency current through his feet and legs, killing any spores or seeds that might have clung to him while he was outside.

He passed on into the building.

A moment later Lieutenant Fulton hurried up to the door. He yanked off his hiking boots and stepped on to the first mat he saw.

The mat folded over his feet.

"Hey," Fulton cried. "Let go!"

He tried to pull his feet loose, but the mat refused to let go. Fulton became scared. He drew his gun, but he didn't care to fire at his own feet.

"Help!" he shouted.

Two soldiers came running up. "What's the matter, Lieutenant?"

"Get this damn thing off me."

The soldiers began to laugh.

"It's no joke," Fulton said, his face suddenly white. "It's breaking my feet! It's—"

He began to scream. The soldiers grabbed frantically at the mat. Fulton fell, rolling and twisting, still screaming. At last the soldiers managed to get a corner of the mat loose from his feet.

Fulton's feet were gone. Nothing but limp bone remained, already half-dissolved.

"Now we know," Hall said grimly. "It's a form of organic life."

Commander Morrison turned to Corporal Tenner. "You saw two mats when you came into the building?"

"Yes, Commander. Two. I stepped on—on one of them. And came in."

"You were lucky. You stepped on the right one."

"We've got to be careful," Hall said. "We've got to watch for duplicates. Apparently *it*, whatever it is, imitates objects it finds. Like a chameleon. Camouflage."

"Two," Stella Morrison murmured, looking at the two vases of flowers, one at each end of her desk. "It's going to be hard to tell. Two towels, two vases, two chairs. There may be whole rows of things that are all right. All multiples legitimate except one."

"That's the trouble. I didn't notice anything unusual in the lab. There's nothing odd about another microscope. It blended right in."

The Commander drew away from the identical vases of flowers. "How about those? Maybe one is—whatever they are."

"There's two of a lot of things. Natural pairs. Two boots. Clothing. Furniture. I didn't notice that extra chair in my room. Equipment. It'll be impossible to be sure. And sometimes—"

The vidscreen lit. Vice-Commander Wood's features formed. "Stella, another casualty."

"Who is it this time?"

"An officer dissolved. All but a few buttons and his blast pistol—Lieutenant Dodds."

"That makes three," Commander Morrison said.

"If it's organic, there ought to be some way we can destroy it," Hall muttered. "We've already blasted a few, apparently killed them. They *can* be hurt! But we don't know how many more there are. We've destroyed five or six. Maybe it's an infinitely divisible substance. Some kind of protoplasm."

"And meanwhile—?"

"Meanwhile we're all at its mercy. Or *their* mercy. It's our lethal lifeform, all right. That explains why we found everything else harmless. Nothing could compete with a form like this. We have mimic forms of our own, of course. Insects, plants. And there's the twisty slug on Venus. But nothing that goes this far."

"It can be killed, though. You said so yourself. That means we have a chance."

"If it can be found." Hall looked around the room. Two walking-capes hung by the door. Had there been *two* a moment before?

He rubbed his forehead wearily. "We've got to try to find some sort of poison or corrosive agent, something that'll destroy them wholesale. We can't just sit and wait for them to attack us. We need something we can spray. That's the way we got the twisty slugs."

The Commander gazed past him, rigid.

He turned to follow her gaze. "What is it?"

"I never noticed two brief-cases in the corner over there. There was only one before—I think." She shook her head in bewilderment. "How are we going to know? This business is getting me down."

"You need a good stiff drink."

She brightened. "That's an idea. But—"

"But what?"

"I don't want to touch anything. There's no way to tell." She fingered the blast gun at her waist. "I keep wanting to use it, on everything."

"Panic reaction. Still, we are being picked off, one by one."

Captain Unger got the emergency call over his headphones. He stopped work at once, gathered the specimens he had collected in his arms, and hurried back towards the bucket.

It was parked closer than he remembered. He stopped, puzzled. There it was, the bright little cone-shaped car with its treads firmly planted in the soft soil, its door open.

Unger hurried up to it, carrying his specimens carefully. He opened the storage hatch in the back and lowered his armload. Then he went around to the front and slid in behind the controls.

He turned the switch. But the motor did not come on. That was strange. While he was trying to figure it out, he noticed something that gave him a start.

A few hundred feet away, among the trees, was a second bucket, just like the one he was in. And that *was* where he remembered having parked his car. Of course, he was in the bucket. Somebody else had come looking for specimens, and this bucket belonged to him.

Unger started to get out again.

The door closed around him. The seat folded up over his head. The dashboard became plastic and oozed. He gasped— he was suffocating. He struggled to get out, flailing and twisting. There was wetness all around him, a bubbling, flow- ing wetness, warm like flesh.

"Glub." His head was covered. His body was covered. The bucket was turning to liquid. He tried to pull his hands free but they would not come.

And then the pain began. He was being dissolved. All at once he realized what the liquid was.

Acid. Digestive acid. He was in a stomach.

"Don't look!" Gail Thomas cried.

"Why not?" Corporal Hendricks swam towards her, grin- ning. "Why can't I look?"

"Because I'm going to get out."

The sun shone down on to the lake. It glittered and danced on the water. All around huge moss-covered trees rose up, great silent columns among the flowering vines and bushes.

Gail climbed up on the bank, shaking water from her,

throwing her hair back out of her eyes. The woods were silent. There was no sound except the lapping of the waves. They were a long way from the unit camp.

"When can I look?" Hendricks demanded, swimming around in a circle, his eyes shut.

"Soon." Gail made her way into the trees, until she came to the place where she had left her uniform. She could feel the warm sun glowing against her bare shoulders and arms. Sitting down in the grass, she picked up her tunic and leggings.

She brushed the leaves and bits of tree bark from her tunic and began to pull it over her head.

In the water, Corporal Hendricks waited patiently, continuing in his circle. Time passed. There was no sound. He opened his eyes. Gail was nowhere in sight.

"Gail?" he called.

It was very quiet.

"Gail!"

No answer.

Corporal Hendricks swam rapidly to the bank. He pulled himself out of the water. One leap carried him to his own uniform, neatly piled at the edge of the lake. He grabbed up his blaster.

"*Gail!*"

The woods were silent. There was no sound. He stood, looking around him, frowning. Gradually, a cold fear began to numb him, in spite of the warm sun.

"*Gail!* GAIL!"

And still there was only silence.

Commander Morrison was worried. "We've got to act," she said. "We can't wait. Ten lives lost already from thirty encounters. One-third is too high a percentage."

Hall looked up from his work. "Anyhow, now we know

what we're up against. It's a form of protoplasm, with infinite versatility." He lifted the spray tank. "I think this will give us an idea of how many exist."

"What's that?"

"A compound of arsenic and hydrogen in gas form. Arsine."

"What are you going to do with it?"

Hall locked his helmet into place. His voice came through the Commander's earphones. "I'm going to release this throughout the lab. I think there are a lot of them in here, more than anywhere else."

"Why here?"

"This is where all samples and specimens were originally brought, where the first one of them was encountered. I think they came in with the samples, or as the samples, and then infiltrated through the rest of the buildings."

The Commander locked her own helmet into place. Her four guards did the same. "Arsine is fatal to human beings, isn't it?"

Hall nodded. "We'll have to be careful. We can use it in here for a limited test, but that's about all."

He adjusted the flow of oxygen inside his helmet.

"What's your test supposed to prove?" she wanted to know.

"If it shows anything at all, it should give us an idea of how extensively they've infiltrated. We'll know better what we're up against. This may be more serious than we realize."

"How do you mean?" she asked, fixing her own oxygen flow.

"There are a hundred people in this unit on Planet Blue. As it stands now, the worst that can happen is that they'll get all of us, one by one. But that's nothing. Units of a hundred are lost every day of the week. It's a risk whoever is first to land on a planet must take. In the final analysis, it's relatively unimportant."

"Compared to what?"

"If they *are* infinitely divisible, then we're going to have to think twice about leaving here. It would be better to stay and get picked off one by one than to run the risk of carrying any of them back to the system."

She looked at him. "Is that what you're trying to find out—whether they're infinitely divisible?"

"I'm trying to find out what we're up against. Maybe there are only a few of them. Or maybe they're everywhere." He waved a hand around the laboratory. "Maybe half the things in this room are not what we think they are . . . It's bad when they attack us. It would be worse if they didn't."

"Worse?" The Commander was puzzled.

"Their mimicry is perfect. Of inorganic objects, at least. I looked through one of them, Stella, when it was imitating my microscope. It enlarged, adjusted, reflected, just like a regular microscope. It's a form of mimicry that surpasses anything we've ever imagined. It carries down below the surface, into the actual elements of the object imitated."

"You mean one of them could slip back to Terra along with us? In the form of clothing or a piece of lab equipment?" She shuddered.

"We assume they're some sort of protoplasm. Such malleability suggests a simple original form—and that suggests binary fission. If that's so, then there may be no limit to their ability to reproduce. The dissolving properties make me think of the simple unicellular protozoa."

"Do you think they're intelligent?"

"I don't know. I hope not." Hall lifted the spray. "In any case, this should tell us their extent. And, to some degree, corroborate my notion that they're basic enough to reproduce by simple division—the worst thing possible, from our stand-point.

"Here goes," Hall said.

He held the spray tightly against him, depressed the trigger, aimed the nozzle slowly around the lab. The Commander and the four guards stood silently behind him. Nothing moved. The sun shone in through the windows, reflecting from the culture dishes and equipment.

After a moment he let the trigger up again.

"I didn't see anything," Commander Morrison said. "Are you sure you did anything?"

"Arsine is colourless. But don't loosen your helmet. It's fatal. And don't move."

They stood waiting.

For a time nothing happened. Then—

"Good God!" Commander Morrison exclaimed.

At the far end of the lab a slide cabinet wavered suddenly. It oozed, buckling and pitching. It lost its shape completely—a homogeneous jelly-like mass perched on top of the table. Abruptly it flowed down the side of the table on to the floor, wobbling as it went.

"Over there!"

A bunsen burner melted and flowed along beside it. All around the room objects were in motion. A great glass retort folded up into itself and settled down into a blob. A rack of test tubes, a shelf of chemicals . . .

"Look out!" Hall cried, stepping back.

A huge bell jar dropped with a soggy splash in front of him. It was a single large cell, all right. He could dimly make out the nucleus, the cell wall, the hard vacuoles suspended in the cytoplasm.

Pipettes, tongs, a mortar, all were flowing now. Half the equipment in the room was in motion. They had imitated almost everything there was to imitate. For every microscope there was a mimic. For every tube and jar and bottle and flask . . .

One of the guards had his blaster out. Hall knocked it down. "Don't fire! Arsine is inflammable. Let's get out of here. We know what we wanted to know."

They pushed the laboratory door open quickly and made their way out into the corridor. Hall slammed the door behind them, bolting it tightly.

"Is it bad, then?" Commander Morrison asked.

"We haven't got a chance. The arsine disturbed them; enough of it might even kill them. But we haven't got that much arsine. And, if we could flood the planet, we wouldn't be able to use our blasters."

"Suppose we left the planet."

"We can't take the chance of carrying them back to the system."

"If we stay here we'll be absorbed, dissolved, one by one," the Commander protested.

"We could have arsine brought in. Or some other poison that might destroy them. But it would destroy most of the life on the planet along with them. There wouldn't be much left."

"Then we'll have to destroy all life-forms! If there's no other way of doing it we've got to burn the planet clean. Even if there wouldn't be a thing left but a dead world."

They looked at each other.

"I'm going to call the System Monitor," Commander Morrison said. "I'm going to get the unit off here, out of danger—all that are left, at least. That poor girl by the lake . . ." She shuddered. "After everyone's out of here, we can work out the best way of cleaning up this planet."

"You'll run the risk of carrying one of them back to Terra?"

"Can they imitate us? Can they imitate living creatures? Higher life-forms?"

Hall considered. "Apparently not. They seem to be limited to inorganic objects."

The Commander smiled grimly. "Then we'll go back without any inorganic material."

"But our clothes! They can imitate belts, gloves, boots—"

"We're not taking our clothes. We're going back without anything. And I mean without anything *at all.*"

Hall's lips twitched. "I see." He pondered. "It might work. Can you persuade the personnel to—to leave all their things behind? Everything they own?"

"If it means their lives, I can *order* them to do it."

"Then it might be our one chance of getting away."

The nearest cruiser large enough to remove the remaining members of the unit was just two hours distance away. It was moving Terra-side again.

Commander Morrison looked up from the vidscreen. "They want to know what's wrong here."

"Let me talk." Hall seated himself before the screen. The heavy features and gold braid of a Terran cruiser captain regarded him. "This is Major Lawrence Hall, from the Research Division of this unit."

"Captain Daniel Davis." Captain Davis studied him without expression. "You're having some kind of trouble, Major?"

Hall licked his lips. "I'd rather not explain until we're aboard, if you don't mind."

"Why not?"

"Captain, you're going to think we're crazy enough as it is. We'll discuss everything fully once we're aboard." He hesitated. "We're going to board your ship naked."

The Captain raised an eyebrow. "Naked?"

"That's right."

"I see." Obviously he didn't.

"When will you get here?"

"In about two hours, I'd say."

"It's now 1300 by our schedule. You'll be here by 1500?"

"At approximately that time," the captain agreed.

"We'll be waiting for you. Don't let any of your men out. Open one lock for us. We'll board without any equipment. Just ourselves, nothing else. As soon as we're aboard, remove the ship at once."

Stella Morrison leaned towards the screen. "Captain, would it be possible—for your men to—?"

"We'll land by robot control," he assured her. "None of my men will be on deck. No one will see you."

"Thank you," she murmured.

"Not at all." Captain Davis saluted. "We'll see you in about two hours then, Commander."

"Let's get everyone out on to the field," Commander Morrison said. "They should remove their clothes here, I think, so there won't be any objects on the field to come in contact with the ship."

Hall looked at her face. "Isn't it worth it to save our lives?"

Lieutenant Friendly bit his lips. "I won't do it. I'll stay here."

"You have to come."

"But, Major—"

Hall looked at his watch. "It's 1450. The ship will be here any minute. Get your clothes off and get out on the landing field."

"Can't I take anything at *all*?"

"Nothing. Not even your blaster . . . They'll give us clothes inside the ship. Come on! Your life depends on this. Everyone else is doing it."

Friendly tugged at his shirt reluctantly. "Well, I guess I'm acting silly."

The vidscreen clicked. A robot voice announced shrilly: "Everyone out of the buildings at once! Everyone out of the buildings and on the field without delay! Everyone out of the buildings at once! Everyone—"

"So soon?" Hall ran to the window and lifted the metal blind. "I didn't hear it land."

Parked in the centre of the landing field was a long grey cruiser, its hull pitted and dented from meteoric strikes. It lay motionless. There was no sign of life about it.

A crowd of naked people was already moving hesitantly across the field towards it, blinking in the bright sunlight.

"It's here!" Hall started tearing off his shirt. "Let's go!"

"Wait for me!"

"Then hurry." Hall finished undressing. Both men hurried out into the corridor. Unclothed guards raced past them. They padded down the corridors through the long unit building, to the door. They ran downstairs, out on the field. Warm sunlight beat down on them from the sky overhead. From all the unit buildings, naked men and women were pouring silently towards the ship.

"What a sight!" an officer said. "We'll never be able to live it down."

"But you'll live, at least," another said.

"Lawrence!"

Hall half-turned.

"Please don't look around. Keep on going. I'll walk behind you."

"How does it feel, Stella?" Hall asked.

"Unusual."

"Is it worth it?"

"I suppose so."

"Do you think anyone will believe us?"

"I doubt it," she said. "I'm beginning to wonder myself."

"Anyhow, we'll get back alive."

"I guess so."

Hall looked up at the ramp being lowered from the ship in front of them. The first people were already beginning to scamper up the metal incline, into the ship, through the circular lock.

"Lawrence—"

There was a peculiar tremor in the Commander's voice. "Lawrence, I'm—"

"You're what?"

"I'm scared."

"Scared!" He stopped. "Why?"

"I don't know," she quavered.

People pushed against them from all sides. "Forget it. Carry-over from your early childhood." He put his foot on the bottom of the ramp. "Up we go."

"I want to go back!" There was panic in her voice. "I—"

Hall laughed. "It's too late now, Stella." He mounted the ramp, holding on to the rail. Around him, on all sides, men and women were pushing forward, carrying them up. They came to the lock. "Here we are."

The man ahead of him disappeared.

Hall went inside after him, into the dark interior of the ship, into the silent blackness before him. The Commander followed.

At exactly 1500 Captain Daniel Davis landed his ship in the centre of the field. Relays slid the entrance lock open with a bang. Davis and the other officers of the ship sat waiting in the control cabin, around the big control table.

"Well," Captain Davis said, after a while, "where are they?"

The officers became uneasy. "Maybe something's wrong."
"Maybe the whole damn thing's a joke!"
They waited and waited.
But no one came.

COLONY:
I TRUSTED THE RUG COMPLETELY

This is a science-fiction horror story, and a good one.

Its author, like all the writers in this book, was someone I admired inordinately and studied indefatigably during the years that I was beginning to learn my craft. But Phil Dick, like Bob Sheckley, held a special place for me in that feverish time. Like Sheckley, he was young, he was clever, he was diabolically prolific. He had stories in all the magazines at once, and that was something I dreamed of doing. Here on my desk now is that dog-eared mimeographed pamphlet listing all the science-fiction stories published in 1953: Dick has almost a whole page to himself. A story in the June *Astounding*, one in the September *Amazing*, one in the September *Beyond*, one in the September *Cosmos*, three in *Fantasy & Science Fiction*, two in *Fantastic Universe*, and on and on and on down to the story in the September *Space* and the one in the May *Science Fiction Quarterly*, twenty-eight short stories in all that year. "Colony" was one of them, from the June, 1953, *Galaxy*, one of the six stories he had published that month alone. Damon Knight, speaking of Dick a few years later, called him "that short story writer who . . . has kept popping up all over. . . . Entering and leaving as he does by so many doors at once, Dick creates a blurred impression of pleasant, small literary gifts. . . ."

Time has shown that Knight had underestimated Dick's "pleasant, small literary gifts," and Knight himself soon backed away from that assessment when Dick's first novel appeared. For me, Dick was far more than a minor writer even in 1953. Like Sheckley, like Kuttner (who was, I think, a model for them both), Dick was a deft and subtle short-story writer with a keen sense of form and a fine understanding of the absurdities of the universe. Like them, he was a hardworking professional who began a new project as soon as he had finished the last, and kept his name constantly before the public with a succession of competent, entertaining pieces that, though they might often be light, were anything but trivial. That was the sort of writer I hoped to be.

"Colony" is early Dick. The standard bibliography of his work indicates that it was his twelfth published story, appearing less than a year after his first. Its brisk, functional prose style—short sentences, plenty of dialog, minimal exposition—is a far cry from the flamboyance of Alfred Bester's writing or the richness of C. L. Moore's. But simplicity of approach doesn't necessarily indicate a shortcoming of craft. Some stories—Pohl's "Day Million," say, or Blish's "Common Time"—draw their power as much from the way they are told as from what they convey. "Colony" is not like that. What matters is what happens, period; the writer's job is to depict the action. Dick's style in "Colony" is lucid and effective, a no-frills technique that conveys the mystifying incidents of the story without excessively calling attention to itself. I prefer it, generally, to the dense, involuted manner of Dick's own later period. To see what I mean, compare this passage from "Colony"—

He stopped, his voice choked off—

Choked off, because the two eyepieces of the microscope had twisted suddenly around his windpipe and were trying to strangle him. Hall tore at them, but they dug relentlessly into his throat, steel prongs closing like the claws of a trap.

Throwing the microscope on to the floor, he leaped up. The microscope crawled quickly towards him, hooking around his leg. He kicked it loose with his other foot, and drew his blast pistol.

The microscope scuttled away, rolling on its coarse adjustments. Hall fired. It disappeared in a cloud of metallic particles.

"Good God!" Hall sat down weakly, mopping his face. "What the—?" He massaged his throat. "What the hell!"

—with this one, chosen at random from an early chapter of Dick's famous 1968 novel *Do Androids Dream of Electric Sheep?* later filmed as *Blade Runner.*

Silence. It flashed from the woodwork and the walls; it smote him with an awful, total power, as if generated by a vast mill. It rose from the floor, up out of the tattered gray wall-to-wall carpeting. It unleashed itself from the broken and semi-broken appliances in the kitchen, the dead machines which hadn't worked in all the time Isidore had lived here. From the useless pole lamp in the living room it oozed out, meshing with the empty and wordless descent of itself from the fly-specked ceiling. It managed in fact to emerge from every object within his range of vision, as if it—the silence—meant to supplant all things tangible. Hence it assailed not only his ears but his eyes; as he stood by the inert TV set he experienced the silence as visible and in its own way, alive. Alive! He had often felt its austere approach before; when it came it burst in without subtlety, evidently unable to wait. The silence of the world could not rein back its greed. Not any longer. Not when it had virtually won.

There's a certain Beckettesque power to the second passage, especially in its invocation of the shabby, decaying world in which *Do Androids Dream of Electric Sheep?* is set. But also it is static; it advances neither plot nor character; and eventually it buries the sense of the scene beneath layer upon layer of abstraction and metaphor. Whereas the unpretentious passage from "Colony" renders a grotesque and absurd incident—"the two eyepieces of the microscope had twisted suddenly around his windpipe and were trying to strangle him"—without editorial comment, without the intervention of abstractions, without even any figures of speech other than one highly concrete simile. The clarity of Dick's earlier style is harder to achieve than it looks, and, at least in a short story, more effective than some of the tortuous effects he reached for in his later work.

Nevertheless "Colony" is unmistakably the work of the writer who eventually would give us *The Three Stigmata of Palmer Eldritch, The Man in the High Castle*, and *Ubik*. Even here at the outset of his career the difficulty of distinguishing between the real and the unreal obsessed him, and the precarious and perilous nature of life in a treacherous universe proves the undoing of his unfortunate characters. Kuttner before him had the same obsession, and moments that we would now consider Dickian recur constantly in Kuttner's work. The microscope scene, one of the funniest pseudoparanoid moments in science fiction, surely owes something to the classic narrative hook with which Kuttner began his 1946 novella, *The Fairy Chessmen*: "The doorknob opened a blue eye and looked at him."

"Colony" opens with a characteristically sly Dickian stratagem: reversing the adage that a story ought to begin with someone in trouble, Dick arouses our suspicions (but not those of Major Hall and Lieutenant Friendly) by depicting an utter *absence* of trouble: "What kind of place is this?" Friendly asks. "No disease germs, no lice, no flies, no rats, no—" The whole place is harmless. Could it be the long-lost Garden of Eden? Well, no, it can't. The moment Friendly goes out of the room, Hall's microscope tries to strangle him. Rebuffed, it comes crawling after him like a demented hound. When threatened it scuttles away, rolling on its own coarse adjustments— a deliciously crazy image. We are getting one of the earliest manifestations of the wondrous Dickian paranoia, that darkly comic view of the universe in which things are *never* what they seem. As the story goes along, the reality slippages grow wilder: Hall is attacked by his towel and his belt, Taylor's office rug rolls him up inside itself, Dodds is killed by his own gun, Fulton is mutilated by a doormat. The progression of attacks is carefully calculated. What is at first perplexing and scary quickly becomes lethal. And nothing can be trusted. Unger, getting into what appears to be his automobile, discovers that he is in a stomach and being digested.

During this phase of the story a simple piling up of horrors, however comic and ingenious, would probably not have been sufficient to keep a reasonably sophisticated reader interested; the story would quickly have become comic-book stuff, fashioned as it is out of comic-book situations. Dick provides an additional level of tension and narrative thrust by intercutting his series of bizarre attacks with a second tried-and-true device of this sort of "Terrible Menace" story: the skepticism of the characters who are not under attack. Not only does Hall have to worry about the malevolent intentions of his microscope, he swiftly finds himself required to defend his own sanity to his fellow officers. Are we reading a story about an alien onslaught or one about Major Hall's mental breakdown? For much of the time we aren't sure. Only when Taylor is engulfed by his rug does Commander Morrison begin to reconsider her assessment that Hall is psychotic.

Dick's deadpan narrative method is important in maintaining our belief in the plausibility of what is going on. A clumsier writer would overload the story with expository nudges to make certain that we were properly terrified by the predicament of the characters. ("It was inconceivably ghastly. The bewildered Earthmen looked harried and worn. Reality itself had come loose from its moorings. Now that such harmless objects as belts and towels had shown themselves to be potential killers, anything at all might happen! Nothing could be trusted! Nothing!") But Dick, even as a 24-year-old novice, knew better. The story is made up entirely of action and dialog. All Dick needs to do is have Hall tell Morrison, "We've got to be careful. We've got to watch for duplicates. Apparently *it*, whatever it is, imitates objects it finds." The plight of the characters is implicit in what they do and say. There's no need to spell it out in heavy-handed exposition.

Because Dick appears to take a stance outside the fabric of the story, carefully limiting it to basic this-happened-and-then-he-said-that-and-then-this-happened narrative, he is able to mix farce and horror without unbalancing the tone. The scuttling microscope is a good example. So is the rug that flops off rapidly toward the open door when it is pulled free of Taylor. (And Taylor, when the rug is brought to him, docile again, a little while afterward, says, "My wife gave it to me. I—I trusted it completely." It's an altogether farcical line, but somehow it doesn't puncture the tension of the moment.)

Of course, we're ahead of the characters most of the way. (Calling them "characters" is charitable. All they are is names. We can't tell Hall from Taylor from Dodds, and it doesn't matter. Once again, as so often in science fiction, attempts at real characterization would be distractions. If we really cared about the characters, knew all about their hopes and fears and childhood aspirations and little imperfections of soul and shipboard romances, the effect of the story would be entirely different, painful and harrowing instead of bright and diverting.) Hall and Taylor and Dodds don't know what they're up against for most of the story, but we, once we've decided that Hall isn't crazy, understand that they're under attack by fiendish mimic life-forms from the planet they're exploring. We know that because Dick has given us a cue in the conventional place, with that opening conversation about how harmless the planet is. The fun for us is in seeing the fulfillment of our expectations. Of *course*, something ghastly is bound to happen, and it does, and then something even ghastlier, and we read on, wanting to know what form the next horrible thing will take, and the one after that.

Because we know the conventions of short fiction, we know that the Earthmen will ultimately begin to fight back, and we assume they ultimately will triumph, as Earthmen always do in this sort of thing. So when the counter attack scene arrives on schedule ("I'm going to release this throughout the lab," says Hall, holding up the spray tank of arsenic and hydrogen. "I think there are a lot of them in here, more than anywhere else") we *naturally* get ready for the ingenious denouement and the dramatic defeat of the aliens.

But if we are ahead of the characters, Dick is ahead of *us*. He knows there's no way that a handful of Earthmen can defeat a planet full of creatures with the power of absolute mimicry, certainly not on their home turf—except in the pages of comic books and pulp magazines. So he sets up our expectations and then goes coolly about the task of demolishing them. The use of the arsenic-hydrogen spray leads not to glorious victory for the gallant spacemen but to the funniest Dickian moment of them all:

> At the far end of the lab a slide cabinet wavered suddenly. It oozed, buckling and pitching. It lost its shape completely—a homogeneous jelly-like mass perched on top of the table. Abruptly it flowed down the side of the table on to the floor, wobbling as it went.
>
> "Over there!"
>
> A bunsen burner melted and flowed along beside it. All around the room objects were in motion. A great glass retort folded up into itself and settled down into a blob. A rack of test tubes, a shelf of chemicals . . .

The aliens are everywhere. There's no hope of defeating them. Inglorious retreat is the only sensible answer. And so the story might have ended with the survivors hurrying aboard the rescue ship and looking back in horror and relief at the implacable, menacing planet from which they were just barely able to escape. Even now, though, Dick shows no mercy. A final manic twist—foreshadowed by the scene in which Unger is digested by his car—and the ultimate catastrophe occurs. With enviable subtlety Dick leaves it undescribed. Telling it by implication is a better way; and that is what he does, with a swift, effective ringing down of the curtain in an economical last scene less than a dozen lines long.

There are no profundities in "Colony," no shattering revelations of the human condition, no searching explorations of the far reaches of physics or biochemistry. For profundity and revelations of the human condition we have to go to the books Philip K. Dick wrote two decades later, just before his much too early death in 1982 at the age of 53; for physics or biochemistry we must turn to the stories of Hal Clement or Larry Niven or Poul Anderson. What we have here instead is a beautifully told minor story, both funny and frightening, a model of expert narrative from a great writer at the start of his remarkable career.

THE LITTLE BLACK BAG
C. M. KORNBLUTH

Old Dr. Full felt the winter in his bones as he limped down the alley. It was the alley and the back door he had chosen rather than the sidewalk and the front door because of the brown paper bag under his arm. He knew perfectly well that the flat-faced, stringy-haired women of his street and their gap-toothed, sour-smelling husbands did not notice if he brought a bottle of cheap wine to his room. They all but lived on the stuff themselves, varied with whiskey when pay checks were boosted by overtime. But Dr. Full, unlike them, was ashamed. A complicated disaster occurred as he limped down the littered alley. One of the neighborhood dogs—a mean little black one he knew and hated, with its teeth always bared and always snarling with menace—hurled at his legs through a hole in the board fence that lined his path. Dr. Full flinched, then swung his leg in what was to have been a satisfying kick to the animal's gaunt ribs. But the winter in his bones weighed down the leg. His foot failed to clear a half-buried brick, and he sat down abruptly, cursing. When he smelled unbottled wine and realized his brown paper package had slipped from under his arm and smashed, his curses died on his lips. The snarling black dog was circling him at a yard's distance, tensely stalking, but he ignored it in the greater disaster.

With stiff fingers as he sat on the filth of the alley, Dr. Full unfolded the brown paper bag's top, which had been crimped over, grocer-wise. The early autumnal dusk had come; he could not see plainly what was left. He lifted out the jug-handled top of his half gallon, and some fragments, and then the bottom of the bottle. Dr. Full was far too occupied to exult as he noted that there was a good pint left. He had a problem, and emotions could be deferred until the fitting time.

The dog closed in, its snarl rising in pitch. He set down the bottom of the bottle and pelted the dog with the curved triangular glass fragments of its top. One of them connected, and the dog ducked back through the fence, howling. Dr. Full then placed a razor-like edge of the half-gallon bottle's foundation to his lips and drank from it as though it were a giant's cup. Twice he had to put it down to rest his arms, but in one minute he had swallowed the pint of wine.

He thought of rising to his feet and walking through the alley to his room, but a flood of well-being drowned the notion. It was, after all, inexpressibly pleasant to sit there and feel the frost-hardened mud of the alley turn soft, or seem to, and to feel the winter evaporating from his bones under a warmth which spread from his stomach through his limbs.

A three-year-old girl in a cut-down winter coat squeezed through the same hole in the board fence from which the black dog had sprung its ambush. Gravely she toddled up to Dr. Full and inspected him with her dirty forefinger in her mouth. Dr. Full's happiness had been providentially made complete; he had been supplied with an audience.

"Ah, my dear," he said hoarsely. And then: "Preposserous

accusation. 'If that's what you call evidence,' I should have told them, 'you better stick to your doctoring.' I should have told them: 'I was here before your County Medical Society. And the License Commissioner never proved a thing on me. So, gennulmen, doesn't it stand to reason? I appeal to you as fellow memmers of a great profession—' "

The little girl, bored, moved away, picking up one of the triangular pieces of glass to play with as she left. Dr. Full forgot her immediately, and continued to himself earnestly: "But so help me, they *couldn't* prove a thing. Hasn't a man got any *rights*?" He brooded over the question, of whose answer he was so sure, but on which the Committee on Ethics of the County Medical Society had been equally certain. The winter was creeping into his bones again, and he had no money and no more wine.

Dr. Full pretended to himself that there was a bottle of whiskey somewhere in the fearful litter of his room. It was an old and cruel trick he played on himself when he simply had to be galvanized into getting up and going home. He might freeze there in the alley. In his room he would be bitten by bugs and would cough at the moldy reek from his sink, but he would not freeze and be cheated of the hundreds of bottles of wine that he still might drink, the thousands of hours of glowing content he still might feel. He thought about that bottle of whiskey—was it back of a mounded heap of medical journals? No; he had looked there last time. Was it under the sink, shoved well to the rear, behind the rusty drain? The cruel trick began to play itself out again. Yes, he told himself with mounting excitement, yes, it might be! Your memory isn't so good nowadays, he told himself with rueful good fellowship. You know perfectly well you might have bought a bottle of whiskey and shoved it behind the sink drain for a moment just like this.

The amber bottle, the crisp snap of the sealing as he cut

it, the pleasurable exertion of starting the screw cap on its threads, and then the refreshing tangs in his throat, the warmth in his stomach, the dark, dull happy oblivion of drunkenness—they became real to him. You *could* have, you know! You *could* have! he told himself. With the blessed conviction growing in his mind—It *could* have happened, you know! It *could* have!—he struggled to his right knee. As he did, he heard a yelp behind him, and curiously craned his neck around while resting. It was the little girl, who had cut her hand quite badly on her toy, the piece of glass. Dr. Full could see the rilling bright blood down her coat, pooling at her feet.

He almost felt inclined to defer the image of the amber bottle for her, but not seriously. He knew that it was there, shoved well to the rear under the sink, behind the rusty drain where he had hidden it. He would have a drink and then magnanimously return to help the child. Dr. Full got to his other knee and then his feet, and proceeded at a rapid totter down the littered alley toward his room, where he would hunt with calm optimism at first for the bottle that was not there, then with anxiety, and then with frantic violence. He would hurl books and dishes about before he was done looking for the amber bottle of whiskey, and finally would beat his swollen knuckles against the brick wall until old scars on them opened and his thick old blood oozed over his hands. Last of all, he would sit down somewhere on the floor, whimpering, and would plunge into the abyss of purgative nightmare that was his sleep.

After twenty generations of shilly-shallying and "we'll cross that bridge when we come to it," genus homo had bred himself into an impasse. Dogged biometricians had pointed out with irrefutable logic that mental subnormals were outbreeding mental normals and supernormals, and that the process was occurring on an exponential curve. Every fact that could be mustered in the argument proved the biometricians' case, and led inevitably to the conclusion that genus homo was going to wind up in a preposterous jam quite soon. If you think that had any effect on breeding practices, you do not know genus homo.

There was, of course, a sort of masking effect produced by that other exponential function, the accumulation of technological devices. A moron trained to punch an adding machine seems to be a more skillful computer than a medieval mathematician trained to count on his fingers. A moron trained to operate the twenty-first-century equivalent of a linotype seems to be a better typographer than a Renaissance printer limited to a few fonts of movable type. This is also true of medical practice.

It was a complicated affair of many factors. The supernormals "improved the product" at greater speed than the subnormals degraded it, but in smaller quantity because elaborate training of their children was practiced on a custom-made basis. The fetish of higher education had some weird avatars by the twentieth generation: "colleges" where not a member of the student body could read words of three syllables; "universities" where such degrees as "Bachelor of Typewriting," "Master of Shorthand" and "Doctor of Philosophy (Card Filing)" were conferred with the traditional pomp. The handful of supernormals used such devices in order that the vast majority might keep some semblance of a social order going.

Some day the supernormals would mercilessly cross the bridge; at the twentieth generation they were standing irresolutely at its approaches wondering what had hit them. And the ghosts of twenty generations of biometricians chuckled malignantly.

It is a certain Doctor of Medicine of this twentieth generation that we are concerned with. His name was Hemingway—

John Hemingway, B.Sc., M.D. He was a general practitioner, and did not hold with running to specialists with every tri-fling ailment. He often said as much, in approximately these words: "Now, uh, what I mean is you got a good old G.P. See what I mean? Well, uh, now a good old G.P. don't claim he knows all about lungs and glands and them things, get me? But you got a G.P., you got, uh, you got a, well, you got a . . . *all-around man!* That's what you got when you got a G.P.—you got a all-around man."

But from this, do not imagine that Dr. Hemingway was a poor doctor. He could remove tonsils or appendixes, assist at practically any confinement and deliver a living, uninjured infant, correctly diagnose hundreds of ailments, and pre-scribe and administer the correct medication or treatment for each. There was, in fact, only one thing he could not do in the medical line, and that was violate the ancient canons of medical ethics. And Dr. Hemingway knew better than to try.

Dr. Hemingway and a few friends were chatting one eve-ning when the event occurred that precipitates him into our story. He had been through a hard day at the clinic, and he wished his physicist friend Walter Gillis, B.Sc., M.Sc., Ph.D., would shut up so he could tell everybody about it. But Gillis kept rambling on, in his stilted fashion: "You got to hand it to old Mike; he don't have what we call the scientific method, but you got to hand it to him. There this poor little dope is, puttering around with some glassware and I come up and I ask him, kidding of course, 'How's about a time-travel ma-chine, Mike?' "

Dr. Gillis was not aware of it, but "Mike" had an I.Q. six times his own, and was—to be blunt—his keeper. "Mike" rode herd on the pseudo-physicists in the pseudo-laboratory, in the guise of a bottle washer. It was a social waste—but as has been mentioned before, the supernormals were still standing at the approaches to a bridge. Their irresolution led to many such preposterous situations. And it happens that "Mike," having grown frantically bored with his task, was malevolent enough to—but let Dr. Gillis tell it:

"So he gives me these here tube numbers and says, 'Series circuit. Now stop bothering me. Build your time machine, sit down at it and turn on the switch. That's all I ask, Dr. Gillis—that's all I ask.' "

"Say," marveled a brittle and lovely blond guest, "you remember real good, don't you, Doc?" She gave him a melting smile.

"Heck," said Gillis modestly, "I always remember good. It's what you call an inherent facility. And besides I told it quick to my secretary, so she wrote it down. I don't read so good, but I sure remember good, all right. Now, where was I?"

Everybody thought hard, and there were various suggestions:

"Something about bottles, Doc?"

"You was starting a fight. You said 'time somebody was traveling.' "

"Yeah—you called somebody a swish. Who did you call a swish?"

"Not swish—*switch*."

Dr. Gillis's noble brow grooved with thought, and he declared: "Switch is right. It was about time travel. What we call travel through time. So I took the tube numbers he gave me and I put them into the circuit builder; I set it for 'series' and there it is—my time-traveling machine. It travels things through time real good." He displayed a box.

"What's in the box?" asked the lovely blonde.

Dr. Hemingway told her: "Time travel. It travels things through time."

"Look," said Gillis, the physicist. He took Dr. Hemingway's

little black bag and put it on the box. He turned on the switch and the little black bag vanished.

"Say," said Dr. Hemingway, "that was, uh, swell. Now bring it back."

"Huh?"

"Bring back my little black bag."

"Well," said Dr. Gillis, "they don't come back. I tried it backwards and they don't come back. I guess maybe that dummy Mike give me a bum steer."

There was wholesale condemnation of "Mike" but Dr. Hemingway took no part in it. He was nagged by a vague feeling that there was something he would have to do. He reasoned: "I am a doctor, and a doctor has got to have a little black bag. I ain't got a little black bag—so ain't I a doctor no more?" He decided that this was absurd. He *knew* he was a doctor. So it must be the bag's fault for not being there. It was no good, and he would get another one tomorrow from that dummy Al, at the clinic. Al could find things good, but he was a dummy—never liked to talk sociable to you.

So the next day Dr. Hemingway remembered to get another little black bag from his keeper—another little black bag with which he could perform tonsillectomies, appendectomies, and the most difficult confinements, and with which he could diagnose and cure his kind until the day when the supernormals could bring themselves to cross that bridge. Al was kinda nasty about the missing little black bag, but Dr. Hemingway didn't exactly remember what had happened, so no tracer was sent out, so—

Old Dr. Full awoke from the horrors of the night to the horrors of the day. His gummy eyelashes pulled apart convulsively. He was propped against a corner of his room, and something was making a little drumming noise. He felt very cold and cramped. As his eyes focused on his lower body, he croaked out a laugh. The drumming noise was being made by his left heel, agitated by fine tremors against the bare floor. It was going to be the D.T.'s again, he decided dispassionately. He wiped his mouth with his bloody knuckles, and the fine tremor coarsened; the snare-drum beat became louder and slower. He was getting a break this fine morning, he decided sardonically. You didn't get the horrors until you had been tightened like a violin string, just to the breaking point. He had a reprieve, if a reprieve into his old body with the blazing, endless headache just back of the eyes and the screaming stiffness in the joints were anything to be thankful for.

There was something or other about a kid, he thought vaguely. He was going to doctor some kid. His eyes rested on a little black bag in the center of the room, and he forgot about the kid. "I could have sworn," said Dr. Full, "I hocked that two years ago!" He hitched over and reached the bag, and then realized it was some stranger's kit, arriving here he did not know how. He tentatively touched the lock and it snapped open and lay flat, rows and rows of instruments and medications tucked into loops in its four walls. It seemed vastly larger open than closed. He didn't see how it could possibly fold up into that compact size again, but decided it was some stunt of the instrument makers. Since his time—that made it worth more at the hock shop, he thought with satisfaction.

Just for old times' sake, he let his eyes and fingers rove over the instruments before he snapped the bag and shut and headed for Uncle's. More than a few were a little hard to recognize—exactly that is. You could see the things with blades for cutting, the forceps for holding and pulling, the retractors for holding fast, the needles and gut for suturing, the hypos—a fleeting thought crossed his mind that he could peddle the hypos separately to drug addicts.

Let's go, he decided, and tried to fold up the case. It didn't fold until he happened to touch the lock, and then it folded all at once into a little black bag. Sure have forged ahead, he thought, almost able to forget that what he was primarily interested in was its pawn value.

With a definite objective, it was not too hard for him to get to his feet. He decided to go down the front steps, out the front door, and down the sidewalk. But first—

He snapped the bag open again on his kitchen table, and pored through the medication tubes. "Anything to sock the autonomic nervous system good and hard," he mumbled. The tubes were numbered, and there was a plastic card which seemed to list them. The left margin of the card was a rundown of the systems—vascular, muscular, nervous. He followed the last entry across to the right. There were columns for "stimulant," "depressant," and so on. Under "nervous system" and "depressant" he found the number 17, and shakily located the little glass tube which bore it. It was full of pretty blue pills and he took one.

It was like being struck by a thunderbolt.

Dr. Full had so long lacked any sense of well-being except the brief glow of alcohol that he had forgotten its very nature. He was panic-stricken for a long moment at the sensation that spread through him slowly, finally tingling in his fingertips. He straightened up, his pains gone and his leg tremor stilled.

That was great, he thought. He'd be able to *run* to the hock shop, pawn the little black bag, and get some booze. He started down the stairs. Not even the street, bright with mid-morning sun, into which he emerged made him quail. The little black bag in his left hand had a satisfying, authoritative weight. He was walking erect, he noted, and not in the somewhat furtive crouch that had grown on him in recent years. A little self-respect, he told himself, that's what I need. Just because a man's down doesn't mean—

"Docta, please-a come wit'!" somebody yelled at him, tugging his arm. "Da litt-la girl, she's-a burn' up!" It was one of the slum's innumerable flat-faced, stringy-haired women, in a slovenly wrapper.

"Ah, I happen to be retired from practice—" he began hoarsely, but she would not be put off.

"In by here, Docta!" she urged, tugging him to a doorway. "You come look-a da litt-la girl. I got two dolla, you come look!" That put a different complexion on the matter. He allowed himself to be towed through the doorway into a mussy, cabbage-smelling flat. He knew the woman now, or rather knew who she must be—a new arrival who had moved in the other night. These people moved at night, in motorcades of battered cars supplied by friends and relations, with furniture lashed to the tops, swearing and drinking until the small hours. It explained why she had stopped him: she did not yet know he was old Dr. Full, a drunken reprobate whom nobody would trust. The little black bag had been his guarantee, outweighing his whiskery face and stained black suit.

He was looking down on a three-year-old girl who had, he rather suspected, just been placed in the mathematical center of a freshly changed double bed. God knew what sour and dirty mattress she usually slept on. He seemed to recognize her as he noted a crusted bandage on her right hand. Two dollars, he thought—An ugly flush had spread up her pipe-stem arm. He poked a finger into the socket of her elbow, and felt little spheres like marbles under the skin and ligaments roll apart. The child began to squall thinly; beside him, the woman gasped and began to weep herself.

"Out," he gestured briskly at her, and she thudded away, still sobbing.

Two dollars, he thought—Give her some mumbo jumbo, take the money and tell her to go to a clinic. Strep, I guess, from that stinking alley. It's a wonder any of them grow up.

He put down the little black bag and forgetfully fumbled for his key, then remembered and touched the lock. It flew open, and he selected a bandage shears, with a blunt wafer for the lower jaw. He fitted the lower jaw under the bandage, trying not to hurt the kid by its pressure on the infection, and began to cut. It was amazing how easily and swiftly the shining shears snipped through the crusty rag around the wound. He hardly seemed to be driving the shears with fingers at all. It almost seemed as though the shears were driving his fingers instead as they scissored a clean, light line through the bandage.

Certainly have forged ahead since my time, he thought—sharper than a microtome knife. He replaced the shears in their loop on the extraordinarily big board that the little black bag turned into when it unfolded, and leaned over the wound. He whistled at the ugly gash, and the violent infection which had taken immediate root in the sickly child's thin body. Now what can you do with a thing like that? He pawed over the contents of the little black bag, nervously. If he lanced it and let some of the pus out, the old woman would think he'd done something for her and he'd get the two dollars. But at the clinic they'd want to know who did it and if they got sore enough they might send a cop around. Maybe there was something in the kit—

He ran down the left edge of the card to "lymphatic" and read across to the column under "infection." It didn't sound right at all to him; he checked again, but it still said that. In the square to which the line and column led were the symbols: "IV-g-3cc." He couldn't find any bottles marked with Roman numerals, and then noticed that that was how the hypodermic needles were designated. He lifted number IV from its loop, noting that it was fitted with a needle already and even seemed to be charged. What a way to carry those things around! So—three cc. of whatever was in hypo number

IV ought to do something or other about infections settled in the lymphatic system—which, God knows, this one was. What did the lower-case "g" mean, though? He studied the glass hypo and saw letters engraved on what looked like a rotating disk at the top of the barrel. They ran from "a" to "i," and there was an index line engraved on the barrel on the opposite side from the calibrations.

Shrugging, old Dr. Full turned the disk until "g" coincided with the index line, and lifted the hypo to eye level. As he pressed in the plunger he did not see the tiny thread of fluid squirt from the tip of the needle. There was a sort of dark mist for a moment about the tip. A closer inspection showed that the needle was not even pierced at the tip. It had the usual slanting cut across the bias of the shaft, but the cut did not expose an oval hole. Baffled, he tried pressing the plunger again. Again *something* appeared around the tip and vanished. "We'll settle this," said the doctor. He slipped the needle into the skin of his forearm. He thought at first that he had missed—that the point had glided over the top of his skin instead of catching and slipping under it. But he saw a tiny blood-spot and realized that somehow he just hadn't felt the puncture. Whatever was in the barrel, he decided, couldn't do him any harm, if it lived up to its billing— and if it could come out through a needle that had no hole. He gave himself three cc. and twitched the needle out. There was the swelling—painless, but otherwise typical.

Dr. Full decided it was his eyes or ssomething, and gave three cc. of "g" from hypodermic IV to the feverish child. There was no interruption to her wailing as the needle went in and the swelling rose. But a long instant later, she gave a final gasp and was silent.

Well, he told himself, cold with horror, you did it that time. You killed her with that stuff.

Then the child sat up and said: "Where's my mommy?"

Incredulously, the doctor seized her arm and palpated the elbow. The gland infection was zero, and the temperature seemed normal. The blood-congested tissues surrounding the wound were subsiding as he watched. The child's pulse was stronger and no faster than a child's should be. In the sudden silence of the room he could hear the little girl's mother sobbing in her kitchen, outside. And he also heard a girl's insinuating voice:

"She gonna be O.K., Doc?"

He turned and saw a gaunt-faced, dirty-blond sloven of perhaps eighteen leaning in the doorway and eying him with amused contempt. She continued: "I heard about you, *Doctor* Full. So don't go try and put the bite on the old lady. You couldn't doctor up a sick cat."

"Indeed?" he rumbled. This young person was going to get a lesson she richly deserved. "Perhaps you would care to look at my patient?"

"Where's my mommy?" insisted the little girl, and the blonde's jaw fell. She went to the bed and cautiously asked: "You O.K. now, Teresa? You all fixed up?"

"Where's my mommy?" demanded Teresa. Then, accusingly, she gestured with her wounded hand at the doctor. "You *poke* me!" she complained, and giggled pointlessly.

"Well—" said the blond girl, "I guess I got to hand it to you, Doc. These loud-mouth women around here said you didn't know your . . . I mean, didn't know how to cure people. They said you ain't a real doctor."

"I *have* retired from practice," he said. "But I happened to be taking this case to a colleague as a favor, your good mother noticed me, and—" a deprecating smile. He touched the lock of the case and it folded up into the little black bag again.

"You stole it," the girl said flatly.

He sputtered.

"Nobody'd trust you with a thing like that. It must be worth plenty. You stole that case. I was going to stop you when I come in and saw you working over Teresa, but it looked like you wasn't doing her any harm. But when you give me that line about taking that case to a colleague I know you stole it. You gimme a cut or I go to the cops. A thing like that must be worth twenty-thirty dollars."

The mother came timidly in, her eyes red. But she let out a whoop of joy when she saw the little girl sitting up and babbling to herself, embraced her madly, fell on her knees for a quick prayer, hopped up to kiss the doctor's hand, and then dragged him into the kitchen, all the while rattling in her native language while the blond girl let her eyes go cold with disgust. Dr. Full allowed himself to be towed into the kitchen, but flatly declined a cup of coffee and a plate of anise cakes and St. John's bread.

"Try him on some wine, Ma," said the girl sardonically.

"Hyass! Hyass!" breathed the woman delightedly. "You like-a wine, Docta?" She had a carafe of purplish liquid before him in an instant, and the blond girl snickered as the doctor's hand twitched out at it. He drew his hand back, while there grew in his head the old image of how it would smell and then taste and then warm his stomach and limbs. He made the kind of calculation at which he was practiced; the delighted woman would not notice as he downed two tumblers, and he could overawe her through two tumblers more with his tale of Teresa's narrow brush with the Destroying Angel, and then—why, then it would not matter. He would be drunk.

But for the first time in years, there was a sort of counter-image: a blend of the rage he felt at the blond girl to whom he was so transparent, and of pride at the cure he had just effected. Much to his own surprise, he drew back his hand from the carafe and said, luxuriating in the words: "No, thank you. I don't believe I'd care for any so early in the day." He covertly watched the blond girl's face, and was gratified at her surprise. Then the mother was shyly handing him two bills and saying: "Is no much-a money, Docta—but you come again, see Teresa?"

"I shall be glad to follow the case through," he said. "But now excuse me—I really must be running along." He grasped the little black bag firmly and got up; he wanted very much to get away from the wine and the older girl.

"Wait up, Doc," said she, "I'm going your way." She followed him out and down the street. He ignored her until he felt her hand on the black bag. Then old Dr. Full stopped and tried to reason with her:

"Look, my dear. Perhaps you're right. I might have stolen it. To be perfectly frank, I don't remember how I got it. But you're young and you can earn your own money—"

"Fifty-fifty," she said, "or I go to the cops. And if I get another word outta you, it's sixty-forty. And you know who gets the short end, don't you, Doc?"

Defeated, he marched to the pawnshop, her impudent hand still on the handle with his, and her heels beating out a tattoo against his stately tread.

In the pawnshop, they both got a shock.

"It ain't stendard," said Uncle, unimpressed by the ingenious lock. "I ain't nevva seen one like it. Some cheap Jap stuff, maybe? Try down the street. This I nevva could sell."

Down the street they got an offer of one dollar. The same complaint was made: "I ain't a collecta, mista—I buy stuff that got resale value. Who could I sell this to, a Chinaman who don't know medical instruments? Every one of them looks funny. You sure you didn't make these yourself?" They didn't take the one-dollar offer.

The girl was baffled and angry; the doctor was baffled too, but triumphant. He had two dollars, and the girl had a half-interest in something nobody wanted. But, he suddenly marveled, the thing had been all right to cure the kid, hadn't it?

"Well," he asked her, "do you give up? As you see, the kit is practically valueless."

She was thinking hard. "Don't fly off the handle, Doc. I don't get this but something's going on all right . . . would those guys know good stuff if they saw it?"

"They would. They make a living from it. Wherever this kit came from—"

She seized on that, with a devilish faculty she seemed to have of eliciting answers without asking questions. "I thought so. You don't know either, huh? Well, maybe I can find out for you. C'mon in here. I ain't letting go of that thing. There's money in it—some way, I don't know how, there's money in it." He followed her into a cafeteria and to an almost-empty corner. She was oblivious to stares and snickers from the other customers as she opened the little black bag—it almost covered a cafeteria table—and ferreted through it. She picked out a retractor from a loop, scrutinized it, contemptuously threw it down, picked out a speculum, threw it down, picked out the lower half of an O.B. forceps, turned it over, close to her sharp young eyes—and saw what the doctor's dim old ones could not have seen.

All old Dr. Full knew was that she was peering at the neck of the forceps and then turned white. Very carefully, she placed the half of the forceps back in its loop of cloth and then replaced the retractor and the speculum. "Well?" he asked. "What did you see?"

" 'Made in U.S.A.,' " she quoted hoarsely. " 'Patent Applied for July 2450.' "

He wanted to tell her she must have misread the inscription, that it must be a practical joke, that—

But he knew she had read correctly. Those bandage

shears: they *had* driven his fingers, rather than his fingers driving them. The hypo needle that had no hole. The pretty blue pill that had struck him like a thunderbolt.

"You know what I'm going to do?" asked the girl, with sudden animation. "I'm going to go to charm school. You'll like that, won't ya, Doc? Because we're sure going to be seeing a lot of each other."

Old Dr. Full didn't answer. His hands had been playing idly with that plastic card from the kit on which had been printed the rows and columns that had guided him twice before. The card had a slight convexity; you could snap the convexity back and forth from one side to the other. He noted, in a daze, that with each snap a different text appeared on the cards. *Snap.* "The knife with the blue dot in the handle is for tumors only. Diagnose tumors with your Instrument Seven, the Swelling Tester. Place the Swelling Tester—" *Snap.* "An overdose of the pink pills in Bottle 3 can be fixed with one white pill from Bottle—" *Snap.* "Hold the suture needle by the end without the hole in it. Touch it to one end of the wound you want to close and let go. After it has made the knot, touch it—" *Snap.* "Place the top half of the O.B. forceps near the opening. Let go. After it has entered and conformed to the shape of—" *Snap.*

The slot man saw "FLANNERY 1—MEDICAL" in the upper left corner of the hunk of copy. He automatically scribbled "trim to .75" on it and skimmed it across the horseshoe-shaped copy desk to Piper, who had been handling Edna Flannery's quack-exposé series. She was a nice youngster, he thought, but like all youngsters she overwrote. Hence, the "trim."

Piper dealt back a city hall story to the slot, pinned down Flannery's feature with one hand and began to tap his pencil across it, one tap to a word, at the same steady beat as a teletype carriage traveling across the roller. He wasn't exactly reading it this first time. He was just looking at the letters and words to find out whether, as letters and words, they conformed to *Herald* style. The steady tap of his pencil ceased at intervals as it drew a black line ending with a stylized letter "d" through the word "breast" and scribbled in "chest" instead, or knocked down the capital "E" in "East" to lower case with a diagonal, or closed up a split word—in whose middle Flannery had bumped the space bar of her type-writer—with two curved lines like parentheses rotated through ninety degrees. The thick black pencil zipped a ring around the "30," which, like all youngsters, she put at the end of her stories. He turned back to the first page for the second reading. This time the pencil drew lines with the styl-ized "d's" at the end of them through adjectives and whole phrases, printed big "L's" to mark paragraphs, hooked some of Flannery's own paragraphs together with swooping re-curved lines.

At the bottom of "FLANNERY ADD 2—MEDICAL" the pencil slowed down and stopped. The slot man, sensitive to the rhythm of his beloved copy desk, looked up almost at once. He saw Piper squinting at the story, at a loss. Without wasting words, the copy reader skimmed it back across the Masonite horseshoe to the chief, caught a police story in return and buckled down, his pencil tapping. The slot man read as far as the fourth add, barked at Howard, on the rim: "Sit in for me," and stumped through the clattering city room toward the alcove where the managing editor presided over his own bedlam.

The copy chief waited his turn while the make-up editor, the pressroom foreman, and the chief photographer had words with the M.E. When his turn came, he dropped Flan-nery's copy on his desk and said: "She says this one isn't a quack."

The M.E. read:

"FLANNERY 1—MEDICAL, by Edna Flannery, *Herald* Staff Writer.

"The sordid tale of medical quackery which the *Herald* has exposed in this series of articles undergoes a change of pace today which the reporter found a welcome surprise. Her quest for the facts in the case of today's subject started just the same way that her exposure of one dozen shyster M.D.'s and faith-healing phonies did. But she can report for a change that Dr. Bayard Full is, despite unorthodox practices which have drawn the suspicion of the rightly hypersensitive medical associations, a true healer living up to the highest ideals of his profession.

"Dr. Full's name was given to the *Herald*'s reporter by the ethical committee of a county medical association, which reported that he had been expelled from the association on July 18, 1941, for allegedly 'milking' several patients suffering from trivial complaints. According to sworn statements in the committee's files, Dr. Full had told them they suffered from cancer, and that he had a treatment which would prolong their lives. After his expulsion from the association, Dr. Full dropped out of their sight—until he opened a midtown 'sanitarium' in a brownstone front which had for years served as a rooming house.

"The *Herald*'s reporter went to that sanitarium, on East 89th Street, with the full expectation of having numerous imaginary ailments diagnosed and of being promised a sure cure for a flat sum of money. She expected to find unkempt quarters, dirty instruments, and the mumbo-jumbo paraphernalia of the shyster M.D. which she had seen a dozen times before.

"She was wrong.

"Dr. Full's sanitarium is spotlessly clean, from its tastefully furnished entrance hall to its shining, white treatment rooms. The attractive, blond receptionist who greeted the reporter was soft-spoken and correct, asking only the reporter's name, address, and the general nature of her complaint. This was given, as usual, as 'nagging backache.' The receptionist asked the *Herald*'s reporter to be seated, and a short while later conducted her to a second-floor treatment room and introduced her to Dr. Full.

"Dr. Full's alleged past, as described by the medical society spokesman, is hard to reconcile with his present appearance. He is a clear-eyed, white-haired man in his sixties, to judge by his appearance—a little above middle height and apparently in good physical condition. His voice was firm and friendly, untainted by the ingratiating whine of the shyster M.D. which the reporter has come to know too well.

"The receptionist did not leave the room as he began his examination after a few questions as to the nature and location of the pain. As the reporter lay face down on a treatment table the doctor pressed some instrument to the small of her back. In about one minute he made this astounding statement: 'Young woman, there is no reason for you to have any pain where you say you do. I understand they're saying nowadays that emotional upsets cause pains like that. You'd better go to a psychologist or psychiatrist if the pain keeps up. There is no physical cause for it, so I can do nothing for you.'

"His frankness took the reporter's breath away. Had he guessed she was, so to speak, a spy in his camp? She tried again: 'Well, Doctor, perhaps you'd give me a physical checkup, I feel run down all the time, besides the pains. Maybe I need a tonic.' This is never-failing bait to shyster M.D.'s—an invitation for them to find all sorts of mysterious conditions wrong with a patient, each of which 'requires' an expensive treatment. As explained in the first article of this series, of course, the reporter underwent a thorough physical checkup before she embarked on her quack hunt, and was found to be in one hundred percent perfect condition, with the exception of a 'scarred' area at the bottom tip of her left lung resulting from a childhood attack of tuberculosis and a tendency toward 'hyperthyroidism'—overactivity of the thyroid gland which makes it difficult to put on weight and sometimes causes a slight shortness of breath.

"Dr. Full consented to perform the examination, and took a number of shining, spotlessly clean instruments from loops in a large board literally covered with instruments—most of them unfamiliar to the reporter. The instrument with which he approached first was a tube with a curved dial in its surface and two wires that ended on flat disks growing from its ends. He placed one of the disks on the back of the reporter's right hand and the other on the back of her left. 'Reading the meter,' he called out some number which the attentive receptionist took down on a ruled form. The same procedure was repeated several times, thoroughly covering the reporter's anatomy and thoroughly convincing her that the doctor was a complete quack. The reporter had never seen any such diagnostic procedure practiced during the weeks she put in preparing for this series.

"The doctor then took the ruled sheet from the receptionist, conferred with her in low tones, and said: 'You have a slightly overactive thyroid, young woman. And there's something wrong with your left lung—not seriously, but I'd like to take a closer look.'

"He selected an instrument from the board which, the reporter knew, is called a 'speculum'—a scissorlike device which spreads apart body openings such as the orifice of the ear, the nostril, and so on, so that a doctor can look in during an examination. The instrument was, however, too large to be an aural or nasal speculum but too small to be anything else. As the *Herald*'s reporter was about to ask further questions, the attending receptionist told her: 'It's customary for us to blindfold our patients during lung examinations—do you mind?' The reporter, bewildered, allowed her to tie a spotlessly clean bandage over her eyes, and waited nervously for what would come next.

"She still cannot say exactly what happened while she was blindfolded—but X rays confirm her suspicions. She felt a cold sensation at her ribs on the left side—a cold that seemed to enter inside her body. Then there was a snapping feeling, and the cold sensation was gone. She heard Dr. Full say in a matter-of-fact voice: 'You have an old tubercular scar down there. It isn't doing any particular harm, but an active person like you needs all the oxygen she can get. Lie still and I'll fix it for you.'

"Then there was a repetition of the cold sensation, lasting for a longer time. 'Another batch of alveoli and some more vascular glue,' the *Herald*'s reporter heard Dr. Full say, and the receptionist's crisp response to the order. Then the strange sensation departed and the eye bandage was removed. The reporter saw no scar on her ribs, and yet the doctor assured her: 'That did it. We took out the fibrosis—and a good fibrosis it was, too; it walled off the infection so you're still alive to tell the tale. Then we planted a few clumps of alveoli—they're the little gadgets that get the oxygen from the air you breathe into your blood. I won't monkey with your thyroxin supply. You've got used to being the kind of person you are, and if you suddenly found yourself easygoing and all the rest of it, chances are you'd only be upset. About the backache: just check with the country medical society for the name of a good psychologist or psychiatrist. And look out for quacks; the woods are full of them.'

"The doctor's self-assurance took the reporter's breath away. She asked what the charge would be, and was told to pay the receptionist fifty dollars. As usual, the reporter delayed paying until she got a receipt signed by the doctor himself, detailing the services for which it paid. Unlike most, the doctor cheerfully wrote: 'For removal of fibrosis from left lung and restoration of alveoli,' and signed it.

"The reporter's first move when she left the sanitarium was to head for the chest specialist who had examined her in preparation for this series. A comparison of X rays taken on the day of the 'operation' and those taken previously would, the *Herald*'s reporter then thought, expose Dr. Full as a prince of shyster M.D.'s and quacks.

"The chest specialist made time on his crowded schedule for the reporter, in whose series he has shown a lively interest from the planning stage on. He laughed uproariously in his staid Park Avenue examining room as she described the weird procedure to which she had been subjected. But he did not laugh when he took a chest X ray of the reporter, developed it, dried it, and compared it with the ones he had taken earlier. The chest specialist took six more X rays that afternoon, but he finally admitted that they all told the same story. The *Herald*'s reporter has it on his authority that the scar she had eighteen days ago from her tuberculosis is now gone and has been replaced by healthy lung tissue. He declares that this is a happening unparalleled in medical history. He does not go along with the reporter in her firm conviction that Dr. Full is responsible for the change.

"The *Herald*'s reporter, however, sees no two ways about it. She concludes that Dr. Bayard Full—whatever his alleged past may have been—is now an unorthodox but highly successful practitioner of medicine, to whose hands the reporter would trust herself in any emergency.

"Not so is the case of 'Rev.' Annie Dimsworth—a female harpy who, under the guise of 'faith,' preys on the ignorant and suffering who come to her sordid 'healing parlor' for help and remain to feed 'Rev.' Annie's bank account, which now totals up to $53,238.64. Tomorrow's article will show, with photostats of the bank statements and sworn testimony that—"

The managing editor turned down "FLANNERY LAST ADD—MEDICAL" and tapped his front teeth with a pencil, trying to think straight. He finally told the copy chief: "Kill the story. Run the teaser as a box." He tore off the last paragraph—the "teaser" about "Rev." Annie—and handed it to the desk man, who stumped back to his Masonite horseshoe.

The make-up editor was back, dancing with impatience as he tried to catch the M.E.'s eye. The interphone buzzed with the red light which indicated that the editor and publisher wanted to talk to him. The M.E. thought briefly of a special series on this Dr. Full, decided nobody would believe it and that he probably was a phony anyway. He spiked the story on the "dead" hook and answered his interphone.

Dr. Full had become almost fond of Angie. As his practice had grown to engross the neighborhood illnesses, and then to a corner suite in an uptown taxpayer building, and finally to the sanitarium, she seemed to have grown with it. Oh, he thought, we have our little disputes—

The girl, for instance, was too much interested in money. She had wanted to specialize in cosmetic surgery—removing wrinkles from wealthy old women and whatnot. She didn't realize, at first, that a thing like this was in their trust, that they were the stewards and not the owners of the little black bag and its fabulous contents.

He had tried, ever so cautiously, to analyze them, but without success. All the instruments were slightly radioactive, for instance, but not quite so. They would make a Geiger-Mueller counter indicate, but they would not collapse the leaves of an electroscope. He didn't pretend to be up on the latest developments, but as he understood it, that was just plain *wrong*. Under the highest magnification there were lines on the instruments' superfinished surfaces: incredibly fine lines, engraved in random hatchments which made no particular sense. Their magnetic properties were preposterous. Sometimes the instruments were strongly attracted to magnets, sometimes less so, and sometimes not at all.

Dr. Full had taken X rays in fear and trembling lest he disrupt whatever delicate machinery worked in them. He was *sure* they were not solid, that the handles and perhaps the blades must be mere shells filled with busy little watchworks—but the X rays showed nothing of the sort. Oh, yes— and they were always sterile, and they wouldn't rust. Dust *fell* off them if you shook them: now, that was something he understood. They ionized the dust, or were ionized themselves, or something of the sort. At any rate, he had read of something similar that had to do with phonograph records.

She wouldn't know about that, he proudly thought. She kept the books well enough, and perhaps she gave him a useful prod now and then when he was inclined to settle down. The move from the neighborhood slum to the uptown quarters had been her idea, and so had the sanitarium. Good, good, it enlarged his sphere of usefulness. Let the child have her mink coats and her convertible, as they seemed to be calling roadsters nowadays. He himself was too busy and too old. He had so much to make up for.

Dr. Full thought happily of his Master Plan. She would not like it much, but she would have to see the logic of it. This marvelous thing that had happened to them must be handed on. She was herself no doctor; even though the instruments practically ran themselves, there was more to doctoring than skill. There were the ancient canons of the healing art. And so, having seen the logic of it, Angie would yield; she would assent to his turning over the little black bag to all humanity.

He would probably present it to the College of Surgeons, with as little fuss as possible—well, perhaps a *small* ceremony, and he would like a souvenir of the occasion, a cup or a framed testimonial. It would be a relief to have the thing out of his hands, in a way; let the giants of the healing art decide who was to have its benefits. No, Angie would understand. She was a goodhearted girl.

It was nice that she had been showing so much interest in the surgical side lately—asking about the instruments, reading the instruction card for hours, even practicing on guinea pigs. If something of his love for humanity had been communicated to her, old Dr. Full sentimentally thought, his life would not have been in vain. Surely she would realize that a greater good would be served by surrendering the instruments to wiser hands than theirs, and by throwing aside the cloak of secrecy necessary to work on their small scale.

Dr. Full was in the treatment room that had been the brownstone's front parlor; through the window he saw Angie's yellow convertible roll to a stop before the stoop. He liked the way she looked as she climbed the stairs; neat, not flashy, he thought. A sensible girl like her, she'd understand. There was somebody with her—a fat woman, puffing up the steps, overdressed and petulant. Now, what could she want?

Angie let herself in and went into the treatment room, followed by the fat woman. "Doctor," said the blond girl gravely, "may I present Mrs. Coleman?" Charm school had not taught her everything, but Mrs. Coleman, evidently *nouveau riche*, thought the doctor, did not notice the blunder.

"Miss Aquella told me *so* much about you, Doctor, and your remarkable system!" she gushed.

Before he could answer, Angie smoothly interposed: "Would you excuse us for just a moment, Mrs. Coleman?"

She took the doctor's arm and led him into the reception hall. "Listen," she said swiftly, "I know this goes against your grain, but I couldn't pass it up. I met this old thing in the exercise class at Elizabeth Barton's. Nobody else'll talk to her there. She's a widow. I guess her husband was a black marketeer or something, and she has a pile of dough. I gave her a line about how you had a system of massaging wrinkles out. My idea is, you blindfold her, cut her neck open with the Cutaneous Series knife, shoot some Firmol into the muscles, spoon out some of that blubber with an Adipose Series curette and spray it all with Skintite. When you take the blindfold off she's got rid of a wrinkle and doesn't know what happened. She'll pay five hundred dollars. Now, don't say no, Doc. Just this once, let's do it my way, can't you? I've been working on this deal all along too, haven't I?"

"Oh," said the doctor, "very well." He was going to have to tell her about the Master Plan before long anyway. He would let her have it her way this time.

Back in the treatment room, Mrs. Coleman had been thinking things over. She told the doctor sternly as he entered: "Of course, your system is permanent, isn't it?"

"It is, madam," he said shortly. "Would you please lie down there? Miss Aquella, get a sterile three-inch bandage for Mrs. Coleman's eyes." He turned his back on the fat woman to avoid conversation, and pretended to be adjusting the lights. Angie blindfolded the woman, and the doctor selected the instruments he would need. He handed the blond girl a pair of retractors, and told her: "Just slip the corners of the blades in as I cut—" She gave him an alarmed look, and gestured at the reclining woman. He lowered his voice: "Very well. Slip in the corners and rock them along the incision. I'll tell you when to pull them out."

Dr. Full held the Cutaneous Series knife to his eyes as he adjusted the little slide for three centimeters depth. He sighed a little as he recalled that its last use had been in the extirpation of an "inoperable" tumor of the throat.

"Very well," he said, bending over the woman. He tried a tentative pass through her tissues. The blade dipped in and flowed through them, like a finger through quicksilver, with no wound left in the wake. Only the retractors could hold the edges of the incision apart.

Mrs. Coleman stirred and jabbered: "Doctor, that felt so peculiar! Are you sure you're rubbing the right way?"

"Quite sure, madam," said the doctor wearily. "Would you please try not to talk during the massage?"

He nodded at Angie, who stood ready with the retractors. The blade sank in to its three centimeters, miraculously cutting only the dead horny tissues of the epidermis and the live tissue of the dermis, pushing aside mysteriously all major and minor blood vessels and muscular tissue, declining to affect any system or organ except the one it was—tuned to, could you say? The doctor didn't know the answer, but he felt tired and bitter at this prostitution. Angie slipped in the retractor blades and rocked them as he withdrew the knife, then pulled to separate the lips of the incision. It bloodlessly exposed an unhealthy string of muscle, sagging in a dead-looking loop from blue-gray ligaments. The doctor took a hypo. Number IX, pre-set to "g," and raised it to his eye level. The mist came and went; there probably was no possibility of an embolus with one of these gadgets, but why take chances? He shot one cc. of "g"—identified as "Firmol" by the card—into the muscle. He and Angie watched as it tightened up against the pharynx.

He took the Adipose Series curette, a small one, and spooned out yellowish tissue, dropping it into the incinerator box, and then nodded to Angie. She eased out the retractors and the gaping incision slipped together into unbroken skin, sagging now. The doctor had the atomizer—dialed to "Skin-tite"—ready. He sprayed, and the skin shrank up into the new firm throat line.

As he replaced the instruments, Angie removed Mrs. Coleman's bandage and gaily announced: "We're finished! And there's a mirror in the reception hall—"

Mrs. Coleman didn't need to be invited twice. With incredulous fingers she felt her chin, and then dashed for the hall. The doctor grimaced as he heard her yelp of delight, and Angie turned to him with a tight smile. "I'll get the money and get her out," she said. "You won't have to be bothered with her any more."

He was grateful for that much.

She followed Mrs. Coleman into the reception hall, and the doctor dreamed over the case of instruments. A ceremony, certainly—he was *entitled* to one. Not everybody, he thought, would turn such a sure source of money over to the good of humanity. But you reached an age when money mattered less, and when you thought of these things you had done that *might* be open to misunderstanding if, just if, there chanced to be any of that, well, that judgment business. The doctor wasn't a religious man, but you certainly found yourself thinking hard about some things when your time drew near—

Angie was back, with a bit of paper in her hands. "Five hundred dollars," she said matter-of-factly. "And you realize, don't you, that we could go over her an inch at a time—at five hundred dollars an inch?"

"I've been meaning to talk to you about that," he said.

There was bright fear in her eyes, he thought—but why?

"Angie, you've been a good girl and an understanding girl, but we can't keep this up forever, you know."

"Let's talk about it some other time," she said flatly. "I'm tired now."

"No—I really feel we've gone far enough on our own. The instruments—"

"Don't say it, Doc!" she hissed. "Don't say it, or you'll be sorry!" In her face there was a look that reminded him of the hollow-eyed, gaunt-faced, dirty-blond creature she had been. From under the charm-school finish there burned the guttersnipe whose infancy had been spent on a sour and filthy mattress, whose childhood had been play in the littered alley, and whose adolescence had been the sweatshops and the aimless gatherings at night under the glaring street lamps.

He shook his head to dispel the puzzling notion. "It's this way," he patiently began. "I told you about the family that invented the O.B. forceps and kept them a secret for so many generations, how they could have given them to the world but didn't?"

"They knew what they were doing," said the guttersnipe flatly.

"Well, that's neither here nor there," said the doctor, irritated. "My mind is made up about it. I'm going to turn the instruments over to the College of Surgeons. We have enough money to be comfortable. You can even have the house. I've been thinking of going to a warmer climate, myself." He felt peeved with her for making the unpleasant scene. He was unprepared for what happened next.

Angie snatched the little black bag and dashed for the door, with panic in her eyes. He scrambled after her, catching her arm, twisting it in a sudden rage. She clawed at his face with her free hand, babbling curses. Somehow, somebody's finger touched the little black bag, and it opened grotesquely into the enormous board, covered with shining instruments, large and small. Half a dozen of them joggled loose and fell to the floor.

"*Now* see what you've done!" roared the doctor, unreasonably. Her hand was still viselike on the handle, but she was standing still, trembling with choked-up rage. The doctor bent stiffly to pick up the fallen instruments. Unreasonable girl! he thought bitterly. Making a scene—

Pain drove in between his shoulderblades and he fell face down. The light ebbed. "Unreasonable girl!" he tried to croak. And then: "They'll know I tried, anyway—"

Angie looked down on his prone body, with the handle of the Number Six Cautery Series knife protruding from it. "—will cut through all tissues. Use for amputations before you spread on the Re-Gro. Extreme caution should be used in the vicinity of vital organs and major blood vessels or nerve trunks—"

"I didn't mean to do that," said Angie, dully, cold with horror. Now the detective would come, the implacable detective who would reconstruct the crime from the dust in the room. She would run and turn and twist, but the detective would find her out and she would be tried in a courtroom before a judge and jury; the lawyer would make speeches, but the jury would convict her anyway, and the headlines would scream: "BLOND KILLER GUILTY!" and she'd maybe get the chair, walking down a plain corridor where a beam of sunlight struck through the dusty air, with an iron door at the end of it. Her mink, her convertible, her dresses, the handsome man she was going to meet and marry—

The mist of cinematic clichés cleared, and she knew what she would do next. Quite steadily, she picked the incinerator box from its loop in the board—a metal cube with a different-textured spot on one side. "—to dispose of fibroses or other unwanted matter, simply touch the disk—" You dropped something in and touched the disk. There was a sort of soundless whistle, very powerful and unpleasant if you were too close, and a sort of lightless flash. When you opened the box again, the contents were gone. Angie took another of the Cautery Series knives and went grimly to work. Good thing there wasn't any blood to speak of—She finished the awful task in three hours.

She slept heavily that night, totally exhausted by the

wringing emotional demands of the slaying and the subsequent horror. But in the morning, it was as though the doctor had never been there. She ate breakfast, dressed with unusual care—and then undid the unusual care. Nothing out of the ordinary, she told herself. Don't do one thing different from the way you would have done it before. After a day or two, you can phone the cops. Say he walked out spoiling for a drunk, and you're worried. But don't rush it, baby—*don't rush it.*

Mrs. Coleman was due at 10:00 A.M. Angie had counted on being able to talk the doctor into at least one more five-hundred-dollar session. She'd have to do it herself now—but she'd have to start sooner or later.

The woman arrived early. Angie explained smoothly: "The doctor asked me to take care of the massage today. Now that he has the tissue-firming process beginning, it only requires somebody trained in his methods—" As she spoke, her eyes swiveled to the instrument case—open! She cursed herself for the single flaw as the woman followed her gaze and recoiled.

"What are those things!" she demanded. "Are you going to cut me with them? I *thought* there was something fishy—"

"Please, Mrs. Coleman," said Angie, "please, *dear* Mrs. Coleman—you don't understand about the . . . the massage instruments!"

"Massage instruments, my foot!" squabbled the woman shrilly. "That doctor *operated* on me. Why, he might have killed me!"

Angie wordlessly took one of the smaller Cutaneous Series knives and passed it through her forearm. The blade flowed like a finger through quick-silver, leaving no wound in its wake. *That* should convince the old cow!

It didn't convince her, but it did startle her. "What did you do with it? The blade folds up into the handle—that's it!"

"Now look closely, Mrs. Coleman," said Angie, thinking desperately of the five hundred dollars. "Look very closely and you'll see that the, uh, the sub-skin massager simply slips beneath the tissues without doing any harm, tightening and firming the muscles themselves instead of having to work through layers of skin and adipose tissue. It's the secret of the doctor's method. Now, how can outside massage have the effect that we got last night?"

Mrs. Coleman was beginning to calm down. "It *did* work, all right," she admitted, stroking the new line of her neck. But your arm's one thing and my neck's another! Let me see you do that with your neck!"

Angie smiled—

Al returned to the clinic after an excellent lunch that had almost reconciled him to three more months he would have to spend on duty. And then, he thought, and then a blessed year at the blessedly super-normal South Pole working on his specialty—which happened to be telekinesis exercises for ages three to six. Meanwhile, of course, the world had to go on and of course he had to shoulder his share in the running of it.

Before settling down to desk work he gave a routine glance at the bag board. What he saw made him stiffen with shocked surprise. A red light was on next to one of the numbers—the first since he couldn't think when. He read off the number and murmured "O.K., 674, 101. That fixes *you*." He put the number on a card sorter and in a moment the record was in his hand. Oh, yes—Hemingway's bag. The big dummy didn't remember how or where he had lost it; none of them ever did. There were hundreds of them floating around.

Al's policy in such cases was to leave the bag turned on.

The things practically ran themselves, it was practically impossible to do harm with them, so whoever found a lost one might as well be allowed to use it. You turn it off, you have a social loss—you leave it on, it may do some good. As he understood it, and not very well at that, the stuff wasn't "used up." A temporalist had tried to explain it to him with little success that the prototypes in the transmitter *had been transducted* through a series of point events of transfinite cardinality. Al had innocently asked whether that meant prototypes had been stretched, so to speak, through all time, and the temporalist had thought he was joking and left in a huff.

"Like to see him do this," thought Al darkly, as he telekinized himself to the combox, after a cautious look to see that there were no medics around. To the box he said: "Police chief," and then to the police chief: "There's been a homicide committed with Medical Instrument Kit 674, 101. It was lost some months ago by one of my people, Dr. John Hemingway. He didn't have a clear account of the circumstances."

The police chief groaned and said: "I'll call him in and question him." He was to be astonished by the answers, and was to learn that the homicide was well out of his jurisdiction.

Al stood for a moment at the bag board by the glowing red light that had been sparked into life by a departing vital force giving, as its last act, the warning that Kit 674, 101 was in homicidal hands. With a sigh, Al pulled the plug and the light went out.

"Yah," jeered the woman. "You'd fool around with my neck, but you wouldn't risk your own with that thing!"

Angie smiled with serene confidence a smile that was to shock hardened morgue attendants. She set the Cutaneous Series knife to three centimeters before drawing it across her neck. Smiling, knowing the blade would cut only the dead horny tissue of the epidermis and the live tissue of the dermis, mysteriously push aside all major and minor blood vessels and muscular tissue—

Smiling, the knife plunging in and its microtomesharp metal shearing through major and minor blood vessels and muscular tissue and pharynx, Angie cut her throat.

In the few minutes it took the police, summoned by the shrieking Mrs. Coleman, to arrive, the instruments had become crusted with rust, and the flasks which had held vascular glue and clumps of pink, rubbery alveoli and spare gray cells and coils of receptor nerves held only black slime, and from them when opened gushed the foul gases of decomposition.

THE LITTLE BLACK BAG:
PRESS BUTTON FOR TRIPLE BYPASS

I first met Cyril Kornbluth at a New York science-fiction convention in 1954, when I was a teenager with one or two story sales to my credit and he was a famous science-fiction writer whose work, nearly all of it first rate, had been appearing regularly in the magazines for thirteen years—which is to say, since just about the time I had learned how to read. We had a long conversation at that first meeting about the difficulty of persuading editors to publish stories that have unhappy endings. (He cited his "With These Hands," from a 1951 issue of *Galaxy*, the harshness of which had been drastically softened at the request of *Galaxy* editor Horace Gold.) Though I was a boy and he was a man of middle years—solemn and portly at that, in a suit and a tie—he spoke to me as if we were equals. I looked upon him with some reverence, as well I should have, considering the quality of the stories he had published.

We were never exactly friends, but we met on a number of

occasions over the next few years—the years in which my career was getting started. He treated me in the same courteous way each time, as though there might actually be something interesting about this hotshot kid from Brooklyn who was writing two stories a day. (Perhaps I reminded him of his own precocious self, publishing stories by the dozens when he was in his teens, although I knew from my reading of old magazines that the work he had done at the outset of his career had been far superior to my own.) Then one winter day in 1958 came the startling word of his death—of a heart attack, after shoveling snow in front of his suburban home and running to catch a train. The newspaper account the following day gave his age as 34. I found that hard to believe. He had been writing nearly twenty years. He had the look and the manner of a man in his middle forties. He had published a dozen novels (among them the superb collaboration with Frederik Pohl, *The Space Merchants*) and perhaps fifty short stories—with time out for World War II and a career in wire-service journalism. That meant he had been hardly past 30 when we had met at that convention and that such memorable early stories as "The Words of Guru" and "Thirteen O'Clock" had been written when he was about seventeen.

(Kornbluth's death, coming only a few weeks after that of Henry Kuttner, shook me deeply. Here were two of the best and most prolific of science-fiction writers dying young of heart attacks—one at 44, one at 34—and here was I, pounding the typewriter daily with manic zeal, perhaps heading down the same grim path. For weeks thereafter I found myself imagining palpitations and chest pains after putting in my daily stint. I was just being silly, of course, and here I am, nearly thirty years and millions of words later, still battering the keyboard. The early deaths of Kuttner and Kornbluth, I came to learn long ago, stemmed from causes other than their high output of science fiction.)

Thinking of Kornbluth, as I still do from time to time, I find myself amazed even now that he was able to accomplish so much in so short a time. Perhaps he looked so much older than his actual age because he had packed a lifetime and a half into the few decades he was allowed to have. I see him now as I remember him from the 1950s: a man much my senior, somber and reserved, a master of the mysteries of the art of writing. To me Cyril Kornbluth was someone who had never been young. The irony of his life is that in fact he was someone who would never be old. Or even middle-aged.

Kornbluth was probably about 26 when he wrote "The Little Black Bag," which was first published in the July, 1950, issue of *Astounding Science Fiction.* Like most of his short stories it springs from a bleak, profoundly pessimistic view of human existence and the future of mankind. (The novels were a little less dark, perhaps because book publishers were able to impose their preferences.) Throughout his short life he saw with total clarity the corruption, folly, and stupidity of his fellow mortals. It both amused and angered him. He used the anger to fuel the engine that produced his graceful, witty, sardonic stories, but I think that in the end it must have gained the upper hand with him, and that that—as much as the heart ailment that darkened his later years and the financial struggles of his professional life—is what took him from the world so soon.

The underlying idea of "The Little Black Bag" is one that he would use again the following year, more explicitly, in his well-known story "The Marching Morons": that the modern tendency for family size to vary in inverse proportion to the intelligence of the parents would, in time, flood the world with a vast population of low-IQ humans barely able to comprehend the complexities of the society they lived in. He saw a future in which, after ten or twenty generations of this sort of selective breeding for dull-wittedness, a tiny elite caste of intelligent people would find themselves surrounded by a vast horde of dopes. To keep the world running at all, it would become necessary for the intelligent few to devise technologies that had ultra-simple operating systems which would lie within the capacities of the blockhead majority. Kornbluth felt that the dumbing-down process was well under way in his own time— symbolized by the advent of commercial television as the prime medium of public entertainment, and the concurrent rise to power of the great advertising agencies—but that it would accelerate in the decades ahead as an increasingly self-absorbed intelligentsia left the task of raising families to the working classes.

By the year 2450, he tells us bluntly in "The Little Black Bag," intelligent human beings would be in such short supply that even physicians and physicists would have to be drawn from the ranks of the *lumpenproletariat*. Of course, a moronic doctor would be a danger to his patients; and so he would have to be supplied with medical instruments that would do most of the thinking for him. The "little black bag" of the story is Kornbluth's brilliantly inventive solution to the problem: a portable kit of self-governing devices with which almost any dimwit could perform miracles beyond the comprehension of twentieth-century medicine.

The story is constructed in a precise and economical way to demonstrate Kornbluth's bitter, sardonic premise. The opening scene introduces us to Dr. Full, defeated and fallen (both literally and figuratively). He is the apparent protagonist, though his death three-quarters of the way through the story will force us to rethink that belief. We are placed right in Dr. Full's consciousness: we feel the pain of his limp and the sting of the winter wind, we sense the warmth that the wine brings, we see through his eyes the bright blood running from the little girl's cut, we think about the bottle of whiskey hidden behind the sink's rusty drain, we wince as he beats his swollen knuckles against the rough brick wall. There is no science-fiction hook: for a thousand words or so what we have is a mainstream story about a disreputable drunken doctor, something out of an old *Saturday Evening Post*.

But the second scene takes care of that. Kornbluth switches abruptly from Dr. Full's viewpoint to that of the omniscient author and states his marching-moron theme in four paragraphs of blunt exposition. Always the crafty technician, Kornbluth chooses this mock-historical mode because he needs to make clear to us *why* Dr. Hemingway and Dr. Gillis are the hapless dopes they are. Simply showing them being dopey would leave us puzzled and confused: how did such lamebrains, we would wonder, get to be doctors and physicists? Kornbluth might have resorted to the clumsy device of having a couple of members of the intellectual-elite ruling class of the future discussing the sad decline of the human race with each other; but why would they talk about something so familiar? (It would be like explaining Election Day to an audience of Martians by having one polling-place official say to another, "Well, so today we continue our 200-year-old custom of choosing our head of state by a vote of the people.") There are times when straightforward exposition gets the job done faster and less foolishly. This is one of them.

Carefully, Kornbluth stays outside the viewpoint of his future-world characters even as he brings them on stage. They are only spear-carriers; he doesn't want to confuse things by making them seem like major protagonists. So he distances us from them by aiming his exposition straight at us in a quaintly old-fashioned way: "Do not imagine that Dr. Hemingway was a poor doctor," he warns us, and a few sentences later he sounds like any Victorian novelist as he says, "Dr. Hemingway and a few friends were chatting one evening when the event occurred that precipitates him into our story." But the reader, too, is precipitated into the story at that point, and Kornbluth now can pull back, letting the omniscient viewpoint disappear and sliding by almost imperceptible stages into the dim Dr. Hemingway's viewpoint, until by the end of the scene Dr. Hemingway's conscious-ness has pervaded the tone of the narrative exposition itself, and it becomes something that is almost but not quite an interior monolog. ("Al was kinda nasty about the missing little bag, but Dr. Hemingway didn't exactly remember what happened, so no tracer was sent out, so—") And then it is time to return to the twentieth century and Dr. Full.

A quick jump cut and we are back in the old doctor's conscious-ness, feeling the cold air and the hangover and his gummy eyelids opening and the tremor in his left leg. But now he has the little black bag from the future. He doesn't know what it is, but we do, and when he peers inside we become tremendously curious. What wonders does it contain? What will happen when this old drunk begins exploiting the little black bag? Almost at once Kornbluth artfully tosses us the possibility that we will be frustrated: the doctor is thinking of pawning the bag to buy liquor. No, we shout. We don't want him to do that. Kornbluth has deeply involved us in the story, just like that, by the simple device of promising us an interesting situation that he threatens a moment later to take away. We have already begun to write the story for ourselves—the roguish doctor and the little black bag of miracles—and Kornbluth's momentary indication of diverging onto some other narrative path arouses the anxiety in us that is one mark of effective storytelling. We are hooked; we want to know what happens next; we don't want the story jumping off in another direction.

Nor does it, though it constantly threatens to. The doctor puts the bag to use and it is just as wonderful as we thought it would be. The little girl's severe infection is instantly healed. The reader, writing his own story alongside the one he is reading, jumps ahead to the next twist: the doctor, fuddled by wine as he is, will grasp the redemptive possibilities of the wondrous black bag and somehow will regain his place in society. Well, yes, that would certainly be heartwarming. But Kornbluth no sooner invites us to conjure up that possibility than he starts to take it away. The older sister, Angie, enters. She has seen the cure. She knows Dr. Full is worthless and the bag has to be stolen, and she will let the police know about it. Suspense, here: a threat to the redemption of Dr. Full that we have begun to anticipate. And a threat to our seeing what else is in that bag. The bag is a fascinating talisman, a true magic box offering us fairy-tale delights skillfully cloaked in hard-edged medical-technology terms. Like all magic boxes it must be jealously guarded. We worry about it as though it is our own. The threat that the sister represents, perversely, pushes the doctor a step toward that very redemption that we hope for him: offered a drink by the girl's mother, he reaches for it and pulls back. He knows he's in a risky situation; he needs to stay sober and protect himself. Anger and fear have begun to heal him.

But the story refuses to become the slick confection we keep imagining. Dr. Full turns down the drink, yes. But he *still* wants to pawn the bag. His next bottle of booze matters more to him than whatever miraculous powers the bag might impart to him. So we are back to our original uneasiness: will Kornbluth deprive us of seeing what else the bag can do? And the sister remains menacing too: she will let him pawn the bag, but she wants half the proceeds. Our sympathies for Dr. Full having been aroused, we are outraged by this, and it is with great relief that we see, a moment later, that the bag is unpawnable. Back and forth, up and down—in a series of beautifully constructed situations, Kornbluth jockeys our emotions around and around, involving us more deeply in his story with every turn. And all of this takes only two or three pages.

Time now to return to the fabulous powers of the bag. We are at the midway point. Dr. Full at last comes to see that the bag is an inexplicable gift from the future. No need to show the doctor reacting with astonishment or disbelief. Of *course*, he's astonished—wouldn't you be?—and disbelief is irrelevant; the thing has already been seen to work. Instead, Kornbluth makes another jump-cut then, and a big one: he skips over the entire business of Full's rehabilitation and return to medical practice, and shows us—via a newspaper article, and a lot of sharply realized journalistic background detail taken straight from his own professional experience, I imagine—Dr. Full at work using the bag. There are aspects of the scene I don't particularly like, notably the implausible prose of Edna Flannery's account of Dr. Full's sanitarium, but it does serve the purpose of taking us through the passage of a great deal of time and many changes for Dr. Full without a lot of plodding detail. When we see Dr. Full again, he is a successful physician once more. More or less a quack, of course— the methods he uses are hardly those of conventional twentieth-century medicine—but one who does do for his patients what he says he will do; and we are allowed to know that he plans to turn the little black bag over to the College of Surgeons for the good of all humanity before much longer.

Which, however, his cold-blooded and unscrupulous young partner Angie will not permit him to do. Suddenly—unexpectedly—she kills him. This is not a story about the redemption of Dr. Full at all. It's a story about the little black bag, which now passes into the hands of someone even more disreputable than the old doctor himself. Will Angie, the girl from the gutter with no medical training at all, be able to set up a lucrative clinical practice using the miraculous bag? That's the intended function of the bag, after all—to make medicine so easy that anyone, no matter how ignorant, can practice it. The story might have ended with that easy irony: fading out on Angie in her well-appointed office, working her way through a full day of patients.

But Kornbluth has harsher ironies in mind. The little black bag is a disruptive force in the stream of time. Its accidental journey, though it has helped to pull Dr. Full out of his alcoholic haze, has not only invoked greed and envy but poses the risk of letting loose the powerful and perhaps destructive forces of anachronism, if these twenty-fifth-century devices remain at large in the twentieth century. And now they have caused a murder. The murder sends a signal to the future. Lost medical bags are nothing unusual up there, but this one has fallen into homicidal hands. The supervisor pulls the plug. The bag, wherever it may be, will be deactivated. Kornbluth now makes clever use of the old fictional device known in the trade as the "biter-bit ending": the villainous Angie meets a grisly but altogether appropriate fate while she is in the process of exploiting the little black bag. At the end we are compelled to contemplate two equally dismal views of the world: the grim, gritty jungle that is 1950, with its seedy alcoholics, venal slum-dwellers, and shallow hypochondriacs, and the dismal utopia of 2450, where a weary elite of super-men strive to keep a vast population of morons from injuring themselves. The bag is full of miracles, yes. But the offhand plug-pulling gesture that breaks the link between future and past—and costs Angie her life—is Cyril Kornbluth's verdict on the extraordinary but flawed species that invented it. And we are left with his final despairing image: rusted instruments and flasks of black slime and the foul gases of decomposition where once there had been marvels beyond the imagining of Scheherazade.

LIGHT OF OTHER DAYS
BOB SHAW

L eaving the village behind, we followed the heady sweeps of the road up into a land of slow glass.

I had never seen one of the farms before and at first found them slightly eerie—an effect heightened by imagination and circumstance. The car's turbine was pulling smoothly and quietly in the damp air so that we seemed to be carried over the convolutions of the road in a kind of supernatural silence. On our right the mountain sifted down into an incredibly perfect valley of timeless pine, and everywhere stood the great frames of slow glass, drinking light. An occasional flash of afternoon sunlight on their wind bracing created an illusion of movement, but in fact the frames were deserted. The rows of windows had been standing on the hillside for years, staring into the valley, and men only cleaned them in the middle of the night when their human presence would not matter to the thirsty glass.

They were fascinating, but Selina and I didn't mention the windows. I think we hated each other so much we both were reluctant to sully anything new by drawing it into the nexus of our emotions. The holiday, I had begun to realize, was a stupid idea in the first place. I had thought it would cure everything, but, of course, it didn't stop Selina being pregnant and, worse still, it didn't even stop her being angry about being pregnant.

Rationalizing our dismay over her condition, we had circulated the usual statements to the effect that we would have *liked* having children—but later on, at the proper time. Selina's pregnancy had cost us her well-paid job and with it the new house we had been negotiating and which was far beyond the reach of my income from poetry. But the real source of our annoyance was that we were face to face with the realization that people who say they want children later always mean they want children never. Our nerves were thrumming with the knowledge that we, who had thought ourselves so unique, had fallen into the same biological trap as every mindless rutting creature which ever existed.

The road took us along the southern slopes of Ben Cruachan until we began to catch glimpses of the gray Atlantic far ahead. I had just cut our speed to absorb the view better when I noticed the sign spiked to a gatepost. It said: "SLOW GLASS—Quality High, Prices Low—J. R. Hagan." On an impulse I stopped the car on the verge, wincing slightly as tough grasses whipped noisily at the bodywork.

"Why have we stopped?" Selina's neat, smoke-silver head turned in surprise.

"Look at that sign. Let's go up and see what there is. The stuff might be reasonably priced out here."

Selina's voice was pitched high with scorn as she refused, but I was too taken with my idea to listen. I had an illogical conviction that doing something extravagant and crazy would set us right again.

"Come on," I said, "the exercise might do us some good. We've been driving too long anyway."

She shrugged in a way that hurt me and got out of the

car. We walked up a path made of irregular, packed clay steps nosed with short lengths of sapling. The path curved through trees which clothed the edge of the hill and at its end we found a low farmhouse. Beyond the little stone building tall frames of slow glass gazed out towards the voice-stilling sight of Cruachan's ponderous descent towards the waters of Loch Linnhe. Most of the panes were perfectly transparent but a few were dark, like panels of polished ebony.

As we approached the house through a neat cobbled yard a tall middle-aged man in ash-colored tweeds arose and waved to us. He had been sitting on the low rubble wall which bounded the yard, smoking a pipe and staring towards the house. At the front window of the cottage a young woman in a tangerine dress stood with a small boy in her arms, but she turned disinterestedly and moved out of sight as we drew near.

"Mr. Hagan?" I guessed.

"Correct. Come to see some glass, have you? Well, you've come to the right place." Hagan spoke crisply, with traces of the pure highland which sounds so much like Irish to the unaccustomed ear. He had one of those calmly dismayed faces one finds on elderly road-menders and philosophers.

"Yes," I said. "We're on holiday. We saw your sign."

Selina, who usually has a natural fluency with strangers, said nothing. She was looking towards the now empty window with what I thought was a slightly puzzled expression.

"Up from London, are you? Well, as I said, you've come to the right place—and at the right time, too. My wife and I don't see many people this early in the season."

I laughed. "Does that mean we might be able to buy a little glass without mortgaging our home?"

"Look at that now," Hagan said, smiling helplessly. "I've thrown away any advantage I might have had in the trans-action. Rose, that's my wife, says I never learn. Still, let's sit down and talk it over." He pointed at the rubble wall then glanced doubtfully at Selina's immaculate blue skirt. "Wait till I fetch a rug from the house." Hagan limped quickly into the cottage, closing the door behind him.

"Perhaps it wasn't such a marvelous idea to come up here," I whispered to Selina, "but you might at least be pleasant to the man. I think I can smell a bargain."

"Some hope," she said with deliberate coarseness. "Surely even you must have noticed that ancient dress his wife is wearing? He won't give much away to strangers."

"Was that his wife?"

"Of course that was his wife."

"Well, well," I said, surprised. "Anyway, try to be civil with him. I don't want to be embarrassed."

Selina snorted, but she smiled whitely when Hagan reappeared and I relaxed a little. Strange how a man can love a woman and yet at the same time pray for her to fall under a train.

Hagan spread a tartan blanket on the wall and we sat down, feeling slightly self-conscious at having been translated from our city-oriented lives into a rural tableau. On the distant slate of the Loch, beyond the watchful frames of slow glass, a slow-moving steamer drew a white line towards the south. The boisterous mountain air seemed almost to invade our lungs, giving us more oxygen than we required.

"Some of the glass farmers around here," Hagan began, "give strangers, such as yourselves, a sales talk about how beautiful the autumn is in this part of Argyll. Or it might be the spring, or the winter. I don't do that—any fool knows that a place which doesn't look right in summer never looks right. What do you say?"

I nodded compliantly.

"I want you just to take a good look out towards Mull, Mr. . . . ."

"Garland."

"... Garland. That's what you're buying if you buy my glass, and it never looks better than it does at this minute. The glass is in perfect phase, none of it is less than ten years thick—and a four-foot window will cost you two hundred pounds."

"Two hundred!" Selina was shocked. "That's as much as they charge at the Scenedow shop in Bond Street."

Hagan smiled patiently, then looked closely at me to see if I knew enough about slow glass to appreciate what he had been saying. His price had been much higher than I had hoped—but *ten years thick!* The cheap glass one found in places like the Vistaplex and Pane-o-rama stores usually consisted of a quarter of an inch of ordinary glass faced with a veneer of slow glass perhaps only ten or twelve months thick.

"You don't understand, darling," I said, already determined to buy. "This glass will last ten years and it's in phase."

"Doesn't that only mean it keeps time?"

Hagan smiled at her again, realizing he had no further necessity to bother with me. "Only, you say! Pardon me, Mrs. Garland, but you don't seem to appreciate the miracle, the genuine honest-to-goodness miracle, of engineering precision needed to produce a piece of glass in phase. When say the glass is ten years thick it means it takes light ten years to pass through it. In effect, each one of those panes is ten light-years thick—more than twice the distance to the nearest star—so a variation in actual thickness of only a millionth of an inch would..."

He stopped talking for a moment and sat quietly looking towards the house. I turned my head from the view of the Loch and saw the young woman standing at the window again. Hagan's eyes were filled with a kind of greedy reverence which made me feel uncomfortable and at the same time convinced me Selina had been wrong. In my experience husbands never looked at wives that way, at least, not at their own.

The girl remained in view for a few seconds, dress glowing warmly, then moved back into the room. Suddenly I received a distinct, though inexplicable, impression she was blind. My feeling was that Selina and I were perhaps blundering through an emotional interplay as violent as our own.

"I'm sorry," Hagan continued, "I thought Rose was going to call me for something. Now, where was I, Mrs. Garland? Ten light-years compressed into a quarter of an inch means..."

I ceased to listen, partly because I was already sold, partly because I had heard the story of slow glass many times before and had never yet understood the principles involved. An acquaintance with scientific training had once tried to be helpful by telling me to visualize a pane of slow glass as a hologram which did not need coherent light from a laser for the reconstitution of its visual information, and in which every photon of ordinary light passed through a spiral tunnel coiled outside the radius of capture of each atom in the glass. This gem of, to me, incomprehensibility not only told me nothing, it convinced me once again that a mind as nontechnical as mine should concern itself less with causes than effects.

The most important effect, in the eyes of the average individual, was that light took a long time to pass through a sheet of slow glass. A new piece was always jet black because nothing had yet come through, but one could stand the glass beside, say, a woodland lake until the scene emerged, perhaps a year later. If the glass was then removed and installed in a dismal city flat, the flat would—for that year—appear to overlook the woodland lake. During the year it wouldn't be merely a very realistic but still picture—the water would ripple in sunlight, silent animals would come to drink, birds would cross the sky, night would follow day, season would follow season. Until one day, a year later, the beauty held in the subatomic pipelines would be exhausted and the familiar gray cityscape would reappear.

Apart from its stupendous novelty value, the commercial success of slow glass was founded on the fact that having a scenedow was the exact emotional equivalent of owning land. The meanest cave dweller could look out on misty parks—and who was to say they weren't his? A man who really owns tailored gardens and estates doesn't spend his time proving his ownership by crawling on his ground, feeling, smelling, tasting it. All he receives from the land are light patterns, and with scenedows those patterns could be taken into coal mines, submarines, prison cells.

On several occasions I have tried to write short pieces about the enchanted crystal but, to me, the theme is so ineffably poetic as to be, paradoxically, beyond the reach of poetry—mine at any rate. Besides, the best songs and verse had already been written, with prescient inspiration, by men who had died long before slow glass was discovered. I had no hope of equaling, for example, Moore with his:

> *Oft in the stilly night,*
> *Ere slumber's chain has bound me,*
> *Fond Memory brings the light,*
> *Of other days around me . . .*

It took only a few years for slow glass to develop from a scientific curiosity to a sizable industry. And much to the astonishment of we poets—those of us who remain convinced that beauty lives though lilies die—the trappings of that industry were no different from those of any other. There were good scenedows which cost a lot of money, and there were inferior scenedows which cost rather less. The thickness, measured in years, was an important factor in the cost but there was also the question of *actual* thickness, or phase.

Even with the most sophisticated engineering techniques available thickness control was something of a hit-and-miss affair. A coarse discrepancy could mean that a pane intended to be five years thick might be five and a half, so that light which entered in summer emerged in winter; a fine discrepancy could mean that noon sunshine emerged at midnight. These incompatibilities had their peculiar charm—many night workers, for example, liked having their own private time zones—but, in general, it cost more to buy scenedows which kept closely in step with real time.

Selina still looked unconvinced when Hagan had finished speaking. She shook her head almost imperceptibly and I knew he had been using the wrong approach. Quite suddenly the pewter helmet of her hair was disturbed by a cool gust of wind, and huge clean tumbling drops of rain began to spang round us from an almost cloudless sky.

"I'll give you a check now," I said abruptly, and saw Selina's green eyes triangulate angrily on my face. "You can arrange delivery?"

"Aye, delivery's no problem," Hagan said, getting to his feet. "But wouldn't you rather take the glass with you?"

"Well, yes—if you don't mind." I was shamed by his readiness to trust my scrip.

"I'll unclip a pane for you. Wait here. It won't take long to slip it into a carrying frame." Hagan limped down the slope towards the seriate windows, through some of which the view towards Linnhe was sunny, while others were cloudy and a few pure black.

Selina drew the collar of her blouse closed at her throat.

"The least he could have done was invite us inside. There can't be so many fools passing through that he can afford to neglect them."

I tried to ignore the insult and concentrated on writing the check. One of the outsize drops broke across my knuckles, splattering the pink paper.

"All right," I said, "let's move in under the eaves till he gets back." You worm, I thought as I felt the whole thing go completely wrong. I just had to be a fool to marry you. A prize fool, a fool's fool—and now that you've trapped part of me inside you I'll never ever, never ever, *never ever* get away.

Feeling my stomach clench itself painfully, I ran behind Selina to the side of the cottage. Beyond the window the neat living room, with its coal fire, was empty but the child's toys were scattered on the floor. Alphabet blocks and a wheelbarrow the exact color of freshly pared carrots. As I stared in, the boy came running from the other room and began kicking the blocks. He didn't notice me. A few moments later the young woman entered the room and lifted him, laughing easily and whole-heartedly as she swung the boy under her arm. She came to the window as she had done earlier. I smiled self-consciously, but neither she nor the child responded.

My forehead prickled icily. *Could they both be blind?* I sidled away.

Selina gave a little scream and I spun towards her.

"The rug!" she said. "It's getting soaked."

She ran across the yard in the rain, snatched the reddish square from the dappling wall and ran back, towards the cottage door. Something heaved convulsively in my subconscious.

"Selina," I shouted. "Don't open it!"

But I was too late. She had pushed open the latched wooden door and was standing, hand over mouth, looking into the cottage. I moved close to her and took the rug from her unresisting fingers.

As I was closing the door I let my eyes traverse the cottage's interior. The neat living room in which I had just seen the woman and child was, in reality, a sickening clutter of shabby furniture, old newspapers, cast-off clothing and smeared dishes. It was damp, stinking and utterly deserted. The only object I recognized from my view through the window was the little wheelbarrow, paintless and broken.

I latched the door firmly and ordered myself to forget what I had seen. Some men who live alone are good housekeepers; others just don't know how.

Selina's face was white. "I don't understand. I don't understand it."

"Slow glass works both ways," I said gently. "Light passes out of a house, as well as in."

"You mean . . . ?"

"I don't know. It isn't our business. Now steady up— Hagan's coming back with our glass." The churning in my stomach was beginning to subside.

Hagan came into the yard carrying an oblong, plastic-covered frame. I held the check out to him, but he was staring at Selina's face. He seemed to know immediately that our uncomprehending fingers had rummaged through his soul. Selina avoided his gaze. She was old and ill-looking, and her eyes stared determinedly towards the nearing horizon.

"I'll take the rug from you, Mr. Garland," Hagan finally said. "You shouldn't have troubled yourself over it."

"No trouble. Here's the check."

"Thank you." He was still looking at Selina with a strange kind of supplication. "It's been a pleasure to do business with you."

"The pleasure was mine," I said with equal, senseless formality. I picked up the heavy frame and guided Selina towards the path which led to the road. Just as we reached the head of the now slippery steps Hagan spoke again.

"Mr. Garland!"

I turned unwillingly.

"It wasn't my fault," he said steadily. "A hit-and-run driver got them both, down on the Oban road six years ago. My boy was only seven when it happened. I'm entitled to keep something."

I nodded wordlessly and moved down the path, holding my wife close to me, treasuring the feel of her arms locked around me. At the bend I looked back through the rain and saw Hagan sitting with squared shoulders on the wall where we had first seen him.

He was looking at the house, but I was unable to tell if there was anyone at the window.

LIGHT OF OTHER DAYS:
BEYOND THE RADIUS OF CAPTURE

This small, quiet, well-nigh perfect short story shows just how much science fiction can accomplish within a span of three or four thousand words. Beautifully it demonstrates how the best science fiction uses speculative science or technology to illuminate its human themes and human themes to illuminate its scientific speculations.

It is built around two interlocking cores: a troubled marriage and a technological wonder. The wonder is "slow glass," one of the most ingenious science-fictional inventions of the last twenty or thirty years—a substance so opaque that the passage of photons through it is vastly hindered, to the point where it may take ten years for a beam of light to travel the width of a single pane. The marriage is tense because an unwanted pregnancy has interposed itself, causing economic and emotional strains. Shaw's handling of each of these cores is distinctive and elegant; but it is his use of each to cast light on the other that makes this story so memorable.

Slow glass, taken by itself, is the sort of notion that comes once or twice at best in a science-fiction writer's lifetime, the sort of thing that stirs his colleagues to lusty applause and bleak bileful envy. Like most brilliant ideas, it's a perfectly obvious one—to anyone with the wit to see it.

Ask any science-fiction writer, even one who prides himself on his ignorance of science, to tell you what the speed of light is, and you'll get an immediate answer: 186,000 miles per second. (The more fastidious of them may give you the figure in kilometers per second.) But scarcely anyone will bother to add the small but vital qualification that that's the speed of light *in a vacuum*. Light passing through any other medium will move less quickly, which is what causes refraction effects: the velocity of light through water is slower than its velocity through air, which is why the twig in the stream seems to be bent. Light passing through glass is slowed even more— what we see through a window gets to us later than it would if there were no windowpane there—though the delaying effect is imperceptible to our eyes. Shaw simply—*simply!*—postulates the existence of a glass in which the velocity of light is slowed to an extreme degree.

His handling of the rationale for this is exemplary. He could have set it up the lazy way, merely saying, "Slow glass, a substance developed by Pilkington in 1997 that had the unique capacity of slowing beams of light down to a crawl. . . ." Or he could have done it the cheap and sleazy way by stringing together some gibberish that sounds scientific, but isn't: "Slow glass, which is fabricated from polymerized molecules of plutonium hexachloride alloyed with an unusual isotope of silicon. . . ." Instead—though Shaw's narrator is a poet and might legitimately be expected not to have the foggiest idea why slow glass works the way it does—Shaw has the man tell us that we should "visualize a pane of slow glass as a hologram which did not need coherent light from a laser for the reconstitution of its visual information." This is nicely done: holography was such a new concept in 1966, when "Light of Other Days" first appeared, that there is no mention of it in that year's edition of the *Encyclopaedia Britannica* or the contemporaneous *Webster's Third International*, yet Shaw, keeping abreast of technology as a professional science-fiction writer should, was familiar with it even then. But invoking holography alone won't explain slow glass, and so we are told also that in these holograms "every photon of ordinary light passed through a spiral tunnel coiled outside the radius of capture of each atom in the glass." How is that achieved? We don't find out, because Shaw's narrator doesn't know and neither does Shaw; but if glass *could* be constructed that way, slow glass might be possible.

What this boils down to, then, is an artfully worded redundancy: slow glass works because it is constructed in such a way that light slows down as it passes through it. We can't ask Shaw for formulas and molecular models. If he really knew how to manufacture slow glass, of course, he'd be out cruising on his yacht right now instead of planning his next story about spaceships or robots. But at least he has taken care to give us something that sounds plausible and shows some knowledge of what actually happens when a beam of light strikes a plate of glass. The lazy writer, ducking the whole business of inventing a plausible rationale, is serving up a mere fable. The sleazy writer, hoping to fool us with comic-book nonsense about plutonium hexafluoride and silicon, is feeding poisoned peppermints to his ignorant readers while losing the respect (and probably the attention) of those who know a little about chemistry. Shaw, though he is no more able to invent slow glass for us than are the scientists in the Corning factory, has worked at providing a plausible-sounding rationale, instead of merely wishing the stuff into being or tossing together whatever has come into his head. The extra effort lends conviction and substance to his story.

A single paragraph suffices for explaining the fabrication of slow glass. The story isn't about how to make the stuff, but about what it does, which is to create visual delay. What we see is light, reflected from the objects about us and converted into images by the miraculous mechanism that is our eye. If the light is coming from a great distance—say, from the galaxy we call the Andromeda nebula—a certain amount of delay must occur before it gets within processing range of our eyes. You can see the light of Andromeda in the night sky tonight; but what you see set out from Andromeda some 2,300,000 years ago. For all we know, the entire Andromeda galaxy was disrupted by a stupendous explosion while the Pharaohs were building their pyramids. The news of that cataclysm, though it has been traveling toward us at 186,000 miles a second, can't possibly reach us for millions of years.

The passage of light through slow glass causes delay too—months or even years: nothing so awesome as those created by the vast gulfs of intergalactic space, but significant enough in human terms. A window made of slow glass becomes a window into the lost and irretrievable past. Looking through slow glass, we see the light of other days; we see the scenes and people of vanished yesterdays, and they seem as real to us as the age-old light of Andromeda that glows in our sky this evening. It is a tremendously poignant and evocative concept, and from it arise any number of powerful fictional possibilities.

(Dedicated nitpickers have pointed out that slow glass is probably impossible: that impurities in the medium, or random movements of subatomic particles, would deflect and scatter the image long before it had completed its slow journey through the glass. Very likely that's so, but at some point the science-fiction writer has to shrug and ignore criticism of this sort, and I think this is the point. Bob Shaw's trade, after all, is fiction, not science. He is working in parables and metaphors, not in blueprints and formulas. Slow glass is simply too good an idea, one that arouses immensely rich and stirring fictional hypotheses; to discard it on the grounds that it probably couldn't be made to work is to go far beyond any reasonable degree of integrity and purity.)

All right, we have slow glass. How do we find an idea for a story to use it in?

One useful starting point is to think about possible uses (and consequences of the use) of slow glass. Decorative uses, certainly: hang a slab of it beside a Polynesian beach for a few months, then fit it into a window of a Scandinavian home, so that the occupants can look out on palm trees and a coral lagoon all winter long. Recording of entertainment events: viewers could look through slow glass to watch "live" performances of plays that were done years ago. Crimes committed behind slow-glass windows will come to light long after the fact, perhaps with complex effects on jurisprudence. The dying could speak to their unborn descendants. Complex business transactions could be recorded to guard against later challenge. And so on and so on. Many such ideas, and others besides, must have occurred to Bob Shaw as he began to sketch out what would become "Light of Other Days," and he set some of them aside for use in later stories. But for the very first slow-glass story he wisely chose a simple and compelling human situation: the power of slow glass to recapture for us a moment of the past that is otherwise forever beyond our grasp.

James Blish, in a valuable essay on his working methods published in the August, 1967, issue of the *Bulletin of the Science Fiction Writers of America*, declared, "Given the story which arrives in my head background-first, I find it works to ask myself next, 'Whom does this hurt?' The leading character comes out of the answer to this question." It's indeed a useful device for finding the emotional focus of a story. But sometimes, as we see here, the emotional focus of the story and the leading character are not necessarily the same person.

Who might be hurt by slow glass? Perhaps someone who has suffered a great bereavement, and who has years of his lost loved ones recorded on slow glass. The images coming through the glass would give him the illusion that the dead are still with him, which perhaps would be some consolation; but yet he must know that it is only an illusion, and he must live with the awareness that the time inevitably will come when the last of the images has worked its way through the spiral tunnels of the slow glass' atoms and then even the illusion would be gone. And Shaw has his tragic glassmaker, the Scots villager Hagan.

Wisely, though, he shows us Hagan at one remove. His narrator, the troubled husband Garland, has his own problems; and it is in the random search for some sort of peace from those that he encounters the glassmaker, and comes gradually to understand the man's true situation, and does indeed find peace in that understanding.

The story's gentle, understated nature is clear from the brief, lovely opening statement: "Leaving the village behind, we followed the heady sweeps of the road up into a land of slow glass." That one-sentence paragraph gives us an image of rural tranquility and then perhaps of mountain starkness, and leaves us finally perplexed by the mysterious phrase "slow glass." It propels us into a long and splendidly worked second paragraph that offers a richer view of the scenery and an even more puzzling glimpse of the slow glass. (It also provides us with one of those offhand bits of background detail rendered in the throw-away manner pioneered by Robert A. Heinlein: "The car's turbine was pulling smoothly and quietly in the damp air." Cars with turbines belong to the future; the point is made but not stressed.)

The third paragraph leads us from the perplexing windows on the hillside to the conflict between Selina and Garland. There are problems in their marriage: she is pregnant, and angry about it. The accidental pregnancy has forced husband and wife to contemplate things about themselves, and about each other, that they had skillfully managed previously to avoid dealing with. All this is a rare touch of emotional realism in a science-fiction story, particularly in one that was written more than twenty years ago. Most science fiction in that time—and all too much of it today—is set in a never-never land of bland emotions where such real-world matters as marriage, childbirth, and divorce are sidestepped entirely or else handled in a perfunctory and almost embarrassed manner.

As we have seen, there are stories in which such things would only dilute and distort the main business of the piece: in this book "Common Time," "Four in One," "The Monsters," "Colony," and perhaps several others would only be harmed if they dwelled on the private problems (as opposed to the problems posed by the science-fiction concept of the story) of their protagonists. But in "Light of Other Days" the marital problems of the Garlands are inseparable from the science-fiction situation: this is a story about love and the loss of love that comes with time. The love that the Garlands must once have felt for each other has been eroded by stress; the love of Hagan for his wife has been sundered more savagely, by a sudden accident. One loss is irrevocable, but has been cushioned by the miracle of slow glass. The other may yet be repaired; and here slow glass is instrumental in bringing that about.

It is only a little story—almost a miniature—built around an enormous concept. Yet in this one-incident tale the tension that exists between husband and wife is resolved by the climactic moment of compassion that springs from the uniquely science-fictional revelation of Hagan's sorrow that the slow glass provides. "Light passes out of a house," Garland tells his wife, "as well as in." It is an astonishing line, a poet's line, encapsulating in a few words the meaning of the whole story, and sending husband and wife away clinging to one another as they have not done for a long time. The effect is profound and moving. There is nothing new about stories of marital reconciliation, which is not a theme usually considered fruitful for science fiction; but this is the only reconciliation ever brought about by the slow movement of photons through a pane of dark glass. It is a story that could not have been told in any way other than as science fiction. It is a story that is marvelously well conceived and marvelously well told.

DAY MILLION
FREDERIK POHL

On this day I want to tell you about, which will be about ten thousand years from now, there were a boy, a girl and a love story.

Now, although I haven't said much so far, none of it is true. The boy was not what you and I would normally think of as a boy, because he was a hundred and eighty-seven years old. Nor was the girl a girl, for other reasons. And the love story did not entail that sublimation of the urge to rape, and concurrent postponement of the instinct to submit, which we at present understand in such matters. You won't care much for this story if you don't grasp these facts at once. If, however, you will make the effort you'll likely enough find it jampacked, chockful and tip-top-crammed with laughter, tears and poignant sentiment which may, or may not, be worthwhile. The reason the girl was not a girl was that she was a boy.

How angrily you recoil from the page! You say, who the hell wants to read about a pair of queers? Calm yourself. Here are no hot-breathing secrets of perversion for the coterie trade. In fact, if you were to see this girl you would not guess that she was in any sense a boy. Breasts, two; reproductive organs, female. Hips, callipygean; face hairless, supra-orbital lobes nonexistent. You would term her female on sight, although it is true that you might wonder just what species she was a female of, being confused by the tail, the silky pelt and the gill slits behind each ear.

Now you recoil again. Cripes, man, take my word for it. This is a sweet kid, and if you, as a normal male, spent as much as an hour in a room with her you would bend heaven and Earth to get her in the sack. Dora—we will call her that; her "name" was omicron-Dibase seven-group-totter-oot S Doradus 5314, the last part of which is a colour specification corresponding to a shade of green—Dora, I say, was feminine, charming and cute. I admit she doesn't sound that way. She was, as you might put it, a dancer. Her art involved qualities of intellection and expertise of a very high order, requiring both tremendous natural capacities and endless practice; it was performed in null-gravity and I can best describe it by saying that it was something like the performance of a contortionist and something like classical ballet, maybe resembling Danilova's dying swan. It was also pretty damned sexy. In a symbolic way, to be sure; but face it, most of the things we call "sexy" are symbolic, you know, except perhaps an exhibitionist's open clothing. On Day Million when Dora danced, the people who saw her panted, and you would too.

About this business of her being a boy. It didn't matter to her audiences that genetically she was male. It wouldn't matter to you, if you were among them, because you wouldn't know it—not unless you took a biopsy cutting of her flesh and put it under an electron-microscope to find the XY chromosome—and it didn't matter to them because they didn't care. Through techniques which are not only complex but haven't yet been discovered, these people were able to determine a great deal about the aptitudes and easements of babies quite a

long time before they were born—at about the second horizon
of cell-division, to be exact, when the segmenting egg is becoming a free blastocyst—and then they naturally helped
those aptitudes along. Wouldn't we? If we find a child with an
aptitude for music we give him a scholarship to Juilliard. If
they found a child whose aptitudes were for being a woman,
they made him one. As sex had long been dissociated from reproduction this was relatively easy to do and caused no trouble and no, or at least very little, comment.

How much is "very little"? Oh, about as much as would
be caused by our own tampering with Divine Will by filling
a tooth. Less than would be caused by wearing a hearing aid.
Does it still sound awful? Then look closely at the next busty
babe you meet and reflect that she may be a Dora, for adults
who are genetically male but somatically female are far from
unknown even in our own time. An accident of environment
in the womb overwhelms the blueprints of heredity. The difference is that with us it happens only by accident and we
don't know about it except rarely, after close study; whereas
the people of Day Million did it often, on purpose, because
they wanted to.

Well, that's enough to tell you about Dora. It would only
confuse you to add that she was seven feet tall and smelled
of peanut butter. Let us begin our story.

On Day Million, Dora swam out of her house, entered a
transportation tube, was sucked briskly to the surface in its
flow of water and ejected in its plume of spray to an elastic
platform in front of her—ah—call it her rehearsal hall.

"Oh, hell!" she cried in pretty confusion, reaching out to
catch her balance and finding herself tumbled against a total
stranger, whom we will call Don.

They met cute. Don was on his way to have his legs
renewed. Love was the farthest thing from his mind. But
when, absentmindedly taking a shortcut across the landing

platform for submarinites and finding himself drenched, he discovered his arms full of the loveliest girl he had ever seen, he knew at once they were meant for each other. "Will you marry me?" he asked. She said softly, "Wednesday," and the promise was like a caress.

Don was tall, muscular, bronze and exciting. His name was no more Don than Dora's was Dora, but the personal part of it was Adonis in tribute to his vibrant maleness, and so we will call him Don for short. His personality colour-code, in Angstrom units, was 5,290, or only a few degrees bluer than Dora's 5,314—a measure of what they had intuitively discovered at first sight; that they possessed many affinities of taste and interest.

I despair of telling you exactly what it was that Don did for a living—I don't mean for the sake of making money, I mean for the sake of giving purpose and meaning to his life, to keep him from going off his nut with boredom—except to say that it involved a lot of travelling. He travelled in interstellar spaceships. In order to make a spaceship go really fast, about thirty-one male and seven genetically female human beings had to do certain things, and Don was one of the thirty-one. Actually, he contemplated options. This involved a lot of exposure to radiation flux—not so much from his own station in the propulsive system as in the spillover from the next stage, where a genetic female preferred selections, and the sub-nuclear particles making the selections she preferred demolished themselves in a shower of quanta. Well, you don't give a rat's ass for that, but it meant that Don had to be clad at all times in a skin of light, resilient, extremely strong copper-coloured metal. I have already mentioned this, but you probably thought I meant he was sunburned.

More than that, he was a cybernetic man. Most of his ruder parts had been long since replaced with mechanisms of vastly more permanence and use. A cadmium centrifuge, not a heart, pumped his blood. His lungs moved only when he wanted to speak out loud, for a cascade of osmotic filters rebreathed oxygen out of his own wastes. In a way, he probably would have looked peculiar to a man from the 20th century, with his glowing eyes and seven-fingered hands. But to himself, and of course to Dora, he looked mighty manly and grand. In the course of his voyages Don had circled Proxima Centauri, Procyon and the puzzling worlds of Mira Ceti; he had carried agricultural templates to the planets of Canopus and brought back warm, witty pets from the pale companion of Aldebaran. Blue-hot or red-cool, he had seen a thousand stars and their ten thousand planets. He had, in fact, been travelling the starlanes, with only brief leaves on Earth, for pushing two centuries. But you don't care about that, either. It is people who make stories, not the circumstances they find themselves in, and you want to hear about these two people. Well, they made it. The great thing they had for each other grew and flowered and burst into fruition on Wednesday, just as Dora had promised. They met at the encoding room, with a couple of well-wishing friends apiece to cheer them on, and while their identities were being taped and stored they smiled and whispered to each other and bore the jokes of their friends with blushing repartee. Then they exchanged their mathematical analogues and went away, Dora to her dwelling beneath the surface of the sea and Don to his ship.

It was an idyll, really. They lived happily ever after—or anyway, until they decided not to bother any more and died.

Of course, they never set eyes on each other again.

Oh, I can see you now, you eaters of charcoal-broiled steak, scratching an incipient bunion with one hand and holding this story with the other, while the stereo plays d'Indy or Monk. You don't believe a word of it, do you? Not for one minute. People wouldn't live like that, you say with a grunt as you get up to put fresh ice in a drink.

And yet there's Dora, hurrying back through the flushing commuter pipes toward her underwater home (she prefers it there; has had herself somatically altered to breathe the stuff). If I tell you with what sweet fulfilment she fits the recorded analogue of Don into the symbol manipulator, hooks herself in and turns herself on ... if I try to tell you any of that you will simply stare. Or glare; and grumble, what the hell kind of love-making is this? And yet I assure you, friend, I really do assure you that Dora's ecstasies are as creamy and passionate as any of James Bond's lady spies', and one hell of a lot more so than anything you are going to find in "real life." Go ahead, glare and grumble. Dora doesn't care. If she thinks of you at all, her thirty-times-great-great-grandfather, she thinks you're a pretty primordial sort of brute. You are. Why, Dora is farther removed from you than you are from the australopithecines of five thousand centuries ago. You could not swim a second in the strong currents of her life. You don't think progress goes in a straight line, do you? Do you recognize that it is an ascending, accelerating, maybe even exponential curve? It takes hell's own time to get started, but when it goes it goes like a bomb. And you, you Scotch-drinking steak-eater in your relaxacizing chair, you've just barely lighted the primacord of the fuse. What is it now, the six or seven hundred thousandth day after Christ? Dora lives in Day Million, the millionth day of the Christian Era. Ten thousand years from now. Her body fats are polyunsaturated, like Crisco. Her wastes are haemodialysed out of her blood-stream while she sleeps—that means she doesn't have to go to the bathroom. On whim, to pass a slow half-hour, she can command more energy than the entire nation of Portugal can spend today, and use it to launch a weekend satellite or remould a crater on the Moon. She loves Don very much. She keeps his every gesture, mannerism, nuance, touch of hand, thrill of intercourse, passion of kiss stored in symbolic-mathematical form. And when she wants him, all she has to do is turn the machine on and she has him.

And Don, of course, has Dora. Adrift on a sponson city a few hundred yards over her head, or orbiting Arcturus fifty light-years away, Don has only to command his own symbol-manipulator to rescue Dora from the ferrite files and bring her to life for him, and there she is; and rapturously, tirelessly they love all night. Not in the flesh, of course; but then his flesh has been extensively altered and it wouldn't really be much fun. He doesn't need the flesh for pleasure. Genital organs feel nothing. Neither do hands, nor breasts, nor lips; they are only receptors, accepting and transmitting impulses. It is the brain that feels; it is the interpretation of those impulses that makes agony or orgasm, and Don's symbol-manipulator gives him the analogue of cuddling, the analogue of kissing, the analogue of wild, ardent hours with the eternal, exquisite and incorruptible analogue of Dora. Or Diane. Or sweet Rose, or laughing Alicia; for to be sure, they have each of them exchanged analogues before, and will again.

Rats, you say, it looks crazy to me. And you—with your aftershave lotion and your little red car, pushing papers across a desk all day and chasing tail all night—tell me, just how the hell do you think you would look to Tiglath-Pileser, say, or Attila the Hun?

DAY MILLION:
A BOY, A GIRL, A LOVE STORY

All science fiction, as I indicated in the foreword to this book, is in truth fantasy; that is, the free play of the imagination in the realms of the unreal. And yet there are degrees and degrees of fantasy, which is why we are able to make the distinction for purposes of publishing categorization between "fantasy" and "science fiction." The dividing point is the matter of *probability*. What we formally call fantasy—that stuff about elves and unicorns, magical staffs and rings of power, gods and goddesses, demons and sorcerers—is based in thematic material that we generally agree is improbable to the point of impossibility. Science fiction is that branch of fantasy that deals with fantastic situations that nevertheless do not seem flatly impossible to us. For example, it is *difficult* but not, so far as we know, impossible to build the sort of spaceship that takes Garrard on his voyage in "Common Time." It's *unlikely*, but not inherently impossible, that such a voyager might meet something like the clinesterton beademung in the course of his journey. If we ever did manage to travel to planets outside our solar system (and if any such planets exist, which as of today is unproven though probable), it would be unsettling but not impossible to encounter life-forms such as those portrayed in "Four in One" or "Common Time." If android humans could be built (and we don't know any law of science that tells us they can't) it would be unlikely but not impossible for one of them to malfunction in the way described in "Fondly Fahrenheit." And so on.

Within these limits, though, it's possible to identify different levels of probability. Consider the three remarkable views of the distant future that are included here—Aldiss' "Hothouse," Cordwainer Smith's "Scanners Live in Vain," and Frederik Pohl's "Day Million." I think the likelihood that any of those possible futures will actually become real is infinitesimal. Each exists only as a self-contained vision, a fantasy of time to come, a poetic construct. But each also represents a different approach to the problem of making a wildly fantastic situation look plausible.

Smith has not actually drawn on the formal resources of science at all: he postulates a hypothetical "great pain" caused by space travel, which we have subsequently learned does not exist, and proposes a surgical operation to desensitize space travelers to it. Taken on its own terms, it is a fascinating and bizarre idea, worked out with great power and intensity. We can interpret it as a metaphorical view of the difficulties of ordinary human interaction, if we like, or we can simply accept it as a gaudy and extraordinarily vivid dream. Smith's cool, stark narrative voice makes the world of the habermans seem probable at least so long as we are immersed in it as readers.

Aldiss has imagined in considerable detail and with some recourse to the realities of the scientific view of the world. His fantastic vegetable monsters, while imaginary, are designed with care and some are based on plants of today—the banyan, for instance, which forms huge thickets in today's jungles and might well span whole continents in those of Aldiss' remote tomorrow. He explains how changes in solar radiation levels have induced the mutations that have so vastly transformed the vegetable kingdom—a genetic explanation, rather than a magical one. Even where he crosses the line into impossibility—the spiderwebs that reach to the moon, a stunning image but one that violates the laws of celestial mechanics—he works at making his gorgeous if nonsensical idea seem valid by speaking of axial revolutions and reciprocal braking effects. "Hothouse," like "Scanners Live in Vain," is a fantasy, but Aldiss, to an even greater extent than Smith, invokes the talismans of science to strengthen the reality texture of his story.

"Day Million" is a fantasy, too: nothing like it will ever happen, we can be pretty sure. But because Fred Pohl has taken immense care to ground his fantastic assumptions in many aspects of contemporary science and technology, his fantasy carries a kind of conviction quite absent from the other two stories. We already know that space travel will involve us in none of the problems that might have required the inventions of habermans and scanners; but because Smith's story is such powerful fiction, we willingly ignore that difficulty and allow ourselves to be drawn into Martel's strange world as *though it were real*. Pedants like Isaac Asimov and James Blish call our attention to the impossibility of Aldiss' 238,000-mile-long spiderwebs; and we shrug and say, "Yes, but the image of the traversers is so beautiful," and forgive the author his trespasses. In "Day Million," though, there is nothing to forgive. Everything is clear-eyed speculation, solidly grounded. A cadmium centrifuge pumps Don's blood. Osmotic filters rebreathe his wastes. Pohl tells you the code names of Don and Dora in angstrom units and knows which way along the spectrum the numbers run. He is aware that XY chromosomes signify males, that australopithecines were the dominant humanoid species five million years ago, that blue suns are hot and red ones are cool. Each paragraph of the story—each sentence, in fact—demonstrates that Pohl has devoted most of his life to attaining the broadest and deepest possible understanding of the universe as *we comprehend it today*. And out of that knowledge he has drawn these dazzlingly brilliant speculations on what human life *could* be like ten thousand years from now. The chances that it *will* be like that are minute. No matter. This is a fantasy, a dream, a vision of the future. But because it is that special kind of fantasy that we call science fiction, the strength and depth of the scientific underpinning gives it unusual solidity. Fiction is lies that we try to pass off as truth; and in writing science fiction, one good way to disguise your lies as truth is to do it as Fred Pohl has done it here, by cloaking them in genuine knowledge rather than in clever subterfuges or outright gobbledygook.

Of course, all the scientific details in the world wouldn't have made "Day Million" the classic that it is if Pohl had not also done such a spectacular job of storytelling. The story is audacious, outrageous, wildly experimental. It shows how far one can deviate from the assumptions and requirements of conventional magazine fiction without rebuffing the reader. It's not a story for every reader; nor ought every story, or even any story but this, be written this way. But it is an extraordinary demonstration of narrative originality, an experiment that works on every level.

The very first clause—"On this day I want to tell you about"— signals that the author, by interjecting himself so strongly, intends to destroy the illusion so favored by writers of fiction that the reader is viewing actual events through a window magically open before his eyes. Pohl says it bluntly: *You aren't really seeing these things happen, I'm simply telling you about it all. It isn't happening ten thousand years from now; it's going to happen, maybe, but what is really happening is that you're sitting in your armchair and I'm telling you a story.* To make sure that we know that it's just a story, Pohl reminds us of it in the second paragraph: "You won't care much for this story if you don't grasp these facts at once." And again and again throughout the piece—right up to the magnificently sardonic and revelatory last paragraph—Pohl speaks directly to the reader, a technique in direct opposition to the practice of every major writer of fiction of the twentieth century. Though they might sometimes have their *narrator* speak to the audience, none would ever step out of the page to do so in their own persons.

But none of those other writers—not Hemingway, not Joyce, not Faulkner, not Bellow, not Henry James—ever wrote a story like "Day Million." Pohl's purpose here is not so much the re-creation of a fictional reality as it is the reorientation of the reader: and so he talks straight to the reader, tough talk at that, saying, *You don't understand a thing, buddy, you have no idea how fast the world is changing around your ears, and let me open your eyes.* In "Day Million" Pohl is gripped by a genuinely revolutionary vision of the future—one of the few in all of science fiction that really tries to take into account the accelerating pace of change. Long before the term "future shock" became a cliché, Pohl realized that the world is in a state of rapid metamorphosis in which change has been coming at an almost unimaginable rate *and in which that rate will continue to accelerate.* Reality makes science fiction look timid; what most writers imagine as the world of 2583 will be old stuff before the year 2050, and if we could see the true world of 2583 it would be virtually unrecognizable to us. So Pohl invents an unfathomable but plausible world of ten thousand years from now—no mere random hodgepodge of oddities, but a rationally conceived set of interlocking transformations—and tells us brusquely, "Dora is further removed from you than you are from the australopithecines of five thousand centuries ago. You could not swim a second in the strong current of her life. You don't think progress goes in a straight line, do you?" "Day Million" is framed in the form of a challenge to our complacency.

But it is also a story, and indeed it's actually less unconventional in form than it seems at first glance. The closer we look at it, the less experimental it appears, which may be one reason for its impact. Pohl lets us know right away that he intends to build it around the most familiar of story materials: "On this day I want to tell you about, which will be about ten thousand years from now, there were a boy, a girl and a love story." Indeed there are; and buried in the narrative we will indeed find boy-meets-girl and boy-gets-girl. (The usual intervening complication, boy-loses-girl, isn't there. That may be the story's most significant deviation from formula.)

There is also a conventional narrative hook: the familiar science-fiction technique of heading immediately into a paradox. "There were a boy and a girl," Pohl says, and a moment later he contradicts himself: the boy isn't really a boy, because he's 187 years old; and the girl isn't a girl, because she's a boy. We are snared by the puzzle of that immediate self-contradiction. (Pohl tells us that we are likely to recoil in horror from the apparent homosexuality of the situation, but even that is quickly contradicted in a way that plants the hook even deeper.) Then comes courtship, marriage, and—a one-sentence substitute for normal plot complications—separation. ("Of course, they never set eyes on each other again.") The remaining few hundred words of the little story resolve the "plot" by telling us how Don and Dora can be happily married while never once meeting again, and then Pohl turns directly to us once more to deliver that final sardonic shove.

In stepping out from behind the conventional twentieth-century shield of auctorial invisibility, Pohl actually places himself in a direct line that goes back to the earliest known storytellers. "The wrath of Achilles is my theme," says Homer in the first line of The Iliad. "The hero of the tale which I beg the Muse to help me tell is that resourceful man who roamed the wide world after he had sacked the holy citadel

537

of Troy," is how *The Odyssey* begins. "I sing of arms and the man who first from Troy's frontier, displaced by destiny, came to the Lavinian shores," Virgil tells us at the outset of *The Aeneid*. Cervantes insinuates himself everywhere in the narrative flow of *Don Quixote*, leaving no doubt that you are reading a story rather than viewing some self-generated set of events. In the nineteenth century it was not at all un-usual for writers like Dickens or Thackeray to break into the text in their own voices: "I know that the tune I am piping is a very mild one (although there are some terrific chapters coming presently)," Thack-eray declares in Chapter Six of *Vanity Fair*, "and must beg the good-natured reader to remember, that we are only discoursing at present about a stockbroker's family in Russell Square." In our own time that kind of interjection became first unfashionable and then taboo. Pohl revives it here for the best of reasons: he wants you to listen to some-thing that he, Fred Pohl, wants to tell you. And he wants you to believe him. "Cripes, man, take my word for it," he urges.

So the mode of telling is part of the effect—sly, insinuating, au-dacious. It seems modern and experimental, and in many ways it is, but actually Pohl has reverted to the earliest storytelling tradition, that of the bard strumming his harp beside the campfire. Because he handles that aspect of the story with such supreme confidence, he carries it off successfully. (A little arrogance is part of every successful writer's equipment. *I have a story to tell you, and you're going to love it: shut up and listen*.) "Day Million" was state-of-the-art science fiction, an astonishing tour de force, when it first appeared in 1966, in an obscure imitator of *Playboy* called *Rogue*. That magazine is long forgotten, but "Day Million" is as fresh and startling now as it was more than two decades ago. It is a model of thoughtful specu-lative vision; it is a model of original and bold storytelling. To think well, and to write well: those are the minimum requirements for writ-ing great science fiction.

High demands; but those who choose science fiction as the cen-ter of their writing lives accept those requirements unresentfully. Fred Pohl has shown again and again, but never more impressively than in "Day Million," that he meets those minimum requirements, and then some. So, in their various ways, have the dozen other writers whose stories are included here. And, I hope, so do I. With the exception of Cordwainer Smith, there is no one in this book who did not devote a major portion of his adult life to the writing of science fiction. By a rough calculation I find that the writing careers of everyone in this book aggregate a total of nearly five hundred years. That's a long time for fourteen people to spend wrestling with the phantoms of the far reaches of time and space.

What we all discovered, during the course of those five centuries at the typewriter or the word processor, is that science fiction can be a wondrously exhilarating, liberating, exciting thing to write as well as to read. It was that exhilaration and excitement that drew us to science fiction in the first place, almost invariably when we were very young; it was for the sake of that exhilaration and excitement that we took up the writing of it; and it was to facilitate the expression of our visions and fantasies that we devoted ourselves with such zeal to the study of the art and craft of writing.

As, perhaps, you have now begun to do yourself. And perhaps you find yourself now as intimidated by all I have said on the subject of narrative technique and the special demands of writing science fiction as I was, back in my teens, when I read with mounting dismay Thomas Uzzell's book and the critical essays of Knight and Blish. I know how you feel. So much to learn! Such intricacies, such complexities! I was overwhelmed by it all. I thought of giving up. But what I wanted to do was write science fiction, and ultimately that was what pulled me onward despite my fears.

And, ultimately, that is what will pull you onward, if you dream, as I did, of taking your place among the tribe of writers. No one ever said it was easy, nor will I pretend it is now. But the rewards are great.

FOR FURTHER READING

I t seems essential to me that anyone who wants to write science fiction be a devoted reader of science fiction. I know there are some honorable exceptions—John D. MacDonald, I believe, wrote some outstanding science fiction in the early years of his career without having read a great deal of the stuff—but there aren't many like him. For one thing, a familiarity with science fiction saves the would-be writer from the bother of reinventing the wheel. Some wonderful ideas are so wonderful that they've already been done to perfection by the likes of Heinlein or Kuttner or Murray Leinster, years ago; everybody within the field knows and reveres those classic stories, and it's hopeless to try to sell a new version of them, even if you did think it up all by yourself. Better to familiarize yourself with the classics of science fiction to avoid the embarrassment of being told that your great new novella is a mere rewrite of "Vintage of Season" or "By His Bootstraps" or "Nightfall," none of which you've ever read or heard of.

But this kind of accidental and unintentional plagiarism of the classics isn't the most serious problem that failing to ground yourself in the existing literature will cause. Much perfectly fine science fiction is written *in reaction to existing stories*. Some concept in a Poul Anderson novel or a Larry Niven piece, say, will set off a reverberation in a writer's head. He'll begin looking at Anderson's idea, or Niven's, testing it, playing with it, arguing with it—and come up with a fine variation on it himself, something that the original author might never have conceived. It's a legitimate and common way to generate story ideas. But you can't do it if you haven't read what's already been published.

Most important of all to a science-fiction writer, though, is the development of a science-fictional way of looking at the universe. I don't want to try to define that: either you have it or you don't, and if you don't, you'll never know what I'm talking about. The ones who do are the people who read science fiction and eventually go on to write it. It's a matter of nuance, of perception, of intellectual style. Perhaps you have to be born with it; but you can certainly cultivate it, if you have it at all, by reading science fiction. And the old garbage-in-garbage-out rule holds here: there's good science fiction and there's bad, and if you read the junk, you'll probably write even junkier junk when you try to produce the stuff yourself.

So here is a reading list for those who have just read this book and are eager to continue their science-fiction education. It comes in two sections: a group of anthologies containing some of the finest short science fiction ever written, and a group of books by the writers whose work is included in *Worlds of Wonder*, so that you can get a broader and deeper view of their approaches to writing science fiction. If I were setting out right now to master the art and craft of science fiction, these are the books I'd be reading as my homework. They are books from which you can learn much. And they will provide hours of remarkable delight besides.

Anthologies

Isaac Asimov, editor. *The Hugo Winners*. Doubleday, various years. A compilation of the annual award winners chosen by science-fiction readers since 1953.

Michael Bishop, editor. *Light and Dark Years*. Berkley Books, 1984. An overview of science fiction by the writers of the 1960s, 1970s, and early 1980s.

Terry Carr, editor. *Best Science Fiction of the Year*. Tor Books, various years. An annual series; an invaluable guide to the best work being done in the science-fiction magazines.

Gardner Dozois, editor. *The Year's Best Science Fiction*. St. Martin's Press, various years. Similar to the Carr series, but much larger in scope, at least a quarter of a million words per volume. These jumbo collections have been appearing since 1984.

Martin Harry Greenberg, editor, with Frederik Pohl and Joseph Olander. *Science Fiction of the Forties*. Avon, 1978. *Science Fiction of the Fifties*. Avon, 1979. Historical survey collections, loaded with splendid stories.

Robert Silverberg and Martin Harry Greenberg, editors. *The Arbor House Treasury of Modern Science Fiction*. Arbor House, 1980. *The Arbor House Treasury of Great Science Fiction Short Novels*. Arbor House, 1980. *The Arbor House Treasury of Science Fiction Masterpieces*. Arbor House, 1983. Three massive volumes encompassing scores of science-fiction classics from Poe, Verne, and Wells to the 1970s.

Robert Silverberg, editor. *The Science Fiction Hall of Fame*, Volume One. Doubleday, 1970; paperback edition, Avon. The best science-fiction stories of all time as selected by the members of the Science Fiction Writers of America in

1967. Subsequently joined by *The Science Fiction Hall of Fame*, Volume Two, edited by Ben Bova (Doubleday and Avon), which includes stories longer than those eligible for the first volume, and two later books in the series (Volume Three, edited by George Proctor, Avon, 1982, and Volume Four, edited by Terry Carr, Avon, 1986), which include the Nebula Award stories of the Science Fiction Writers of America from 1965 to 1974.

Donald A. Wollheim, editor. *World's Best Science Fiction*. DAW Books, various years. The third of the three regular annual collections of the year's best science fiction. Wollheim has been observing the science-fiction scene for more than half a century, and his tastes are deeply rooted in historical perspective: an important series of books.

Individual Author Story Collections

Who Can Replace a Man? Brian W. Aldiss. Harcourt Brace Jovanovich, 1965.

Hothouse. Brian W. Aldiss. Baen Books, 1984.

The Light Fantastic. Alfred Bester. Berkley/Putnam, 1976.

Star Light, Star Bright. Alfred Bester. Berkley/Putnam, 1976.

Galactic Cluster. James Blish. Signet, 1959.

The Best of Philip K. Dick. Ballantine, 1977.

The Best of Damon Knight. Pocket Books, 1976.

The Best of C. M. Kornbluth. Ballantine, 1976.

The Best of Henry Kuttner. Ballantine, 1975.

The Best of C. L. Moore. Ballantine, 1975.

The Best of Frederik Pohl. Ballantine, 1975.

Other Days, Other Eyes. Bob Shaw. Ace, 1972.

Is That What People Do? Robert Sheckley. Holt, 1984.
Beyond the Safe Zone. Robert Silverberg. Donald I. Fine, 1986; Warner, 1987.
The Best of Cordwainer Smith. Ballantine, 1975.
The Best of Jack Vance. Pocket Books, 1976.

Criticism

A couple of books of criticism of science fiction will be valuable, too, if you can find them. They were published years ago by Advent, a semi-professional Chicago publishing house, and are still in print and available through specialty bookstores:

The Issue at Hand, James Blish.
In Search of Wonder, Damon Knight.